Child Art Therapy

Child Art Therapy

25th Anniversary Edition

Judith Aron Rubin

WILEY

John Wiley & Sons, Inc.

Contents

Illustrations   *xi*

DVD Contents   *xv*

Acknowledgments   *xxxiii*

Preface: 25th Anniversary Edition   **xxxix**
Background   xxxix
Changes in Art Therapy and Mental Health   xl
Changes in Organization and Content of the Book   xli

PART I   The Context

1   Roots: Personal and Professional   **3**
Personal   3
Professional   6
Personal/Professional Passage   8
A Personal Experience of the Creative Process   9
Making Pictures Helps My Mourning Process   13
About This Book   14

2   A Framework for Freedom   **19**
Conditions for Creative Growth   29

3   Understanding Development in Art   **34**
Progression in Normal Artistic Development   34
Where a Child Is   46
General Issues in Development   48

4   A Picture of the Therapeutic Process   **57**
Testing   58
Trusting   61
Risking   62
Communicating   63
Facing   64
Understanding   66
Accepting   68
Coping   69
Separating   70

5   Some Ways to Facilitate Expression   **73**
A Starter (A Scribble)   73
A Theme   74
A Medium   77
A Dream   78
A Mask   81
A Target   83
A Tape Recorder   85
A Poem   88
A Story   89
A Picture-Taking Machine   90
Flashlights and Candles   90
Extending the Range   92
Conclusion   92

PART II   The Individual

6   An Individual Art Evaluation   **97**
Background   97
Initiating the Interview   99
Getting Started   103
The Art Materials   106
The Space   110
Talking about the Artwork   113
Abstract Artwork   115
Some Things Are Easier to Say and to See in Art   117
Productivity   118
Recommendations   119

7   Decoding Symbolic Messages   **121**
To Write or Not to Write?   121
Verbal Communications   122
To Talk or Not to Talk?   122

Contents

Nonverbal Communications   123
Interaction with the Therapist   123
Response to the Task   124
Response to the Materials   124
The Working Process   125
Products: Form   126
Form and Process as Content   128
Products: Content   129
Common Themes   129
Self-Representations   131
Degree of Disguise   131
Attitude toward the Product   132
Making Sense   134
Reporting   135

8   **Some Case Studies**   **137**
Ellen: An Elective Mute   138
Dorothy: A Child with Schizophrenia   145
Randy: A Boy with Encopresis   150
Conclusion   152

9   **Case Illustration: Understanding and Helping**   **153**
Individual Art Evaluation   156
Group Art Therapy   158
Joint Mother-Child Art Sessions   160
Family Art Evaluation   161
Family Art Therapy   162
Joint Nonverbal Drawing   167

PART III   **The Family and the Group**

10   **A Family Art Evaluation**   **173**
Format   174
Scribble Drawing   177
Family Representations   178
Family Mural   180
Free Products   182
Making Sense   182
Characteristics   183
Modifications   185

11   **Family Art Therapy**   **188**
Family Member Dyads   188
Conjoint Family Art Therapy   193

Occasional Conjoint Family Art Sessions   196
Multimodal Family Art Sessions   197

12   **Art Therapy with Parents**   **200**
Individual Art Therapy   200
Mother-Child Art Therapy Group   202
Short-Term Parent-Child Art Therapy Groups   214
Mothers' Art Therapy Groups   215
Conclusion   217

13   **Group Art Therapy**   **218**
History and Development   218
Deciding What to Do   220
Activities in Art Therapy Groups   222
Groups and How They Grow   225
The Use of Structure in Unstructured Groups   228
Group Themes and Concerns   229
Creative Play with Food   230
Role-Taking in Interviews   231
Interviewing Each Other   231
Reviewing in a Group   233
Individual Growth in a Group: Don   233
Group Growth: New Members and Endings   234
Conclusion   236

14   **Multimodality Group Therapy**   **237**
Relationships among the Arts   237
The First Art–Drama Therapy Group: Latency-Age Boys   240
The Second Art–Drama Therapy Group: Adolescents   249
Role of the Leader   257
Conclusion   258

PART IV   **Art Therapy for Disabled Children**

15   **Art as Therapy for Children with Disabilities**   **263**
The Universality of Creativity   263
Children with Schizophrenia in a Psychiatric Hospital   264
Children with Physical Disabilities in a Residential Institution   266
Deaf Children in a Day School   268
Children with Developmental Delays in a Preschool   271
Blind Children with Multiple Disabilities in a
   Residential School   272
Changes over the Years Since the First Edition   276

Special Considerations in Art for Children with Disabilities   277
Values of Art for Children with Disabilities   278

16   Art Therapy with Disabled Children and Their Parents 285
Similarities and Differences   285
Coming to Terms with Blindness   300
Outpatient Mothers' Therapy Group: Sustenance
    and Support   307

PART V   Art as Therapy for Everyone

17   Helping the Normal Child through Art   311
Therapeutic Values in Art Education   311
Dealing with Normal Stresses through Art   313
Loss of Parental Figures   326
Conclusion   328

18   Helping Parents through Art and Play   330
Art as Therapy for Normal Adults   330
Education in the Community   331
Family Art Workshop: Elementary School   332
Parent Art Workshop in a School   334
Mothers and Toddlers in a Church   334
Parent Play Groups   338
Sample Activities to Help Parents Understand
    Developmental Phases   339
Possible Ways to Proceed   343

PART VI General Issues

19   What Child Art Therapy Is and Who Can Do It   347
Art Therapy and Art Education   348
Art Therapy and Play Therapy   350
Qualities of Good Child Art Therapists   351

20   Why and How the Art Therapist Helps   356
The Need and Capacity to Create   356
The Creative Process as a Learning Experience   357
The Art Therapist as a Real Person and Symbolic Other:
    Transference   359
An Artist and a Therapist   363
The Art Therapist as a Change Agent   364
Extending Opportunities: Art Therapy Consultation   365

21   How the Art Therapist Learns through Research   368
Introduction and Issues   368
Objective Observation   369
Subjective Clinical Assessments   370
Grouping and Goal-Setting   370
Assessing Change in Blind Children I   371
Assessing Change in Blind Children II   373
A Phenomenological Investigation   375
Self-Assessments of Art Products   376
Measurement of Media Popularity   376
Group Drawings and Group Dynamics   377
Diagnostic Questions about Child Art   378
Variability in Children's Art   380
Free Association in Art Imagery   381
Relationships between Creativity and Mental Health   382
Comparing Products from Art and Drama Interviews   383
Conclusion   384

A Cautionary Note   387

References   389

Index   407

About the DVD   419

Illustrations

Color files of the illustrations for each chapter are found on the DVD in the folder for that chapter (i.e., folder DVD 1.0 contains the figures for Chapter 1, DVD 2.0 contains the figures for Chapter 2, etc.).

Chapter 1

1.1   "The Scariest Dream" (Two Dead Grandmothers). Age 8. Chalk
1.2   Painting of My Children. Acrylic

Chapter 2

2.1   A Blind Boy Finger Painting in a Tray
2.2   A Blind Boy Mixing Clay and Water in a Bowl
2.3   A Person Drawing by a Brain-Damaged Boy. Age 9
2.4   A Girl Who Is Absorbed in Her Work (Photo by Jacob Malezi)

Chapter 3

3.1   A Toddler Can Manipulate a Paintbrush and Enjoy the Process
3.2   (a) A Head-Body (Cephalopod) Figure. Three years, 10 months. Crayon
      (b) A Person (Mommy) 8 Months Later by the Same Girl. Crayon
3.3   A Partially Sighted Boy Fills in His Own Outlines
3.4   Some of Jenny's Varied Human Figure Drawings Around Age 4
3.5   "Daddy in Front of Our House," by Jim. Age 5. Marker
3.6   "X-ray" Drawing of a Mother with a Baby in Her Tummy. Age 5. Marker
3.7   A Family Eating Dinner around a Table. Age 6. Marker
3.8   A Boy's Pictures of a Clown (a) and of Himself (b). Age 5. Crayon
3.9   (a) Lisa's Usual Style of Painting
      (b) Lisa's Smeary Picture
3.10 A Family Doing Things Inside Their House ("X-ray"). Age 5. Crayon

Chapter 4

4.1   Jeremy's Drawing of Battles and Action. Age 7. Marker
4.2   Donny Filming a Drawing-in-Progress for Animation

Chapter 5

5.1   Carla's Nightmare Monster. Age 8. Scribble drawing, marker
5.2   "A Girl Was Mad" by Eleanor. Age 15. Marker

5.3 (a) A Clay Head, All One Color, by Jerry. Age 11

(b) A Multicolored Clay Head, by Jerry. Age 11

5.4 Chip's Drawing of a Dream about Godzilla. Age 8. Marker

5.5 Lori's Scary Monster Mask. Age 5. Crayon on cardboard

5.6 (a) Drawing an Enemy and (b) Punching Him on a Bag. Boy, age 6

5.7 Glen's Drawing of the USS Constitution. Age 11. Pencil

5.8 The Pencil-Snatcher Sneaking Away, by James. Age 13. Pencil

Chapter 6

6.1 (a–g) Jamie's Products from His Art Interview, in Order

6.2 Melanie's Lonely, Hungry Eagle. Age 15. Scribble drawing, chalk

6.3 Jim's Painting of a "Design," Later Called a "Boat." Age 9. Tempera

6.4 A Statue of a Person Being Born, by Ben. Age 12. Clay

6.5 (a–c) Three Products from a 1-hour Interview, in Order. Age 9

6.6 Head of a Man, by Marilyn. Age 16. Clay

6.7 (a) A Tree, by Evelyn. Age 16. Paint, marker

(b) "Fred," by Evelyn. Age 16. Paint, marker

Chapter 8

8.1 A Pirate with an Eye Patch, by Ellen. Age 12. Marker

8.2 Ellen's First Drawing after a 6-week Interruption. Marker

8.3 Ellen's First Enlargement of Her "Creature," 1 Week Later

8.4 One of Dorothy's Many Bird Drawings. Age 10. Pencil and tempera

8.5 Dorothy's Pencil Drawing of a Destructive Eagle and Its Victim

8.6 The "Tortoise Shell Family" of Cats, by Dorothy. Marker

8.7 Randy Giving the Art Therapist a Gift. Age 10. Marker

8.8 Randy Holding On to the Art Therapist with a Belt. Marker

Chapter 9

9.1 "A Runed Work" (a Crane), by Tim. Age 5. Mixed media

9.2 A House by Tim, Done in Group. Age 5. Wood scraps and glue

9.3 A Boy Holding On to a Pet Snake, by Tim. Age 6. Marker

9.4 A Fire-Breathing Dinosaur, by Tim. Age 6. Marker

Chapter 10

10.1 Mr. F.'s Scribble Drawing: A Bum or a Clown. Chalk

10.2 F. Family Creating Family Portraits

10.3 F. Family Working on Their Dinosaur Mural. Poster chalk

10.4 Mrs. Y.'s Teepee. Free Drawing. Marker

Chapter 11

11.1 Billy and Mrs. K. Drawing Each Other at the Easel

11.2 Josh and Mrs. W. Working Together on a Clay Sculpture

11.3 Family Drawing by Girl with Anorexia

Chapter 12

12.1 Mrs. J.'s Family Drawing. Marker

12.2 Mrs. K.'s "Life Space" Picture. Marker

12.3 A Mother and Son Working Together on a Drawing
12.4 A Young Widow's "Life-Space" Drawing of Her Many Concerns

Chapter 13

13.1 Two Girls Working Together on the Same Space without Talking
13.2 "Joe Frazier" or "The Stupid Man," a Boxer Who Got Beaten Up. Marker
13.3 Three Works by Don
    (a) A Tight Drawing
    (b) A Bloody Sculpture
    (c) A Free Painting

Chapter 14

14.1 Matt's Drawing of a Man Trying to Shoot a Woman. Age 9. Marker
14.2 Soap Crayon "Makeup" Turns Jack into Frankenstein. Age 9
14.3 Two Boys Help Each Other Use Paint to Become "Generals"
14.4 Three Sculptures by Sam
    (a) An Early Undulating Mass
    (b) "Need"
    (c) A Late Head of a King
14.5 A Head with Distorted Features, by Sam. Age 16. Pencil
14.6 Sam's Drawing of the View from His College Window. Pencil
14.7 (a) An Early Athlete, by Jim
    (b) A Later Athlete, by Jim

Chapter 15

15.1 A Boy in a Wheelchair Paints His Ceramic Slab Pot
15.2 A Drawing of the Art Therapist, by Claire. Age 10. Crayon
15.3 Claire's Drawing, Done Immediately after a Visit to the Dentist. Marker
15.4 Eleanor's Drawing of "What She Would Like to Do." Marker
15.5 Carl Making One of His Many Wood Scrap Compositions
15.6 A Blind Child Experiencing Finger Paint

Chapter 16

16.1 Mr. C.'s Picture of His Wife: "The Rock of Gibraltar." Marker
16.2 Mrs. C.'s Picture of Her Husband and His Many Interests. Marker
16.3 Tommy's Super-Powerful Sculpture: "Bionic Susquash"
16.4 Two of Larry's Many Clay Rockets Used for Space Fantasies
16.5 Larry Playing a Recorder during a Therapy Session
16.6 An Artist-Mother "Helps" Her Blind Child to Paint Better

Chapter 17

17.1 A Boy Crying because He Lost His Bike. Age 10. Tempera
17.2 A Bird Knocking Another Bird off the Nest. Age 5. Marker
17.3 A Girl Crying because Her Brother Broke Her Doll. Age 5. Crayon
17.4 A "Bad Scissors" about to Cut Off a Brother's Nose. Age 5. Pencil
17.5 "I Hope This Didn't Happen." Age 5. Pencil
17.6 Ugly Drawing of Older Sister Jenny, by Nona. Age 8. Pen
17.7 Ugly Drawing of Older Sister Nona, by Jon. Age 7. Pencil

17.8 Ugly Drawing of Parents, by Jenny. Age 5. Crayon
17.9 Killer Shark Devouring Bad Mother, by Jon. Age 8. Pencil
17.10 Ugly Drawing of Father by Jon. Age 9. Pen
17.11 A Flying Superhero with a Little Boy Hanging On to Him. Age 5. Marker
17.12 Ugly Picture of Dr. Rubin's Face. Age 7. Marker

Chapter 18

18.1 Children and Parents Working on an "Endless Easel" at an Arts Festival
18.2 (a–b) Mothers and Children at a "Family Art Workshop" in a School
18.3 Mothers and Toddlers at a Parent-Child Workshop in a Church
18.4 An Adult Blowing Soap Bubbles in a Parent Play Group

Chapter 20

20.1 An Ugly Picture of the Art Therapist During a Period of Angry Feelings

DVD Contents

A Note to the Reader/Viewer

Illustrations, not Instructions

Because the book covers a great deal of ground, the DVD is meant to illustrate rather than to instruct. In order to show a wide variety of examples, I have opted for breadth rather than depth. Another reason for the brevity of most of the film clips is to minimize the likelihood of revealing any sensitive information or material about the participants.

Although the majority of the illustrative clips are from unfinished film and tape materials, some are excerpts from finished works, a few of which may still be available for purchase. I have therefore included any relevant information, as well as a listing of those individuals and institutions who have generously given permission for their inclusion. This can be found in the Acknowledgments.

A Reminder About Confidentiality

One reason for the brevity of most of the film clips on the DVD is to minimize the likelihood of revealing any sensitive information or material about the participants. This is a concern that I hope will be understood and honored by you, the reader/viewer.

Although not all of the people on this DVD are patients, it is important to note that many were at the time these images were made, and that in the majority of instances, they agreed to be photographed specifically for the purpose of professional education.

Since this book is addressed to those in the helping professions, I trust that you will respect the need for privacy of anyone allowing themselves to be filmed, and will maintain the same kind of confidentiality normally accorded to any kind of clinical material.

As all Codes of Ethics state, any personal information about people in treatment is privileged information, intended only for professionals. The need for confidentiality extends to the artwork on this DVD, as well as to all stills and video images of those whose generosity will allow others to be helped.

We remain forever in their debt, and therefore owe them the courtesy of neither reproducing nor showing their images to individuals who are not using this book for educational purposes.

Although art therapy publications have long utilized reproductions and photographs in order to train others; this is the first time that so many images have been made available in a single book, in order to better inform those wanting to learn ways of using art in their clinical work.

As one of those individuals, your strict adherence to keeping these images confidential will help future generations of therapists to be educated more fully and more richly in the use of this active modality than ever before. It is up to each person using this text to respect this request.

It is therefore essential that you refrain from copying these images to your computer's hard drive or sharing them with others, and that you use them solely for your own education as a mental health professional.

On behalf of those who agreed to be photographed so that you might better learn, and on behalf of those who can be helped through art, I thank you and wish you good fortune in your own efforts.

Judith Aron Rubin, Ph.D.
January, 2005

Chapter 1. Roots

1.1 Personal
  A. After Peter's Death
  B. Nightmare
  C. My Mother
1.2 Memorial for a Wife
1.3 Spontaneous Art of the Mentally Ill
  A. A Patient and His Art
  B. On Calendar Pages
  C. On Toilet Paper
  D. Painting by a Patient
  E. Aloyse Korbaz——An Artist with Schizophrenia ("Magic Mirror of Aloyse")
1.4 Child Art Therapy Pioneers
  A. Viktor Lowenfeld
  B. Margaret Naumburg
  C. Edith Kramer
1.5 Drawing Helps My Mourning Process
  A. Pain
  B. My Mother in the Hospital Bed
  C. Mama-Breast-Love
  D. I Love You, I Need You
  E. Can You See?
  F. Together Again
  G. Screaming
  H. Cold and Lonely
  I. All Together
  J. Mom—Inside Me Forever

Chapter 2. *Framework for Freedom*

2.1 Carla Frees Herself
- A. "Personality Globs"
- B. "Mind Picture"
- C. Shopping Center at Night
- D. House

2.2 A Schizophrenic Boy Organizes Himself
- A. The Dead King
- B. How a Pumpkin Grows From a Seed

2.3 Containment
- A. Coloring Book
- B. Natural Enclosures
- C. Filled Enclosures

2.4 Conditions for Creative Growth
- A. Choices and Autonomy ("We'll Show You What We're Gonna Do!")
  Art Therapist: Judith A. Rubin, Ph.D.
- B. Things to Draw With
- C. Things to Paint With
- D. Things to Model and Construct With
- E. Choices of Materials and Where to Work
  1. Papers
  2. Paints
  3. Drawing and Modeling Materials
  4. Working Surfaces
- F. Unstructured Media ("Children and the Arts")
- G. Choices and Self-Definition ("Children and the Arts")
  Art Therapist: Judith A. Rubin, Ph.D. (F & G)
- H. Options in Media and Location
  Therapists: Judith A. Rubin, Ph.D. and Eleanor C. Irwin, Ph.D.

Chapter 3. *Understanding Development in Art*

3.1 Stages of Development
- A. Manipulating
- B. Forming
- C. Naming
- D. Representing
- E. Consolidating
- F. Only One Arm Needed to Throw Ball
- G. Only One Arm Needed to Hold Balloons
- H. Wizard of Oz (Age 6)
- I. Naturalizing—Wizard of Oz (Age 8)
- J. Personalizing
- K. Adolescent Finds Her Style
- L. One of Her Paintings

3.2 Barbara and Joyce
- A. Barbara's Careful Style ("We'll Show You What We're Gonna Do!")
- B. Barbara Next to Joyce ("We'll Show You What We're Gonna Do!")
  Art Therapist: Judith A. Rubin, Ph.D. (A & B)

Chapter 4. A Picture of the Therapeutic Process

4.1 Carla and Her Monsters
  A. A Nightmare Monster
  B. Another Monster
  C. Carla as a Monster Attacking Me
4.2 A Mad Scientist by Laura
4.3 Lori Finds Her Anger
  A. Lori Drawing
  B. Lori's Picture
  C. Lori's Finger Painted Monster
4.4 Carla's Goodbye
  A. A Bird on Her Nest
  B. Mother and Baby Turtle
  C. Carla's Film
4.5 Larry's Doctor Play
  A. Going to the Dentist
  B. Going to the Doctor
  C. Giving/Getting a Shot ("We'll Show You What We're Gonna Do!")
     Art Therapist: Judith A. Rubin, Ph.D.
4.6 Lori's Farewell
  A. Lori and the Art Therapist
  B. Ugly Mrs. Rubin
  C. Soap Crayon Makeup
  D. Sad Girl

Chapter 5. Some Ways to Facilitate Expression

5.1 Bars to Cage the Nightmare Monster
5.2 A Later Head by Jerry
5.3 A Microphone
  A. Using a Microphone
  B. A Brush "Microphone"
     Art Therapist: Judith A. Rubin, Ph.D.
5.4 From Art to Drama
  A. A Clay Gun
  B. Being Shot at with a Clay Gun
  C. Being Attacked with a Sword
  D. The Clay Becomes a Hat
5.5 Flexible Space Usage
  A. Making a Hideout
  B. Entering the Hideout
  C. Creating a House
  D. Decorating the House

Chapter 6. An Individual Art Evaluation

6.1 Doing and Undoing
  A. In Clay
  B In Finger Paint

    C. Angry Cat with Big Teeth

    D. Taco the Horse

    E. Electric Potter's Wheel

6.2 Looking Intently

    A. Witness Writing—Open Studio

       Art Therapist: Dayna Block

    B. Witness Writing—RAW Art Works

    C. What Do You See? ("Luis and the Big Fish")

       Art Therapist: Mala Betensky, Ph.D.

6.3 Talking About Artwork

    A. Ralph Describes His House

    B. Lisa Finds Images

       Art Therapist: Judith A. Rubin, Ph.D. (A & B)

6.4 Multiple Products

    A. Lisa Beginning Her Art Interview

    B. Lisa Finishing Her Session

       Art Therapist: Judith A. Rubin, Ph.D. (A & B)

    C. Two Dinosaurs

    D. Dinosaur Attack

    E. Sad Dog

    F. Dog who Got Kicked Out

    G. Bars/Prison/Crib

6.5 Single Product

    A. A Dragon

    B. Two Heads

    C. Andy's Art Evaluation

       Art Therapist: Judith A. Rubin, Ph.D.

    D. Andy's Painting

Chapter 7. Decoding Symbolic Messages

7.1 Spontaneous Verbalization

    A. A Story While Drawing ("Stevie's Light Bulb")

       Therapist: Sara Dubo, M.D.

    B. Associations While Painting ("We'll Show You What We're Gonna Do!")

       Art Therapist: Judith A. Rubin, Ph.D.

7.2 Donny's Buildings

    A. Separated

    B. Touching

7.3 Symbolic Associations

       Art Therapist: Laurie Wilson, Ph.D.

7.4 Pride in the Product

    A. A Girl and Her Clay Figures

    B. A Girl and Her Construction

    C. A Boy and His Drawings

7.5 Positive Self-Evaluations

    A. A Boy Is Proud of His "Beautiful Pot"

    B. Greg Feels Like an Artist ("We'll Show You What We're Gonna Do!")

C. Carl Likes His Construction ("We'll Show You What We're Gonna Do!")
D. Ellen Feels Talented
  Art Therapist: Judith A. Rubin, Ph.D. (A–D)

Chapter 8. *Some Case Studies*

8.1 Ellen—An Elective Mute
A. Ellen's Drawing from the Second Session
B. A Girl Playing Ball
C. A Girl With Head Taped On
D. Dyadic Drawing
E. My Painting of Ellen
F. Girl with Man on Stage
G. A Drag Race
H. A Mean Female Bird
I. Two Swans Swimming
J. My Anguished Creature
K. Different Colors
L. Different Hairdo
M. Shell Around Face
N. One of the Last Creatures

8.2 Dorothy—A Girl with Schizophrenia
A. A Bird
B. Another Bird
C. Bird Painting
D. Bird Feeding Babies
E. Free Painting
F. Monster
G. The Eagle and the Dummy
H. Painted Bird
I. The Kids on the Unit
J. Activities on the Unit
K. Going on a Picnic
L. A Field Trip
M. All the Kids
N. Throwing Doll Away
O. A Cat
P. Another Cat
Q. My Best Cat Costume
R. Watching in a Cat Costume
S. Mrs. Rubin
T. Mrs. Rubin Having a Baby
U. Mrs. Rubin Attacked for Being Bad

8.3 Randy—A Boy with Encopresis
A. Zebra and Fox
B. Zebra
C. School
D. Civil War Scene
E. A Design

F. Mars and Constellations

G. Mrs. Rubin and the Martian

H. Castle

I. School on Fire

J. Dinosaur and Volcano

K. Cover—Space Series

L. Cover—Earth Series

M. Woman on a Cliff

8.4 Andrew-A Boy who Set a Fire ("Art Therapy and Children")
Art Therapist: Roger Arguile, M.A.

Chapter 9. Case Illustration: Understanding and Helping

9.1 Individual Art Evaluation

A. A Runed Work

B. The Dinosaur House

9.2 Group Art Therapy

A. Clay Cave

B. Chalk Stripes

C. Chart

D. Tim in Group

E. Enjoying Finger Paint

F. Tire Swing

G. Self-Portrait

H. Tim and Jamie

9.3 Mother-Child Sessions

A. Tim's Painting

B. Mother's Drawing

C. Tim's Imitation

D. Girl Operating Crane

E. Tim Bosses Mom

F. Mom Bosses Tim

G. Working Together

H. Joint Sculpture

9.4 Family Art Evaluation

A. Basket for Boredom Blues

B. Kabuki Actor

C. Family's Use of Space

D. Mommy Going to a Party

E. Tim's Attempt at "Family"

F. Me and Daddy Playing Ball

G. Family Square Dancing

H. Two Versions of Family

I. Family Mural Task

J. Part of the Mural

9.5 Family Art Therapy

A. Birthday Cake by Tim

B. Birthday Cake by Sister

C. Fort

    D. Pool Table
    E. House
    F. Me in the Rain
    G. Boy on Sled
    H. Snowman who Might Melt
    I. Me and Mommy
    J. Beautiful Gisella
    K. Dopey
    L. Sister's Tummy
    M. Tim Punching Me
    N. A Meanie
    O. Me and Dad Playing Tennis/Mom Divin' Down
    P. Two Dinosaurs

9.6 Family Themes and Tasks
    A. Four Houses
    B. A Motel
    C. New House
    D. Main Problem by Father
    E. Main Problem by Mother
    F. A Walk in the Woods
    G. Me and Dad on the Boat Vacation
    H. Mother's Wish
    I. Father's Wish
    J. Calling Home
    K. Weekend Companions
    L. On the Beach
    M. Joint Construction
    N. Roller Coaster
    O. Seesaw

9.7 Joint Nonverbal Drawing
    A. Tim Leaves Silent Family Drawing
    B. Father Joins Tim
    C. Father Rejoins the Females
    D. Tim Adds Something to the Picture
    E. Tim Making Clay Bank

Chapter 10. A Family Art Evaluation

10.1 The F. Family
10.2 Scribble Drawings
    A. Making a Small Scribble
    B. Developing and Discussing a Scribble
       Art Therapist: Judith A. Rubin, Ph.D. (A & B)
    C. Describing a Scribble
    D. Making a Large Scribble ("Art Therapy: Beginnings")
       Art Therapist: Elinor Ulman, D.A.T
    E. Barbed Wire Fence
    F. Carl's Monster
    G. Carol's Monster

10.3 Family Representations
- A. Another Option-Abstract Family Portrait
  Art Therapists: Patti Ravenscroft, M.A. and Mari Fleming, M.A.
- B. Teenager's "Family Portrait"
- C. Jody's Family Representation
- D. Observing Jack Drawing
- E. Mr. F.'s Family Drawing
- F. Jack's Family Drawing
- G. Mrs. F.'s Family Drawing
- H. Viewing All Family Pictures
- I. Comparing Family Pictures
  Art Therapists: Patti Ravenscroft, M.A. and Mari Fleming, M.A.
- J. Describing a Family Picture
  Art Therapist: Judith A. Rubin, Ph.D.

10.4 Family Mural
- A. A Joint Family Drawing
  Art Therapists: Patti Ravenscroft, M.A. and Mari Fleming, M.A.
- B. J. Family's Mural
  Art Therapist: Judith A. Rubin, Ph.D.
- C. Working Together
- D. Finishing Up
- E. Discussing Mural
- F. F. Family's Mural
- G. I. Family's Mural

10.5 Free Products
- A. Tim's Free Drawing
- B. Glen's Free Drawing

Chapter 11. Family Art Therapy

11.1 Billy and His Mother
- A. Joint Picture—"Our House"
- B. Mother's Picture of Billy
- C. Billy's Picture of Mother

11.2 Donny and Ross

11.3 Mother and Son with Both Therapists
- A. "Lake Erie" by David and Mother
- B. David Painting "A Beautiful Mess"
- C. David Working on the Painting

11.4 Conjoint Family Art Therapy
- A. Dr. Homann and Younger Child Blowing Paint with Straws
- B. The W. Family Discussing Their Art
- C. Bill and Dad Starting Their "Smoking Picture"
- D. Bill and Dad Working on Their Picture

11.5 Laura and Her Family
- A. Laura's Family Silently Settles the Territory
- B. The Finished Product

11.6 Sloane and Her Mom
- A. Bringing a Picture to Mommy

Art Therapist: Cindi Westendorff, M.A.
B. Working Together
Art Therapist: Laura Greenstone, M.A.
11.7 A Multimodal Family Session
Art Therapist: Judith A. Rubin, Ph.D. and
Drama Therapist: Eleanor C. Irwin, Ph.D.
11.8 Lila and Her Family
A. All Head, No Heart
B. Starving Man
C. No Body #1
D. No Body #2

Chapter 12. Art Therapy with Parents

12.1 Mrs. Braver
A. Working on Her Head
B. The Finished Portrait
C. "Who Am I?"
D. A Collage about Herself
E. Showing Me Her Collage
12.2 Mrs. Silver
A. Mrs. Silver Painting
B. Image of Relationships
C. "Roads"
D. "Like Hell, a Storm with Lightning and Turmoil"
12.3 Mrs. Lord
A. Mrs. Lord Painting
B. The Painting—"Sea Mist"
C. Looking at the Painting
D. Working on a Drawing
E. "Shock"
F. "Ambivalence, Dilemma, Uncertainty, Confusion"
12.4 Mother-Child Art Therapy Group
A. Mother Cat by Other Mother + Baby by Child
B. Mother Cat by Child
C. Baby Kitten by Child
D. Working Together
E. Mother Interviews Son
F. Lady with a Weiner and a Black Eye
G. Jamie's Poop Picture
12.5 Parent-Child Dyad Art Therapy Groups
Art Therapist: Lucille Proulx
12.6 Single Mothers Discuss Pictures
12.7 Head Start Mothers Group
A. A Hat She Made
B. A Ring She Made
C. A Group Session
Therapists: Judith A. Rubin, Ph.D. and Eleanor C. Irwin Ph.D.

12.8 Substance Abuse Problems
  A. Sojourner House Group
  B. Women Working in Group
  C. Concentrating
  D. Painting Figure
  E. Statements by Group Members
     Therapists: Judith A. Rubin, Ph.D. and Eleanor C. Irwin Ph.D.

Chapter 13. Group Art Therapy

13.1 Values of Art in Groups
  A. Values of Group Art Activity ("We'll Show You What We're Gonna Do!")
  B. Social Benefits of the Arts ("Children and the Arts")
     Art Therapist: Judith A. Rubin, Ph.D. (A & B)
13.2 Warmup Activities
  A. Closing Eyes Can Reduce Anxiety
  B. A Clay Scribble
     Art Therapist: Linda Gantt, Ph.D.
  C. Drawing on a Shared Space
     Art Therapist: Mary Flannery
  D. Nonverbal Group Mural (Floor)
  E. Working Together Silently (Table)
  F. Round Robin Clay Pass
     Art Therapist: Judith A. Rubin, Ph.D.
  G. Round Robin Exercise ("Art Therapy")
     Art Therapist: Patsy Nowell-Hall, M.A.
13.3 Getting to Know Each Other
  A. Introductions in Clay ("Art Therapy: The Healing Vision")
  B. Making a Bridge Together ("Art Therapy: The Healing Vision")
     Art Therapist: Byron Fry, M.A. (A & B)
  C. Using Initials as Starters
     Therapists: Paul Levy and Judith A. Rubin, Ph.D.
13.4 Group Activities
  A. Each Does the Same Topic
     Art Therapist: Diane Safran, M.S.
  B. All Make Feeling Masks (Ukraine)
     Art Therapist: Olena Woloszuk
  C. Working Together as Instructed
     Art Therapist: Kit Jenkins, M.A.
  D. Making an Island Together (Russia)
  Art Therapist: Doris Arrington, Ph.D.
  E. Sharing Space Informally
     Art Therapist: Judith A. Rubin, Ph.D.
  F. Free Choice-Multifamily Group
     Art Therapist: Donna Betts, Ph.D.
  G. Same Topic, Choice of Media
  H. Same Medium, Choice of Topic
  I. A Mix of Structured and Unstructured Activities
     Art Therapists: Kit Jenkins, M.A. and Mary Flannery

13.5 Group Issues Explored in a Puppet Drama ("Green Creature Within")
    Therapists: Eleanor C. Irwin, Ph.D., Judith A. Rubin, Ph.D., and
    Guillermo Borrero, M.D.
13.6 Reflecting in a Group
    A. Sharing Privately
       Art Therapist: Kit Jenkins, M.A.
    B. Sharing during Discussion Period ("Drawing From the Fire")
       Art Therapist: Kristin Mendenhall, M.S.
    C. Sculpture Serves Artist and Other Members ("Green Creature Within")
       Therapists: Eleanor C. Irwin, Ph.D., Judith A. Rubin, Ph.D., and
       Guillermo Borrero, M.D.
    D. Members Interview Each Other (RAW Art Works)
    E. Re-Viewing as a Group ("Green Creature Within")
       Therapists: Eleanor C. Irwin, Ph.D., Judith A. Rubin, Ph.D.,
       Guillermo Borrero, M.D.

Chapter 14. Multimodality Group Therapy

14.1 Multimodal Expression Is Natural
    A. Spontaneous Singing while Drawing
    B. Spontaneous Singing while Modeling
14.2 Shifts Happen Spontaneously
    A. A Clay Horsie Speaks ("We'll Show You What We're Gonna Do!")
    B. Sound Effects Enliven ("We'll Show You What We're Gonna Do!")
       Art Therapist: Judith A. Rubin, Ph.D. (A & B)
    C. Soap Crayon Mask
    D. Clay Leads to an Attack ("We'll Show You What We're Gonna Do!")
    E. Clay Leads to a Party ("We'll Show You What We're Gonna Do!")
       Art Therapist: Judith A. Rubin, Ph.D. (D & E)
    F. About to Pound the Clay
14.3 Some Pariscraft Casts
    A. Making a Cast
    B. Putting It on an Arm
    C. Creating a Finger Cast
14.4 Latency Art-Drama Group
    A. Finger Painting Wearing a Scary Mask
    B. Speaking of Peace (Boy with Spina Bifida)
       Art Therapist: Judith A. Rubin, Ph.D.
    C. Matt's Pirate Mask
    D. Matt as a Pirate
    E. Putting the Fight on Paper in a Mural
    F. Bombing a German Plane (Mural)
    G. War Mural by Group
14.5 Adolescent Art-Drama Group ("Green Creature Within")
    A. Multiple Modalities
    B. Writing and Poetry
    C. "Need" by Sam
    D. Art and Meanings

E. A Filmed Drama
Therapists: Eleanor C. Irwin, Ph.D., Judith A. Rubin, Ph.D., and Guillermo Borrero, M.D. (A–E)
14.6 The Story of Sam
A. Change over Time ("Green Creature Within")
Therapists: Eleanor C. Irwin, Ph.D., Judith A. Rubin, Ph.D., and Guillermo Borrero, M.D.
B. One of His Paintings
14.7 The Story of Jim
A. Jim Drawing an Athlete
B. Growth Over Time ("Green Creature Within")
Therapists: Eleanor C. Irwin, Ph.D., Judith A. Rubin, Ph.D., and Guillermo Borrero, M.D.
C. Jim as a Big Shot
14.8 Role of the Leader ("Green Creature Within")
Therapists: Eleanor C. Irwin, Ph.D., Judith A. Rubin, Ph.D., and Guillermo Borrero, M.D.

Chapter 15. Art as Therapy for Children with Disabilities

15.1 Animal Artists
A. Congo the Chimpanzee Painting a Picture
B. Chimp Painting
Art Therapist Observer: David Henley
C. Dolphin Painting
Art Therapist Observer: Barbara Ann Levy
D. Elephant Painting (*CBS News* Reporter: Bob Simon)
15.2 Viktor Lowenfeld
Audiotape of Lowenfeld Lecture: John A. Michael
15.3 Schizophrenic Children
A. One of Karen's Danced Paintings
B. One of Teddy's People
C. Another Person by Teddy
D. Teddy's Boy Schema
E. Uncle's Farm (Tempera)
F. Uncle's Farm (Watercolor)
15.4 Physically Handicapped Children
A. The Art Program
B. In the Art Room
  1. At the Table
  2. In a Wheelchair
  3. On Rolling Beds
C. A Feather Collage
D. A Tempera Painting
E. A Wood Scrap Person ("Outa Shape")
Art Therapist: Judith A. Rubin, Ph.D. (D & E)
F. Claire in a Drama
G. Talking Book Picture

15.5 Deaf Children
   A. A Boy Is Pleased with His Artwork
   B. Same Boy, Another Day
   C. A Girl Enjoys Finger Paint
15.6 Retarded Children
   A. A Teacher Observing
   B. The Children at Work
15.7 Blind Children
   A. Terry's Pre-Program Assessment
   B. Peter's Pre-Program Assessment
   C. Expectations—Art Program ("We'll Show You What We're Gonna Do!")
   D. David—Art as Sublimation ("We'll Show You What We're Gonna Do!")
   E. Peter's Pride and Poetry ("We'll Show You What We're Gonna Do!")
      Art Therapist: Judith A. Rubin, Ph.D. (C– E)
   F. Larry in a Group
   G. Larry Speaks of Blindness
15.8 Current Developments
   A. Emotional Difficulties
      Art Therapist: Janet Bush, M.S.
   B. Social and Emotional Problems
      Art Therapist: Alice Karamanol, M.P.S.
   C. Learning Disabilities
      Art Therapist: Simone Alter-Muri, Ph.D.
   D. Neurological Impairments
      Therapist: Ralph Rabinovitch, M.D.
   E. Physical Handicaps
      Art Therapist: Nina Viscardi Ochoa, M.A.
   F. Blindness ("Access to the Arts")
      Art Therapist: Maureen Coghill-Moran, M.A.
   G. Deafness ("Art Therapy: the Healing Vision")
      Art Therapist: Terry Ouderkirk, M.A.
15.9 Special Considerations
   A. Karen is Proud ("We'll Show You What We're Gonna Do!")
   B. Peter Remembers His Operation ("We'll Show You What We're Gonna Do!")
      Art Therapist: Judith A. Rubin, Ph.D. (A & B)
   C. Organization of Materials ("Creating for Me")
   D. Responsive Materials ("Creating for Me")
      Art Therapist: Susan Aach-Feldman (C & D)

Chapter 16. Art Therapy with Disabled Children and Their Parents

16.1 Candy
   A. Family Art Evaluation
   B. Candy's Family Picture
   C. Her Brother's Family Representation
   D. Couple Drawing Together Silently
16.2 Tommy
   A. Larry with a Big Finger
   B. Tommy with a Big Hand

C. Tommy Martian in Outer Space
D. "Dead" in Outer Space
E. An Angry Clay Puppet
16.3 Julie Enacts a Drama
16.4 Janice Tells a Story
16.5 Larry
A. Larry Using Clay
B. Rocket by Larry
C. Larry Playing a Gong
D. Larry Singing
16.6 Mothers' Group
A. Mother-Child Session
B. Terry's Mother's Life-Space Picture
C. Pizza by Larry and Mother
D. Painting by Larry and Mother
E. Larry and Mother Painting
F. Larry, Terry, and Their Mothers
G. Larry and Mother Working Independently
H. Terry and Mother Working Together
I. Peter's Mother Painting
J. Peter and Mother Painting
K. Jimmy and His Mother

Chapter 17. Helping the Normal Child through Art

17.1 Fred Rogers (*Mister Rogers' Neighborhood*)
Art Lady: Judy Rubin
17.2 Art as Therapy
A. Self-Definition ("Children and the Arts")
B. Expression of Feelings ("Children and the Arts")
C. Self-Actualization ("We'll Show You What We're Gonna Do!")
Art Therapist: Judith A. Rubin, Ph.D. (A–C)
17.3 Normal Stresses
A. Man Scared of the Dark
B. Going to a New School
C. Babies inside Mommies
D. Jon Painting a Monster
E. Jon's Monster Painting
F. Jon's Fantasy Creatures (3)
G. Family Drawing by Jenny
H. Later Family Drawing
I. Mrs. Funny Bunny
J. Jerky Teacher
K. A Girl Who Has Grown Long Hair and Locked Her Mother in the Garage
L. The Girl Has the Key
M. Funny Clown Family
N. Boy Shooting Man
O. Batman
P. Well-Armed Battleship
Q. A Sad Girl

DVD Contents

17.4 A Concentration Camp
  A. Child Art from Terezin
    1. I Never Saw Another Butterfly—Book of Poems and Drawings
    2. Nightmares—Horrors of the Camp
    3. The Seder—A Happy Memory
  B. Edith Kramer on Friedl Dicker-Brandeis
    ("Edith Kramer: Artist/Art Therapist")
  C. Frederick Terna—Child Artist in Terezin ("The Story of Butterfly")
17.5 A Firestorm ("Drawing from the Fire")
  Art Therapist: Kristen Mendenhall, M.S.
17.6 Wars and Violence
  A. Israeli Child
  B. Second Israeli Child
  C. Croatian Child
  D. American Child
  E. Fires and Looting
  F. Yesterday (Riots)
  G. Tomorrow (Hope)
17.7 Medical Stresses
  A. Eddie Draws about His Diabetes ("Stevie's Light Bulb")
    Therapist: Ralph Rabinovitch, M.D.
  B. Draw Your Asthma as a Creature
    Art Therapist: Robin Gabriels, Ph.D.
  C. After an Operation
  D. After Severe Burns (KQED-TV)
    Art Therapist: Pat Levinson, M.A.
17.8 Abuse and PTSD
  A. Someone Being Shot
  B. Warning Sign on Door
  C. A Happy Bunny Family
  D. A Goodbye Card
  E. A Goodbye Valentine
17.9 Loss of Parental Figures
  A. Mother Died in an Accident
    Art Therapist: Sandra Graves-Alcorn, Ph.D.
  B. Uncle Died in a Fight ("Listening to Children")
    Therapist: Robert Coles, M.D.
  C. Parents Died of Cancer ("When Children Grieve")
    Art Therapist: Paula Shaefer, M.A.
  D. Fathers Died on 9/11 ("Tender Hearts")
    Art Therapist: Laura Loumeau-May, M.P.S.
  E. Group for Bereaved Children ("A Child's Grief")
    1. Draw the Person who Died
    2. Talk about the Person who Died
    3. Draw the Weather Inside
    4. Talk about the Weather Inside
      Therapist: Mavis Hines, Ph.D.

17.10 Parental Suicide
  A. Billy Being a Daddy
  B. Christopher's Flag
  C. Other Side of the Flag
  D. A Dog (Scribble Drawing)
  E. A Person Falls Off a Road

Chapter 18. Helping Parents through Art and Play

18.1 Therapeutic Art Classes
  A. The Cane School of Art
  B. Classes for All Ages
  C. Robert Ault and Student
  D. Growth Group—Warming Up ("Gestalt Art Experience With Janie Rhyne")
  E. Growth Group—Self-Definition ("Gestalt Art Experience With Janie Rhyne")
     Art Therapist: Janie Rhyne, Ph.D. (D & E)
18.2 Three Rivers Arts Festival
18.3 Animated Film Program
  A. Setting Up for Animation
  B. Doing Animation
  C. Filming Animation
18.4 Family Art Workshop
  A. Family Art Workshop
  B. A Mother Observes Her Child
  C. Grandmother and Grandson
18.5 Parent Art Workshop
  A. Parents Modeling
  B. Parents Constructing
18.6 Mothers and Toddlers in a Church
  A. A Mother and Son
  B. Another Mother and Son
18.7 Parent Play Group
  A. Blowing Soap Bubbles
  B. Moving Freely

Chapter 19. What Child Art Therapy Is and Who Can Do It

19.1 A Therapy Group Can Look Like a Class ("Stevie's Light Bulb")
19.2 Art Therapy and Art Education ("Children and Art Therapy")
     Art Therapist: Roger Arguile, M.A.
19.3 Some Child Art Therapy Pioneers at Work
  A. Margaret Naumburg ("Art Therapy: Beginnings")
  B. Edith Kramer ("Art Therapy: Beginnings")
  C. Mala Betensky ("The Scribble")
  D. Violet Oaklander ("A Boy and His Anger")
  E. Helen Landgarten ("Lori: Art Therapy and Self-Discovery")

Chapter 20. Why and How the Art Therapist Helps

20.1 Transference
  A. Larry and the Therapist

B. Positive Transference—Terry ("We'll Show You What We're Gonna Do!")
   Art Therapist: Judith A. Rubin, Ph.D.

Chapter 21. How the Art Therapist Learns through Research

21.1 Assessing Change in Blind Children
   A. Pre-Program Session
   B. Pre-Program Assessment
   C. Post-Program Session
   D. Post-Program Assessment
21.2 A Phenomenological Investigation—Tactile Aesthetic Study
   A. Sculpture by Blind Child
   B. Sculpture by Partially Sighted Child
   C. Sculpture by Sighted Child
   D. Blind Judge Responds
   E. Blind Judge Compares
   F. Partially Sighted Judge with Blindfold
   G. Partially Sighted Judge Responds
   H. Sighted Judge Responds
   I. Sighted Judge with Blindfold Compares
21.3 Diagnostic Questions-Paired Comparisons (* = Schizophrenic Child)
   Paired Comparisons (6): One by Schizophrenic*, One by Non-Schizophrenic
   Child as Presented to Judges in Study-Left and Right Slides (i.e., R1, R2, etc.)
21.4 Intra-Individual Variability
   A. Intra-Individual Variability by Age
   B. Person, Day 1, M4
   C. Person, Day 2, M4
   D. Person, Day 3, M4
   E. Person, Day 4, M4
   F. "A Nut" Day 1, M12
   G. "A Martian" Day 2, M12
   H. "My Cousin" Day 3, M12
   I. "My Friend" Day 4, M12
21.5 Outcome Study-Glasswork as Therapy
   Art Therapist: James Minson, M.A.

Acknowledgments

Though I alone must take responsibility for what is written here, I wish to thank some of the many individuals whose support and teaching have nourished both me and my work. I begin with my childhood family—my warm grandmother who always understood, my proud father with his high expectations and steady affection, my patient mother with her calming manner, and my companion brother.

I thank too my present family—my dependable husband, who has been patient throughout the long gestation period and two revisions of my first printed offspring; our three children—now adults with children of their own—whose drawings and words appear within, who helped with proofreading and typing the original, and who were most understanding at times when I was less available to them than any of us wished; and our four grandchildren, who provide lively evidence of the therapeutic benefits of art, and who constantly inspire me with their considerable creativity.

I thank too the many teachers and colleagues, friends and helpers, who provided good models as well as good ideas, and who, over the past 40 years, helped me to learn about myself, children, and art. A great many of them, like my parents, are no longer among the living, so it is a source of comfort that their values live on in this book.

In addition, I want to thank my friend and colleague Ellie Irwin, who has been a steady and stimulating companion throughout my career. I am grateful to Edith Kramer, who gave generously of her time and expertise in suggesting revisions for the 2nd edition. I also wish to thank the three experienced art therapists who reviewed the book for this 25th anniversary edition: Audrey Di Maria, Ikuko Acosta, and Joan Phillips, whose detailed and thoughtful suggestions were most helpful to me.

My employers—in 1978 the Pittsburgh Child Guidance Center, and in 1984 the Western Psychiatric Institute and Clinic—provided support services for the first two editions. Norman Rabinovitz and Sheila Ramsey took most of the photographs, along with some by Jim Lenckner, Jacob Malezi, and Lynn Johnson. Those which are technically poor are from slides taken with my own inexpensive camera.

I should also like to express my gratitude to the following organizations and publications to reprint material which first appeared in their journals or books: American Dance Therapy Association, American Foundation for the Blind, American Journal of Art Therapy, American Society of Psychopathology of Expression, Art and Activities, Association for the Advancement of Psychotherapy, Association for the Education of the Visually Handicapped, Beacon House, Brunner-Routledge, Doctor Franklin Perkins School, High Fidelity/Musical America, Karger Publishers, Mental Research Institute and Nathan Ackerman Family Institute, National Art Education Association, Pergamon Press, and the Pittsburgh Area Preschool Association.

Most of all, as in earlier editions, I want to thank the children and their families, who have been my very best teachers. Their generosity in allowing me to tell their stories and to reproduce their art and pictures of them at work has permitted many others to learn from our collaborative efforts. I believe that they have been willing to share because they wanted others to have the same opportunity to be understood and to grow through art therapy.

Thanks to the following for permission to excerpt material for the DVD:

ABC News Archives (Tony Brackett)
   "Tender Hearts"

Accessible Arts, Inc. (Paul Lesnik)
   "Access to the Arts"

Sandra Graves Alcorn, Ph.D.
   Videotape of Interview with Child after Mother's Death

Simone Alter-Muri, Ph.D.
   "Creative Arts Therapies at the Pace School"

American Art Therapy Association
   "Art Therapy: Beginnings"

Doris Arrington, Ph.D.
   Videotape of Art Therapy with Russian Orphans

Acknowledgments

Robert Ault, M.F.A. and The Menninger Foundation
"Art Therapy: The Healing Vision"

Dayna Block
Videotape of Open Studio Process Group

Ian Brownell, Bushy Theater, Inc.
"Access to the Arts"

Janet Bush, M.A.
Videotape of an Art Therapy Session in a School

Norma Canner, ADTR
"Access to the Arts"

CBS News Archives
"The Big Picture" (60 Minutes), "Middletown, U.S.A." (48 Hours)

David Crawley, KDKA-TV
"The Art of Healing"

Expressive Media, Inc.
"Art Therapy Has Many Faces," "Children and the Arts: A Film About
Growing," "The Green Creature Within: Art and Drama in Group Psycho-
therapy," "'We'll Show You What We're Gonna Do!' Art With Multiply
Handicapped Blind Children"

Family Communications, Inc., WQED-TV
Excerpt from Mister Rogers' Neighborhood

Thomas Frank, M.D. and Kate Frank, Ph.D.
Photographs of Margaret Nawnburg (Frank)

Robert Frye, Bolthead Communications
"The Journey of Butterfly"

Robin Gabriels, Ph.D.
Med*Source Program on Art Therapy for Asthma

Frank Goryl, Ph.D.
Videotape of Clay Workshop Led by Linda Gantt, Ph.D.

Janet Greenwood, Ph.D.
"Gestalt Art Experience with Janie Rhyne"

Richard Greenberg
"Ventilator Dependent Children at School"

David Henley, Ph.D.
Videotape of Chimpanzee Painting

Chris Holmes, Chris Holmes Productions
"Drawing From the Fire"

Paula Howie, M.A.
Videotapes of Art Therapy from the Walter Reed Army Medical Center

Simcha Jacobovici, Associated Producers, Ltd.
"A Child's Grief"

Kit Jenkins, M.A.
Videotapes from RAW Art Works

Alice Karamanol
"Classroom Closeups"

KQED-TV
"Without Words"

Edith Kramer, D.A.T.
"Edith Kramer: Artist and Art Therapist"

Helen Landgarten, M.A.
"Lori: Art Therapy and Self-Discovery"

James Lenckner
"Creating for Me" with Susan Aach-Feldman

Barbara Ann Levy, M.A.
Videotape of Dolphin Painting

Laura Loumeau-May, M.P.S.
"Tender Hearts" (ABC News Archives)

John A. Michael
Audiotapes of Viktor Lowenfeld Lectures; Photographs of Viktor Lowenfeld

James Minson, M.A.
"The Transition of Indigenous Guatemalan Youth Living in Foster Care as
Assisted by Glass Craft Training and Practice" (Master's Thesis DVD)

New Jersey Education Association
"Classroom Closeups" (2 Shows on Art Therapy)

Aina Nucho, Ph.D.
"Luis and the Big Fish," "The Psycho-Cybernetic Model of Art Therapy,"
"The Scribble"

Violet Oaklander, Ph.D.
"A Boy and His Anger: A Therapy Session"

Nina Viscardi Ochoa
"Ventilator Dependent Children at School"

Ralph Rabinovitch, M.D.
"Stevie's Light Bulb: Graphic Art in Child Psychiatry"

Patti Ravenscroft, M.A.
Family Art Evaluation

Mary Cane Robinson, ATR
Photographs of Florence Cane

Acknowledgmants

Diane Safran, Ph.D.
    Videotape of ADHD Art Therapy Group

Max Solomon, MaxSound Productions
    "A Boy and His Anger: A Therapy Session"

Buddy Squires, Filmmaker
    "Listening to Children with Dr. Robert Coles"

Arthur Ulene, M.D.
    "When Children Grieve"

Very Special Arts, Massachusetts
    "Multi-Arts Resource Guide"

Harriet Wadeson, Ph.D.
    Videotape of Couple Art Therapy

Diane Waller, Ph.D. and John Beacham, Ph.D.
    "Children and Art Therapy "

Laurie Wilson
    Videotape of Art Therapy with a Young Boy

Olenka Woloszuk
    "Let Us Save the Children: Olenka's Workshop" (Ukraine)

Preface
25th Anniversary Edition

Background

There is an interesting irony to the genesis of this 25th anniversary edition. Having changed homes several times since 1978, *Child Art Therapy* was still in print, but the price had increased each year, so that it had become prohibitively expensive for art therapy students, its main audience. Wiley, the current parent, had offered me a contract for *Artful Therapy* (Rubin, 2005), a book addressed to mental health workers from other disciplines. I realized that I liked the idea of my latest book being housed where my first one now resided.

My only problem was the constantly escalating cost of the former. I was therefore delighted when Peggy Alexander, the publisher at Wiley, agreed to offer *Child Art Therapy* at a more reasonable price, if I would do another revision. I suggested that since it would soon be 25 years since the original publication, this could be an anniversary edition. Peggy liked the idea as well. It is indeed gratifying to have a book-child be useful to people for so long.

I was especially pleased that she was also willing to have me create DVDs to accompany both books, since I was working at the time on a videotape about the field, *Art Therapy Has Many Faces*[1] (Rubin, 2004). Having made educational films since the 1970s, the notion of audiovisual modes of teaching was not new to me, and I had recently discovered that today's technology allowed even a therapist to edit films using a laptop computer.

---

[1] *Art Therapy Has Many Faces* is available in VHS and DVD formats from Expressive Media, Inc. at 128 N. Craig St., Pittsburgh, PA 15213. Available from www.expressivemedia.org.

I had also found during the past six years that using film and video in courses and presentations added something very special.

The prospect of both a lower price for the book and an accompanying DVD made the idea of a revision appealing. I became even more engaged when I received the reviews from three experienced colleagues, all with excellent ideas for modifications. Since they have used the text in teaching more often than I, I was especially grateful for their suggestions, most of which I have tried to implement.

Thus, like many worthwhile projects, this one began somewhat serendipitously, and evolved into an enjoyable endeavor. It has been fun to reread a book first written as a dissertation 30 years ago. It has been reassuring to discover that my basic values have not really changed very much, and that I am still in accord with most of what I wrote then.

Changes in Art Therapy and Mental Health

There is no question that the world has changed greatly in the last 30 years. It is much harder to conduct the kind of long-term therapy sometimes described in this book, although I believe the principles are equally applicable to short-term work, of which there are also many instances. Fortunately, it is considerably easier now for troubled children to obtain therapy, since it is much more acceptable than it was 25 years ago.

Although the field of art therapy expanded rapidly in the six years between the first two editions, this growth has continued exponentially in the last 20, not only in the United States, but around the world. The literature has grown at a faster rate than I could ever have predicted, which is evident in the many additional citations herein.

Not only are there more and better training programs; there is also a certification exam, allowing art therapists to be credentialed, first as Registered (ATR) and then as Board Certified (ATR-BC). In addition, art therapists are now licensed in many states, and many are trained at the doctoral level. The work of the professional association, the American Art Therapy Association (AATA) is responsible for many of these developments, but the main reason art therapy has grown is that it works so well where other methods often do not (see Chapter 20).

Art therapy, while still found in hospitals and clinics, has expanded well beyond the psychiatric settings where it began. As a result, art therapists now serve children in new places: schools (Bush, 1997; Moriya, 2000), medical hospitals (Bach, 1990; Furth, 1988; Malchiodi, 1999), hospices (Bertoia, 1993; Zambelli, Clark, & Heegaard, 1989), detention centers (Gussak & Virshup, 1997), shelters (Malchiodi, 1997), and specialized settings for those with eating disorders or substance abuse. Art therapists may do forensic evaluations (Cohen-Liebman, 2003), and may also offer immediate help to youngsters who have suffered traumas (Hagood, 2000; Klorer, 2000; Murphy, 2001; Steele, 2003).

But in spite of all the changes in art therapy and mental health treatment, children are still children, and the psychological issues they cope with—such as anxiety or loss of control—are not fundamentally different from what they were 25 years ago, whatever the cause. Their diagnostic labels have changed, though I am no more comfortable with them now than I have ever been. I prefer to see people as fellow humans, and have never found it terribly helpful to categorize them as having one or another disorder, although I willingly select the condition which best fits, so that their treatment can be supported.

During the past 25 years, the names of disorders have changed. Children who were once called "minimally brain damaged" or "learning disabled" are now described as suffering from "attention deficit disorder," with or without hyperactivity. The language used to identify children with physical and cognitive disabilities has also been modified, but the problems from which they suffer have not, except that thanks to advances in medical science, more severely disabled children are surviving (Evans & Dubowski, 2001). Psychiatric syndromes like major depression and bipolar disorder have been identified more often in children; they frequently receive medication which sometimes helps greatly, and sometimes not. Their suffering is still immense, and still needs to be addressed empathically.

The field of child therapy, including the sort that uses art as the primary modality, has—like adult therapy—experienced many fads and fashions over these years. Yet, although there is much to be learned from current approaches, such as the selective use of cognitive and behavioral strategies, many new ideas seem quite familiar. As I reviewed the art therapy literature of the past 20 years, what struck me was that—regardless of the stated approach or length of treatment—effective art therapy with children and families usually involves a thoughtful and flexible clinician, who proceeds with care and respect.

Changes in Organization and Content of the Book

This edition is not simply a cosmetic revision, but rather a substantial one. Based on suggestions by the reviewers, the book has been reorganized, new material has been added, and some portions which are no longer relevant have been omitted. Most of the original content remains, but some is found in new locations, and some has been renamed.

PREFACE

This book, unlike *Art Therapy: An Introduction* (1999) or *Approaches to Art Therapy* (2nd ed., 2001), is not meant to represent the child art therapy domain in a balanced fashion. Rather, first written partly to sort out my own thoughts in the area which was then my specialty, it consists primarily of my own experiences and ideas. I have tried, as much as possible, to note work done in the area of art therapy with children since the last revision, for those who wish to pursue any topic in greater detail.

PART I

THE CONTEXT

1

Roots

Personal and Professional

Although my personal roots and those of my chosen discipline are not identical or even parallel, I believe it is useful for the reader to know something of the background of the practitioner as well as of the origins of the profession. Both provide the context within which this book was written and can best be understood. I begin, therefore, with some thoughts about the sources of my own childhood interest in art, in order not only to introduce myself, but also to offer some ideas about how and why art is therapeutic.

Personal

The roots of my interest in art are deep and old and personal. And even after many years of psychotherapy, I am still not sure of all of the meanings for me of making, facilitating, and looking at art. I know that sometimes my pleasure was primarily visual. Like all children, I was curious about what could not be seen, what was hidden inside the body or behind closed doors. So it was exciting to be able to look with wide-open eyes, because in art looking was permissible, while it was so often forbidden elsewhere. I still find it fascinating to look at art, which is, after all, private feeling made into public form.

Just as my often-insatiable hunger felt somehow appeased when receiving art supplies, especially brand-new ones, so looking at art had a nourishing quality as well. It was a kind of taking-in, a drinking-in with the eyes of a delicious visual dish. Viewing a whole exhibit of work I liked was at least as fulfilling for me as eating an excellent meal.

If looking at art was a kind of validated voyeurism, the making of products was a kind of acceptable exhibitionism. So too the forbidden touching, the delight in sensory pleasures of body and earth, put aside as part of the price and privilege of growing up—these were preserved through art in the joy of kneading clay or smearing pastel.

Not only was art a path to permissible regression; it was a way to acceptable aggression as well. The cutting up of paper or the carving of wood, the representation of hostile wishes—these were possible through art, available to me, as to others, in the many symbolic meanings inherent in the creative process.

Many years ago, I found a drawing made when I was 5. It contained some aesthetically interesting designs and was developmentally appropriate. It allowed me to articulate what I knew about the human body and to practice my decorative skills. More important symbolically, it represented the fantasied fulfillment of two impossible wishes: to be my king-father's companion as princess-daughter (or even queen) and to be *like* him—to have what he had (the phallic cigarette) that I lacked (the legs are missing on the girl). The drawing was also done *for* him, a gift that probably brought praise for its very making and giving.

Sometimes art became for me, as for others, a way of coping with trauma too hard to assimilate (DVD 1.1). When I was 17, my friend Peter suddenly died. He had been young, handsome, and healthy; president of our class, ready to go on to a bright career in college and the world. In a crazy, senseless accident at high altitude, he stepped off the edge of a Colorado mountain and crashed to his end. Numbly, I went home to the funeral from the camp where I was working as an arts and crafts counselor. Numb, I returned to camp, then succumbed to a high fever for several anguished days and nights.

When I awoke, there was a strong need to go to the woods and paint. On my first day off I did, and it was good. The painting was not of Peter, but of a person playing the piano, making music in dark reds, purples, and blacks (1.1A). It was a cry, a scream caught and tamed. It was a new object in the world, a symbolic replacement for he who was lost, a mute, tangible testament. The doing of it afforded tremendous relief. It did not take away the hurt and the ache, but it did help in releasing some of the rage, and in giving form to a multiplicity of feelings and wishes.

So too with a remembered nightmare, finally drawn and then painted, given form and made less fearful (1.1B). Years later I was to discover, much to my surprise, that drawing a recurrent scary dream (Figure 1.1) would help my daughter to finally sleep in peace. Only now do I begin to understand the mechanism, the dynamics, the reason behind this miracle of

1.1 "The Scariest Dream" (Two Dead Grandmothers). Age 8. Chalk

taming fear through forms of feeling. I think it is what the medicine men have known for so long: that giving form to the feared object brings it under your own symbolic control.

Waking as well as sleeping fantasies evoked images that invited capture on canvas. A powerful, insightful revelation of ambivalent feelings toward my formerly idealized mother during my analysis stimulated a rapidly done expressionistic painting, which still evokes tension (1.1C). As an externalization of how and what I was feeling, however, it gave both relief and a greater sense of understanding. The push and pull of conflict was translated into paint, reducing inner anguish through outer representation.

Not only the making but also the perceiving of art was of vital importance to me as I grew up. As a young child I stared long and hard at a Van Gogh reproduction that hung on our living room wall. The *Sunflowers* were so big and alive, so vivid and powerful, that even in a print they seemed to leap forth from the canvas. And later, as a teenager, I recall the drunken orgy of a whole exhibit, with room after room full of original Van Goghs, wild and glowing. Each picture was more exciting than the last—the intensity and beauty of the images, the luscious texture of the paint—like the "barbaric yawp" of author Thomas Wolfe, another of my adolescent passions.

Many a weekend afternoon was spent sitting transfixed before some of my favorite paintings in the Museum of Modern Art. I think I must have studied every line in Picasso's *Guernica*, yet I am still moved by its power. A large Futurist painting called *The City* was an endlessly fascinating, continually merging sea of images. And another large painting by Tchelitchew, *Hide and Seek*, never ceased to magnetize my mind, to both repel and attract, with its heads and guts and fleeing figures. Surely there is much in art that feels therapeutic to the viewer, as well as to the artist.

As I write many images return, all vivid and bright and full of the feelings they stimulated and echoed. No wonder I embraced the art history major required for studio art courses at Wellesley. For there I experienced what André Malraux (1978) called the "Museum Without Walls"—the projection of an image magically magnified, glowing forth in the darkened room, giving one the illusion of being alone with a "presence"—despite the many other students, equally transfixed by its power and the music of the lecturer's voice. As an artist said once in a television interview, "Art is the mediating object between two souls. You can actually feel there's somebody there who's trying desperately to communicate with you."

Professional

This "magic power of the image" (Kris, 1952) is also one of the ancient roots of the discipline of art therapy. The use of art for healing and mastery is at least as old as the drawings on the walls of caves; yet the profession itself is a youngster in the family of mental health disciplines. In a similar paradox, while art therapy itself is highly sophisticated, the art process on which it rests is simple and natural.

On a walk through the woods some years ago, I came across a self-initiated use of art to cope with an overwhelming event, reminding me of my own painting after the tragedy of Peter's death. A rural man—a laborer—had carved a powerful totemlike sculpture out of a tree trunk, as part of mourning the untimely death of his young wife (DVD 1.2). His explanation to me was that he "just had to do something," and that the activity of creating the larger-than-life carving had seemed to fit his need, perhaps helping to fill the void left by his loss.

Similarly, people caught in the turmoil of serious mental illness and threatened by loss of contact with reality have sometimes found themselves compelled to create art (DVD 1.3) as one way of coping with their confusion (1.3A). Such productions (1.3B), even found on scraps of toilet

6

paper or walls (1.3C), intrigued psychiatrists and art historians in the early part of the twentieth century (Prinzhorn, 1922/1972). Fascinated by these outpourings of the troubled mind (1.3D), they collected and studied such spontaneous expressions, hoping to better understand the creators and their ailments (1.3E).

With the advent of depth psychology (Freud, 1908, 1910; Jung, 1964), therapists looked for ways to unlock the puzzle of primary process (unconscious, illogical) thought, and tried to decode the meanings of images in dreams, reverie, and the art of the insane (Jakab, 1956/1998; MacGregor, 1989). The growth of projective testing in the young field of clinical psychology stimulated further systematic work with visual stimuli such as the Rorschach inkblots or drawings, like those of the human figure, primarily for diagnostic purposes.

While these developments were occurring in the area of mental health, educators were discovering the value of a freer kind of artistic expression in the schools. Those in the progressive movement (Naumburg, 1928) were convinced that the creative experience was a vital part of any child's education, essential for healthy development (Cane, 1951). Some art educators were especially sensitive to the value of personal expression in helping children deal with frustration and self-definition (DVD 1.4). One, Viktor Lowenfeld (1952, 1957, 1982), developed what he called an "art education therapy" for children with disabilities (1.4A). During that time, art was beginning to be offered as therapy to patients in general hospitals (Hill, 1945, 1951) and in psychiatric settings.

The two women most responsible for defining and founding the field of art therapy began their work with children—in a hospital (Naumburg, 1947) and in a special school (Kramer, 1958)—on the basis of their experiences as educators. Both were Freudian in their orientation, though each used different aspects of psychoanalytic theory to develop her ideas about the best therapeutic use of art.

For Margaret Naumburg (1950, 1953, 1966) art was a form of symbolic speech coming from the unconscious, like dreams, to be evoked in a spontaneous way and to be understood through free association, always respecting the artist's own interpretations (1.4B). Art was thus conceived as a "royal road" to unconscious symbolic contents, a means of both diagnosis and therapy, requiring verbalization and insight as well as art expression.

For Edith Kramer (1971, 1979, 2000, 2001) on the other hand, art was a "royal road" to sublimation, a way of integrating conflicting feelings and impulses in an aesthetically satisfying form, helping the ego to control, manage, and synthesize via the creative process itself (1.4C). Both approaches are still visible in a field that has grown extremely rapidly over the

7

last 50 years. This rapid development reflects the power of art as a therapeutic modality. I never cease to be amazed at the potency of art therapy, even in the hands of relatively naive practicum students.

Since it is so powerful, it is fortunate that no longer can "anyone with a paint brush and a patient" declare him- or herself to be an art therapist (Howard, 1964, p. 153). Indeed, my own learning experiences—in the era before formal education was available in the field—bear witness to the need for clinical training for anyone whose background is solely in art and education.

Personal/Professional Passage

The roots of my interest in art, as noted earlier, lay deep in the soil of my childhood and adolescence, before blossoming into a variety of roles— teacher of art to neighborhood children in high school, arts and crafts counselor at summer camps, art major in college, and later, art educator (of children, then of teachers), art researcher, "art lady" (*Mister Rogers' Neighborhood* on PBS), art consultant, and—eventually—art therapist.

When I first discovered the field, I felt like the ugly duckling who found the swans and no longer saw himself as a misfit. As an artist, I never felt talented enough to make a career of my painting. And, as a teacher, although I loved working with children, I was often uncomfortable with the methods of my fellow teachers—like asking children to fill in stenciled drawings, or using a paddle for discipline.

In 1963, when the Child Development Department at the University of Pittsburgh invited me to offer art to schizophrenic children, I was in no way a clinician. But the work was such a pleasure and a challenge, and the support from others was so available, that I was able to find places to grow and people to help me.

I first sought the guidance of the two pioneers in art therapy mentioned earlier, each of whom gave generously of her time and thought. Both suggested that I learn about myself through personal therapy and that I learn about being a therapist through supervised work under an experienced clinician.

I was fortunate to find both a mentor and a setting where I was able to learn the necessary skills and practice my trade. As I began to feel like a real therapist, I also became aware of a need for further didactic learning. This need was met through intensive study of adult and child analysis at a psychoanalytic institute, supplemented by graduate work in counseling at a university.

Although one reason for writing this book was the required doctoral dissertation, I was also responding to inner tensions. Like most creative activities, it began with the perception of a problem or felt concern that increasingly demanded a solution. I had reached a point at which I could no longer comfortably pursue any of the many directions I had by then explored without first finding some order for myself in all that I had learned about children, art, and growing. When I began writing, I felt uncertain about what would emerge on the blank paper, just as I had so often felt anxious about what would come from painting on a clean canvas.

One of the best ways for an art therapist to understand therapeutic work is through reflection on his or her own creative endeavors. Shortly after becoming a therapist, I found myself reflecting on an unusually intense painting experience. Because I was so moved by it at the time, I tried to put the event into words, in an effort to clarify and to understand it for myself. Here is some of what I wrote, 3 weeks after it happened.

A Personal Experience of the Creative Process

"I would like to try to give words and form to an essentially nonverbal and formless experience, an experience of such power and intensity that it demands clarification and invites sharing. I wonder to myself, how universal or how personal was this happening? And I wonder, too, what it can tell me about the meaning of art in therapy.

"I was painting this past summer, with a strange awareness of functioning on several levels simultaneously. I was the mother who responded to the child who called from his bed for a drink of water. I was also the technician who periodically changed brushes and added colors to my acrylic palette in order to achieve the desired effects. Yet further, I was the artist, deeply and actively engaged in the creative process, which simultaneously involved every layer of my psyche.

"The painting had begun as a group portrait of my children, full of conscious loving of their exterior and interior selves. I strove intently to draw them as they sat painting around a table, concerned with reproducing both their features and the warm, proud feelings they evoked. This first stage of the picture seemed to be conscious, careful, with sincere and very deliberate attempts at naturalistic representation.

"Then they went to bed, and I continued with the painting, having temporarily interrupted the process to play my maternal bedtime role. I was aware of my resentment at having to stop work in order to bed them, but even more powerfully conflicted feelings rose to the surface, as I continued to apply the paint. An onrush of diffuse and intense destructive impulses impelled me to work more rapidly. I found the activity gathering a momentum which did not seem to be under my voluntary control.

"Before, I had worked slowly, deliberately, and carefully to make them beautiful. Now, I worked with a somatic sensation of pressure, as if the intensity and perhaps the guilt of the propelling feelings required such speed. With quick, short strokes I modified—and partially obliterated—their forms.

"My husband remarked sadly that I was destroying what had recently been so attractive, but his criticism was acknowledged only intellectually as reasonable. On another level, I resented the intrusion, and went on at an accelerated tempo, doing what at that moment had to be done. The sense of both compulsion and excitement was almost too great to bear. Yet it was thrilling as well as painful, as the tension quickly mounted. Coexisting were love and hate, creation and destruction, joy and pain.

"And yet the figures remained, less clear but perhaps more intense for their ambiguity. I found them more beautiful now, as they reflected the full complexity and ambivalence of my emotions (DVD 1.1F). And I was aware of another kind of tension—between the need to modify and the desire not to destroy, but to enhance. Though executed at a quick pace, each stroke felt crucial.

"While working so intensely, I felt simultaneously a high level of ego control and an equally high level of communication with the unconscious forces that threatened the very control I prized so dearly. At the end of the painting process, my working pace slowed down. With deliberate calm and rather cool control, I found myself standing back and looking, modifying, and completing the portrait (Figure 1.2).

"And now, weeks later, I reflect upon the event. Perhaps it was that very experience of teetering at the brink, of allowing such a powerful upsurge of unconscious and irrational feeling—while maintaining a tight control over it—that is the essence of at least one aspect of the 'therapy' in art. For without the experience of near-loss of control, it must be feared as catastrophic. It is only by letting go as fully as possible that one learns that the fantasied fear is a somewhat myth. If one always holds tight the reins of conscious control there is no danger—yet the danger still exists by implication. The more unknown and unfelt, the more it is feared.

"Indeed, one might question whether it is ever possible to learn self-control in the deepest, most secure sense, without allowing oneself at times to loosen the bonds of control as well. What is vital is that this was felt as a 'peak experience' (Maslow, 1959), both thrilling and frightening, both

1.2 Painting of My Children. Acrylic

soaring and plunging. It was aesthetic as well as personal, as was the resultant painting.

"...To experience in any sphere 'letting go' yet remaining simultaneously aware and ultimately in charge, is a profound lesson. Whether or not the content of the art is affectively toned, the dynamics of the creative process itself provide a powerful learning experience.

"One might also argue that limiting, or in any way protecting the client from letting go, might serve to reinforce already-crippling fears of loss of control. The art therapist who prematurely limits the client's activity in the name of safety or security may actually be saying, 'Yes, you are right. Loss of control is disastrous in its consequences, so I will set limits and help you keep a brake on your dangerously strong and destructive feelings and impulses.' Yet learning to be in charge of the self may only be possible when one has allowed conscious control to relax sufficiently to explore the consequences of strong expression of feeling, then to find that one may still be master of one's fate.

"What is emerging is not a position which suggests no limits at all. Rather, the creation of a work of art has its own built-in limits, which provide sufficient safety, along with the opportunity for constructive abreaction and channeling of strong feelings. Indeed, the expressive arts are vital both to healthy personality growth and to therapy precisely because they allow for a channeled, controlled 'letting go.' The very nature of each art form sets the limits which, when broken, negate the art. Throwing paint on the wall is not the same as making a vibrant picture by slashing with the brush, and random body movements are not the same as those which are in tune with the music.

"Nevertheless, it has been my experience that many disturbed youngsters, whether their superficial behavior is inhibited or hyperactive, need initially to release, in a cathartic and often formless fashion, at first unfocused and heretofore repressed feelings. Only when this has been safely experienced can the child then give a genuinely artistic form to such feelings. Perhaps it is only then that he or she feels in control of him or herself and in charge of the process, not in a compulsively tight but a relaxedly free way.

"Surely my painting process involved regression with control, and while form was given to feeling, feeling was also given to form. They intermingled in an inseparable fashion, each one evoking the other, neither one the chronological precursor of the other. My painting was not meant primarily as a communication to others, but rather as a kind of self-communication, a rhythmic dialogue between picture and creator which gradually rose and finally fell in intensity. I think the process was neither primarily cathartic nor primarily integrative, but was both simultaneously, and was meaningful just because of the tension and interplay between constructive and destructive forces. It was both an aesthetic and an intellectual experience, producing art as well as insight."

Making Pictures Helps My Mourning Process

Many years later, stimulated by my psychoanalytic training, I was intrigued by the idea of "Free Association in Imagery." An artist friend and I decided to offer a class through the Psychoanalytic Center, in which participants would be invited to choose a medium and then allow each emergent image to follow the previous one, until the sequence felt complete. Modeled on the basic method of free association in analysis, it turned out to be amazingly powerful (Rubin, 1981a).

For myself, the imaging course came at a stressful time; the first class was a week after my mother's unexpected death. I found it surprisingly helpful to my own mourning process to engage in a freely associative use of materials. A review of the drawing series that emerged that day may help you understand how therapeutic a series of spontaneous images can be, even without discussion (DVD 1.4).

The first, red and black, sharp and angular, felt like "Pain," and was tense and angry in the doing (1.4A). The second became "My Mother in the Hospital Bed," hooked up to the oxygen tank, as I had last seen her the week before her demise. I was surprised at how much she looked like an infant (1.4B).

The third began abstractly but became a pair of breasts with large dark nipples. I titled it "Mama-Breast-Love" (1.4C). The fourth is a child reaching up to a mother who is mostly a smiling face. When I looked at it I thought it was me saying "I Love You, I Need You" (1.4D).

The fifth began as a stark, angular tree, then became an image of a tombstone, and then I thought of sun and eyes shining . . . looking down from above. "Can You See?" was the title that came to mind, the pre-logical, wishful/fearful magical thinking that had been flowing through my usually skeptical head (1.4E). The sixth was an image of my mother and (already-dead) father meeting in some other life, he welcoming her, the two "Together Again"—another magical thought (1.4F).

The seventh arose from intense affect, a feeling of tension and pain, first expressed in the heavily scribbled red and black lines, then in the face, which emerged in tears, mouth open, hungry, and angry, "Screaming" (1.4G).

The next image began as a bleak white-and-gray landscape, then a

13

night sky with a moon and a star, each of which got covered over. Then I thought of a droopy lonely figure—our eldest daughter, far away in France, having to bear her pain separated from the family—and then I thought of the rest of us (my husband and two other children) leaning sadly on each other: "Cold and Lonely" (1.4H). The ninth was a kinesthetic impulse to make tangles of different colors; the title-thought was "All Together" (1.4I).

The tenth began as a wavy-line tree on the left, then a wavy line in the center that turned into a dance, which then turned into a person with a large glowing womb inside; then I thought of a baby in that. When that image came, in a kind of birthing process, I felt relieved of much of the tension I had experienced throughout the others, as if something had been, at least for the moment, eased. My thought on looking at it along with the others was "Mom-Inside Forever," certainly one way to cope with loss (1.4J).

While I can easily share my thoughts about the images, it is more difficult to put into words my emotional experience of the process. A similar experience took place the following week with clay, the next week with paint, then with collage, and with the final week's product—for me, a painted portrait of my mother.

I was not aware of thinking in the usual sense, but of allowing myself to be led by the materials and by my impulses. Each image came quite naturally, almost always with heightened emotion. There was a feeling of activity and internal tension, though "absorption" fits it better, and a sense of being "done" at the end. I did not feel particularly involved in the products as art; indeed, I found them unappealing aesthetically. But I did feel intense involvement in what may have been a kind of visual thinking process.

Most significantly, perhaps, I found the entire set of experiences to be extremely helpful in the work of mourning. Instead of the class being a burden as I had feared, it became a welcome respite for me, a chance to deal wordlessly with my grief. I believe that the use of media provided much more than a catharsis. Of course, it wasn't the whole story; I remained involved in a grieving process for some time after that class, but I was frankly surprised at how helpful it had been.

Such personal experiences of the power of art in my own life are no doubt what led me to feel so at home in art therapy and to want so much to make the healing benefits of creative endeavor available to others.

About This Book

This book is about children, art, and growing, through a distillation of the reflections and visions of an art therapist. It is about children, how they can grow in and through art experiences, and how to help them to do that in a healthy, therapeutic way. It is a message to those who care for children about some ways in which one may facilitate their becoming through art.

Knowing what to do and what not to do, when to do it, and how to do it, are difficult learnings to convey to others. One learns these things over time, through experience and reflection, and they become less and less simple in the process. Nevertheless, this work is an attempt to communicate such understandings as I now possess, in the hope that they may be useful to others.

This book is about children from the time they can use art materials in a meaningful way until they can no longer be called children. It is about all children, including those who simply need to be provided with the most facilitating conditions for growth and development. It is about normal, healthy children and their normal, healthy needs for expression, mastery, self-definition, and ways to cope with stress.

It is also about children with special needs and problems—those for whom growing has been painful because of unchangeable disabilities or hurts that are hard to bear—those who have stopped growing in a healthy way, who have turned back, gotten stuck, and perhaps become distorted and ugly to themselves and to others.

This book is about all children, and about their right to an opportunity to become themselves and to deal with their hurts in a creative way through art. In yet another way, it is about the youngster in each of us, our understanding of that inner child, and our use of both little and grown-up selves in the service of another person's growth.

This book is about growing in and through art, especially the visual and plastic arts (though other forms are highly respected siblings and allies). At times it is about responses to art, to work done by self or others. Mostly it is about the work that children do with creative media, the process and the product of an encounter between a youngster and art materials.

And it includes all aspects of that dialogue: the approaching and manipulating, as well as the forming and refining. All are seen as inseparable aspects of art, from sensory exploration to complex intentional configurations, from playful to solemn making. It includes the toddler stacking blocks, the teenager constructing a stabile, the infant molding sand and water, and the 10-year-old modeling clay.

This book is about growing deeper as well as bigger, broader as well as taller, freer as well as older, stronger inside as well as outside. It is mostly about growing affectively, about gaining an awareness, understanding, acceptance, liking, and control of one's feeling-self through art. Growth in art includes perceptual, motor, cognitive, and social development as well.

15

The interest here, however, is in these dimensions mainly as they relate to emotional maturation and integration.

For me growing is growing, wherever it happens; and art is art, whether it occurs in a home, a classroom, or a therapy room. The relative emphases may be different, and indeed the goals are best made explicit. Thus, growth in art education may have to do mostly with the acquisition of skills and concepts about art, whereas these are seen as a means to a different end in art therapy.

There, the growth is primarily in the development of the capacity to be a freely creative person, with firm but flexible inner controls. Nevertheless, the emotional components of art may become central at times in the classroom, just as the acquisition of skills may become focal in the clinic. Many things are seen as common to growth in both contexts, like the conditions and attitudes that foster personally meaningful work.

Helping, like growing, can take many forms. Helping a child to grow through art can involve giving, showing, or telling. It may also mean watching and, often, waiting. Many times it means moving in, doing or saying something in an active way. At other times it means being present but silent, respectful of the other's primary absorption in the creative (versus the human) dialogue. Helping means many different things, but always it means being tuned in to the other person—behaving in a way that respects their right to their own space and makes it possible for the individual to gain control and freedom within it.

My own understanding of *art therapy* is that it refers broadly to understanding and helping a person through art and that it encompasses a wide variety of dimensions. These include the integrative aspects of the creative process itself, as well as the use of art as a tool in the service of discharge, uncovering, defense, or communication.

Art for any child can and does become different things at different times. I find it impossible to characterize the process, even with one human being or in one setting, as being any one thing alone or always. Rather, it seems that for anyone, the art activity ranges over time from being central and integrative to peripheral and adjunctive and back again, serving many different possible functions.

What is important is to know what is occurring when it is happening, and to have some sense of its meaning and function for that person at that moment in time. What seems equally vital to me is that the therapist have the flexibility and openness to permit the individual to flow in different directions over time, and the wisdom and creativity to stimulate, unblock, or redirect the flow when necessary.

It is my hope that what I write will have some meaning and some utility for all who care about children. This book is especially for art and play therapists, but it is truly for anyone who values the creative process in the child, who wishes to nurture and strengthen it, and in so doing to help a child to become the best he or she can be.

Such a person might be any clinician who works with children—a counselor, psychiatrist, social worker, or psychologist, or an occupational, recreational, or speech therapist. Such a person could also be a teacher (especially an art teacher), or a pediatrician, a nurse, or a child care worker. Such a person might even be a parent—and could, most certainly, be an artist.

Since it is my hope to communicate experiences and ideas to others from a variety of disciplines and frames of reference, I have tried to avoid terminology that belongs exclusively to one or another professional field and to find a language that will be common enough to make sense, yet rich enough to convey complex meanings. I know that in so doing I may risk oversimplification and lack of depth, yet it seems so important to reach those who work directly with children in art that it is worth that risk.

In this way, I hope to talk meaningfully about the conditions that facilitate creative growth in art, and the ways in which one may use art with children in order to better understand (assessment) as well as to help (treatment). I shall explore understanding and helping in a variety of contexts, including work with individuals, families, and groups. I shall also suggest implications and applications of art therapy in educational and recreational settings as well as in clinical ones, and attempt some preliminary suggestions of useful theoretical constructs.

The profession of art therapy was young in 1978, and although it is much more mature in 2005, I think it is fair to say that it is still working on defining its identity for itself as well as for others. In one sense, it is still, as I wrote then, "a technique in search of a theory." Indeed, since art is versatile, art therapists have been able to ground their work in a wide variety of psychological frames of reference, including psychodynamic, humanistic, developmental, cognitive, behavioral, solution focused, narrative, and spiritual (cf. Malchiodi, 2003; Rosal, 1996; Rubin, 2001).

In the course of my own development over the past 40 years as an art therapist, I have read, studied, and worked with many different theoretical perspectives, and I have usually found in each one or more concepts relevant to my work. At one point, I thought that the solution to my problem would be a kind of patchwork—a mosaic or collage of different ideas from different theories that together would account for what seems to happen in art therapy. This kind of additive eclecticism may still be the answer, but I now doubt the value or validity of such a heterogeneous mix.

In 1978 I had thought that a theory of art therapy would emerge from art therapy itself. I expected that it would partake of elements of other perspectives but would have its own inner integrity in terms of the creative process of which it consisted. Indeed, there have been some significant efforts to construct such art- or studio-based theories, most significantly those articulated by Allen (1995) and Moon (2001).

Like the field itself, however, there is not only an art part, but there is also a therapy part, and the artistry of the work consists of putting the two together—something I devoted my second book, *The Art of Art Therapy* (Rubin, 1984), to spelling out. Probably for that reason, in 1987 I asked a group of colleagues to contribute to a book called *Approaches to Art Therapy: Theory and Technique*, which has been recently revised, with the addition of newer approaches and reflective commentaries (Rubin, 2001).

In the conclusion to that book I returned to a theme first hinted at in this one: that of the frame into which one must insert different lenses, in order to clearly perceive different aspects of the phenomena observed, analogous to the use of stains to illuminate different aspects of an organism on a microscopic slide. I believe that the many different theories of personality and psychotherapy allow art therapists, like other clinicians, to insert different lenses into their listening ears and viewing eyes (cf. Hedges, 1983). They also allow them to use different methods with different patients at different times.

In 1978 I didn't feel ready to develop and articulate a definitive theoretical statement about art as, in, or for therapy. Although I've since made one rather feeble attempt (Rubin, 1984), I am now, after 40 years of practice, more eclectic and pragmatic than ever. And even though I have studied, have taught, and value psychoanalytic theory, I have never felt that it had all the answers or that other ways of understanding were not also helpful and relevant.

In 1978 I wrote that it was "my intention to review what I *know*, what I think I have gleaned from books, from articles, from teachers, from colleagues, from children, and from myself. It is equally my intention to review what I *feel*, what I *believe in* most sincerely and often passionately, the values which have come to guide my seeing, knowing, and doing. My thoughts and understandings about children, art, and growing will certainly evolve over time, in the future as they have in the past. This statement is for now, for me as well as for others." In 2004, all of that remains true.

2

A Framework for Freedom

To create conditions which assist children in releasing that which lies dormant and waiting within them so they may paint their impressions on life's canvas in rich, bright, bold, brave colors is the challenge for all who guide children
—NIXON, 1969, p. 301

Three years after the profound painting experience—and reflections on it—described in Chapter 1, I was invited to participate in a seminar on the arts in education, and to think and write on the topic of "order and discipline in art as models for effective human behavior." I did not consciously recall the painting paper, long put aside, but instead thought over my current notions about order, and found myself continually thinking of freedom as well. Feeling by then more secure about the ideas hinted at earlier, I searched the literature to find what others had concluded about freedom, order, and control in art, especially as they related to conditions for creative growth for children.

This later attempt to review and organize ideas around a central topic was more precise and academic than my earlier expression of my vague thoughts. Though different in style, the two stem from the same source and mind, and represent different stages in an ongoing problem-solving process. What follows is an attempt to clarify ideas about a concept that is still vital to me now, 33 years later.

For me, the notion of order in creative activity is intimately and inextricably intertwined with that of freedom. Man's religious mythology, after all, describes the Almighty as creating a world of order out of a universe of chaos. Neither the extreme of order—rigidity—nor the extreme of freedom—chaos—is conducive to creative function.

Yet in most definitions of the creative process, whether by psychologists, aestheticians, or artists, we encounter seemingly opposed and incompatible states: reverie and alertness, fantasy and reality, disintegration and integration, unconscious and conscious thought. Art, so often defined as characterized by order and discipline, is as frequently related to chaos (Peckham, 1965).

There is no clear agreement on the precise relationship between these two sides of the creative coin. They are sometimes described as simultaneous, as in "contemplative action" (Milner, 1957, p. 153) or "unconscious scanning" (Ehrenzweig, 1967). Sometimes they are seen as a "flexible alternation of roles [because] it is impossible to produce free associations, to be freely imaginative, to be freely creative, if at the same time and in the very moment of 'freedom' one attempts to maintain a watchful, critical scrutiny of what one is producing" (Kubie, 1958, p. 54).

At times the emphasis is on a passive receptivity to spontaneity and freedom, as in the "creative surrender" of Ehrenzweig (1967), followed by more ordered activity: "In other words, succeeding upon the spontaneous is the deliberate; succeeding upon total acceptance comes criticism; succeeding upon intuition comes rigorous thought; succeeding upon daring comes caution; succeeding upon fantasy and imagination comes reality testing. . . . The voluntary regression into our depths is now terminated, the necessary passivity and receptivity of inspiration or of peak-experience must now give way to activity, control and hard work" (Maslow, 1959, p. 92).

It is my own feeling that the relationship between these two clusters of experiential states may be at one time simultaneous, at another alternating, and at yet another sequential, as true for children as for adults. What seems most critical is the recognition that in creative expression there can be no true order without some experience of genuine freedom, and that the provider of art for children must make possible a productive and integrated relationship between the two.

Barron (1966), discussing "the paradox of discipline and freedom," describes the job well: "The task we face is to avoid sacrificing one possibility to the other. We must be able to use discipline to gain greater freedom, take on habits in order to increase our flexibility, permit disorder in the interests of an emerging higher order, tolerate diffusion, and even occasionally invite it, in order to achieve a more complex integration" (p. 86). If the control, order, and discipline are to come from within the creator, then that child or adult must be enabled to confront whatever confusion, vagueness, or inner reality they need to understand and organize, if it is at all possible for them to do so.

Without passion, energy, intensity, or absorption, the process of working with creative media can hardly be called "art." One cannot be "on fire" with inspiration (Dewey, 1934, p. 65) or lose oneself in an aesthetic experience (Neumann, 1971) without free access to joy and spontaneity. "Art is the quality that makes the difference between merely witnessing or performing things and being touched by them, shaken by them, changed by the forces that are inherent in everything we give and receive. Art education [and therapy] then, means making sure that such living awareness results when people paint pictures" (Arnheim, 1967, p. 342).

I believe from my own painting experience, as well as from work with others, that learning how to "let go" is essential for genuine absorption in a creative process. Even in work with people who have lost confidence in their own creativity, it has been my happy learning that it is not destroyed, but simply dormant, capable of reawakening. While creativity "*may* be weakened . . . its expression *may* also simply become muted, or be altogether behaviorally silent, while the capability remains" (Barron, 1972, p. 162).

Why then, do we so often find in our treatment of children a "restriction of a natural tendency . . . towards play, music, drawing and painting, and many forms of non-verbal sensory grasping and symbolizations?" (Barron, 1966, p. 87) What has made it so hard for us to provide them with an opportunity to freely let go and to express themselves openly in both the form and content of their art? While the Puritan value of work versus play may be partly to blame, it seems to me that a more fundamental problem is our natural human "fear of chaos" (Ehrenzweig, 1967). We are afraid, for ourselves and for those in our care, of the consequences of loss of self, of fusion, of dissociation, of disorganization, and of regression.

While regression may not sound as dangerous as disintegration, we *do* fear the tantrum and other forms of disorderly infantile behavior. We conceive rightly—but rigidly—of regression as associated with stress, as in the "Q" paintings of the Easel Age Scale which are said to indicate disturbance (Lantz, 1955). But we forget that periods of stress also coincide with increased creative productivity. "Every challenge and every emergency in man's life may lead to new creative behavior. Let us not forget that creativity is often closely linked with periods of biological upheaval" (Meerloo, 1968, p. 11).

We forget that in the development of graphic skills there are periodic returns to earlier forms of behavior; and that in art, as in all normal growth, "while the child attains more mature levels of action and cherishes his recent acquisitions, there is also a continual homecoming to earlier gratifications" (Peller, 1955, p. 3). We fear that the learner is losing ground, forgetting that in work with any new medium, at any age level, it is natural to begin with a period of free, playful exploration and experimentation.

Regression in the creative process was first described as "regression in the service of the ego" (Kris, 1952)—regression, in other words, that is symbolic, controlled, and voluntary. We forget, too, that in any transitional growth phase, in order to restructure, previous structures must be in some way broken down. Arnheim (1969) illustrates progress toward three-dimensional graphic projection in a child's drawings, noting the many intermediate forms of disorientation. He stresses the necessity, during a time of risk and growth, of some degree of "ugliness" (p. 266).

All who work with children in art have seen many instances of both temporary and prolonged regressions in the service of growth. For the child who finds security in rigid control, this may be seen in a return to compulsively careful work. More often, it is evident in a return to a less structured and perhaps more playful use of materials. For some constricted children, forced too early perhaps to be clean and neat, the capacity "to enjoy constructive work with clay or paint is possible only after a veritable orgy of simple messing with the stuff." Similarly, "a very angry child may not be able to settle down to work unless he first gives vent to his anger directly" (Kramer, 1971, p. 160).

For many children, both hyperactive and inhibited, experimenting with a freer, more honest form of creating may be essential to convince them that, in this symbolic mode, they can indeed let go, express strong feelings with free movements, and remain in control of impulses that turn out neither to be as destructive nor as disorganizing as anticipated. It is only after such a symbolic letting loose that familiarity with the feared experience permits them to grow.

Both regression and aggression are difficult for most people to handle. We fear the violence as well as the vitality of children's fantasy life. Even those trained in clinical work sometimes have difficulty controlling their own disgust and horror, in response to the mess and mayhem of a disturbed child's inner life. One helpful beginning is to recognize one's own honest responses and to get in touch with one's own feared feelings and impulses; through introspection if possible, through therapy if necessary. Indeed, it is my sincere belief that the adult who has not yet made some kind of open-eyed peace with his or her own fantasy life is ill-equipped to help children deal with theirs.

Given an acceptance of one's own violent propensities and most bizarre fantasies, the task is to create those conditions under which freedom can be safely and supportively facilitated. What Milner has said of her own creative efforts applies equally well to the provision of an appropriate environment for children: "the spontaneous urge to pattern in the living organism . . . comes about not by planned action, but only by a planned framework, within which the free play of unplanned expressive movement can come about" (1969, p. 263). The framework is thought of broadly, "in time as well as in space" (1957, p. 157). If indeed there is, as she suggests, "the necessity for a certain quality of protectiveness in the environment," it is because "there are obviously many circumstances in which it is not safe to be absent-minded; it needs a setting, both physical and mental" (1957, pp. 163–164).

The provision of limits and structure are vital in creating a framework for freedom. "Limits define the boundaries of the relationship and tie it to reality . . . they offer security and at the same time permit the child to move freely and safely in his play" (Moustakas, 1959, p. 11). Overwhelmed and frightened by the sometimes "undisciplined outpourings of the unconscious" (Bettelheim, 1964, p. 44) often caused by lack of appropriate limits, those who work with children have too often "overstepped their function of providing a secure frame for the free activities and tried to dictate the activities themselves" (Milner, 1957, p. 105). Worse yet, they may prohibit certain activities because of their anticipated disorganizing effect on the child, prematurely restricting and constricting his or her world. One cannot help but agree with Bettelheim (1964, p. 60) that all too often, "despite loud assertions to the contrary, these adults . . . remain afraid of permitting children to think and act for themselves."

I believe that the most critical psychological variable in the freedom/order equation is that of the adult offering art—that person's attitudes (trust versus mistrust), expectations (positive versus negative), and personal qualities (empathy versus distance). If we hope to promote individual development we must learn to trust the child as a human being with an inherent and natural tendency toward growth, order, and integration. We will not be able to provide opportunities for choice, for independent movement, and for self-initiated decision making, without "faith in the inner potential of [children] so that [we] will trust them when they wish to explore on their own" (Haupt, 1969, p. 43).

In my own work with seriously ill schizophrenic children, where they had freedom of media choice, it was striking that those with poor ego boundaries consistently avoided such fluid materials as finger paints. They often provided their own kinds of structure, such as one agitated 12-year-old who always pulled a chair up to sit at the easel, in order to contain his usual aggressive hyperactivity. He further controlled his work through repetitive movements, letting his arm go up and down rhythmically, like a Japanese Sumi painter, calming himself with a motion like an infant's rocking.

Another child, blind and developmentally delayed, contained his experimentation with finger paint, previously threatening to him, through the use of a tray. He had chosen finger paint and paper at the first group session, but had been both excited and frightened by the texture and by the threat to control posed by the hard-to-find edges of the paper when covered with paint. He had ripped up the product, quite agitated. An observing child psychiatrist had advised against allowing finger paint again.

Not having heard the doctor, however, the next week Bill again requested finger paint. When it was refused and alternatives were suggested, he put up a loud fuss. Because of his exasperation, he was given the gooey substance, this time in a plastic tray hastily borrowed from the school cafeteria (Figure 2.1). He was surprisingly calm and relaxed throughout; the physical boundaries of the tray apparently allayed his anxiety about loss of control, thus permitting him to enjoy tremendous sensory pleasure and delight, which was frequently repeated in subsequent sessions. This boy had once told of accidentally squeezing a soft, gushy worm to death in bed, a

2.1 A Blind Boy Finger Painting in a Tray

2.2 A Blind Boy Mixing Clay and Water in a Bowl

memory stimulated while manipulating clay. Perhaps finger painting was a way of working through some of the feelings associated with that event, this time under his control, and now safely bounded.

Larry, another blind boy, contained his exploration of the effects of mixing clay and water within a bowl (Figure 2.2). In fact, when a group of totally blind children were given the choice of a tray or paper for finger paint, all selected the tray with its clearly defined edges because, as one of them explained, "it helps you to stop."

Clearly defined limits of time also facilitate creative work (DVD 2.1). Carla, a partially sighted teenager, once explained to me how she molded what she called "personality globs," (2.1A) and how she drew "mind pictures" (2.1B). In both cases, as she proudly demonstrated, she would pause, close her eyes, sit meditatively still, and then with clay or marker do "whatever my brain and hands tell me to do."

She made a distinction between drawings done under these conditions, in which she was relaxed and unconcerned about realistic rendering (2.1C) and those produced with eyes close to paper, a strained attempt at reproduction of the visual world (2.1D). "I'm more *free*," she explained, "like I feel more like *myself* when I draw something indirect. . . . I feel *good*, you know."

Such concrete means of organizing time, space, and the self are often

25

supplemented by symbolic means through art. For art itself offers a kind of protective framework, a boundary between reality and make-believe, that enables children to more daringly test themselves and to more openly state their fantasies than is possible without its aesthetic and psychic distance. "Only in protected situations, characterized by high walls of psychic insulation" can a person afford to let himself "experience disparities, tensions, etc. . . . . art offers precisely this kind of experience" (Peckham, 1965, p. 313).

Thus it was possible for Don, a constricted 10-year-old boy almost crippled by compulsive tension, to explore symbolically in clay the impulse to hurt his younger brother; then to explore smeary-messy "uncontrolled" painting; and, finally, to achieve a freer kind of order in his work (see also Chapter 13, Figure 13.3).

Similarly, Dorothy, a psychotic girl of 10 with a serious speech defect, spent several weeks in the rigid and repetitive representation of birds, with whom she identified, then boldly experimented with the free use of paint and brush without her usual prior pencil drawing. This venture, both exhilarating and fearful, was followed immediately by the pictorial expression of powerful unconscious fantasies of monsters and birds that her inarticulate tongue had never spoken. This outburst, lasting several weeks, was succeeded for many months by an attempt to make sense out of the real world in which she lived, through pictorial lists of cats, clothes, and the other children on the ward (see also Chapter 8, Figures 8.4 and 8.5; DVD 8.2).

One day, a schizophrenic youngster, a boy of 11, spent perhaps half an hour in the careful mixing of brown paint—his first attempt at combining colors. Then, rhythmically and somewhat compulsively, he covered the entire surface of a large white paper with the brown mixture, followed by a drawing, along with an elaborate story, of his central unresolved (oedipal) conflict (DVD 2.2).

The painting was of a "Dead King" in his coffin underground (2.2A), who, according to the long and complex story, had been accidentally killed off and then succeeded by his son, the prince. Having succeeded in articulating at least a part of his inner wish-world, he was then free to begin to organize the outer one, creating pictorial diagrams and maps of concepts, places, and processes, like "How a Pumpkin Grows from a Seed" (2.2B).

In art or play children can do the impossible. They may symbolically fulfill both positive wishes and negative impulses, without fear of real consequences. They can learn to control the real world by experimenting with active mastery of tools, media, and the ideas and feelings expressed in the process. They can gain symbolic access to and relive past traumas, and can rehearse and practice for the future. They can learn to be in charge in a symbolic mode, and thus feel more competent to master reality.

But it is my conviction that children cannot learn to control and organize themselves if the structure does not ultimately come from within (DVD 2.3). It has been argued that prepared outlines (2.3A) are useful to children because they need to learn motor control. Yet a careful look at what children produce spontaneously in the course of their graphic growth demonstrates the normal self-creation of boundaries or outlines (2.3B) within which they color (2.3C), actualizing an age-appropriate desire for self-set limits on their own strong impulses.

Teddy, who was neurologically impaired, might have escaped into abstraction rather than struggle with his confused body image. Given a secure, dependable setting, and an attentive adult, he was able to confront his confusion graphically, to work to clarify his conception, to make sense out of what was formerly chaotic by "figuring it out" on paper (Figure 2.3; see also DVD 15.3B and 15.3C).

Because children are small and dependent, however, they need an adult to provide them with a physical and psychological setting, within which they can freely struggle to order and control. They need an adult to provide empathic support, accepting understanding, a reflective mirror; to be a "container," a vessel into which they can freely pour their feelings and fantasies; and a responsive, articulate voice, that can help them to clarify, explain, and make sense out of what's inside.

So it follows that the adult offering art and therapy must provide a framework or structure within which the child can be free to move and to think and to fantasize; not a structure which imposes, controls, and makes a child dependent, for such a framework is a straightjacket and not conducive to growth. Such a restrictive framework may take many forms, from the use of prepared outlines, kits, and step-by-step guides, to generalizations about the best size of paper or brush, or an invariant description of the "right" way to offer art to children. The arrogance of those who have found the one correct way to work with all children in art is equal only to the disrespect on which it is based.

Surely an adult has both the right and the responsibility to set strict limits on destruction of property or dangerous ingestion of art media; but does he or she also have a right to decide that preschoolers should be restricted from free access to tempera paint because of a fear that that the child will "drown the graphic patterns of its scribbling in water colour?" (Grözinger, 1955, p. 91) Although the supposedly limited capacities of a child who is cognitively impaired are often used to justify constant supervision, does

2.3 A Person Drawing by a Brain-Damaged Boy. Age 9

any human being have the right to decide for another that "creative activity must be held to a reasonable minimum?" (Wiggin, 1962, p. 24)

Fortunately there are many who still believe in the often untapped creative resources of all human beings, who assume the growth potential of others; like the man who works with slow learners and feels sure that the "children have a rich inner life waiting to be developed in a . . . setting of love and approval" (Site, 1964, p. 19).

But *love is not enough* in many cases (Bettelheim, 1950); what is also needed is a safe and supportive framework for freedom in growing. As Milner discovered in her own struggle to paint: "Fearful subservience to an imposed authority either inside or out, or complete abandonment of all controls, neither of these was the solution." Instead, she found that it was necessary to "provide the framework within which the creative forces could have free play" (1957, p. 101). In therapy as well as in education, in art as in any other form of creative expression, this concept has continued to deepen in meaning and validity for me over time.

Conditions for Creative Growth

A framework for freedom is one way of thinking about facilitating conditions for growth, something I assume necessary to help human beings actualize their inner creative potential. It translates into the provision of a physical and psychological setting that makes it possible for each child to become him- or herself. In order to do that we need to think carefully about materials, space, and time. We may need to provide alternative expressive modalities, like music or drama, for those who cannot find their way comfortably in paint or clay (DVD 2.4).

In order to help individuals discover their own styles and selves, we must accept and value whatever they do or say that is genuinely and truly theirs. Thus, individuality, uniqueness, and originality should be affirmed. Similarly, autonomy, independence of thinking and function, and the taking of risks ought to be stimulated and reinforced when they occur (2.4A).

Materials are of many sorts: those to draw with (2.4B), those to paint with (2.4C), those to model with, and those with which to construct (2.4D). Children need to have at least some of each available, as well as surfaces and tools with which to use them successfully (2.4E). If art materials are cared for lovingly, they will not only remain most usable; children will also learn respect for the tools of the trade. I believe that, for the most part, art media are best if primarily unstructured, allowing maximal alternatives for idiosyncratic expression (2.4F). If there is enough variety, then children can discover and develop their own unique tastes and preferences, their own favorite forms of expression (2.4G).

If they are available in a state of readiness, children can use them spontaneously, without unnecessary frustration or delay in the actualization of a creative impulse. They must be sturdy, of reasonable quality, and appropriate for the children who are expected to use them—appropriate to their developmental level, degree of coordination, previous experiences, particular interests, and special needs.

Space includes not only dimension, but also places and surfaces for materials, work, storage, and cleaning up. If basic expressive media and equipment are kept in consistent and predictable places, then children will know where to go to get and to use them. If they are clearly arranged and organized, it will be easier for children to make choices. If they are placed so that they may be procured and used them independently, then excessive intervention will not be necessary.

A child needs adequate, well-lit, uninterrupted spaces for art, with sufficient definition to provide closure when necessary. A child needs places where it is all right to spill or to mess without fear of adult disapproval. A child does best with options, choices in spaces as well as in materials, so that there are ways to be close or far, alone or with others (2.4H).

Time for art means often enough and long enough to sustain interest and to become involved in a genuine creative process (Figure 2.4). If the same basic materials are available all or most of the time, they will become familiar. Only then can children truly get to know them and have sufficient opportunity to practice their use, and only through such practice can they achieve genuine mastery and competence.

Whatever the context, whether individual, group, or family, children need to know how much time is available; it helps to have a warning at the point where the time is drawing to a close. Ending times are often hard for youngsters, and we need to provide ways for them to adjust to having to stop and to leave.

Order means clarity and consistency in the organization of materials, working spaces, and time. This is helpful for all children; for children with little inner order it is absolutely essential. An alone-with-another time in art can be a powerfully peaceful and organizing experience. Even in a group, such an atmosphere is possible. It is most probable where children's bodies, working spaces, materials, and products are protected from disruption by others. Psychological safety is as important as physical protection, for children's feelings need the same kind of respect and concern.

Safety means that many kinds of expressive activity are accepted: bizarre as well as realistic, regressive as well as progressive, those with negative as well as positive subject matter. Limits help to protect children from their own impulses, so that while it is safe to smear chalk or to draw destructive fantasies, it is not safe to allow smearing people, or destroying property.

In work with children, it is important to protect them whenever possible from outer as well as inner psychological dangers, such as practices that would limit or stunt their creative growth. I think especially of the danger of imposing outside ideas or standards on children, invalidating or crippling their own developing images—telling them what to do and how to do it.

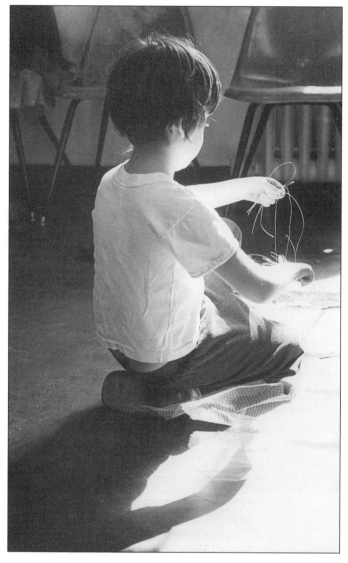

2.4 A Girl Who Is Absorbed in Her Work (Photo by Jacob Malezi)

Respect for children is shown by allowing them the freedom to choose to become involved or not to participate; to take a superficial and fleeting "taste," or to become deeply engrossed; to select their own medium and topic; to work alone or with others; to explore and experiment at their own pace and in their own way. Respect for each child's uniqueness is also shown by allowing and helping every one to explore and discover their own most congenial ways of expressing themselves, their preferred modalities, personal themes, and styles (see DVD 2.4A and 2.4G).

Respect for children's opinions is expressed through listening and interviewing in a way that encourages them to express their own thoughts and associations about both process and product. Respect for children as artists is expressed through helping them set their own goals and standards, and to evaluate for themselves how well they have achieved them. Respect for children's tangible productions, extensions of themselves, is shown through handling and preserving, or sharing and displaying them, with loving care.

Interest in youngsters and in their personal explorations and expressions must be sincere, because children are acutely sensitive to phoniness. Such interest may be expressed in sensitive, unintrusive observation, genuine listening, and gentle verbal intervention. Interest is shown by being available as a facilitator during the creative process, if they express or show a need for the adult's help, support, or appreciation.

Support for the child's inner creative strivings is expressed through consistent provision of conditions like those noted above. This is different from a passively permissive attitude, which may represent (or at least communicate) a lack of interest or concern on the part of the adult. Support for all children requires an awareness of normal stages of development in art, in order to help them to take the next steps.

This is part of the framework child art therapists need to have, and is delineated in detail in Chapter 3, "Understanding Development in Art." Support for growth in therapy requires an awareness and understanding of normal stages in psychotherapy, which are described in Chapter 4, "A Picture of the Treatment Process."

Support also requires knowledge of each individual child's developmental and psychological state, his "frame of reference" (Henley, 1992; Lowenfeld, 1957), within which you both must meet if you are to lead him forward. This is probably best illustrated in the many case studies in this book, beginning with Chapter 8, which describes work with an elective mute, a psychotic girl, and an encopretic boy.

Chapter 16 describes work with blind children, including two anxious girls, one oppositional boy, and another boy who would probably be described now as having a borderline personality disorder. Two case studies of adolescents are found in Chapter 14: the story of Sam, who had been diagnosed as suffering from a schizo-affective disorder, and the story of Jim, who was struggling with depression.

Support for children who are blocked, or "stuck," requires especially thoughtful understanding and assistance from the adult. With timid children, for example, active participation in the artwork alongside them may be a helpful, concrete expression of adult permission for their own involvement with media. Indeed, there are numerous ways to help, limited only by the imagination and flexibility of the therapist. Although examples are found in many places, these ideas are perhaps best illustrated in Chapter 5, which details a number of ways to facilitate expression.

In a broader sense, support for any child's struggle to grow in and through art requires genuine empathy on the part of the adult, and its communication to the child in a manner best suited to enhance that individual's own expressive development. I understand the role of a therapist primarily as a facilitator of another person's growth, the shape and form of which vary tremendously from one child to another. If there are no big blocks to creative development, the provision of facilitating conditions like those previously noted may be sufficient to enable the youngster to flower.

If, however, the blocks are large and severe, some reparative work is probably in order, and will vary in form, depending on the capacities and needs of the child. All such work for me is a challenging, unpredictable, creative endeavor. Each new person is a new puzzle, like but unlike others, with untapped potential for symbolic communication and healthy growth.

3

Understanding
Development in Art

Progression in Normal Artistic Development

The normal sequence of development in child art has been observed, collected, described, and categorized since the nineteenth century by specialists in child development, psychology, and art education; work has focused, probably for practical reasons, on graphic expression, including a number of recent studies (Arnheim, 1954; Cox, 1992, 1993, 1997; Di Leo, 1970, 1974, 1977, 1983; Dubowski, 1984; Gardner, 1980, 1982; Golomb, 1974, 1992, 2002; Goodnow, 1977; Harris, 1963; Koppitz, 1968, 1984; Lowenfeld, 1957; Malchiodi, 1998; Mortensen, 1991; Thomas & Silk, 1990; Van Sommers, 1984; Winner, 1982).

Despite the fact that some beginnings have been made in looking closely at painting (Alschuler & Hattwick, 1947; Lantz, 1955; Simon, 1992; Smith, 1981) and at clay modeling (Brown, 1975; Golomb, 1974, 2002; Hartley, Frank, & Goldenson, 1952); these efforts have been spotty and as yet unintegrated. Although, like others, I have found Lowenfeld's (1957) stages to be helpful ways of conceptualizing graphic development, I have not found them to be as useful when applied to painting, modeling, or constructing. I have therefore felt a need for a broader set of developmental categories, which could apply more comfortably to work in all two- and three-dimensional media.

All attempts to describe art development make clear that there is a predictable sequence of events for what most children will do in art as they mature. This sequence has a kind of cyclical rhythm—moving forward and backward, expanding and contracting, with a progressive thrust over time.

The stages defined by different workers reflect not only the regularity of this process, but the fact that the same developmental sequence may be divided in a variety of ways, each with its own logic, and may be analyzed in more or less detail from diverse perspectives, each one appropriate to its own frame of reference.

As an art therapist, I find I share with others an interest in both the cognitive and affective aspects of art behaviors, and that I must account for both the process and the product. I also find, since I often work with those whose growth is uneven and delayed (see Wilson, 1977), that I need to understand in more detail the beginning phases of art development—an area to which some workers have made helpful contributions (Gardner, 1980; Grözinger, 1955; Kellogg, 1969; Rutten-Sarris, 2002). Because I have found no existing set of stages comfortably applicable to all modes and to the earliest periods of creating, I have needed to find relevant ways of thinking about art development for my own work.

At the risk of oversimplifying what is always a complex and ultimately individual sequence of events, I should therefore like to propose yet another way of describing normal development in art—a way that includes drawing, painting, modeling, and constructing, and that deals in some detail with the earliest period of expression. The stages that make sense to me are as follows: *Manipulating, Forming, Naming, Representing, Containing, Experimenting, Consolidating, Naturalizing, Personalizing.*

The steps are not so discrete in reality. Indeed, they always overlap, and in a very real sense live on forever as possible modes of doing. Manipulation, for example, is always present when using media, though it does not remain the primary focus of attention and absorption as children mature. The stages refer to what is most central for each period, and must be seen as complex, multilayered, and persistent. The separation, therefore, is artificial, but hopefully helpful—in emphasizing descriptively and conceptually those aspects of creating that take successive prominence in normal growth and development.

It is probably not worth debating when "art" begins, but it is important to remember that it is a logical development of the earliest forms of encountering the world through the senses (J. Erikson, 1988). From the rattle in the mouth, to the stick in the sand, to the crayon on the paper, is not a series of hops, but part of a continuous sequence.

Different children have different developmental rhythms as they do working rhythms, which may have genetic as well as environmental bases. In any case, norms are wide and must remain so, thus calling into question the usefulness of things like drawings for developmental diagnosis, when so many relevant variables are unspecified.

35

Some have requested that I specify ages for each of the stages. I have not done so before, because the variability in normal art development is so great that age ranges are nothing more than extremely approximate guidelines, to be stretched as needed to fit individual growth patterns. However, as long as that is understood—that is, that a stage can start as much as a year or more before and can end as much as a year or more after the ages noted here—I have done so for this third edition (DVD 3.1).

Manipulating (1 to 2 Years)

The first stage of any encounter with materials is a manipulative one. Of course, the manipulation may be inappropriate, for example, putting clay into the mouth or crayon on the wall. These behaviors are not wrong from the infant's or toddler's point of view, but are defined as such by the environment, which decrees that you may smear your food in the high chair tray or play with mud and sand in the yard, but may not mark the wall with the crayon or eat the clay (which indeed looks and smells like food to the very young). In any case, we generally permit infants and toddlers to smear, mark, model, and construct with natural materials as soon as they are able, but restrict them from using art materials until they can do so within our societally defined limits.

The sensory qualities of materials are vital during this manipulative phase—the feel of paint or clay, the texture of sand or wood. Equally important are the kinesthetic aspects of the experience—the movement of hands, arms, and often the whole body in making marks, molding, or putting things together (3.1A). When one observes a toddler or preschooler manipulating clay or scribbling with crayon, one becomes aware of how central the motor-kinesthetic aspects of such an experience are for the young child.

As the child becomes aware of the fact that it is *she or he* who has squeezed the clay or marked the paper, the youngster becomes increasingly interested in the visual aspects of the experience, in the shape of the clay or the color of the scribbles. Attention starts to focus not just on the making process, but on that which is being made, despite the fact that there is no real concern about a finished product at this stage (Figure 3.1). Although there is great individual variability, this stage usually lasts from about ages 1 to 2.

Forming (2 to 3 Years)

As children mature intellectually and physiologically, they gain increasing control over their movements, and begin to take more deliberate charge of what happens when using crayons or clay. They practice, and

3.1 A Toddler Can Manipulate a Paintbrush and Enjoy the Process

soon demonstrate their control over materials by repeating certain motions or activities, as in longitudinal or circular scribbling, rolling or flattening clay. They start to consciously vary manipulations of materials—to make first dots and then lines, or lines and then masses, to pound and then squeeze, to build in a way that is more than just picking up and putting down.

They then begin to make gestalts, separate shapes or objects which have an existence of their own. Although not representational at first, these represent a forward step of great magnitude in the creation of intentional forms. One such example is beginning and ending a line in the same place in a drawing, thereby making an enclosure. By so doing, the child creates a separate shape which is perceived as such, and is then related to with other lines, shapes, or extensions. Although there is great variability, this stage usually occurs between ages 2 and 3 (3.1B).

Naming (3 to 4 Years)

Perhaps because adults want so often to know what has been made, or perhaps because children have reached a point where they begin to think of making a "something," the next step for almost every child is the naming of marks or objects as real things. Grownups are usually puzzled, because these masses of paint or clay or configurations of wood in no way resemble the objects they are said to represent.

But they do stand for something else, in the same way that a block can symbolize a car or a gun in the hands of a 3-year-old. Their identity often shifts in a fluid fashion because it is not fixed in any quality of the creation, but rather in the child's association to the form at a particular moment (see Wilson, 2001, on symbolization). This stage, which often overlaps with the previous one, generally occurs from 3 to 4 (3.1C).

Representing (4 to 6 Years)

There does come a time, however, when true representations emerge from the manipulating, forming, and naming processes of children using materials. They are often strange to adult eyes, hard to recognize, and frequently mixed on the same picture space or clay board with nonrepresentational items. Yet they are distinct, because they do involve qualities of the object being represented.

The early human figures, the well-known cephalopods, for example (3.1D), do have a shape which stands for head-body, extensions which legitimately stand for limbs, and usually one or more features which resemble that to which they refer (eyes, mouth, and so on). Here is one version by a little girl (a), and a drawing of her Mommy (b) 8 months later (Figure 3.2).

There are many strange variations and odd features in early representational art—in drawings, sculptures, paintings, and constructions—which refer in some meaningful way to the objects they are said to be. One way of explaining this early work has been to say that children draw what they *know*, not what they *see*. There is some truth in that notion in this sense: that what children make represents, as far as they are able, those things they know about the object which seem important to them at the moment of making. But at three or four or five years of age, and for a long time thereafter, children can represent far less than they either know or see. Instead,

38

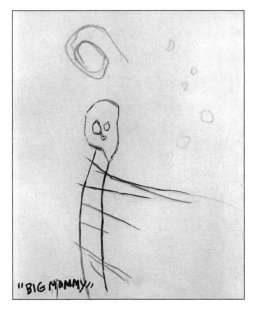

3.2a A Head-Body (Cephalopod) Figure.
Three years, 10 months. Crayon

3.2b A Person (Mommy) 8 Months
Later by the Same Girl. Crayon

their work is a condensed form of symbolization, showing what they are able to about that which *interests* them.

It is also during this period that designs become not only configurations of line or mass, but that the filling-in of lines and the creation of boundaries become both possible and important. For children's growth and expansion have to do not only with an increasing capacity to do more things better, but also to control themselves and their strong impulses.

Young children often delight in practicing and demonstrating their ability to stay within the lines in their own artwork, just as they are learning to stay within bounds in other areas. They do this quite spontaneously, creating and filling in their own boundaries (see DVD 2.3), a far healthier activity both psychologically and creatively than filling in other peoples' spaces, like stencils or coloring books (Figure 3.3).

During this early representational phase, children experiment in a way similar to but different from their manipulative explorations. They explore different ways of doing, of making, and of saying things. Their human figures are a good index of the freedom and flexiblity of their capacity to experiment, for they are still the most frequent symbol. Lowenfeld (1957) called this period the "pre-schematic" stage, indicating that it precedes chronologically a time of settling on specific symbols or "schema" for specific objects.

3.3 A Partially Sighted Boy Fills In His Own Outlines

But I do not believe that this exploration and expansion of graphic vocabulary is simply a search for a set of symbols. Rather, it is a time of expansion—intellectually, and in all areas of development. It is a time when children stretch, try their wings, and hopefully are encouraged to explore their environment and their own capacities. In this context, exploration in art in this early representational period is a similar kind of mental and visual thinking, roaming, and discovery. Part of this experimental phase involves the discovery of many graphic ways to say the same thing, such as Jenny's human figures, all done within a 6-month period in her fourth and fifth years, each one quite unique (Figure 3.4). These beginnings of representation usually occur between ages 4 and 6, though here too there is great individual variation.

Consolidating (6 to 9 Years)

At about the time most children enter school, a kind of consolidation takes place in their art work, as in other areas of behavior. They begin to find preferred ways of saying things pictorially and tend to repeat them, rather than to go on as before, trying out different ways (3.1E). These schemata or symbols are both simple statements, like Jenny's way of representing the human figure, and complex ones, like John's way of represent-

a

b

c

3.4 Some of Jenny's Varied Human Figure Drawings around Age 4

ing relationships between objects in space with a baseline to indicate the ground on which they stand (Figure 3.5).

Some of these configurations look fairly realistic, while others, like the "X-ray" (Figure 3.6), or "mixed plan and elevation" conventions (Figure 3.7), look quite strange. For example, the catching and throwing arms of two baseball players might be represented, while the inactive arms are

3.5 "Daddy in Front of Our House," by John. Age 5. Marker

omitted (3.1F). While not naturalistic, these pictorial conventions have a kind of inner logic and tend to be utilized for a period of time, varying from child to child (3.1G). The degree of flexibility in the work of any individual during this stage (which Lowenfeld called "schematic") also varies considerably. Although children at this stage delight in using color, it is not yet consistently realistic.

The shift to a different kind of order in schematic symbols, and ways of relating them, is paralleled by a shift from a rather egocentric point of view

3.6 "X-ray" Drawing of a Mother with a Baby in Her Tummy. Age 5. Marker

to a more social one. The earliest subject matter for most children is the human figure, most often labeled as self or family members. Gradually, however, as their world and horizons broaden, they include other people, trees, plants, houses, vehicles, and, eventually, people and places both near and far away. While there are cultural variations in popular spontaneous subject matter, there is a general widening, broadening, and expanding of the child's creative horizons over time in all societies. This stage usually occurs between the ages of 6 and 9.

43

Naturalizing (9 to 12 Years)

Throughout the preceding phases, paralleling the increasing elaboration and sophistication in nonfigurative work, children's art becomes more and more naturalistic. Parts of the body are represented in gradually more realistic proportions, spatial relationships become more and more accurate, and relative sizes and colors of objects get closer and closer to those of reality. The change is evident in two versions of "Wizard of Oz" by the same child, done at ages 6 (3.1H) and 8 (3.1I).

During the early phase of attempts at naturalizing their art, children's products often reflect some awkwardness, associated with the abandonment of the old, comfortable, but no longer acceptable schemata of earlier years. They struggle with proportions, shading, and attempts to control the quality of line and color, and feel increasing concern about the realism of both two- and three-dimensional products.

Whereas before most children were satisfied or even delighted with their efforts, now most children are dissatisfied, often discouraged and self-

3.7 A Family Eating Dinner around a Table. Age 6. Marker

critical. There comes a time, in fact, when the discrepancy between what they have represented and the visual facts apparent to their eyes becomes distressing to the majority of youngsters. At this point they experience anxiety and frustration, attempting to make things as they are, but rarely feeling satisfied with their efforts.

This inner dissatisfaction occurs at different ages for different children, and no doubt has multiple cognitive, affective, and social roots. Whatever the cause, it seems to be an inevitable stage in normal development, one at which many children give up in discouragement, turning to other (mostly verbal) forms of expression which are more manageable and in which they feel more competent. This stage is usually from age 9 to 12.

Parenthetically, there are many possible ways to help discouraged children continue to create during this period. As with any other intervention, trial and error is best. I will note a few, but the list is hardly exhaustive. One is to shift to another modality where, because it is new, they have fewer expectations about their performance. This could be another medium, like a new kind of clay; another activity, like creating puppets; or another technique, like using a potter's wheel.

Or, it could be the use of magazine photos or three-dimensional materials to create something new, like a collage or sculpture. Here, the activity involves putting preexisting elements together, rather than creating everything from scratch. These kinds of two- and three-dimensional constructions are not only less threatening to those discouraged about their representational ability; they are also excellent alternatives for self-representation, something highly appealing to most adolescents.

Another approach is to focus on abstraction, whatever the medium, and to suggest the making of designs or patterns or symbols that have something to do with themselves. Yet another is to use some sort of assist, such as a "visual starter," like a scribble, on which to project imagery, especially fantasy (so their worries about being able to succeed in realism can be put aside).

One method which sometimes works is to respond directly to the expressed feelings of inadequacy and to focus on drawing from some sort of model (still or human or pictured). However, to make this less threatening, it is best to use techniques which seem to help people to get unstuck at any age, such as contour and gesture drawing, or using the nondominant hand (B. Edwards, 1979, 1986; Rogers, 1993).

Personalizing (12 to 18 Years)

For most children, the period of naturalizing goes on for a long time, throughout the later elementary school years and into early adolescence. If youngsters experience sufficient success in these endeavors, and have enough instruction and practice, they can develop an impressive degree of skill in naturalistic rendering in any of the large variety of media they can now manage. Some, less successful with naturalism but with a strong aesthetic sense, turn to abstract work, and often show a preference for creative activities in nongraphic media, including crafts, where the youngster's increasing fine-motor control can be contained and made productive within a designated skill activity.

Those youngsters who remain active in art during adolescence usually reflect their increasing concern with themselves, characteristic of this phase, by intentionally personalizing their work, self-consciously exploring different styles, for example, as a way of expressing their own emerging identity. Whether their interest is primarily in how things look or in how they feel about events, teenagers tend to search for their own particular media and themes, in order to express their personal perceptions of both inner and outer worlds (3.1J).

Their self-criticism and concern with quality increases, and is eventually focused not only on naturalism, but also on other expressive and aesthetic goals. The work may be simple or complex, rich or stark, figurative or nonfigurative. What characterizes all of it, however, is the self-conscious and deliberate quality of the adolescent artist. Whether they work in a free or controlled style, they are more intentionally in charge than ever before, in great contrast to the rather unself-conscious spontaneity of the earliest periods (3.1K).

During adolescence, children's concern with the world often becomes secondary to their preoccupation with themselves, and the subject matter of their art reflects this increasing egocentrism. Whether they represent themselves or someone like them, or choose to specialize in a specific medium, subject matter, or type of abstraction, they are basically looking for personally syntonic themes, just as they are searching for a personally congenial style (3.1L). This period lasts through adolescence.

Where a Child Is

While most children function within normal developmental limits, there are also youngsters who are well behind age norms, and there are some who are functioning beyond what would be expected for children their age. How are we to understand such variations? This is a complex area to be sure, yet one that is vital for our work.

When a child is behind peers in artistic development there are two critical questions that need to be addressed. The first is whether the youngster is consistently delayed, or is rather more variable in artistic performance. The second, which is more difficult to answer, is whether the lag is caused by something organic, such as a neurological deficit, or is caused by something psychodynamic, such as an internalized conflict, resulting in performance anxiety. Each would be treated quite differently.

When a child is beyond peers in artistic development, the questions are equally complex. As with lagging behind, the consistency or variability of the youngster's artistic performance needs first to be addressed. If the child's art is significantly ahead that of agemates, he or she is gifted in art, usually having progressed rapidly through normal developmental stages. The role of talent in all of the arts is generally acknowledged as innate, but as also requiring the support of the environment. Not all children who are gifted become artists as adults, and few become famous, though the childhood drawings and paintings of most recognized artists are usually dramatically advanced.

On the other hand, the child may be delayed in other areas of development, sometimes dramatically so. A girl named Nadia, like a small number of other autistic savants, was able to draw pictures at a most sophisticated level, even though her speech and other functions were well below the norm (Selfe, 1977). Although many theories have been proposed for such remarkable gifts in cognitively impaired children, there is no consensus regarding the cause of this phenomenon (Golomb, 1992, 2002).

The child who is delayed can be helped with a carefully conceived and executed developmental approach, which recognizes tiny steps and promotes the taking of further ones (Aach-Feldman & Kunkle-Miller, 2001; Malchiodi, Kim, & Choi, 2003; Roth, 2001).

The gifted child artist is likely to please the art therapist in ways that have little to do with the problems that brought him or her to treatment. As an artist, the art therapist will no doubt enjoy working with a youngster who produces attractive artwork, just as a talk therapist enjoys working with an articulate patient of any age. The risk is that the art therapist's attention to and perception of the issues for which the child is in therapy could be distorted or compromised because of inevitable pleasure in the youngster's talent.

It is essential for the art therapist to put aside the aesthetic gain of witnessing the production of good art, and to focus throughout on the person who made it and the problems that brought him or her into treatment. I was not so convinced of this problem until I had supervised hundreds of art therapists, in training and with experience. I now have no doubt that the seductive appeal of a child (or adult) with talent requires self-awareness and vigilance on the part of the art therapist, so that it does not interfere with being able to help them.

General Issues in Development

Source of the Child's Imagery

Some issues span all developmental levels—for example, the source of the imagery in the art of the child. While one might think that it is more likely to be kinesthetic at the earliest manipulative stages (Grözinger, 1955; Kellogg, 1969), other variables may also predispose the youngster to respond more to the body and less to vision, as with Lowenfeld's (1957) *haptic* type, first evident in adolescence. Many stimuli for artistic imagery seem to be largely internal, like instinctual drives, and those body parts, zones, and processes of special significance (Erikson, 1950). Neurobiological sources also seem critical, affecting both responsive and productive image behavior (Berlyne, 1971; Horowitz, 1983).

In addition, there is provocative evidence for the possibility of innately preferred sensory modalities and for universal visual propensities, such as archetypes (Jung, 1964; J. Kellogg, 1978; R. Kellogg, 1969; Robertson, 1963)—further internal sources of imagery in child art. Significant maturational factors affecting art imagery include cognitive development (Arnheim, 1954; Piaget, 1950, Piaget & Inhelder, 1956, 1971); phase-appropriate growth-tasks (Colarusso, 1992; Erikson, 1950; A. Freud, 1965; Tyson & Tyson, 1990); and defense mechanisms (A. Freud, 1936; Levick, 1983).

In addition to internal forces, external influences on the child's art imagery are significant at all developmental stages. The influence of others—first mother, then father, then siblings and peers—on what the child produces to please or to compete is probably impossible to quantify, but is important nonetheless (see Cassidy & Shaver, 1999; Lowenfeld, 1957; Kramer, 1958; Wilson & Wilson, 1978).

Of course, the visual world itself is the source of most art imagery at all ages, but what is most intriguing is how the inner pressures affect the perception and selection of external imagery for art. In 1969 I met with Dr. Ernst Harms, a child psychologist, a pioneer in the use of art in therapy (1948), and founder of the journal, *Art Psychotherapy* (now *The Arts in Psychotherapy*).

Dr. Harms scoffed at the notion, proposed by child psychiatrist Lauretta Bender (1952), that the children in Bellevue's psychiatric unit painted boats on the water because it symbolized the separation from their mothers. With some scorn, Dr. Harms made the point that they drew boats because the hospital was on the East River, and that was all they saw! Despite such persuasive skepticism, one must still account for the *selection* of stimuli, given the fact that there are always many things to choose from, even in a relatively restricted environment.

This interaction of internal needs with external stimuli is one of the most fascinating aspects of the study of child art. Some individual youngsters develop preferred art images which carry a special power because of their connection with experiences of intense meaning and feeling (McFarland, 1978). While such images are characterized by differing degrees of disguise, they seem to occur at all developmental levels, with multiple cognitive and affective determinants.

There is no question that the meaning of the art activity changes as children mature, as different aspects become more prominent and others less so. Because of these shifts over time, and because of the ongoing maturation of body and mind, issues like mastery, ordering, or finding aesthetic "rightness" are different for a 3-year-old than for a 13-year-old. The interaction of variables like affect and cognition is a complex one, and yet a separation of the two seems highly artificial when one is dealing with such multifaceted acts as drawing, painting, sculpting, or constructing.

Certainly, how one feels about what one is doing will influence many things, from choice of materials to selection of subject matter to style of work. Whether a 3-year-old or a 13-year-old works in a calm and deliberate or sloppy and impulsive manner has more to do with affective than with cognitive factors. The interaction of these is complex developmentally, for while it is true that most 4-year-olds are freer than most 10-year-olds when they paint, within each age group there is an equally great range of differences, due as much to personality as to developmental level.

Whether a 2- or a 12-year-old uses more or less picture space is probably more a reflection of personality than an index of cognitive or motor development. What is important here from the point of view of assessment is the need to understand all relevant variables—the cognitive, the affective, and the motoric—and to relate these within a developmental framework that takes into account what is known about most children, as well as what can be discovered about any particular child.

Parenthetically, while the emphasis in this chapter is on normal development in art as a framework within which art therapists need to ground their diagnostic and therapeutic work, such knowledge needs to be placed within a larger frame of reference regarding normal child development. All therapists who work with children should be familiar with its characteristics, both in and out of therapy (see Lewis & Blotcky, 1997).

Regression in Children's Art

To understand where and how someone is functioning in art it is vital to remember the cyclical and variable nature of normal development. While signs of progress are to be found in the art of most children as they grow, so too are signs of regression. For the growth process is not a simple linear movement forward, but rather a cyclical one, well-characterized in the folk wisdom of "two steps forward, one step backward" (A. Freud, 1965). There is certainly a degree of variability at any one moment in time in most youngsters' work (Figure 3.4).

It is particularly essential to know the norms alluded to above, and to know them in some detail, in order to be able to discriminate regression from some of the strange, illogical, but developmentally normal characteristics of early figurative stages—characteristics such as "cephalopods" (Figure 3.2a; DVD 3.10), transparencies or "X-ray" pictures (Figure 3.6), mixed plane and elevation in the treatment of space (Figure 3.7), or value-rather than reality-based relative sizes (Figure 3.5).

It is only within a framework of normal growth and development in art, and within the narrower framework of a particular child's past and present work, that the concept of regression becomes meaningful. Thus, knowing that a physically disabled boy of 5 can draw a detailed clown (Figure 3.8a), we are entitled to label as dramatically regressed his portrait of himself (Figure 3.8b), a poignant expression of his sense of his body as a disorganized entity. About his self-portrait, Jimmy, whose lifeless legs were in a wheelchair, said, "His legs got lost in the grass."

His picture of the clown, on the other hand, showed how bright he was, since it was a superior human figure drawing for a child his age. The massive difference in the developmental level of his self-portrait indicated not only Jimmy's body image, but also his rage and helplessness about his physical state. The Self drawing is particularly poignant in contrast to his choice of a clown, who can not only walk, but who can also jump and hop—and perhaps even fly on a trapeze.

While not always pure, it may help to think of regression in children's art as being manifest in four major ways: Form, Content, Organization, and the Thought processes evident in the work. Regression in Form, the return to earlier modes of representation, is perhaps the most common and most easily identified, as in the examples already noted. In Content, one may see the representation of symbolic material relating to earlier phases of development. This may be more or less overt, as in 15-year-old Melanie's oral-aggressive hungry eagle (Figure 6.2), may be disguised through a symbol, or may be hidden in an abstraction.

The other forms of regression may be thought of as more vertical than

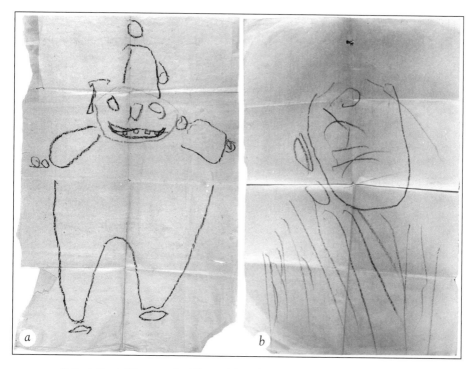

3.8 A Boy's Pictures of a Clown (a) and of Himself (b). Age 5. Crayon

horizontal, that is, regression downward from the conscious, rational level of the mind to deeper ones (versus regression backward in form or content). It is evident at times in disorganization—in the disintegration of form, in fragmentation, or even in chaos—the loss of order.

A related kind of regression is manifest in the appearance of thought processes characteristic of that part of the mind dominant in dreams as well as in psychosis—the socalled "primary process" of the unconscious. This is seen in the use of such devices as condensation, like a teenager who drew her family as a head with a feature from each member (DVD 10.3B); or displacement, as in Sam's bizarre head with its distorted features (Figure 14.5). The absence of real time or space in pictures with a dreamlike, surrealistic quality may also be thought of as a regression to deeper, more primitive, less logical modes of thought.

It should be noted that not all instances of progressive or regressive behavior in art are evident in the product itself. While one can sometimes guess from a product that aggressive-destructive impulses gained control over progressive-constructive ones, one cannot observe in a picture the growth in a child's autonomy which may have accompanied its production.

Causes of Regression

There are a variety of reasons for regression in children's art, and it may be useful to note the more common ones. Some involve external stimuli, such as the medium. Chalk, for example, invites smearing and loss of boundaries more easily than crayon, as can be seen in two drawings by a boy done in the same hour (Figure 6.5a, b).

At times the social situation seems to be the primary impetus to regression, through contagion from others. Tim, usually neat and well-organized in his portraits of people, rarely let go in his work unless the person next to him in his art therapy group made it permissible to do so (see DVD 9.2E). Barbara (DVD 3.2), whose work was generally very careful (3.2A), loosened up when she sat next to Joyce (3.2B).

Other causes seem more internal, such as fatigue. The last two pictures in a series of 16 done by a 4-year-old boy were significantly less organized and differentiated than his first two drawings. The most common cause of all seems to be stress. 5-year-old Lisa, for example, reacted by abandoning her normally well-organized decorative painting style (Figure 3.9a) for a smudgy smear (Figure 3.9b) on the day her mother went to the hospital to have a baby.

Sometimes, however, the major determinant for regression in form seems to be a kind of naive logic, as in Jenny's family picture (Figure 3.10). Most of the figures inside her house are not as detailed, since they were less important than the mother, who is more elaborated. Di Leo (1970) sees this phenomenon as due to a shift in the child's "cognitive-affective ratio." The same kind of logic, equating size with importance rather than reality, is visible in John's picture, where Daddy is clearly more important than the house (Figure 3.5); or that dictates that only one arm be drawn when throwing a ball (DVD 3.1F), or holding balloons (DVD 3.1G).

Paradoxically, another major determinant of regression in children's art seems to be progression or growth. A certain amount of awkwardness, even disorganization, may accompany the struggle involved in giving up an old schema and developing a new one. As Rudolf Arnheim said of this phenomenon, "the resulting disorder, though perhaps unappealing in itself, gives evidence of the searching mind in action" (1969, p. 266).

At times an art therapist may deliberately suggest the loosening of controls through a regressive, playful approach, in order to allow more personal imagery to emerge. Such was the case with Dorothy, whose rigidly stylized birds were painted in carefully drawn pencil outlines week after week (Figure 8.4). Only after giggly experimentation with free painting, which I had suggested (DVD 8.2E), did she articulate her powerful projections of the symbolic meanings of those birds in her fantasy life (Figure 8.5; DVD 8.2G).

3.9a Lisa's Usual Style of Painting

3.9b Lisa's Smeary Picture

3.10 A Family Doing Things inside Their House ("X-ray"). Age 5. Crayon

The experience of safe but permissible regression may be an essential learning for the constricted child. "When it frees the individual from crippling inhibitions, temporary regression to crudely aggressive art may be an emotional victory" (Kramer, 1971, p. 161). In another sense, "temporary regression is a necessary phase in every creative act" (Kramer, p. 14), particularly in terms of gaining access to unconscious and preconscious processes.

Perhaps the ability to be playful, to let go of some measure of conscious control, "is not regression, [but] courageous progression" (Barron, 1972, p. 162). While the kind of "regression in the service of the ego" described by Ernst Kris (1952) is probably less common with small children than with adults, it does sometimes occur that a child with full awareness deliberately lets go of their usual controls, allowing less conscious processes to dominate. Such was the case with Carla, the partially sighted girl of 13 described in the previous chapter (see DVD 2.1).

Whether the regression is experienced as liberating and freeing, or as disorganizing and paralyzing, may best be judged from the child's ensuing behavior and work. "Healthy regression is relaxing and releases energy for further growth; unhealthy regression stops growth" (Rabin & Haworth, 1960, p. 29). This becomes clear very quickly when one observes what happens both during and after a regressive interlude. The more one considers progression and regression in children's art, the more complex they seem. Both can be seen in behavior; sometimes they are reflected in the products themselves—in their form, content, organization, and the thought processes evident therein.

Regression seems to be caused by a number of possible determinants, both internal and external, such as the medium, the social context, the child's state of alertness or fatigue, comfort or stress, and even growth itself. Regression seems sometimes to be under the child's control—a useful, healthy phenomenon. At other times, it seems to be out of his or her control—a destructive, disorganizing, frightening experience. It can be evaluated only in the context of normal child development in general and in art, the growth of any particular individual, and the sequence of graphic and behavioral events that precede and follow its appearance.

Stages of Normal Child Development

In work with parent education groups, my expressive arts therapy colleagues and I developed activities for adults which were designed to stimulate their memories and awareness of key issues in normal development. Described in Chapter 18 (pp. 339-343), they turned out to be useful in training clinicians as well, helping child psychologists, psychiatrists, and others attend to the key themes of different age groups (Table 3.1).

Table 3.1

Core Issues in Normal Development

I. Infant
    Trust vs. Mistrust
    Sensori-Motor Exploration
    Differentiation of Self and Non-Self
    Primacy of Oral Zone

II. Toddler
    Impulse Control
    Autonomy
    Ambivalent Power Struggle with Mother
    Independence/Dependence
    Control of Locomotion

III. Preschooler
    Curiosity
    Inclusion/Exclusion
    Rivalry and Competition
    Intense Fantasy Play
    Concern about Retaliation and Punishment
    Sex-Role Identification

IV. School-age Child
    Competence, Mastery and Learning
    Peer Group Interaction and Acceptance
    Same-Sex Groups
    Development of Rules and Standards

V. Adolescent
    Revival of Oedipal Wishes
    Dependence/Independence
    Autonomy and Control
    Concern for Privacy
    Future and Work Choice
    Sex-Role Orientation Established
    Interest in Identity
    Self-Consciousness
    Self-Definition
    Self-Esteem

4

A Picture of the Therapeutic Process

Inevitably one develops some notions about the problems that children have in growing that bring them to the attention of the adults who care for them, and sometimes to therapists for help. Almost always, they reflect conflict, some kind of battle which has not been successfully resolved. Sometimes the conflict is primarily between the child and the environment, so that work with parents or teachers may be all that is needed to resume free-forward movement. Frequently, however, although the child may have gotten into trouble with his world, the conflict has also become internalized.

I find it useful to think about both developmental and dynamic aspects, in trying to help as well as to understand. Is the battle between an impulse and a prohibition? If so, is it the sort of issue common to the earliest years of life (such as nurturance or security), or is it characteristic of some later phase (such as competition or identity)? How is the child trying to cope, what kinds of defense mechanisms are being used, and how primitive or sophisticated are they?

In this area, I have found the psychoanalytic perspective to be most helpful in conceptualizing both the developmental (Blos, 1962; Cassidy & Shaver, 1999; Erikson, 1950, 1959; Fraiberg, 1955; A. Freud, 1965; Sarnoff, 1976; Tyson & Tyson, 1990) and the psychodynamic (A. Freud, 1936, 1946, 1965) aspects of conflict and the meanings of symptomatology.

I think it matters not so much which frame of reference one uses to understand children's difficulties. I feel it is essential to have one, however, preferably one that is fairly consistent and relevant for a variety of problems. Without a conceptual framework to which to relate the child's symbolic and behavioral messages in assessment or treatment, one's work remains fuzzy and unfocused, without form or aim. Often one must begin in just such a state of confusion, since the signals sent by the child initially may be unclear, inconsistent, disguised, and misleading. But one hopes and works for clarification.

It is helpful in the appreciation of a Renaissance painting to have some understanding of the physical and conceptual structure within—the underpainting, the perspective, and the iconography of the time. It is equally helpful to have some sense of what is beneath the surface in work with a child. Without such awareness, one is working in the dark, and may do little good, perhaps even harm. Moreover, it is my conviction that the more one understands, the more one can help.

With these notions in mind, I should like to attempt some generalizations about the therapeutic process with individuals in art, with the full awareness that there will always be exceptions to any such statements. Nevertheless, it seems to me as I review work with different children (most of whom came for weekly sessions for 3 months to 3 years) that some common patterns emerge, although their individual shape and form varies considerably (see also Betensky, 1973).

At the risk of oversimplifying, I should like to hazard the notion that progress in child art therapy consists of a series of steps, most often including: *Testing, Trusting, Risking, Communicating, Facing, Understanding, Accepting, Coping,* and *Separating.* These have to do with a child's relationship to the therapist as well as to their own difficulties. Like stages in art development, the separation is an artificial one, since the phases in therapy also involve overlapping, regression, and the persistent presence of all throughout the process.

Testing

Though children vary considerably in how readily they relate to a new adult, there is always some degree of uncertainty and testing in the early stages of the relationship. Even the most needy child, though hungry for the adult's attention and approval, is likely, because of past disappointments, to have trouble believing in the dependability of a new adult. During this initial period of uncertainty some testing often occurs, and takes many forms, including demands for extra-therapeutic supplies or attention, and literal testing of the limits of time, space, or behavior in the therapy hour.

It is not surprising to find that individual child therapists set different limits in their playrooms, no doubt because they differ in what each is comfortable with (Ginott, 1961). It seems that child art therapists are similarly varied. What matters most is that a therapist be clear in his or her own mind about limits for child patients, and that they enforce them clearly and consistently, in an empathic and kindly fashion.

For myself, the most important limits have to do with not allowing destructive aggression against either property or people, in both individual and group therapy. If the aggression can be redirected to an acceptable act, that can be helpful to children, such as throwing clay "bullets" at a target, not a person. My own preference is not to state limits in advance, but to deal with each as they come up in behavior.

As with *when* to set limits, *how* one does so depends on many variables, including social and institutional norms,[1] personal comfort, and the nature of the child's disturbance. Here, too, clarity, consistency, firmness, and kindness seem to me to be essential. What is vital during this initial phase, however, is that the adult be firm about his or her chosen limits, yet convey the clear and consistent message that within these, he or she is totally available to the child.

It is tempting to try to build a "good" relationship by being lenient, by overlooking mild limit-breaking—but such a stance does not create security. While it may be immediately gratifying, it is ultimately threatening to the child, who wants and needs a secure framework in order to feel free to expose and to take risks.

Adults have different reasons for going into service professions, and a common motivation is related to their own needs for nurturance. It is not surprising, therefore, that one of the most frequent problems for inexperienced therapists is setting limits and withholding gratification of the child's urgent demands. It is understandable that one might identify with the hurt and needy child, and in so doing feel compelled to give.

It is a hard lesson to learn, but an essential one, that such behavior in the long run does not promote a secure therapeutic alliance, and that one must be firm (albeit friendly) from the start. Understanding the reasons for such a stance helps, and I have no question of its validity. Because limits

---

[1] In my first career, as an art teacher, I ran into a conflict between what I was comfortable with and the culture of the school in which I taught. I was in fact scolded by the principal for *not using a paddle*, routine in the Pittsburgh public schools of 1959. I was also told that I was undermining other teachers' ability to control their classes. I had no need to use a paddle, since the children loved art and behaved well; but it is also true that I would have had a hard time using one because of my own discomfort with doing so.

are essential to creating the kind of secure framework described in Chapter 2, I believe they need to be set and enforced in both the assessment and treatment phases of the therapeutic work.[2]

The beginning is also a time for helping children to learn what is expected of them in both doing and reflecting upon their artwork, for initiating them into the rules of this particular "game." Therapy is very different from any other situation in which children find themselves, so it is essential to help them discover how it can be helpful to them.

In these early sessions, in which one wants children to develop trust and a generally positive relationship with the therapist, it is important to be not only consistent but also as nonthreatening as possible. The time for interpretations or confrontations may come later; the early period is a time for making the situation as pleasant as possible, so that children want to return—clearly essential for becoming engaged.

Some people think this means becoming the child's "pal," and though there may be a few cases in which this is the only possible way to achieve a working alliance, it is to be avoided in general. Indeed, one can be friendly without being familiar, warm without being effusive, and interested without being either nosy or chummy.

To be open about one's own life-realities is generally not a good idea. Some think that is what is meant by being "authentic," but I understand authenticity to mean honesty, integrity, and genuineness with another human being; not providing details about one's own feelings, fantasies, and private life. Besides, it is infinitely more fruitful to respond to children's questions about oneself by wondering just what they *think* the answers might be. Though this might be frustrating, it should be explained that it will help you to help them more if you know their ideas and fantasies (the stimuli for the questions) than if you answer them directly.

Needless to say, one need not be rigid, and sometimes it makes therapeutic sense to convey some information after exploring the child's fantasies. If that is done, however, it must be with a full awareness of its possible and probable impact, and an alertness to the effects on the child and the treatment of answering any personal inquiry.

---

[2] I generally don't set limits in assessment sessions with families, since part of what I need to learn is whether and how the parents will do so with their children. In the course of family art therapy, however, whether conjoint sessions are occasional or regular, I feel most comfortable stating and enforcing the limits which make sense to me with the children. One of the most interesting aspects of family art therapy is to see whether and how, over time, the parents participate in limit setting in "my" space.

Trusting

Developing a feeling of trust and confidence takes different periods of time for different children, and one must be patient. If the therapist can be clear and consistent about all facets of the encounter, from time and rules to materials, space, and interaction, this stability will help to provide a clear and secure framework for further work.

Thus, it matters that one meets with the child at a consistent place and time, that one has the same supplies available in the same locations, and that one handles routine transactions (greeting, cleaning up, leaving) in a predictable manner. There is enough uncertainty and anxiety already in a troubled child; nothing can be gained by increasing these through inconsistent behavior on the part of the adult.

Protecting the child from unnecessary intrusions or betrayals is also essential. This means making sure that the space and time to be used are kept free from disruption. It also means being clear and open about the purpose of note-taking, if that occurs, while exploring the child's fears and fantasies concerning who might see the notes.

Obviously, it is both unprofessional and unethical to discuss a child's confidences with anyone not legitimately involved in the treatment, and one must never disclose private information to parents, schools, or others, without involving the youngster openly in such an act. While it may not be easy for a child to believe that the therapist will really treat communications as private, it is essential to convey this protective framework—at the same time exploring whatever distrust and concern they may feel.

If one wishes to have an interview observed, for any reason, such as the training of students, it is only ethical to obtain the child's consent—in spite of the fact that it might be possible here as elsewhere to do so without his or her awareness. It is difficult enough, under the most ideal conditions, for children to risk openness about their innermost fears and fantasies; it is unfair and dishonest to expect them to do so, if the therapist is not behaving according to the highest standards of personal and professional integrity.

The development of trust is a gradual process, and like any other kind of growth can regress under stress. It becomes apparent in the child's behavior and interaction with the therapist, and is especially obvious as the verbal communications become more confidential. It is also evident in the child's symbolic communications, as these move from more disguised and defensive ones to more open and expressive ones.

Carla (DVD 4.1), a youngster frightened by vivid nightmares, required a long time and some active help from the therapist, in the form of a sug-gested "scribble drawing," before she was able to risk drawing the monsters of her scary dreams (see Figure 5.1; DVD 4.1A). Once she began, Carla drew monsters of all shapes and sizes, using a variety of media (4.1B). For a while, she cut out the monster drawings and placed them inside cut-paper cages she had carefully constructed. And, for 2 weeks, she insisted that the caged monsters be locked in my desk drawers so they couldn't escape.

As she became more familiar and comfortable with these images, it was possible for her to extend the fantasy in dramatic play. One week, she spon-taneously used soap crayons and painted my face as the monster, asking me to pretend to attack her. The next week, she reversed roles and became the monster, attacking me as the fearful child (4.1C). It was during this period of work that the nightmares stopped. Art allowed Carla to *see* the scary-mad monster, while drama allowed her to safely *feel* her anger. She went on to repeat and work through in her drawings and dramas, and was thereby able to risk confrontation of the images, and then to risk confronting the aggression as her own, as well as belonging to others.

Risking

The process of risking disclosure of previously buried thoughts and feel-ings, hidden often from the child himself, is inevitably a slow one, even when it seems otherwise. Laura opened up rapidly at first, despite years of having been tightly closed up, according to parents and teachers. Her cre-ation in the first session was an elaborate but rigid wooden robot (probably a self-representation), and the story was told with much hesitation and dis-comfort. In the second session, however, she relaxed after using some fin-gerpaint, and produced a flood of fantasy material based on a picture of a mad scientist (DVD 4.2). The stories poured out of her, as if a dam had been forced open, suggesting intense pressure for release.

Following this open meeting, she withdrew dramatically, coming in and working with materials silently, resisting interviewing about the products, and even finding the art creation itself difficult for several weeks. It was many months, with forward and backward movement over time, before she could even hesitantly convey the confused fantasy world that had burst forth so prematurely in that early hour.[3]

---

[3] One might well wonder whether the flooding in the second session could have been avoided, if I might have been able to help Laura to titrate her outburst. Even with the hind-sight of experience, including years of work with Laura at different stages of her life ex-tending into adulthood, I rather doubt that there was much I could have done, except to

Communicating

To establish trust and enable a child to risk facing the fears within, it is necessary to find ways of communicating which are meaningful for both parties. It may take time, and even some trial and error, to discover the words and images and frames of reference that make sense to a particular child. While this is especially difficult with nonverbal, retarded, or psychotic youngsters, it is an essential condition for effective work with all children.

Generally, one finds a combination of verbal and nonverbal ways of relating. They may change over time with any youngster, requiring constant alertness. Finding an appropriate and workable wavelength on which to communicate is a challenge, and may require a good bit of risk-taking and creativity on the part of the therapist, but very little work can get done without effective communication.

Communicating with a child who cannot or will not speak is an especially arduous task, and one where the articulation of themes in art becomes an obvious asset. Jeremy, age 7, was an elective mute—a child who was capable of speech but who chose not to talk to all adults and most children. His early drawings, however, were clearly meant as communications, with little disguise of his pressing concerns. Jeremy's pictures are a marvelous example of the articulation power inherent in art, when a child wants badly to send symbolic messages.

A typical drawing shows family members involved in mutual battles (Figure 4.1). First, he drew the two roads on either side, with a chasm filled with water in between. A car, identified as his mommy's, was drawn over the water, then a triangular rock, which has caused the car to "trip." He was uncertain whether it would drown or make it over to the other side of the water, reflecting his ambivalence and anxiety regarding aggressive feelings toward his mother.

He then drew a car on the edge of the other cliff, then a helicopter, then an airplane (upper left)—both shooting at the car, and, finally, a rescue car at the left, shooting back at the helicopter. His younger sister was said to be in the car on the edge, his father in the helicopter, and his older brother in the rescue car on the left. He, Jeremy, was in the only plane not involved in the battle (middle left). This information was conveyed by pointing at himself and nodding his head yes or no in response to my questions. Sometimes I was unable to understand him, and he would write words in order

---

ask that she pause while telling her stories, which I suspect would have been felt as a painful rejection, and might well have stopped the therapy before it could get started.

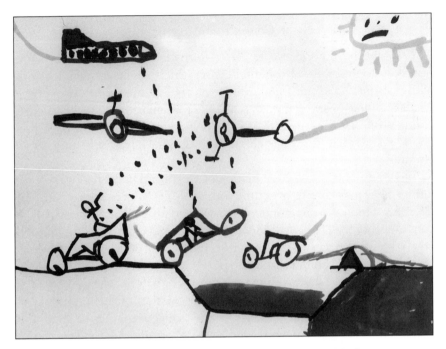

4.1 Jeremy's Drawing of Battles and Action. Age 7. Marker

to communicate. It is clear that despite his unwillingness to talk, Jeremy was quite eager to convey messages, and was able to do so very dramatically through his action-filled story pictures and accompanying gestures.

Facing

Probably the hardest part of all therapeutic work with children is the time when the child has not only communicated something risky, but is then ready (albeit ambivalently) to face that information. It was one thing for Tommy to tell a story about a snake whose eyes were going bad because he was too greedy; it was quite another for him to relate that story to himself and to his progressive blindness (see Chapter 16; DVD 16.2).

It is not always necessary to insist on a confrontation of such issues. For some, especially the very young and not too disturbed, it seems possible at times to play it out; for most communications to remain at a symbolic level (Klorer, 2000). Lori (DVD 4.3) was able to work through her anger at her mother and father, as well as her guilt and fears about their divorce, in art (4.3A) and dramatic play, with only rare, spontaneous references to herself and her own feelings (4.3B).

In one session, for example, this 4½-year-old girl identified her finger-painted creature first as "a Monster" (4.3C), then as "a 4½-year-old boy playing outside by himself." She explained that his older brother had gone in to eat, but he didn't go in, because "he doesn't like his mother's food." When asked why that was so, she replied, "He hates her." I noted that he must be awfully mad about something, so mad that he wouldn't let her feed him. She grinned and then asked if it was okay to be angry. I said it certainly was okay to be mad, but wondered if the boy would be getting hungry soon, to which she jauntily replied, "Then he'll go in and eat!"

Larry, on the other hand, could have gone on playing out dramas of injury, abandonment, and wishful fantasies forever, it seemed, with little change in his disruptive behavior at home and in school. For him it was necessary to go beyond a reflective or nondirective approach to a more interpretive one, in order to help his ego gain cognitive as well as affective understanding of his feelings and their consequences. It was long, hard work—6 years, in fact, and there were many periods of quiet and stormy resistance—but I think that without such connections, he would have continued to deny his blindness in private fantasy play, to act out his aggression in his environment, and to miss out on the learning and growing opportunities available to him. You will read more about his story in Chapters 15 and 16 (see also DVD 4.5).

It is not easy to decide in advance when a child may need to do more than gain integration through a sublimated expression in order to get well. When art therapy is adjunctive to other forms of psychotherapy, this is certainly a sufficient goal. But art therapists are often asked to work independently, especially with children who can relate in no other way. When it is the sole mode of treatment, then art alone may not be enough, and it becomes essential to expand the therapy both in depth and breadth—sometimes into other forms of communication, like drama, movement, music, and poetry. This has occurred spontaneously so often in my own work that I am convinced it is a natural thing for children to search for congenial forms of expression, and unnatural to restrict them to any one creative modality.

Had Carla stopped at the representation and locking up of her nightmare monsters, for example, I think she would not have been so well able to feel and then understand how much of the aggression she feared was her own (projected). By taking the role of the monster in a spontaneous drama, she was able to experience her own angry feelings, and later, to see how those angry monsters in the dreams and drawings might not only be scary grownups, but might also be scary angry wishes in herself (DVD 4.1).

Such experiences suggest that even though an art therapist's primary tool is art, it is important to be able to comfortably utilize other expressive modalities, including words. Facing fearful fantasies or feelings may be easier in some forms than in others. All of the arts offer some distance and disguise, which may be left undisturbed if a reflective approach seems to enable the child to move along, both in and out of therapy.

When it is necessary to intervene more actively, to help children see connections between their expressions and themselves, the facing process may be a painful one; often taking much time, with many attempts to avoid or resist. Understanding these defensive maneuvers, and respecting children's need to protect themselves, is just as important as accepting the bizarre and "bad" fantasies against which they defend. I believe that defenses should be left alone unless it seems necessary to undo them. Usually this is done to free a child because they are crippling, and in order to help achieve awareness and mastery of a disabling conflict.

The facing of previously unconscious—and therefore unacceptable—wishes and thoughts is difficult for anyone, child or adult. It is not too difficult to get at them symbolically. It is much harder, but sometimes necessary, to get at them directly. If done with caution, and with the general cooperation (trust) of the child—despite many inevitable moments of anger and anxiety—it can be hard work well done, and a sense of accomplishment can be felt jointly, even with a young child. The degree of understanding of which any child is capable will vary according to age and intellectual endowment. What is needed is enough understanding to be able to integrate this newfound awareness, and to move on to more adaptive ways of thinking, feeling, and behaving, through internal changes.

Understanding

It takes a long time, from the first glimmer of hard-to-handle, conflicted aspects of the self, to reach the point at which the child can accept, without undue anxiety, these previously hidden secrets. Carla was in weekly therapy for a full year following her first drawing of the nightmare-monster (see Figure 5.1). Toward the end of our work (DVD 4.4), the focus of her concerns shifted to issues of nurturance (4.4A), identity, and separation (4.4B), which intensified when termination was decided upon.

When the time came for her therapy to end, Carla was sad. It was not easy for this little girl, the oldest of four children—of an immature, needy mother and an unavailable father—to give up her special relationship with a therapist. Given 6 months and the opportunity to set the final date herself, however, she managed to work through the rage and hurt she felt. In the course of feeling anger at me for abandoning her (kicking her out), she was frequently reminded of her early angry monster dreams, drawings, and dramas.

For her last project Carla decided that she would make a film, "The Monster of Night Mystery," suggesting that I show it to other children with fears like hers. Using a Super 8mm camera, tripod, light, and simple animation techniques (Figure 4.2), Carla cut out monster heads that were moved around the walls (magically), finally scaring a little girl who was at the sink. After this, the girl and her sister come to see me, we return to look at the heads together, and the girl makes them disappear by throwing a magic disappearing potion on them (4.4C). It was a creative way for

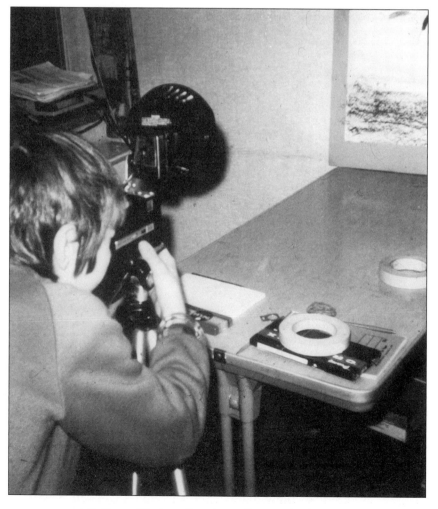

4.2 Donny Filming a Drawing-in-Progress for Animation

Carla to "re-view" the main problem for which she had been in therapy, reminding herself of what she had learned. It was also a way to deal with her envy of future patients (siblings), transforming her rage (via reaction-formation)into a wish to provide understanding (the film).

While she no longer had the nightmares, and had not had them for over a year, it had taken her some time to integrate her slowly dawning awareness, understanding, and acceptance of her own aggressive impulses. This *working-through* process is often accomplished by repetitive confrontations with the feared idea or through drawing or playing out a loaded theme, often with a limited amount of modification. While this process may seem like a "stuck" one to the therapist, it is a necessary one for the child, who may be going through something analogous to *desensitization*, gradually becoming more and more comfortable with previously unacceptable ideas and feelings.

Accepting

Larry, who was totally blind, came to the clinic on a weekly basis for almost 6 years (DVD 4.5). He was a complex boy with long-standing problems. For one period, lasting almost a year, he played and replayed scenes of doctor and patient (4.5A), dentist and patient (4.5B), and nurse and patient, in settings labelled first "the clinic," then "the doctor's office," and finally "the hospital."

He often took both roles, and sometimes involved me as mother, doctor, or child. He played himself at his chronological age and at earlier ages, sometimes saying the patient was someone else. He created a series of doctors, some good and kind, some harsh and insensitive, some permissive, some demanding (4.5C).

While there was variation in the dramatic play (which was usually stimulated and facilitated by water, cotton, or clay tools), there was much repetition. Yet it is not surprising that Larry, who had been hospitalized over fifty times before he was 5, should have needed to master these traumatic experiences by replaying them (Erikson, 1950). Nor is it surprising that he needed not only to relive the events, but also to relieve the rage by taking the active role, when in reality he had been passive and helpless.

A baby sister of whom he had been jealous had died of cystic fibrosis shortly before the final removal of Larry's eyes at age 5. It seemed as if his repeated dramatizations around doctors and operations were related not only to the trauma itself, but also to his unconscious guilt for the death of his sister, presumably punished by the removal of his eyes. He needed to accept both his "badness" (anger) and his blindness.

Coping

Twelve-year-old Pete began to see himself as possibly able to function independently of me, then of his mother, after 2 years of intermittent weekly therapy. But it took him another two to consolidate the gains in his autonomy and self-esteem. Only hesitantly was he able to try out a more assertive self, first at school and with peers, then at home with his parents. In the course of his therapy, Pete had begun by working primarily in art—first compulsively, then regressively and aggressively. For several months he shifted primarily to dramatic play, killing off rubber parent figures with clay "bombs." He then spent another few months making elaborate constructions with wood scraps and other materials, actively competing with the other kids whose sculptures he saw in my office.

In the early spring, Pete asked if we could walk to a nearby park, where he made a fairly serious attempt to become proficient at sketching what he saw, then recreating it with different media in my office. During the next phase, he brought his favorite music to play in my office while, for the first time, we had direct discussions about him and his life.

Separating from me and from therapy after 4 years was as anxiety-ridden for Pete as the development of a self that was independent of his mother. He vacillated for months, openly ambivalent about both coming and leaving. In a giant stride, Pete announced that he had decided to "take a break" for the summer. With just a few phone calls during the 3 months to touch base, he returned to wrap up his work in a most creative way.

Pete spent the next 4 months writing a book, dictating it to me each week (after finding his own typing too slow for his ideas). The following week he would reread his last section before going on. Although Pete had an attention-deficit disorder, his work on the story never wavered. The story, "What Will We Do?", was about two boys who ran away from home, representing two facets of Pete himself. One was cautious and fearful, like the old Pete. The other was bold and daring, as Pete longed to be and indeed was becoming. The story, which went on for weeks with ups and downs, seemed like a symbolic review of his own treatment—including a long trip into a well where the boys met strange, messy creatures—perhaps representing his unconscious fantasies.

At the end of the book, Pete announced that he was ready to end therapy, and was able to follow through. He provided himself with some transitional objects by taking photographs of his artwork, of the office, and of me, carrying them proudly as he left. Being in charge of how and when he terminated was, I believe, vital to the success of Pete's treatment.

Although developmentally delayed with organic impairment, Pete had improved significantly in his schoolwork and his peer relationships. He no longer suffered from nightmares, nor did he feel the depression behind the suicide attempts that had brought him to me for treatment. Perhaps because of the disabilities he had probably inherited from his seriously disturbed mother, Pete's therapy took a long time. After achieving the ability to take risks and to face things, it was a struggle for him to understand and to accept them enough to be able to cope effectively. Although his comprehension was never profound, it was sufficient. This was evident in his story, which reflected some understanding of the relationships between feelings, ideas, and actions, as well as between fantasy and reality.

Separating

Pete, in coping with the termination of a 4-year therapy process, was, during much of the time described above, working on and working through issues related to separation. At the end of any process of therapy—whether mutually arranged or unilaterally imposed, after 6 weeks, 6 months, or 6 years—children will have mixed feelings about ending a relationship that has become important in their life.

As with earlier separations, the step out of therapy represents growth and progress, but also entails loss. While there is often decreasing dependency on the therapist and increasing competition of other interests ("Why do I have to come on such a nice day? I'd rather play ball!"), there is still usually some anger at the adult, who is realistically in charge, whatever attempts may have been made to involve the child in the process of setting the termination date. Even a child who's no longer depressed often feels upset about ending. After 7 months of weekly art therapy, Lori spoke directly as well as symbolically in her last session.

Lori's Farewell

Lori, by then age 5, reminded me that it was her last day, and announced at the beginning of her session that she intended to use some of *everything* in the room. Accidentally spilling some paint, she played at being a bossy mother while we both sponged it up, saying, "Do what I say! Don't step in this while it's wet!" Then she stopped abruptly—a "play disruption" (Erikson, 1950) because of anxiety about her anger (DVD 4.6).

Lori said she didn't want to make-believe that day, and wondered if I had hidden the ice pick that we used to open clogged paint-shaker holes (4.6A). When she found it in its usual place, she pantomimed stabbing me with it, saying that she wasn't *really* going to kill me, but was only pretending (4.6B).

Lori then put on soap crayon makeup (4.6C) looking in the observation mirror, and commanded me imperiously not to watch: "If you look, I'm going out the door!" When I suggested that perhaps she wanted to go out the door on her own, rather than have me tell her it was time to leave on the last day, she nodded, and said, "I know this is the last day, and I'll cry and I said I'll miss you and Dr. M."—whom she also saw weekly (4.6D).

Going on with her fantasy of walking out on me, Lori said, "I'm gonna leave here, and I'm gonna drive my own car, and leave my mommy. But I might *lost* myself. Then I might walk at your place cryin' 'I lost myself!'" She wondered if I might buy her play clothes for her birthday, and if we could exchange telephone numbers.

Lori then made a huge sloppy painting, and said a farewell message on the tape recorder: "Goodbye. I'm not gonna see you no more, but I'm gonna cry if I don't see you no more." I told her that I would miss seeing her too, and she went on: "Well, see, if I don't see you no more, I might cry. I wanna hear myself talk." After listening to her speech on the tape recorder, a faint smile occasionally brightening her sad face, she said we should kiss goodbye, which we did. She was thus able in her last session to express her true feelings—anger, sadness, and affection.

Chip's Ending Process

Chip was twice Lori's age when it came time to say goodbye; he had come to the clinic for almost three times as many sessions, over a 2-year period. Arranging for alternate weeks during the last 2 months seemed to help in his weaning process, as he struggled to master an ambivalent mixture of anger, sadness, and pride. In his final session, Chip reviewed his therapy pictorially, by drawing a "Time Line." On the left he put the number "6," his age when his troubles began, when his mom, who had been his "girlfriend," remarried.

Next on his time line was a picture of his parents with a little Chip in between and the word "Married" above. To the right he drew a judge in a courtroom, saying it was him going to have his name changed when his stepfather adopted him. Describing it, he made a transparent oedipal slip: "*We* were married—I mean mom and dad—and then I went into court for my name change."

The next picture was of "mean Dr. S. with his knife and fork doing that operation on me." Chip had undergone an operation for an undescended testicle, which—coming at the time he felt he had lost his mother to a rival—had greatly intensified his fear of punishment for hostile wishes—what is known as "castration anxiety."

The final image in Chip's time line was a building: "And then I went to school—first, second, third, and fourth grade. Now I'm going into fifth. Here's a picture of my school with its smokestack. This is white." At this point in his narration, he added a door to the school building. He entitled his picture "The Impossible Dream." Therapy for Chip was a place to confront his many fearful dreams, like those of Godzilla attacking him (Figure 5.4). It was also a place to explore and to give up on impossible wishes, such as wanting me or mom as his girlfriend.

Chip then went on to review more explicitly: "At the beginning, I was really worried about my mother and father. Sometimes I got furious at her, like I am today, but now I can love her, too. I really was worried that they didn't care about me, but now I know they do." His mother, who had seen a psychologist while I saw Chip, said that she felt therapy had enabled each family member to like himself and the others more.

Indeed, one might think of the entire process of therapy through art as involving separating—separating fact from fancy, reality from fantasy, and, in a deeper sense, separating a child from the conflicts that have caused unhappiness. In the course of such work a strong attachment to the therapist is formed, in which the child can trust and then open up, and through which, symbolically, some of the conflicted issues can be made apparent and resolved—the "transference" (see also Chapter 20, pp. 359–363).

In the same way that unconscious material is projected onto unstructured media, so past expectations and unresolved interpersonal issues are projected onto the neutral therapist. By accepting and trying to understand distorted transference reactions, just as one tries to understand symbolic representations, one gets a sense of the child's inner world. The separating from the parent-therapist in the transference, toward whom the child has experienced strong emotional reactions, takes place along with separating from the real person-therapist, who has accepted the child and helped him or her to create a more contented self through art.

5

Some Ways to Facilitate Expression

There are many resources with which to help a child in the context of art therapy, some environmental and some personal. The former include the manipulation of space, time, furniture, lighting, and materials, as well as the introduction of possible themes or formats for work. The therapist may choose to be a quiet observer, an active questioner, a parallel participant, or a joint creator with materials.

Possibilities for expression in other modalities may be enhanced by the availability of tools, such as a computer, a tape recorder, musical instruments, puppets, miniature life toys, and props. One can facilitate dramatization by interviewing in an official sort of way, using a fake or real microphone, as well as engaging in a drama by taking a role.

Most often, such variations in technique arise out of a feeling that the child is stuck—unable to proceed easily without some help—though sometimes they emerge out of a feeling that they will further enhance an already comfortable flow of creative material. Much of my awareness of such possibilities has been given me by the children themselves—a continuous, ongoing process.

Though it is impossible to choose typical sessions, since each child and each moment are in a very real sense unique, it might help to look at a selection from different stages in treatment, and from work with children at different age levels with a variety of problems.

A Starter (A Scribble)

The scribble drawing is often used by art therapists as a way of helping patients to overcome their inhibitions about drawing, and is especially helpful for children who are stuck on a particular schema, or blocked in their imagery in a more global way. It enables patients to find and draw images they would probably not have created from scratch, and often assists in the emergence of imagery that is waiting in the wings.[1]

Carla, who had been referred for treatment by her mother because of frightening nightmares and disobedience, hid her worries behind colorful, abstract paintings during the early weeks of art therapy. Many of these paintings were striped, and were soon described as "bars," behind which the feared monsters of her dreams were waiting (DVD 5.1). When asked, after several weeks of talking about them, if she could draw the nightmares, Carla said it would be much too risky.

In a rare directive intervention, I suggested the next week that she might like to try a game, the "scribble drawing," in the hope that some of these images would emerge. Carla must have been ready to find and to represent her "Nightmare Monster," for that is what she created from her scribble, telling the story as she drew (Figure 5.1). The monster caught first one little girl, then another, then Carla, too. After showing all three girls in the monster's clutches, she drew one yelling, "Help!" Picking up a red tempera marker, she pounded vigorously on the paper, calling the blotches "soldiers," who she hoped would be able to rescue the children. Throughout most of the drawing-drama, Carla was uncertain about the outcome. At the very end, however, she declared with relief that the soldiers would win and the monster would be killed.

A Theme

While the most significant themes usually emerge spontaneously in art therapy, there may be times when it helps to suggest a specific topic to the child. Eleanor, a depressed deaf teenager, dealt with an unstructured art evaluation by first using colored pencils to draw two flowers on a 12-by-18-inch piece of manila paper. She was very careful, outlining first, then fill-

---

[1] At about the same time, a playful British analyst named Winnicott (1964–68, 1971b) and an inspired American art teacher named Cane (1951) independently came up with the notion of using a scribble as a visual starter, that is, developing a picture from a self-made scribble. For Winnicott, it provided a rapid and nonthreatening way to get to know a child he was assessing; because his interest was in communication rather than composition, a pencil and a small piece of paper suited his *Squiggle Game*. Cane, on the other hand, wanted to stimulate freedom and spontaneity in art expression; her *Scribble* technique included preparatory breathing and movement exercises, and was done on large drawing paper with colored pastels. Introduced by her sister, art therapy pioneer Margaret Naumburg (1947, 1966), it is extremely popular among art therapists.

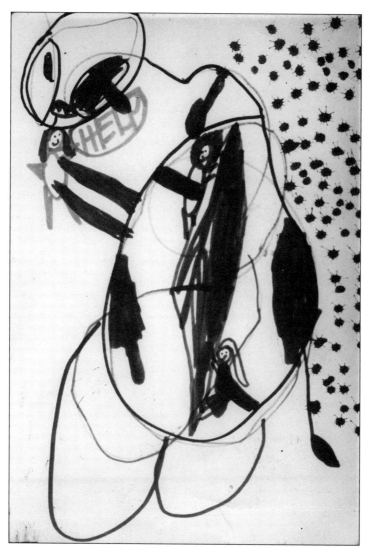

5.1 Carla's Nightmare Monster. Age 8. Scribble drawing, marker

ing in, often looking at me as if to make sure that what she was doing was acceptable. She indicated that the flowers would be hers, titled the picture "Rose," and then pointed to the words she had written when finished drawing: "I don't have more idea."

In response to her distress at having to make yet another selection, I wondered if she could draw "A Feeling," probably suggesting that topic because I sensed that she was feeling a great deal, but not showing it in her art or associations. Since Eleanor still seemed quite tense and unable to move spontaneously, I said she might want to find a color of paper that was like the feeling she had in mind. She grinned, selected a 12-by-18-inch piece of red construction paper, asked in writing how much more time we had, and then expressed her concern more directly by writing, "I think something's hard."

Despite her anxiety, however, Eleanor proceeded to draw a picture of a girl with an angry mouth and eyes, adding the ears at the end (Figure 5.2). On the side she wrote, "A girl was mad." When I asked why the girl was mad, she wrote, "Because she fight with her friend." When asked what the fight was about, she responded, "She stole your girlfriend's purse. Your friend was very mad with her."

When I asked what sort of things made her mad, she wrote, "with school" and "bad swear." When asked if there was any person who made her mad, she wrote the name of a person in authority at the school; but when I asked if this woman was mean, she quickly responded that she was a "nice lady and explained to people." She looked uncomfortable about having identified this woman as the target of her anger, but quickly indicated, in response to my query, that she would like to come again for art.

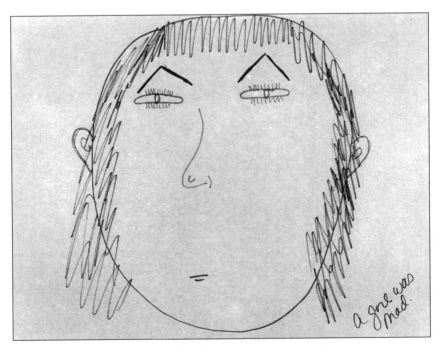

5.2 *"A Girl Was Mad" by Eleanor. Age 15. Marker*

A Medium

While it is usually best to allow a free choice of materials, there may be times when a suggestion is helpful. Sometimes it is a technical matter—letting the child know that a thin brush is available and will work better for the picture they have sketched out, or that plasticine might be more appropriate than water-base clay for the sculpture they have in mind. Such technical assistance requires familiarity with art media and their properties, and is a vital tool in the armamentarium of an art therapist.

In a different way, one might suggest the use of a medium or a process for more psychodynamic reasons. It is my firm belief that to "prescribe" is in error—that to "tell" a constricted child to use fingerpaint so it can help him or her to loosen up is not only to promote an authoritarian relationship, but to potentially cause anxiety as well. There are times, however, after a fairly stable alliance between patient and therapist has been formed, when one might offer some specific suggestions, being as explicit as possible about the reasons.

One day, Jerry, a partially sighted boy suffering from encopresis, made a clay head using plasticine. Since he had chosen to use clay of a single color, his limited vision made it very hard for him to see where to put the facial features. Indeed, he was quite upset with his finished product, saying that the head looked "all messed up" (Figure 5.3a).

I therefore suggested that it might be easier if he made the features with clay that was of different colors than the face. He proceeded to make a large head of a man, with a moustache and beard like his father's, and finally said that it was his Dad (Figure 5.3b). He was much more satisfied with this product than he had been with the first.

He also went on to use the differences between the two heads in a most creative way. He played out a story, calling the first head "A Little Squished-up Man with a Little Squished-up Face," and the second, "A Big Man with a Big Face." In addition to his blindness, Jerry had a growth hormone deficiency which made him look "squished-up." In the story the little guy ends up killing the big one, who has been very critical.

Jerry had finally found a way to play out, using the two heads, his angry death wishes toward his father, whom he held responsible for his mother's desertion of the family following their violent fights. It was likely that his anal messing was an unconscious expression of this hostility, directed partly toward the caretaking parent who literally had to clean up the mess.

At the end of the session, Jerry said that the little guy in the story was wishing for something that was hard to say. After much encouragement on

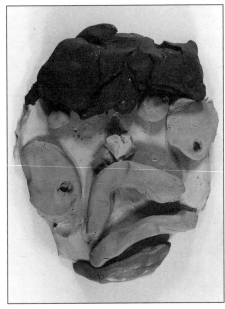

5.3a A Clay Head, All One Color,
by Jerry. Age 11

5.3b A Multicolored Clay Head,
by Jerry. Age 11

my part, he whispered, "blind." Then he said there was another word he was also finding hard to say, which turned out to be "handicapped." I wondered if the little boy in the story was wishing to get rid of those, and he nodded vigorously in the affirmative.

I asked if he had any idea why the little boy had that problem, and he whispered, "'Cause he's bad!" I asked if he was bad for wanting to kill the big guy, and he nodded yes. This suggested that the little "squished-up" person was in such a bad physical state *because* he was so angry, and that his blindness was a punishment for his badness (see Chapters 15 and 16). In this instance, the suggested use of the medium facilitated the making of a more organized sculpture, which became even more coherent over time (DVD 5.2). This then enabled the child, through subsequent dramatic play, to articulate further the unconscious fantasies underlying his conflicts and symptoms.

A Dream

Sometimes it is helpful to suggest to the child that something being discussed could be represented, especially if the topic happens to be one with a potentially high therapeutic yield, like a dream. It is a reversal of the more common situation in art therapy of asking the individual to tell about what has been created; here, one asks the person to create what is being talked about.

In the middle of a year of weekly art therapy sessions, 8-year-old Chip began an hour by mentioning that he had been having scary dreams. I wondered if he could draw one, and he agreed with the notion that he could tell me better that way than with words. He proceeded to use markers on a large (18-by-24-inch) piece of paper to create a rather elaborate, detailed drawing of what he called a "Nightmare" (Figure 5.4). He said, "This monster is known as Godzilla. He's a monster on television." He then asked if I had to take notes,[2] to which he was by then accustomed, worrying that I "might show it to like, say, Dr. H." (his parents' therapist). Reassured that the notes would not be shown to anyone—doctor, parents, or teachers—he went back to telling the story.

Godzilla, with his outstretched arm and pointing finger, is saying, "Kill!" while a plane and a tank try to attack him. He then described how the bullets would "ricochet and hit the tank, then ricochet and hit the plane. I'm gonna make another plane that's being blown up. . . . I'm making a smaller plane, like an F-11, the yellow one on the right." While he drew, he dramatized, making noises like "bang-bang," as the bombs crashed into the ground. The black airplane on the upper left was said to be a B-52, and was also attempting unsuccessfully to shoot at the monster, its bullets boomeranging, too.

The last item drawn was the little figure held in the monster's hand, yelling, "Help!" a boy whom Chip thought would not be rescued. Indeed, his conclusion about the nightmare dream-drawing was that Godzilla would probably kill everyone, including Chip and his buddies. Then, as if to defend against those helpless feelings, he reminded me, "I'm a better artist than you, so watch out!"

This statement was followed by a seductive invitation, "Wanna make a castle with me?" I commented that I would enjoy watching *him* make a

---

[2] I began taking notes during child art therapy sessions largely because I had been asked to report what happened in detail by most supervisors. As noted in Chapter 4, being scrupulous about issues of privacy is vital to establishing and maintaining trust. I would therefore offer to let the child look at the notes any time they wished in their own notebook (one for each patient), and was clear about not sharing with anyone except with permission. In addition to learning how to look and write at the same time, I believe there are two advantages: (1) having a record of sequences within a drawing, painting, or sculpture, and (2) conveying the idea that what a child says and does is important and worthy of being carefully recorded. Despite some anxiety at first, most youngsters grew used to the note-taking and in fact might comment if I stopped for a long period, wondering why.

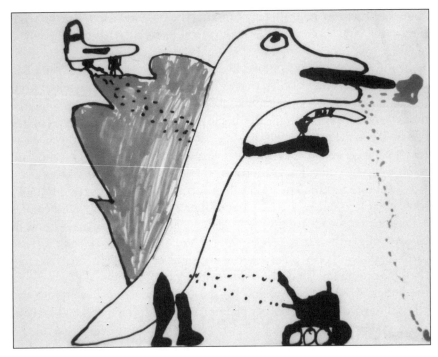

5.4 Chip's Drawing of a Dream about Godzilla. Age 8. Marker

castle, and he replied, "I'd rather *you* help."[3] I then noted that he often wanted help with things, and wondered what it had to do with needing to get help from his mother, in order to be sure of her love. He nodded in a way that signified some real understanding, and proceeded to build a castle with blocks, describing it as "a little shelter in case of Indians." He got inside it, then went behind it and yelled, "Crunch!" followed by, "He killed himself!" He asked me to push him in the "cart" (a large wagon he could

---

[3] I have described several instances of agreeing to a request to participate in dramatic play, like being a monster or frightened child with Carla or a child to Lori's bossy mother (Ch. 4). I believe that such role-taking under a child's direction allows them to better explore their fantasies. I have also described times when I agreed to a child's request, like letting Lori give me a hug and a kiss as part of saying goodbye, or taking Pete to the park as a way of helping him take his new bolder self out of the clinic with me as support.

Even though there are rare times where working together in art can be helpful, like making a mask alongside Lori (pp. 81–82) or dyadic drawing with Ellen (p. 139) for the most part I prefer encouraging children to work independently. With Chip it was especially important not to gratify his oedipal victory fantasies, which his divorced mother had done before when he was indeed her "partner"—a role which had been both gratifying and anxiety-provoking, leading to some of his symptoms.

sit in), then turned and yelled with mock fury, "Get out of my castle, you!" He agreed with my notion that perhaps he was feeling angry because I did not agree to build with him, and left in a cheerful mood.

The suggestion to draw the dream not only helped Chip to clarify his scary experience, but also led to some play, which helped both of us to understand better the relationship of the angry impulses— symbolized in the dream—of his wishes for protection and for a more exclusive relationship with his mother.

Though at one point he turned the aggression inward ("He killed himself!") as he often did in reality (being accident-prone and voicing suicidal ideas), he was able finally to direct it to the adult, where it belonged. The shift from art to drama in his session often occurs in just such a spontaneous way, and can sometimes be facilitated through simple suggestions, as in the following session (the 8th of 25) with Lori, a 4½-year-old girl you have already met.

A Mask

Lori went immediately to the sink, mixed powder paints from shakers in their dry form, and said it looked like salt and pepper. "My mom uses pepper on her eggs," she said, adding that she herself *hates* pepper. About the paint, she instructed me rather imperiously, "You better get more . . . whatever I ask for, you'll get!"

While mixing orange paint with water to make "orange juice," she said, "My mom's with Dr. M." Asked how that made her feel, she said, "It makes me feel *real bad*—and I don't like it. It feels like my mom leaves and she forgets me." A few minutes later she said, "Oh, that was just a *dream* about my mom leaving me. . . . Would you take me home with you if my mom went out and left me here?"

Seeming quite anxious with these thoughts of abandonment, she recalled a hide-and-seek game she had initiated in past sessions. When I suggested that there were other hiding games she could play, like hiding behind a mask,[4] Lori responded eagerly with the idea that we should each make a "Scary Monster Mask." She made one on a piece of cardboard (Figure 5.5). On the back of it, Lori drew a "Happy Monster" and explained: "I hurt you and you get dead—not for real, just for pretend."

---

[4] In this instance, I suggested a mask rather than hide-and-seek, a separation game Lori had played a great deal; in order to help her to feel more comfortable with her anger at her mother (and me, in the transference). For this reason I also agreed to make a mask myself, as a way of modeling being angry in a make-believe, acceptable fashion.

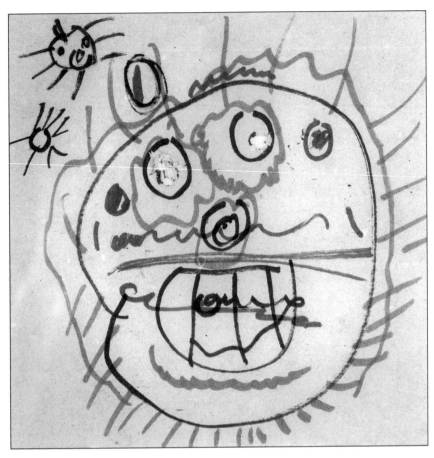

5.5 Lori's Scary Monster Mask. Age 5. Crayon on cardboard

She then used her mask and pretended to be an angry monster who was very scary, saying repeatedly in a growly voice, "I'm going to kill you!" She also periodically turned the mask around and played the role of a happy, conciliatory monster. She drew several more "Happy Monsters," and directed me to draw a "Scary Monster Lady Mask." In the middle of this intense drama, she said, "I get scared a lot. I get scared, like monsters."

Lori was very much involved in trying out both angry (scary) and conciliatory (happy) roles with the masks, growling and gesturing aggressively at me in true monster fashion. At the end of her dramatic play, she said, "I ain't mad no more," explaining that she was mad "sometimes, but not all the time."

In the few remaining minutes, she got some clay and began by pounding it very hard. She drew a "happy" face into the clay with a tool, and then used another tool to poke holes all over the clay, attacking the face vigorously and aggressively. She left the session in a very bouncy mood, in contrast to how she had been when she entered.

Lori had been quite anxious about the potency of her anger, fearful that it might lead to being abandoned by her mother, as she felt she had been by her father, since he had left home at the time of her parents' separation. Her worries about loss were evident in the beginning of the session, while the anger only emerged in the course of the drama, facilitated by the monster mask.

A Target

Chip, the 8-year-old described earlier, came to the clinic one day full of unfocused anger, and expressed a wish to hit the punching bag in the large room where he had once been part of a group. I suggested that it might help to imagine a more specific target, to pretend that the bag represented different people, a suggestion to which he responded with enthusiasm.

First he said the bag was his mother, hugging and kissing it passionately, saying over and over again, "I love you, I love you." He then decided it would represent his stepfather, whom he kissed and hugged, but then punched and yelled at, speaking of his stepdad's "yelling anger." Then he said the bag was "Mamorelli, the worst kid in town. He's older. He beats me up."

Slugging as hard as he could, it was clearly more comfortable for Chip to pound Mamorelli than either parent. However, he returned to the idea of the bag as mother, again saying, "I love you," then shifted to his stepfather, alternately loving and hitting with vehemence. At the end he said to the bag-father, "I want to be your friend. You've been mean and nasty and cruel, but I really want to be your friend." Then he turned, and told me about how his parents fought violently, got angry and hit each other—and how scary that was for him.

I reminded him that once before he had drawn a picture of the target of his anger (a peer) and had thrown clay bullets at it. He decided to paint a picture of a boy, which he then taped onto the punching bag, and hit again with vigor (see Figure 5.6). He commented, "Love and violence can't go together." I wondered if indeed one couldn't have violent, angry feelings, and loving ones, toward the same person at different times, or even at the same time? He seemed intrigued with this notion, but wasn't ready to accept it, asserting again that they couldn't possibly go together.

His next activity was a tempera spatter painting on huge paper, that was described as a picture of a friend with "black and blue marks all over."

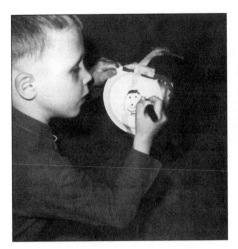

5.6 (a) Drawing an Enemy, and (b) Punching Him on a Bag. Boy, age 6

When I wondered how the person had gotten them, Chip said, "He must have been punched by somebody else." While he then swung on the tire swing in the same group room, he wondered aloud, "Don't you get scared with all this violence?" and, "How can you stand all that violence?" We talked together about how scary it was for him.

Such explicit dramatizations of children's hostility allow for release of affect and for a temporary discharge of surplus energy. In addition, they provide the child with an experience of expressing intense aggression without harm to anyone. But it is vital that the therapist make it continually clear to the child that all of this aggression, while very *real* as an impulse, is *pretend* as an action, against a *make-believe* adversary.

Moreover, it is the therapist's responsibility not only to permit such experiences as ways of discharging and focusing overwhelming affect, but also to help the child see that the task in growing up is to find more constructive ways of expressing such energies, while learning how to put his angry feelings into words rather than actions. In fact, if one can learn to integrate loving and aggressive impulses, as Chip was struggling to do, then one can use the energy in a healthy, constructive fashion.

Some therapists fear that encouraging such dramatizations of aggression might promote its use in reality against, for example, the person chosen as the pictured or imagined target. In 40 years of practice, I was not made aware of such an effect, and I am sure I would have heard about it from an angry parent or teacher. In fact, what seemed to happen most often, was that the outside behavior—whether aggressive toward others or the self— tended to lessen after this kind of pretend experience about very real feelings and impulses. I felt that this confirmed what I had been groping toward in my early writing—about the place and function of limits (Chapter 1), and the idea of a framework for freedom (Chapter 2).

Like any other interpersonal transaction in therapy, such an invitation or suggestion is loaded, and no doubt the "music" I tried to convey was as important as the words. My "tune" was that it was normal to have such impulses, and all right to feel them fully in a symbolic context. The "coda" was that the creative challenge was to find ways to express these impulses in real life that were constructive rather than destructive. Perhaps I was influenced by a Fred Rogers song, "What do you do with the mad that you feel / when you feel so mad you could bite?"

What is also significant is that these children were so conflicted that they usually didn't feel the anger toward the actual (love) object, but rather were suicidal or depressed. And even if they did feel or express anger or op-positionalism, it was often unfocused or displaced, getting them into lots of trouble—which tended to be repeated until they first understood and accepted the rage. Only then could they work to integrate it and to find acceptable outlets, in order to be able to move on in a healthy fashion.

A Tape Recorder

Some children have great difficulty talking freely about their products, but can often be helped through the use of props, such as a tape recorder. Glen, an 11-year-old boy who had recently attempted suicide, was almost finished with 10 months of biweekly sessions in art (alternating with meetings with a child psychiatrist). He had by then learned how to describe his artwork, but was still not too comfortable doing so, usually restricting his remarks to brief comments.

He loved the microphone and tape recorder, however, and responded to my introduction of these with a much more elaborate description of his picture than usual. The drawing, sketched in pencil on a large (18-by-24 inch) piece of white paper, was of a ship, about which he had expressed some uncertainty regarding the addition of a sail (Figure 5.7). When I handed him the microphone, he performed as if he were truly on the air, and his first nonstop statements were as follows:

"This is Glen Smith talking about his latest art piece. Now in this drawing I have a sketch of the USS frigate, *Constitution*, being fired upon by an un-known British ship in the background. Now this scene—many scenes like this have happened during the Revolution, with *Bonhomme Richard* and John Paul Jones and many other ships, especially the privateers, who guarded along the coast and attacked on small British ships. This I chose to

5.7 Glen's Drawing of the USS Constitution. *Age 11. Pencil*

have the sails down, with the anchor in the water, and the ship is not moving, as you can see. Now, I have crows' nests, but I didn't sketch any people. Now, this British ship is firing upon the *Constitution* and soon, when the *Constitution* is alerted, it will turn, pull in its anchor, pull up sails, turn around, and prepare for battle. Of course, in the background, I drew a smaller ship. It looks better, I think. On the forward masts, you will see banners, flags, and on the real ship, these banners never were. Only on Spanish ships were these banners placed; and when I drew the United States flag. I drew it pretty large, because I have been on a ship, and I saw Admiral Perry's ship, and the flag was very large. Now, over in the forward part, the bow, I have riggings shown where there were ropes with crossings going up to the forward mast. And on my model ship there were many riggings, but of course I cannot place all of the riggings on the ship I have here.

"Now as you can see, on the British ship I have smoke around one of these cannons, a symbol that it has been fired, and the splashing in the water near the ship, the USS *Constitution*. If you would look toward the forward part of the ship, you would see the front forward pole where lines and masts and ropes from the mast come down, and seamen use these ropes to lower the sails down and leave them up, so that the ship will run under full speed. In the back you'll notice I have a rudder, which is controlled from the back of the ship, and it moves the ship back and forth whichever way it is turned.

On this ship I have placed many cannons, but really, the *Constitution* has two decks of cannons, which I only drew one. But of course in this small drawing, I couldn't possibly fit two. So, settle for the best I guess. On the mast I have the sails lowered, on really the opposite sides of the mast—the poles, see. Really, the sails are rested on the top, and they slide down so that they'll be easier for the seamen to lower the sails. But in this fashion of drawing, I put the sails on the bottom, for they were really on the bottom of the ship, and it would take too long to get the sails up. And, if you'll notice, toward the middle of the *Constitution*, you'll see a lifeboat here. Now, really on the *Constitution* there were about six lifeboats, but see, on this kind of drawing, you can't put that much detail in. This is Glen Smith, just talking about his latest art piece. Bye."

After that rather obsessive but rich description poured into the microphone, I decided to ask Glen some questions, in order to clarify for him and for myself the nature of the conflict suggested in the drawing. Our interchange went as follows:

JR: Mr. Smith, I just have a few questions to ask you about that battle that's going to be waged. Is that cannonball going to hit the *Constitution*, or just what's going to happen to it?

Glen: Well, uh, his, on this particular ship, the cannonballs weren't explosive. They would hit the ship, making a very big hole, or hitting the mast, knocking it down, and if it hit the right place, it would sink the ship. But his cannonball isn't hitting the ship.

JR: I see. Well, now, you said that the *Constitution* is going to realize that this other ship is attacking it, and is going to kind of turn around and gird itself up for battle. What do you think the outcome will be of that battle? In other words, who's going to win?

Glen: Well, the *Constitution*, really. Because the *Constitution*, throughout all its history, has won all the battles it's ever fought. And now it is in Boston harbor, and it's a tourist attraction, attracting many tourists. . . .

JR: Glen, if you were going to be in this scene, where would you want to be, and what would you want your role to be? In other words, which ship would you want to be on, and what would you want to be doing?

Glen: Really, I'm not sure of the Captain on the *Constitution*, but I wouldn't like to be him, 'cause during all the battles of the *Constitution*, this captain has had many troubles and many hard battles. But, uh, this question is sort of hard for me to answer. Supposedly, I'd like to be, uh, really, I'd like to be the crewman on the *Constitution*. I'm not sure of the position I'd like to be on the ship, at the time.

After clarifying aloud in some detail what different crewmen do, Glen decided,

> "I think I'd like to be—I guess, a gunner. I'm not sure which gunner I'd like to be, but it really doesn't matter. And the gunner is—being gunner is a very dangerous job too. Like the battle of the *Bonhomme Richard* and the *Serapis*, these two ships were actually locked together, and the gunners were in very serious trouble. The *Constitution* won, because while the battle was going on, men climbed up the riggings, got onto the crow's nest, and threw hand grenades and shot rifles down on the other ship. That's mainly what won the battle. See, smart maneuverings by John Paul Jones swirled the ship away from the other, giving the *Serapis* straight shots from the rear. But luckily, they missed the ship altogether. The *Bonhomme Richard* turned, and gave it a broadside of all her guns, and eventually sank the *Serapis*."

I then commented on how much history I was learning from Glen, and asked "If you had been in that battle, what do you wish you would have done?" to which he replied:

> "Well, really, I don't know. Well, let's look at the facts. These two ships were locked together. The captain of the British ship was mortally wounded while leaning over the railing, leading his men. He was in a sword fight with John Paul Jones on the main deck of the ship. While they were fighting, another crew member—a crew member aboard the British ship—accidentally shot their captain. Now, in this battle, I would have preferred to be John Paul Jones, showing courage and strength in this battle."

At this point, having not only talked enough, but having just brushed perilously close to his core conflict by "accidentally" killing off the captain (father), Glen abruptly said, "Let's play it back now," indicating a wish to stop as well as to review his long, exhibitionistic recording.

A Poem

The tape recorder (DVD 5.3) was an asset to Glen, as to others, in satisfying and channeling his wishes to show off (5.3A), to hold the phallic microphone, and to be a big shot, as if on television (5.3B). It enabled him to say much more about his picture than had previously been the case when I asked him to talk to me about drawings.

For some, writing words down is easier than saying them aloud. Evelyn, whose assessment interview is described in Chapter 6, spontaneously began writing poetry as well as making art while hospitalized after a suicide attempt. Sometimes her poems were as simple and stark as her tree (Figure 6.7a):

"I wanna cry
Cry until there is no water left in my body
BECAUSE
GOD DAMN IT
I AM AFRAID!"

Sometimes they were a bit more complex, and conveyed ideas that were perhaps best put in verbal form:

"Your mind is a safe place to stay
Because no one can hurt you there . . .
Not even your *friends*
You do not have to plead, beg, cry!!!
For someone to believe you
When you tell the truth.
Oh hell man!"

A Story

Evelyn was a very bright girl, for whom poetry was, as for many adolescents, a highly appealing, expressive modality. Alan, a preadolescent boy, was a slow learner with a learning disability and suspected neurological dysfunction. He had always had difficulty in school, and was generally fearful, confused, and frightened by the angry feelings toward his dad which were becoming apparent in his art therapy. One week he said he wanted to type a story, then dictated it to me as my secretary (at my suggestion, since the typing was becoming too frustrating for him). This is the story he told (his father was practically blind in one eye):

THE LUCKY SOLDIER
Just as the soldier entered the battlefield, he saw only two things: dead bodies all over the field, and people dropping from every direction. He was so scared that he ran to an old shack. After 2 hours of hiding, a German force raided the shack. A captain saw him hiding. He said to the captain, "Please don't shoot me." The captain said, "I'll give you a 50/50 chance. If you can tell me which eye is artificial, I will let you go. If not, I shall have to kill you." The soldier stuttered for a moment. At last he whispered, "The left." The captain replied, "You are free! But don't ever come back again!"

In this scary but wishful story, the soldier-boy's deficit helps him escape the dangerous captain-father; while in reality Alan was still struggling with wishes to act autonomously, in defiance of his stern, punitive father, whose rage he had good reason to fear. The telling, as well as the subsequent illustration, rereading, and photocopying of the story, helped Alan to review and rethink it, something that was usually difficult for him. The simple fact that, by rereading the story, he could stay in touch with the feelings and wishes involved, enabled him to talk about them in relation to himself.

A Picture-Taking Machine

Just as the tape recorder or computer preserves sounds or words, so those magic machines which preserve images (including still and moving picture cameras) can be helpful in art therapy. Making instant photocopies of drawings to which children are deeply attached, or which they may wish to give as gifts to significant people in their lives, is a way of facilitating the work, recognizing its importance, and keeping a record for both therapist and patient.

Thirteen-year-old James, a shy, constricted boy, was keen on keeping his book about his newly created character, "The Pencil Snatcher." The book itself had been the result of a deliberate ploy, for when this very tight, in-hibited child, who drew compulsive and impersonal pictures, commented in a mumble that he wished he had a sketchbook, I had impulsively given him a plain pad I had just gotten for scratch paper.

He had come in the following week with a series of rather aggressive hu-morous cartoon drawings of kids and teachers he disliked. He had then re-vealed his secret fantasy character, probably a self-representation—"The Pencil-Snatcher" (Figure 5.8). Pictures of the pencil-snatcher and his bird friend were brought in week after week as the story emerged, but James could not part with any pages from the pad. Thus, it was helpful to make copies on the machine, both preserving the images for my file and giving them additional importance in our therapeutic detective work.

For Tommy, who was going blind, the existence of a machine that made images through light took on additional meaning. He often wanted to make copies of his black line drawings, ostensibly to give them to family and friends, and because he took tremendous delight in making the magic eye of the photocopying machine work with the push of a button. Often, the pictures related to the feelings he was experiencing as his sight worsened from his retrolental fibroplasia. His story is told in detail in Chapter 16 (pp. 290–292).

Flashlights and Candles

A child who was afraid of the dark wanted to turn off the lights and use flashlights or candles. From this experience I discovered that both art and drama sometimes come more easily in a dimly lit room than in a bright one,

90

5.8 *The Pencil-Snatcher Sneaking Away, by James. Age 13. Pencil*

especially when the fears or fantasies center on what happens in the dark. Carla, who suffered from nightmares, used candles, flashlights, and even spotlights for several months to create changing atmospheres for changing productions.

Her pictures and stories were of scary sounds heard while people slept at night. At one point I was cast in the role of a punitive mother who finally abandoned a frightened little boy (Carla). Later *she* became a mother—first a mean one, and later a kind one—who stayed and comforted and even fed the hungry child (me), despite my naughty curiosity.

Extending the Range

Tommy was distressed by his progressive loss of vision, but found it hard to put his anger into words. Some of this feeling was first expressed through banging hard on a drum and later on a xylophone. In the process, we both discovered a marvelous rhythmic and melodic gift in this little fellow, and recorded his compositions and concerts on tape.

Musical instruments, puppets (Irwin & Shapiro, 1975), miniature life toys—toys that can be moved around in clay worlds or on sand trays or tables (Carey, 1999; Kalff, 1980; M. Lowenfeld, 1971, 1979)—and the willingness of the therapist to move in other creative directions can help a child to find the most appropriate and comfortable means of expression—just as, within art, the therapist can help the child find the best medium for his or her particular message.

Conclusion

Although it may seem strange to be describing so many dramatic interventions in a book on art therapy, I find all expressive modalities to be intimately related, especially in work with children. To restrict a child rigidly to work in any one art form would be to inhibit artificially a natural, organic flow of expression. In my work with children, related modalities often emerged spontaneously (DVD 5.4), as with Carla. A child might use finger paint as makeup and create a role. He or she might create a prop, such as a gun (5.4A) or a sword, and then use it to attack (5.4B) in a drama (5.4C). He or she might pick up a clay sculpture and start to speak for it as if it were a puppet (see also Oaklander, 1988; Rogers, 1993; DVD 14.2A). Or the clay might become something really unexpected, like a hat (5.4D).

In some of the instances described in this chapter, expanding the range of expression was made possible simply by having other modes available and being receptive to their use. In others, it involved making a specific suggestion, which seemed likely to facilitate the child's ability to say—creatively—what was on his or her mind. It is probably in this area, and especially when interviewing about products, that the child art therapist's own creativity can be most useful—indeed, the more imaginative the idea the better, as long as the inventiveness is used to serve the child's needs for expression and understanding, and not the therapist's.

In a broad sense, the challenge and the task are always to use whatever resources seem best at the moment, and to be open and creative about the many possibilities inherent in space (DVD 5.5), materials, and oneself. Whether one attempts to uncover or to support defenses depends on many complex issues involving the dynamics of the child's psyche and of change over time—issues best learned in close clinical supervision.

With most children, it is possible to trust the youngster's own ability to use defenses when necessary—to stop or to change gears if things become too threatening. As time goes on in work with individuals, one gets a pretty good sense of how much anxiety and frustration they can handle, and when it is necessary to intervene. One learns to trust not only the child's self-protective system, but also one's own sixth sense, "third ear," and in art therapy, "third eye."

There are many ways in which an art therapist can facilitate the child's struggle to grow; a challenge to one's own ingenuity and creativity. Active intervention is a tricky business, to be done only with acute awareness of internal and external motivations, and of the possible effects on the child and his treatment. It is fortunate that, with a solid therapeutic alliance and a sense of trust, art therapy with a child can tolerate a fair number of missteps. So trial and error are still the rule—there are no formulas.

PART II

THE INDIVIDUAL

6

An Individual Art Evaluation

Background

Many psychologists who have used drawings as a respectable way of finding out where children are developmentally (Harris, 1963; Koppitz, 1968, 1984) have also found the drawing of a person and or other subjects to be helpful as ways of understanding the child's personality. While large samples of drawings by normal children of different ages were being collected in order to determine characteristic features at different stages, interest also grew in such questions as what a child's drawings can tell us about his or her emotional state and possible psychopathology (Buck, 1948; Di Leo, 1974, 1983; Drachnik, 1995; Klepsch & Logie, 1982; Machover, 1949; Malchiodi, 1998; Oster & Crone, 2004; Schildkrout, Shenker, & Sonnenblick, 1972).

Most diagnostic drawing procedures have followed what Hammer calls "psychology's demand for standardization" (1958, p. 54), and control rather stringently the topic and the medium. In copying (DiLeo, 1970, 1974, 1983) and in completion tasks (Kinget, 1952), a small piece of paper and a pencil are the rule. Assigned topics, such as human figure (Machover, 1949), family (Appel, 1931; Burns & Kaufman, 1970; Hulse, 1952), animal (Levy & Levy, 1958), and House-Tree-Person (Buck, 1948; Burns, 1987; Hammer, 1958) specify not only what may be drawn, but the medium to be used as well.

Free choice of subject matter is sometimes combined with assigned topics in procedures requiring a series of drawings, such as those reported by Schmidl-Waehner (1946), Cohen, Hammer, and Singer (1988), Levick (1983, 1989), and Betensky (1995). Free choice is more common in interviews using media other than pencil or crayon, as in Napoli's work with finger paint (1951), or Woltmann's with clay (1964b). In 1983, Edith Kramer and Jill Schehr (2000) proposed an art assessment consisting of a *series of activities:* drawing, painting, and working with clay, and in 1988, Ellen Horovitz suggested a similar assessment using the same three media (Horovitz-Darby, 1988). In these procedures, the child is required to draw, paint, and model, but can select the topic (cf. Brooke, 2004; Silver, 2002).

Rarely, however, is a wide range of media offered along with a free choice of subject matter, except where the workers have studied artwork produced spontaneously in school or treatment settings under naturalistic conditions (Alschuler & Hattwick, 1947; Bender, 1952; Elkisch, 1945; Hartley, Frank, & Goldenson, 1952; Schmidl-Waehner, 1942). In research or in the clinic, where it seems important to standardize what is offered and to control extraneous influences, only a few reported investigations come close to offering a range of media and a free choice of subject matter (Dewdney, Dewdney, & Metcalfe, 1967; Pasto & Runkle, 1955; Schmidl-Waehner, 1946).

Yet, in work with children in both educational and clinical settings, I have almost always found it most useful to allow such an open choice. When I began working at a child guidance center and was asked to develop some kind of art evaluation, I originally planned for a combination of free and assigned topics, feeling that pictures of self or family would indeed be informative. What I discovered, however, as I began doing art interviews with different children, was that the youngsters themselves would inevitably structure the hour in such personally syntonic and revealing ways, that any imposition of required media or topics seemed an unnecessary and distorting interference.

There are indeed times when it has seemed appropriate to use assigned topics or media, as in a family art evaluation (see Chapter 10), or in some research projects (see Chapter 21). For the general purpose of getting to know children, however, finding out where they are, what concerns them, and how they are dealing with those concerns internally, the unstructured approach has proved to be most useful to me in a variety of settings.

Perhaps the closest example of an analogous invitation to freely structure time and space, given a variety of materials, would be a play interview for a young child (Axline, 1947; Chazan, 2002; Gil, 1991; Haworth, 1964; Moustakas, 1953; Schaefer & O'Connor, 1983). One major difference between a play session and an art interview is the latter's applicability to a broad range of ages.

Just as a child at a pre-representational level of graphic development could not draw a person or a family, so a teenager is not likely to play freely with dolls or sand. Both, however, can respond appropriately to a range of art materials, each using them at their own developmental level. Before going any further, it would be helpful to look briefly at what can happen in such an art evaluation.

Initiating the Interview

I prefer to have as little information as possible prior to an initial evaluation, for the simple reason that it allows me to be more open to whatever the child is telling me. I can also honestly say to them that I don't know anything (or much) about them, but since they are the experts on themselves, I expect they'll be able to show and tell me what matters. I also prefer meeting first with the child rather than the parents, so that it is clear to everyone that the youngster is my main interest and concern. It is possible to proceed this way even with very young children.

Initially, the therapist must set the stage, both physically and psychologically, in order to make meaningful work possible. This means providing a range of art materials in a clear and pleasing arrangement that may be easily explored, and providing suitable options in working space and surface for maximal comfort. The invitation is simple: to use whatever they want and to make whatever they wish, in the time available.

If a child asks the reason for the art interview, I say that it gives me a way to get to know them, and gives them a way to tell me about themselves, along with whatever they want to say in words. Sometimes I add that it will help both of us decide if art therapy might be helpful to them. If they further question the rationale, I explain that images sometimes give clues to things that aren't yet conscious, and that it has nothing to do with art but rather uses another language familiar to the mind, as in dreams.

While observing the child's way of coping with the task (see Chapter 7), the art therapist must also be ready to intervene at any point in order to facilitate the flow of material. Such intervention may mean helping a child to get started, which is sometimes a simple matter of restating options, or asking questions that aid in decision-making. It may mean giving explicit permission to touch or to use a medium in a particular way, or it may mean giving technical help in order for the child's apparent creative goals to be actualized. On rare occasions, it means helping a child to stop, pause, and regroup, after becoming confused or disorganized.

The guiding principle that makes the most sense to me is: the least possible—"least restrictive"—intervention for the most tolerable and authentic flow. It is especially important not to interfere or to subtly influence the child's ideas, thus contaminating the data, which is most valid when coming completely from the individual being assessed.

If it is necessary to intervene in any way, the effect of that intervention must be kept in mind, and as soon as possible the adult should return to the role of a neutral observer. The more unobtrusive, acute, and perceptive such observation, the more information one has available for making sense out of the material (the focus of Chapter 7).

Jamie's Dramatic Hour

Jamie, a fearful boy of 6, came with me to the playroom. He had just met me, and had separated easily from his mother in the lobby. As he entered, he saw an easel and a table, drawing papers in a range of sizes and colors, a sink on which were many kinds of paint (finger paint, powdered tempera in saltshakers, liquid tempera, water colors), and brushes of all shapes and sizes. On another table he saw both familiar and novel drawing tools: chalk, crayons, markers, paintsticks, and tempera markers. He could also see wood scraps and glue, clay, cardboard, clay tools, tape, and scissors. He was told that he could use any materials, work wherever he liked, and make whatever he wanted.

After carefully inspecting this wide array of materials, Jamie decided to use paintsticks (something new). Standing at the table, he carefully drew a triangular shape, using a different color for each side, on the largest size of paper available, 18-by-24 inches (Figure 6.1a).

He then brought some small shakers of powder paint and a bowl of water to the table. Sprinkling and pounding the shakers of color, he talked about his little sister who is "bad—she kicks me!" (Figure 6.1b). Next, Jamie used creamy finger paint (Figure 6.1c) and, while rhythmically smearing, told a make-believe story about how "the police got me one time. I cut someone's nose off." In a confidential tone, he added that his mother has a rule about cutting noses off—presumably a rule *against* it.

After washing his hands and joking about things going down the drain, he moved away from me and worked on the floor with wood scraps and glue, quietly and carefully constructing a tall rocket (Figure 6.1d). Again choosing the largest size of white paper and using thin markers, he proceeded to draw a picture of a spaceman who went all the way up to the moon, but who would starve, because the people on earth had not supplied him with enough fuel to return or food to stay alive (Figure 6.1e).

After meticulously arranging the markers to match the colors on the box, Jamie used thick poster chalk to draw a picture of "Hansel and Gretel and a Dirty Old Witch" (Figure 6.1F), working quickly so he would have

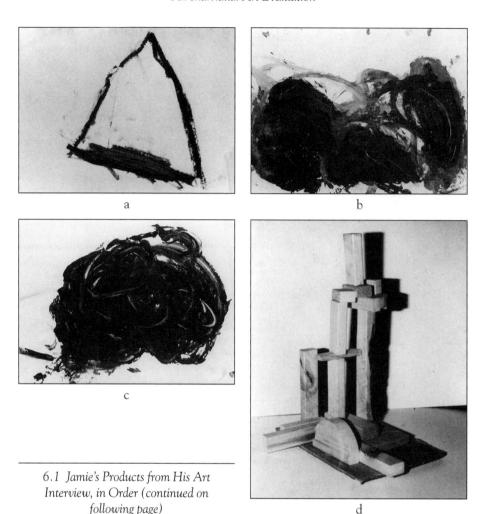

a

b

c

d

6.1 *Jamie's Products from His Art Interview, in Order (continued on following page)*

time to paint. In his version of the story, the witch is first destroyed, her face literally scribbled over, but then wins, pushing both children into the oven because they were too greedy.

Then, bringing every jar of tempera to the table, Jamie painted a picture on large paper with a short flat brush, excitedly narrating the story as he worked (Figure 6.1g). First came the house, then the fire, then he yelled, "Help! Help! Fire!" He explained that the "little kid" in the house is yelling for help and wants to get out. But the parents—all the other people in fact—are dead, and the child is the only one left.

Jamie then proceeded to try to rescue the boy, by adding a fire engine with a hose, two firemen, and a policeman, all of whom have come to save

e

f

g

the child. He agonized over how the story would end, concluding sadly that the boy would probably perish in the fire despite the rescue attempts. When asked how the fire had gotten started, he said that the boy himself had started it, implying that his death was in part punishment for having acted on that naughty impulse. Jamie was deeply and passionately involved in both the telling of the story and the painting of the picture, the product barely reflecting the intense dynamism of the process.

Indeed, Jamie told a great deal in his hour, through his behavior as well as through the form and content of his products and his associations to them. I got a picture of a little boy who was under pressure (very busy), but coping constructively and productively with this potentially threatening, uncertain, unstructured situation. He demonstrated his capacity to work at an age-appropriate developmental level in his figurative drawings. He also showed his ability to tolerate frustration, to sustain his efforts, and to coordinate hand and eye in a complex manner in his construction of the rocket out of differently sized wood scraps and glue.

He stimulated some hypotheses about why he was having trouble at home and in school: that his major concerns centered around the control of his impulses (his neediness, his curiosity), and the anxiety provoked by his fantasies of the probably disastrous consequences of his anger (injury, abandonment, or death). In the course of the hour he loosened up considerably in his artwork, from his first careful triangle, and not only became quite free, but also increasingly figurative and symbolically communicative, especially in his last three productions.

Jamie did not want to leave, but reluctantly accepted the termination of the 1-hour session. What may be one of the most important features of such an art interview is that it is typically perceived as fun and nonthreatening, unlike most testing situations. Though many children spontaneously request another such session, a single 1-hour art interview typically provides a sufficient wealth of material that significant data is available for treatment planning. As an introduction to outpatient treatment in a mental health clinic or office, there is much to be said for an activity that is pleasant, cathartic, and expressive, serving both therapeutic as well as diagnostic purposes.

Getting Started

Jamie had no difficulty getting started, and indeed such a response is the rule rather than the exception. In part this may be due to my confident expectation that the youngster will be able to find something to work with and a way to use it, a conviction no doubt conveyed to the child. Although the choice of a topic is sometimes difficult, it has never been necessary to give even the most dependent child a specific suggestion.

While most children begin by visually, verbally, or manually exploring the available materials, a few seem almost immobilized by the task of initiating activity. Most often it is possible to help them to begin by simply articulating the kinds of choices available. Fourteen-year-old Donald, for example, stood rigidly and stared at the materials for perhaps 3 or more tense, silent minutes. However, when I asked if he would prefer to draw, paint, model, or construct, he was able to make a choice, and to begin an elaborate wood construction.

Only rarely, in thousands of such interviews, has it been necessary—usually with adolescents or adults—to suggest that the client create a *scribble* upon which to project and then draw an image. This procedure of creating and then responding to one's own ambiguous stimulus has been used by many (Cane, 1951; Elkisch, 1948; Naumburg, 1947, 1966; Winnicott, 1964–68; 1971b). Like the doodles produced on the pad which Hammer (1958) places near his clients, pictorial projections on such self-made Rorschachs may indeed represent a shortcut to unconscious material (Elkisch, 1948; see footnote 1, p. 74).

Melanie, age 15, had been reluctant to draw spontaneously, but was able to project and develop an image of a bird in her scribble (Figure 6.2). In regarding it, she first decided that it was an eagle, but then shifted, saying, "I think it's a hawk or something." She continued, saying that she would either like to *be the bird* or to *take care of it*, finding the latter idea a more comfortable one. She went on to explain that eagles were in danger of becoming extinct through people's neglect, and that she would like to work for the preservation of the species.

In response to a question about whether she thought the bird had anything to do with her she agreed, relating her comments to her own strong and largely unmet dependency needs—she was living with her brother, but didn't feel happy or accepted in his home. I thought that the eagle/hawk probably expressed both her hunger and her oral aggression, evident also in the explosive, sullen, angry quality of her speech.

Tim, age 16, was acutely uncomfortable about drawing freely, since he felt inadequate as an artist. He agreeably made and developed a scribble, however, and described it as the head of "A Person" who was sad and crying, a teardrop coming from his eye. "Maybe he lost something, like a friend . . . the friend might have died, might have been the same age." In a spontaneous insight, Tim exclaimed, "Hey! I just thought of something! I'm talking about myself!" He then told of his friend who had died from drugs two years ago, and how "the exact same thing almost happened" this

6.2 Melanie's Lonely, Hungry Eagle. Age 15. Scribble drawing, chalk

week to his girlfriend, about whom he felt responsible, having introduced her to drugs himself.

Tim's capacity for self-awareness in his first art interview, despite a long history of resistance to court-mandated therapy, was a hopeful sign that he might be able to face and to know himself. Indeed, he did come for 2 years to an Art-Drama therapy group (Chapter 14) and made significant changes, helped by the modalities, the therapists, and his peers.

Woltmann (1964a, p. 325) commented that "the less structured a nonverbal activity is, the greater are the potentials for projective communication," and since I agree that "not all children do equally well on all non-verbal projective activities," it would seem appropriate to extend the range of choices offered. Certainly, individuals differ in their preferences as well as abilities, perhaps in accord with innate or learned preferred expressive modalities.

The Art Materials

Perhaps even more significant for the purpose of assessment are the differential responses and associations stimulated by different media—tactile, kinesthetic, and visual, as well as verbal. Equally important are the inherent capacities and limitations of each medium, and how the individual deals with them. There is no doubt that "materials have behavior-propelling qualities of their own" (Ginott, 1961, p. 55), and that different media "have different potentials and are adapted to different ends" (Dewey, 1934, p. 226).

Each medium has intrinsic qualities, central to what it evokes, demands, and stimulates in the child (cf. Kramer & Schehr, 2000; Lusebrink, 1990). In that sense, media and processes have inherent personalities, capacities and limitations, characteristics and idiosyncrasies. Thus, what someone chooses enables us to observe how they deal with both its possibilities and its pitfalls.

For instance, there are many possible responses to the frustration of dripping paints at the easel. How a child handles this kind of problem is one index of his or her ability to deal with frustration in general, his or her flexibility. While creating his "old-fashioned boat" (Figure 6.3), for example, 9-year-old Jim had been rigidly compulsive in his choice of paint colors for successive parallel lines. Having repeatedly but unsuccessfully tried to get me to select the next color for him, he resolved the problem by settling on a magical ritual. He would repeat the rhyme, "Ocka-bocka soda crocka, ocka-bocka-boo, Ocka-bocka soda crocka, I choose you!" bouncing his brush in the air over each paint jar in the easel, using the color he landed on at the end. After painting each horizontal stripe, he would carefully remove the color just used from the easel tray. When only one color was left in the tray, he still compulsively repeated the magical rhyme.

Jim's potential for more flexible behavior, however, was demonstrated in his handling of the "accidents" occurring in the course of the process. When the purple paint dripped, for example, he said, "Whoo," grinned, paused, and then proceeded, rhythmically pressing the brush against the paper to create more purple spots at patterned intervals.

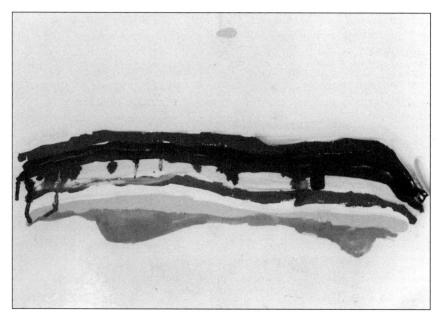

6.3 Jim's Painting of a "Design," Later Called a "Boat." Age 9. Tempera

Both finger paint and clay are regressive and messy, and have the capacity to be done and undone multiple times (DVD 6.1), providing the opportunity to smash down or remake a clay sculpture (6.1A), or to make a series of images in finger paint, smearing over between each (6.1B). One 6-year-old girl established a dramatic, repetitive rhythm, finger painting with two hands at the easel. She would rapidly draw or scratch a picture into the paint, then, just as quickly, cover it over, smearing, scratching, and clawing aggressively at the medium. Her final image was consonant with her gestures, called "An Angry Cat, with his Big Teeth" (6.1C).

Rose: A Story in Fingerpaint

A picture of "Taco, the Horse" (6.1D) was only the last word in a long sentence of images and associations by 5-year-old Rose. She began by angrily banging the powder paint container, saying, "I'll show this bottle who's the boss!" Although she said she hated getting her fingers messy and really hated finger paint, she looked longingly at the moist finger paint jars, while mixing powder paint and water with a large brush. Brushing on the paint, Rose continued to express concern about cleanliness: "I'll clean up every mess I make, after each little mess, not one big mess. No wonder I never get stuff cleaned up at school. All the kids mess around and piss!" She then went and got the creamy finger paint and glossy paper, vigorously smearing huge gobs of paint on the surface, expressing her ambivalence with a combination of grins and verbal ejaculations of words like "Yuck!" and "Ick!"

Rose's series of images began with a *Scribble*, which was followed by a *Bell*. She then drew a *Heart*, which was reworked several times. Next were squiggle lines called "*Snakes Tangling Up*," then two squiggles with faces meeting in the center, called "*Two Snakes Kissing.*" "Every day they're tangling up!" After that, Rose tried to draw a "Boy" into the paint, with much reworking and dissatisfaction: "I'm not an expert on this. Ooh! That's a bad boy!" He was quickly erased, and was followed by an attempt to "just make a *Snake*," during which Rose became concerned: "I gotta find the end. He can't got a *tail!* It looks more like a *Horse.*"

This same animal was finally developed into "*Taco*," who was later described, in an interview about the picture, as "a boy horse who is goin' to eat grass. His mom is callin' him for supper right now, but he's not comin' to eat. If he's hungry, why doesn't he come to eat? His father is gonna spank him if he doesn't come. His mother will spank him too. He's not allowed to eat any more grass. He didn't hold his temper, 'cause he hit the baby horsie! He told his mom and his mom spanked him. The others are telling his mom too, 'cause he hit his baby!"

Rose's behavior with the materials, as well as her series of images and associations, provided a wealth of information, including: her attraction to and intense anxiety about the messy finger paint, her anger with the materials, her kissing dyad, her difficulty drawing the boy and the snake's tail, and her image of a boy horse—without a tail—who is hungry but doesn't want his mother's food, who is bad for wanting other food, as well as for hitting his baby. Together these suggested Rose's feelings of being excluded from the parental couple, as well from the mother-baby dyad. Her rage and hunger were both seen as "bad," as was her wish to be messy, like the baby. It will probably come as no surprise to discover that she was the eldest of two, and that her younger sibling was a newborn baby brother.

Ellen: A Drama in Clay

Ellen, a shy 8-year-old, placed a piece of red clay onto an electric potter's wheel, which could be made to turn by pressing a foot pedal (see 6.1E). Putting her hands on either side of the clay, she called it "a *Little Lump*." She then pushed her right index finger into the center, saying she was making "a *Little Hole*." Ellen pressed the top down, trying to flatten the clay. Then she squeezed it a little and announced, "I'm makin' a *barrel*, one of those *Wooden Barrels*." With a grin, she commented, "This is a smooth feel, it feels so good. This one's gonna be for my mom. This'll be of '*Beer.*' She loves beer!"

She then added a piece of clay, covering a hole in the side, and called it "a *Patch* for any holes." Ellen commented that the clay felt like "*Mud*," and said it was getting "*Tall.*" She proceeded to put one, then two, then four fingers in the center, making a larger hole, and commenting that "I made it pretty *Deep!*" She announced, "This isn't gonna be a *Barrel*, now it's a *Vase*." At this point a piece of the clay broke off, and Ellen said she wanted to "start all over again. This clay *Stinks*! It smells awful!"

Having expressed her frustration over being unable to control the clay on the wheel, Ellen announced, "I'm just gonna let it do what it wants to do. If it goes to the side, it goes to the side." As the clay started to form an amorphous shape under her hands, she said, with some anxiety, "It looks like a *Ghost*. I don't like ghosts. I'm not gonna make it into a ghost. I was gonna make a *Bell*. I dunno. You'll see." She then commented that the shape under her hands didn't look like a *Bell*, but more like "a *Hump*."

Grinning as she put more pressure on the foot pedal of the wheel, which made it turn faster, Ellen said "This is doin' a *Hula Dance!*" I asked if it was a boy or a girl, and she said she wasn't sure, as the shape became more phallic inside her hands. Then she giggled and said "*Someone's Takin' a Bath!* This is weird! I'm gonna make it *Smooth!*"

I commented that the clay was getting taller and taller and Ellen said, "I want it *Shorter and Shorter.*" She then poured water on it and put her finger in, so that she made spiral shapes on the wheel, protesting as if she'd been chastised, "It's not *babyish!*" At that point she wondered if the time was up, and when told there was more, decided to stop using the wheel and paint the vase she had made the preceding week. She spent the next few minutes doing so rather compulsively, despite a few drips along the way.

There seems to have been a shift at the moment when the clay broke off, and Ellen noticed the "awful smell." It was then that she decided to "let it do what it wants to do," simultaneously denying responsibility for what might emerge, and permitting herself more leeway. It was at this point that the imagery become unbidden, first scary (the ghost), then exciting (the hula dancer, taking a bath). Shortly after, there was what Erik Erikson (1950) called a "play disruption." The ideas stirred up by the series of images were probably threatening, so she abruptly stopped using the wheel and proceeded to decorate something already completed, the vase.

Knowing that her mother was an alcoholic, I heard the wish to provide beer in a barrel for her as stemming from Ellen's longing for her mother's approval. She was the least liked of the four children, the odd one in her mom's eyes, the one she just couldn't relate to. Ellen couldn't acknowledge her anger at that point, nor her fear of her mother's loss of control when drunk. Like the images Ellen projected onto the clay on the potter's wheel, her mother's alcoholic behavior was both exciting and frightening. For when she was drunk, she was more loving toward Ellen, yet more volatile as well.

Ben, age 12, worked long and hard on a clay statue of a person to go on the flat slab pedestal he had carefully made. He first worked on the body, then added the legs, carefully building in armature-like supports for the limbs. As he added the head and neck, he began to describe the figure as no longer a "*Boy*" as first indicated, but rather a "*Girl*" of thirty-four, whom you could tell was "nice" because "she wouldn't holler much." At this point he began to discuss grownups who holler, male and female, and squeezed the body, making it taller and thinner. Next, Ben began to press down on the figure, then grinned and smashed it with his fist.

He went and got a bowl of water, and spent the remainder of the hour experimenting with clay and water, saying it reminded him of "*Mud Pies*." He shook some powder paint on the clay, rubbed it in, and admired his curved form, saying it reminded him of "*Somebody Being Born*," and that next week he would "make a *Man* this time." He liked the shape so well, however, that he decided to save it, his final statement in an hour marked by regression (Figure 6.4).

The Space

Because there are options in addition to media and topic, there are other useful diagnostic indexes in such an unstructured interview, such as how the child uses the available space. With a choice of working surfaces and locations, the child may decide to stand or to sit, to be close to or far from the therapist, to look at or work with his or her back to the adult. Many children try out several options, and often seem more relaxed and more freely verbal when not facing the therapist.

One boy sat at the table next to me as he drew his first neat, careful, somewhat stereotyped crayon scene of a farmhouse and pumpkins in a field (Figure 6.5a). He then moved to the easel, his back to me, and began to experiment with thick poster chalk, relaxing and swinging rhythmically as he explored the new, looser medium (Figure 6.5b). His projected title for his line-swinging multicolored abstraction was "A Colorful Cloud." When asked how the cloud felt, this meek, polite boy said in a soft voice, "Well, the way the eyes are, she's pretty mad . . . at the sun, for drawing all the water out." When he next returned to the table, he animatedly created,

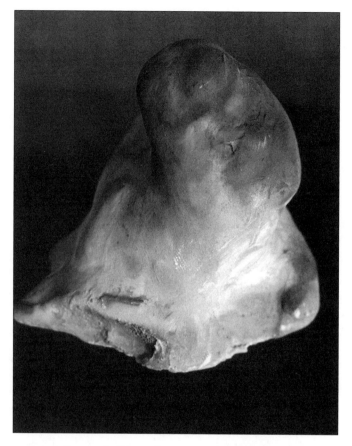

6.4 A Statue of a Person Being Born, by Ben. Age 12. Clay

wore, and spoke through (in significantly louder tones) an openly angry "Monster" mask (Figure 6.5c).

While some children remain at the same spot for the duration of the session, many choose different locations for different activities, the sequence varying for individuals. Daniel made his first product, a conical paper "Fire-Starter" containing feces-like balls of clay and wads of paper, while standing with his back to me the whole time. He then chose to paint at the table near me.

He became so self-conscious and even paranoid about the observers, however, whom he knew to be on the other side of the two-way mirror, that he quickly taped his painting on the mirror because, as he explained, "They could spy." When asked who he thought they were going to tell, he whispered, "Mothers!" Although he was reassured to the contrary, he spent his remaining time covering the entire observation window with paper,

a

b

6.5 *Three Products from a 1-hour Interview, in Order. Age 9*

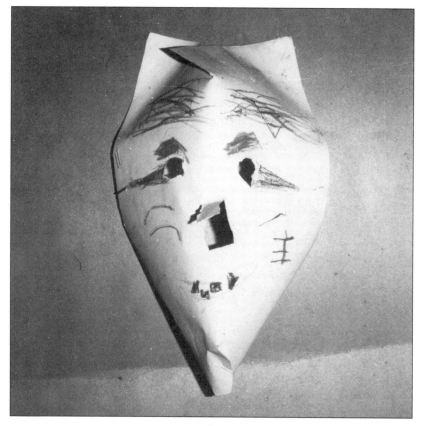

c

drawing bars of steel with chalk so that "them little sneakies" couldn't see or hear what was happening in the room.

Talking about the Artwork

Just as it is up to the child to decide what to use, and how and where to use it, so the youngster may choose to speak spontaneously or to work in silence. If there is little or no spontaneous verbalization by the middle of the hour, I might actively encourage the child to talk about ideas and feelings while using the art media.

Some children are so self-conscious that the more casual interviewing during the process is the only kind which does not produce acute anxiety, blocking, and defensiveness. As a teenager once said while we both looked at her clay cave, it was easy for her to talk to me, "because I'm not looking in your eye. If I was looking in your eye I couldn't say all this."

Children are given the option of deciding whether to be interviewed about each product directly after it is finished or at the end of the session. Although some verbalize freely and spontaneously while they work, they can be helped to further associate to the product through open-ended interviewing after the artwork is completed.

It is always helpful to attempt some kind of formal interviewing around the product (and perhaps the process), and it seems to help if this is separated in time and space from the creation of the artwork. With many, it helps to be open about the notion that "we might get some more ideas [about what's bothering you] if together we look at what you've made and either think about what it reminds you of or tell a story about it" (or some other ego-syntonic form of association). Finding a way of tuning in to the child's vocabulary, mental capacities, interests, and concerns is a challenge to the adult attempting to enter and clarify the child's world.

It often helps to encourage the child to gain some aesthetic and psychic distance by placing the product in a place both can see easily without distraction—like the easel, table, floor, or wall (DVD 6.2). The first step is to suggest that the youngster start by looking intently at whatever has been created, as in the "witness writing" of the Open Studio Process (Allen, 1995; DVD 6.2A), which has been widely adopted by art therapists (6.2B). The simple question, "What do you see?" (Betensky, 1995, 2001) can also elicit many useful responses (6.2C).

The interview is best if conducted mainly in an open-ended fashion (DVD 6.3), with questions that allow maximum freedom of response, such as, "Can you tell me about your picture?" (6.3A) "Does that have a story to go with it?" "What comes to mind when you look at your artwork?" or, "Does it remind you of anything?" (6.3B).

Sometimes it is also helpful to ask clarifying questions about just what might be represented, such as the age, sex, and character of figures, or the location or activity either shown or implied in the product. Questions which help the child to relate to the representation are useful, such as, "If you were in that place, *where* would you be?" or, "If you were in that story, *who* would you be?" Questions which help the youngster to extend associations can help as well, such as, "What might have happened *earlier*?" or, "What do you think will happen *next*?"

Often, children spontaneously speak for their artwork, especially when small, three-dimensional products make it possible to use them like puppets (see DVD 14.2A). Should this not occur, however, it is not too difficult to stimulate such activity by questions like, "I wonder what that _____ (dog, person) would say if it could talk?" or, "Could you speak for your sculpture as if it were a puppet?" Such invitations are yet another avenue for projection. Whatever the question, the job of the interviewer is to encourage children to clarify and to extend their personal associations and ideas, without imposing or intruding the therapist's own projections—a challenging but rewarding creative task.

Even the most silent child can speak eloquently through art, as in the case of Tommy, a timid boy of 8. He first worked on a wood scrap and glue "*Hobby Horse,*" while sitting on the floor, at the opposite end of the room, with his back to me. While waiting for part of it to dry, he came back to the table and quietly squeezed and manipulated a small piece of clay, still avoiding eye contact.

When asked what it might be, he first called the clay a "*Rowboat,*" then made it into a "*Snake,*" with which he hissed softly in a meek but playful manner. Then he formed it into a "*Ball,*" which he dropped on the table, gradually throwing it down with increasing force, ostensibly to flatten it in order to make a "*Pancake.*" Tommy finally poked features into the pancake and called his creation a "*Monster Face.*" When encouraged to use it as a puppet, he was able, with mounting volume and intensity, to express the boy monster's anger at both his mother and his sister, who "bother him."

Other youngsters, like 16-year-old Marilyn, speak freely from the moment they enter, perhaps aided by the materials. Marilyn used clay, commenting frequently about the pleasure of playing with it, and about its sensory qualities, noting that the clay "feels good. It's cool. It's nice and smooth." While she worked, Marilyn spoke in depth and detail about the realities of her current confused state.

When she was finished, she described her head of a Man (Figure 6.6) as "a guy—very strong, with high cheekbones. And the way I made him, he looks mean, because his eyes are so far in. His eyebrows stick out. He looks like he's looking straight at me . . . because I'm so depressed." In elaborating, she described him as telling her to "straighten up" with a "strong voice," and, when requested, she spoke for the man, and answered for herself in a powerfully moving dialogue. The character was portrayed as an idealized father-lover-saviour figure, upset not out of meanness, but out of deep concern for her welfare. If we see the head as a possible self-representation, the gaping eyes, mouth, and ears seem to scream out her own inner panic, anxiety, and emptiness.

Abstract Artwork

Even when a child's product is nonrepresentational, it is still possible to utilize it as a stimulus for projection (as with a Rorschach). Derek's abstract wood scrap sculpture was finally seen by him as a crowd of people, yelling,

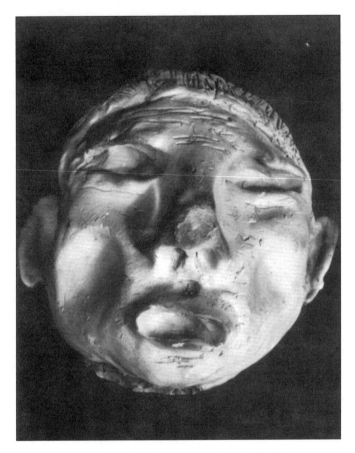

6.6 *Head of a Man, by Marilyn. Age 16. Clay*

each going his or her own separate way. When asked if he knew any group like that, he said it reminded him of his own large family, with its busyness and lack of communication.

Cathleen began by saying that her painting was "just a design," but upon looking at it longer, said it reminded her of "flowers" or maybe "suns." When asked who the flowers or suns might be if they were people, she quickly identified the smaller one as a girl and the larger one as a woman, stronger than the younger one. Asked if they reminded her of anyone, she said they were like her mother and herself, angrily asserting, "I feel like people are dominating me. I feel like everyone's dominating me!"

Similarly, the multicolored finger painting that 9-year-old Max produced with powdered tempera paint reminded him of "something you have for lunch." At one point, while engaged in the process, he made a mock-aggressive gesture toward me with his messy hands. At the end of the hour he titled the painting "Something Pretty, like a Rainbow," but went on to modify that image in a more aggressive direction: "Eruptions, Something Erupting, like a Volcano." When asked what might be erupting, he said, "Different colors of gems. . . . Jet is the black one, the blue one is lapis lazuli, the red one is ruby, the white spots are diamonds, the green ones are emeralds, and the yellow is topaz." He elaborated further, explaining that the volcano was spurting out not only beautiful jewels, but also fire and lava.

He then shifted in his associations from this anal image to an oral one, saying that the multicolored picture now reminded him of a "Fruit Bowl." Pointing to the colors, he explained, "The purple would be grapes, the green could be grapes, the black could be . . . a rotten bunch of bananas, the red could be apples, and the orange could be oranges." When asked what he might like to eat, Max replied, "Apples," and when asked who was probably going to get the fruit in the bowl, he said that no one would, because his grandmother would throw the bowl in the fireplace unless he stopped her by plugging it up.

Some Things Are Easier to Say and to See in Art

Sometimes an art interview is a peculiarly sensitive instrument where others are not. Evelyn, a painfully shy adolescent of 16, was thought to be mildly inhibited but not grossly disturbed. Since it was so difficult for her to talk, the psychiatrist who was doing the diagnostic workup requested an Art Assessment.

She first did a painting on a large piece of white paper; a stark, split, barren purple "Tree" (Figure 6.7a). Asked what sort of place it was in, she said it was "nice" and that she would like to be there, right next to the tree. She then said she might "*be*" the tree itself, an odd choice. Evelyn next chose fine-tipped markers and drew a bizarre figure she named "Fred" (Figure 6.7b). When I asked her to tell me about "Fred," she described her as "an 18-year-old girl." She then told me that the other kids called her "crazy," and that "Fred" talked to herself, because it was better than talking to others. Her final product was a clay turtle who she said was scared to come out of his shell. Given her timidity, the turtle seemed a self-representation.

Although the referring psychiatrist remarked that Evelyn's art looked "sicker" than anything else, it was a subsequent suicide attempt which validated the confusion and withdrawal evident in her artwork and associations to the imagery. Fortunately, she was able to be treated through adjunctive art and dance therapy while hospitalized, which was especially helpful during a time when she became electively mute. Retrospectively,

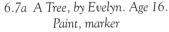

6.7a *A Tree, by Evelyn. Age 16.*
Paint, marker

6.7b *"Fred," by Evelyn. Age 16.*
Paint, marker

the glove on Fred's hand and the denial of the body in that drawing, as well as the vaginal split in the tree, were clues not only to the depth—but also to the nature—of her pathology, which became more apparent in her therapy over time.

Productivity

For most children, several products emerge spontaneously from a 1-hour session, the average being two-and- one-half. Younger children tend to be more prolific, while older youngsters tend to spend more time on individual products. In a sample of 50 Subjects (Ss) ages 5 to 17, the mean number of products created by 13-to-17-year-olds (17 Ss) was 1.76, by 9-to-12-year-olds (14 Ss) 2.71, and by 5-to-8-year-olds (19 Ss) 3.42.

The availability of more than one item per child is helpful in countering the problem of intraindividual variability (R. Kellogg, 1969; Rubin, Schachter, & Ragins, 1983). This is in accord with the recommendation of many that a sample of several art products is more reliable for assessment than one or two (DVD 6.4). Certainly, all of Jamie's products taken together present a richer, truer reflection of him than any one alone.

Younger children, like Lisa, tend to be more prolific in their output, often creating one or more products in the course of the hour. It is evident that she was stimulated by the many media choices available (6.4A), and that making many items was significant to her (6.4B).

The sequence often unfolds with increasing clarity and a lessening of disguise. A boy who had become electively mute had recently begun to destroy his own toys, leading to a clinic referral. In his first picture (6.4C), two dinosaurs are poised for action, the den and babies of one clearly visible underground. In the second drawing, the action becomes clear, as the blood flows from one dinosaur being attacked by the other (6.4D).

An adolescent who had been sexually abused and had been herself abandoned, first drew a sad dog (6.4E), then modeled a "mutt" who was later said to have been "kicked out" of its home (6.4F). Her last product (6.4G) was first said to be "a crib," reminding her of the baby she had recently aborted; but then was seen as the "bars" of someone trapped in a prison, as she felt herself to be with her foster mother.

Some youngsters, mostly older children and teenagers, work throughout the session on a single creation (DVD 6.5), like the two-headed dragon (6.5A) created by one boy, who explained that the dragon couldn't decide whether to be good or evil (6.5B). Similarly, Andy, a 17-year-old boy (6.5C) worked hard on one painting (6.5D) throughout the entire session.

Harris concluded from his review of the literature that "free drawings are more meaningful psychologically than assigned topics" (1963, p. 53). The assumption implicit in the unstructured art interview is that "we do best for any diagnostic purpose if we give the patient 'complete freedom' to reveal his own unique reaction" (Harms, 1948, p. 243). The manner in which the child approaches and structures the hour, plus what he or she produces and how he or she does it, add up to a rich storehouse of data that may then be fitted together like the pieces of a puzzle to make diagnostic sense.

Recommendations

The number of media and space options can be many fewer than those described earlier, but the principle is still the same; that most children, given choices in an unstructured situation, will convey a great deal about themselves. Even if the choice is much more limited, you will usually learn more than if you prescribe what's to be used. If you are willing and have the space, I suggest that you offer the following options:

1. Drawing surfaces (white and colored paper—9″ × 12″ and 12″ × 18″)
2. Something to draw with (markers, oil crayons, pastels)

3. Something to paint with (watercolors, tempera paints)
4. Something to model with (plasticine: assorted colors; clay: gray and terra-cotta)
5. Something to construct with (magazines, scissors, wood scraps, glue)
6. Tools: brushes (flat, pointed, short handled)

If you want to add more, the following are desirable: assorted colors of paper—three sizes of both white and colored paper; thin and thick markers; thin and thick (poster) chalk; colored pencils; finger paints; tempera markers; clay tools (wires, points, serrated). For adolescents, it helps to have more adult materials, such as charcoal, artist's pastels, acrylic paints, and gouache (cf. Linesch, 1988; Moon, 1998; Riley, 1999).

It also helps to have options about where to work as well as what to use and to make. So, if you don't have space for a floor easel, a wall or table easel can be stored in a closet. If you suggest that children can decide where to work, they can choose whether to sit across from you, next to you, catty-corner, with their back to you, on the floor, and so on.

In addition, especially when time or contacts are limited (as in the managed care world of mental health), it may be helpful to include a Self Portrait, a Kinetic Family Drawing (Burns & Kaufman, 1970), or any other subject matter that appeals to you and seems relevant. A great number of evocative themes have been proposed by clinicians (Hammer, 1958, 1997), such as a Bridge (Hays & Lyons, 1987), a Person Picking an Apple from a Tree (Gantt & Tabone, 2003), a Mother-Child Drawing (Gillespie, 1994); Two People Doing Something in a Place (Gerber, 1996); and A Favorite Kind of Day (Manning, 1987).

Of course, there are different strokes for different folks, and not every art therapist is comfortable with an open-ended approach. I am certain that anyone will do best to proceed in a way that is congenial to their temperament and compatible with their training.

What seems most important to remember is that the art made in therapy is not only a source of information for the therapist; it is also a *mirror* for the youngster, as Edith Kramer once wrote, "Paintings are valuable not so much because they can tell the adult something about the child, but also because the very act of creating helps the child to learn something new about himself. This process of self-discovery and self-acceptance through art is the core of art therapy" (personal communication, 1959).

CHAPTER

7

Decoding Symbolic Messages

In order to utilize the unstructured art interview effectively, it is important to know *how* to look, what to look *at*, what to look *for*, and how to make *sense* out of what has been observed. Children respond rapidly, perhaps unconsciously, to the invitation to reveal themselves through a creative modality. They do so in a variety of ways, sending messages at many levels and in many guises. If one wishes to understand these messages, it is necessary to determine what children are saying by looking both at *what* they say and *how* they communicate (cf. Irwin & Rubin, 1976).

Any interview provides a wealth of interpersonal behavior within the hour, from the initial meeting to the final leave-taking. Since the session probably represents a novel situation to the child, there are also all of the meanings implicit in the child's response to and ways of coping with this new, unstructured task. There are also symbolic communications inherent in the child's working process, as well as in the form and content of the product(s) created. In all of these areas, there are direct as well as disguised messages being sent both verbally and nonverbally by the child and responded to by the therapist. It is in the evoking, observing, deciphering, and relating of these multiple sources of data that some of the many questions about the child may be answered.

To Write or Not to Write?

Even though it is not essential to do so routinely, it is a good idea to make written notes of what goes on during an art assessment, paying special attention to the aspects of both process and products discussed in the following section. The note-taking need not be elaborate, but unless an art therapist has an exceptional visual memory, it is likely that recalling things like sequences within a drawing, or the connection between artistic behaviors and facial expressions, will not be that easy.

One way to explain the need to write things down is that it helps in remembering the details of the artistic process. If done casually, as if it is taken for granted that they will accept it, children are more likely to do so. If youngsters are uneasy about note-taking, they can be invited to look at their notebook. One notebook for each child is a good way to keep records separate, to insure privacy, and to give them a place to write or draw as well, if they wish.

Verbal Communications

In the course of such an interview, some of the communications are verbal, including those associated with the making of a product, as well as in response to questions about it. One looks not only at *what* children say, but also at the *way* in which they say it—the form and quality of the speech: its tempo, pitch, intensity, stress, articulation, vocal quality, and its overall flavor (confidential, belligerent, fearful, etc.).

Spontaneous verbalizations, especially those made when the child is engaged in work with media, often give a gestalt of feeling/ideation (DVD 7.1). For example, the child who pinches the clay and breaks off pieces while talking about how his baby sister gets in his way may be commenting both verbally and gesturally about his negative feelings and aggressive impulses toward her.

Active listening, like active observing, is a skill that improves with practice, primarily because it is continually rewarded by what is learned. If children speak spontaneously while they work they may talk about the process or the product (7.1A), or they may discuss something else, like what they dreamed last night, or their worries about a friend or teacher (7.1B). It is best to let them lead the way, partly because they will be more comfortable, but also because what they say is revealing about whatever they are creating while they say it, even if it seems at first to be completely unrelated.

To Talk or Not to Talk?

Once children have begun using art materials, it is best to let them do what is most comfortable. That means that if they want to work quietly, it is wise not to intrude. On the other hand, if they want to talk while they work, that's fine, too.

What matters is to respect their spontaneous response to using art materials, and to react sensitively as well as supportively. Although I know of no studies of this phenomenon, after over 40 years of doing art therapy it is clear to me that some children can operate on more than one expressive channel with comfort, even facilitation of one or both, while others cannot. It appears that this is not something they can modify, which leads me to hypothesize that it is based on innate differences in neurological wiring.

If you interrupt a single-channel artist with a question, he or she will stop creating in order to answer, or will continue working as if you weren't heard. Conversely, doodling or fooling around with clay seems to dramatically loosen the tongues of others. Paradoxically, therefore, using art materials may facilitate or inhibit spontaneous verbalization during the creative process.

In any case, it is best to adopt an interested, unintrusive stance. If you feel that you must question people while they work, just ask them to let you know if talking with you interferes with their concentration on the task (see DVD 6.5C). If children talk spontaneously about what they're making while creating, it is always best to let them lead the way. This is because any question or statement on your part may be heard as a value judgment. What you say can also affect the end product, so that it's not the same as what the child might have created without your commentary.

Nonverbal Communications

Nonverbally, the child speaks just as eloquently. A glance "talks," as a child looks at the adult for permission, blame, punishment, or approval. The closeness or distance from the adult says something, as do the position and muscle tone of the body, facial expressions, and gestures. When Tommy first sat far away with his back facing me, he might have been symbolically saying any or all of the following: "I am afraid," "I don't want you to see what I'm doing," "I don't trust you," or, "I wish you weren't here." Similarly, in moving his chair extremely close to me while he worked on his sculpture with its contiguous wood scrap structures, Jim seemed to be saying, "I want and need to be next to you in order to feel good."

Interaction with the Therapist

How children approach and interact with the adult in general is often an important communication of attitudes and expectations. They may be fairly confident and unafraid to ask for help, or they may be fearful, even paralyzed in silence.

Whether shy, friendly, controlling, or helpless, a useful assumption is that children project upon this new person feelings and expectations related to significant others, just as they project wishes and concerns onto the unstructured media. One observes to see if a child is suspicious or trusting, withdrawn or outgoing, fearful or comfortable, hostile or friendly, dependent or independent—and if these change in the course of the hour.

Response to the Task

How children deal with an essentially unstructured creative task may give some indication of their usual way of coping with a new and somewhat ambiguous situation. Children respond in a variety of ways to the initial request to decide what to use and how to use it. Some respond impulsively, like Jill, who hastily grabbed many different art materials almost at random, working in a pressured yet disorganized manner. Gary also brought a range of many different media to the working space, but chose them very deliberately, and then used some of each in his picture as a way of avoiding a selection among them. *What* is used as well as *how* it is used are indeed of symbolic significance.

Response to the Materials

The materials may be approached enthusiastically or gingerly, at times with a dramatic display of approach-avoidance behavior. Finger paint is often looked at, commented on, and verbally rejected early in the hour, only later to be used with (guilty) gusto, as did Rose (see Chapter 6, pp. 107–108).

Some youngsters are "feelers," touching and sometimes tasting or smelling whatever they can, as though still learning primarily through their senses. They actively explore the media and often question what was purchased where and by whom, their behavior reflecting curiosity as well as a kind of sensory hunger. Some children gobble up all the materials in sight, grabbing large quantities, suggesting problems with impulse control as well as anxiety about whether there will be "enough." They may also ask to take them home, as though their needs are insatiable.

Once a medium is selected, the way in which it is manipulated gives important clues. Clay may be squeezed or stroked, attacked or caressed, pinched or patted, handled in many possible, and always meaningful, ways. Aggressive impulses may peek through, as when a child forcibly squeezes off a tiny piece of clay, or presses hard enough to break a crayon or to crumble a piece of chalk.

Getting to know a medium is like making a new acquaintance. Sometimes it starts with a circling around, a looking-at and observing for a long time without direct contact. Eventually there may be tentative touching, fingering, and handling, perhaps followed by a pulling-away, or, conversely, by a plunging-in. Yet another way of making contact may be impulsive, an initial decision made without hesitation to use something familiar or to try something new. Children may go about this initial contact in any number of ways—deliberately, cautiously, casually, freely, or impulsively—always telling us, through what is chosen and rejected, as well as how they proceed, important things about themselves.

The Working Process

Once the child begins to work, the process that follows is as revealing as the decision-making that preceded it. As the child works the therapist can observe the manner or style of working, the overall form of the working process, and the way in which it changes over time. In the course of the hour, children reveal their individual rhythms, tempos, and energy levels. Some are consistent throughout the session, working at a steady pace. Joanna, for example, carefully executed three slowly drawn paintings, while Jill was impulsive throughout the hour, not completing any of her carelessly-done products.

Most children, however, show variations within the session, usually gradually relaxing and loosening up. As time goes on, the majority become more spontaneous and more open—physically, verbally, and symbolically. The relaxation seems to be stimulated by the materials themselves, as well as by the implicit permission to express feelings and fantasies freely.

Some children, on the other hand, become increasingly threatened and anxious, and seem to either tighten up or to let go, exploding or being flooded with sudden, overwhelming feeling and loss of control, sometimes crossing the boundary between fantasy and reality. A rapid regression and disorganization in behavior and in the form of art products is often associated with the use of fluid and messy tactile media, especially finger paint and clay. A material's similarity to body products may exert a strong regressive pull, stimulating memories and feelings associated with early childhood, as well as forbidden impulses.

Fifteen-year-old Hannah, for example, playfully hit and kissed the art therapist with the clay "Loving Duck" she had just made, acting out the impulse with the figure rather than talking about it or using it symbolically. Sometimes the emotional flooding in an art session is reflected in a noticeable regression in the form of the products, as with Sam's bizarre head (Figure 14.5), and occasionally in a perceptible impairment of ego functions, manifested in such forms as immature speech, forgetting, or associations to products with a primary process flavor.

In his art evaluation, Sam had revealed the fragility of his ego boundaries in his painting—a fluid, flowing, amorphous, wet watercolor—and his projections: "It's like a landscape, a turbulent sea with a cloudy sky. . . . A person, a man or a woman, is running into the sea holding a handbag, like it's running toward the red object, which must be another person . . . playing the violin or some instrument. He's standing there as a lure, like Circe." He then commented that the lady with the handbag had at first resembled a chicken, and that another ambiguous form in the painting might be "a cat or a bird going up out of the water and then flying away."

Conversely, fearful Richard's products became tighter and smaller, as he withdrew verbally in the course of his art interview. Less often, a child's working style alternates between states of clarity and confusion, like Peter, who was disorganized between working periods, but was able to focus as soon as he settled down to work on a product.

Whatever the child's process over time—whether more relaxed or more tense, more open or more closed, more organized or disorganized, smooth or disconnected—observing and noting the evolution is helpful in understanding its dynamic meaning.

An art interview provides a unique opportunity for simultaneous multi-level communication. Some children verbalize freely about real or imagined concerns while working with the material in either a playful or planful way. A youngster may play with a medium in a most meaningful fashion with no end product, as when Donald systematically trimmed, smoothed, and sliced up clay, which he later identified as a "monster."

Because of the conscious energy spent on the conversation, a child is often unaware of what his hands are saying, as when Sherry squashed her partly-formed clay figure each time a sibling was mentioned (albeit lovingly) in her verbalization; or when Cindy made and unmade breasts and a large (pregnant?) belly on her Buddha-like figure, while she talked about various forms of escape from a painful situation with her mother at home.

Products: Form

Most approaches to understanding children through art focus on the products themselves. While there is indeed much to be learned from these wonderfully permanent records of expression, those process elements previously noted seem to me to be equally eloquent clues, especially when observed in the context of what is being created. Formal aspects of art products (line, organization, and so forth) may offer important clues to the state of the child's cognitive apparatus; indeed, they are the most dependable index of developmental level—far more useful than content.

Some widely held notions about the meanings of certain formal qualities, however, such as shading, are questionable. It is my feeling that, like universal symbolic meanings, such correlations as that of excessive shading with anxiety may often be valid; that is, perhaps in many cases (maybe even the majority) there is such a connection. However, to assume when one sees shading that it *always* indicates anxiety, or that small figures *invariably* indicate constriction, is to make what seems to me to be a grave error.

Attempts to validate such indices in the drawings of adults have been less than successful, and are even more doubtful with children, who are in a dynamic process of development (Harris, 1963; Kaplan, 2003; Malchiodi, 1998; Swenson, 1968). What makes more sense is to be aware of such common relationships; to have them available as hypotheses, but to remain open to other possibilities. Observing the creation of a product and listening to clues of symbolic meaning (like the kinds of associated comments and nonverbal signals noted previously) seem more valid.

Certainly, one may look at art products in terms of their degree of organization, clarity, completeness, symmetry, movement, or color. Such qualities are helpful ways to describe and perceive, and at times to attempt diagnostic classification (Gantt & Tabone, 1998, 2003; Mills, 2003). But it is equally important to utilize formal indices with caution—to approach all generalizations about invariant meanings with skepticism, and to rely heavily on what is observed and what makes sense in the context of the actual encounter with a child in art.

Many resources relate color to symbolic meanings (Lüscher, 1969), associating black, for example, with depression, and yellow with pleasure. Yet black, for a black child, may signify pride, and yellow may relate to fear (Axline, 1964); color choice must always be seen in the context in which it occurs. One study, in fact, showed that preschoolers tend to select easel paint colors on the basis of their position in the easel tray, usually working from left to right (Corcoran, 1954).

One of my favorite (supposedly true) stories is of the child who used only brown in her drawings. Her sophisticated mother was concerned about possible problems, and took the girl to a psychologist for testing. At the end of a comprehensive battery, the psychologist, having won the child's confidence and finding nothing wrong, asked her frankly why she always drew in brown. The girl answered quite straightforwardly, "Well, I sit in the back row, and by the time the crayon box gets to me, brown is the only color left" (Kaye, 1968, p. 17).

There is no question in my mind that in most cases of *deliberate* color selection there is indeed a meaning in the child's color choice. Similarly, varying with developmental level, there is significance in his or her degree of organization or elaboration. I am equally convinced, however, that to make blanket generalizations about such formal qualities—as if they were applicable to all children—is folly, and is often responsible for the all-too-common misuse, abuse, and pseudo-psychologizing about children's art on the part of educators, clinicians, and laypersons.

To divorce the final product from the process which created it is equally foolish. Often, it is not so important to know *how much* space was finally filled as to know the *manner* in which that filling came about. Certainly, this is as true of content as it is of form, where the *sequence* of objects drawn may be at least as significant as the nature of the objects themselves.

Looking at formal aspects of children's art tells us not so much *what* is being said as *how* it is being conveyed. Jane, for example, fills her picture with carefully-executed elaboration, telling us about her concerns clearly, deliberately, and with detail. Sally, on the other hand, smears and erases, includes little, and creates an ambiguous form that communicates not only her own confusion, but also perhaps her ambivalence about telling someone else.

Form and Process as Content

Sometimes form may be viewed as content, where vague and inarticulate feelings or ideas are conveyed in the form or process more than in the subject matter. For example, Mickey, in all of his paintings, was continually concerned with making and staying inside the lines, suggesting worries about impulse control. Linked with his stories of aggression and punishment, told while painting innocuous pictures at the easel, the implicit concern with loss of control becomes an even more probable hypothesis.

Max spent a good deal of time while doing his two finger paintings in making and then "covering over"—by smearing out what he had drawn into the paint, much as he "covered over" his feelings and impulses with his clever rationalizations and intellectualizing.

Donny moved his chair closer and closer to me during the joint making of a city of wood blocks in which he had insisted I participate (DVD 7.2). Although he had begun by suggesting that we make separate buildings (7.2A), he eventually placed them together (7.2B). Making sure that his buildings were touching those already glued down by his partner, his wish for closeness and his unmet dependency needs were even more apparent in his manner than in what he made or the story he told.

Products: Content

The content of an art product can be considered in terms of:

1. The verbal and nonverbal communications occurring during the process of making the object—which may or may not be consciously related to the medium or topic;
2. The manifest or surface topic or subject matter, including abstraction;
3. The associative content, in the form of the title or projected images and stories related to the product, during or after its completion;
4. The implied latent content, evident in distortions (exaggerations or omissions) or symbol selection, but not necessarily alluded to or in any way conscious to the maker.

I find that it makes sense to assume the validity of *psychic determinism*—that all behavior (including expressive behavior) is not random, but has meaning, though not always easily discovered. Noting the sequence of all events in any encounter between a child and art, and assuming an associative link, can be extremely helpful in trying to decipher the meaning(s) of any particular communication. What precedes and what follows a particular creative act, like the sequence of forms within a product, is assumed to be meaningfully related in a (psycho)logical way (cf. Baruch & Miller, 1952).

In regard to universal symbols, it is my assumption that such connections must have some degree of validity or they would not have been made in the first place. And, indeed, it is striking in one's work over time to discover the frequency with which a sun seems to represent the father or a house the mother. Nevertheless, as with formal signs, such correlations are considered as hypotheses, which may or may not be confirmed by the child's own associations. Thus, extensions may often be phallic, or containers feminine, for indeed they do resemble those body parts in their form—but the particular meaning of a specific symbol is only available to the listener and/or observer with a mind genuinely open to the child's own associations (gestural, physical, verbal, and so on).

Common Themes

The meanings of symbols in a child's art are not so mysterious if one listens and looks with care, and assiduously avoids allowing one's own projections to obscure what the child is trying to communicate. Common themes are fairly few in number, centering around universal human and developmental concerns. Most relate to aggression (anger) or to love and needs for affection.

The aggression may have an oral, biting, devouring quality, as when Tommy's clay monster head was said to eat up mothers, sisters, and others who got in its way. Or, it may have an anal, explosive quality, as when Mack's fingerpainted volcano was said to erupt, spilling fire and lava all over. Finally, it may have a thrusting or phallic quality, as when Lance's clay knife was to be used to cut up enemies.

Related are themes concerning autonomy and struggles with authority, as when Evan's female figure in a painting of a man and woman was described as being the boss: "She rules the house, huh? *I'll* rule the house in *my* house!" Often in art such aggressive ideas are implied or potential rather than being directly shown, as when Mickey's painted cannon was said to be available for use, but not necessarily to be fired.

In the area of sexuality, children often express oral themes relating to nurturance, or to maintenance of physical comfort, as when Cindy's clay figure reminded her of "my mother. She's big and round and warm . . . that gives me happiness."

Conversely, themes relating to lack of protective care, rejection, or abandonment sometimes appear, as when, in Peggy's story, her clay dog was kicked out and left to die by a mean aunt (See DVD 6.4F). Pregenital wishes for a kind of symbiotic union or merger are sometimes expressed, as when Donny's two wood scrap houses came together to hug and kiss. Sometimes what predominates is curiosity, especially visual, as when, in his painting, Mickey wanted to look into all the windows on Captain Hook's boat.

Closely related are themes of competition, often with an older and stronger adversary (suggesting an oedipal quality), as when John's painted Mustang was to be "the winner" in a big car race. At times the major concern is with some kind of injury to the self, suggesting anxiety about bodily injury as punishment for "bad" aggressive or sexual impulses, as when Ava's deer was missing one leg, or John's painted "super plane" (in a battle with a larger one) exploded because "some guys shot him down."

Older as well as younger children sometimes express confusion or ambivalence about their sexual identity, as when Sally's boat rower was alternately identified as a boy and as a girl—the figure, drawn in chalk, was also visually ambiguous. Wishes for genital sexuality in a romantic sense are sometimes expressed, as when Heather's two clay blobs got married and quickly produced a clay baby.

When a particular theme is repeated several times in a child's products, then one can assume its special importance in their inner life. Thus, John created a drawing, a painting, and a scarred clay head, all of which involved self-injury; and Donny not only glued together his two wood houses, but also projected an image onto his crayon drawing of "Two People Hugging," underlining the intensity of his symbiotic yearnings.

It is not at all uncommon (in fact, it is usual) for a symbol to contain more than one idea; some of its power coming from the peculiar characteristic of condensation, and the possibility of multiple meanings at multiple levels. Thus, Melanie could identify with her oral-aggressive eagle's rage, as well as with its hunger for food and care (Figure 6.2). Pete wished both to stay *far away* from the snake he saw in his abstract construction, and to *be* the snake, so that he could bite those who tease him—both projections referring to aggression but in different ways.

Self-Representations

Sometimes it seems quite clear that the child is representing her- or himself in some way in the art product, often creating more than one in the course of the hour. Thus, Eva, an 8-year-old girl, made a clay "boy bird, Twinkle," who is strong and lives happily with friends in a clay nest, even though the mother and father birds have left home (as did Eva's father in reality).

She also modeled "a Plain Old Deer" with no horns and one leg missing, who said plaintively, "I'm a sloppy little thing, 'cause I don't know how to walk yet. I'm eight, too." This girl, who was indeed damaged both physically and psychologically, communicated how she *felt* (the deer) as well as how she *wished* to be (the bird). She then created a drawing of yet another wishful self-image: "a Boy Angel" who can "fly to meetings" to find his lost father.

On rare occasions, spontaneous inclusion of the real self occurs, as when her clay blob in dramatic play asked me what I thought of "poor Heather," or when Ava's painted house was said to contain "me and my pets and my friends." It is important to keep in mind that self-representations may reflect the way things realistically are, or may be projections of children's fantasies—they may convey how they wish or fear themselves to be, or they may represent different facets of personality.

Degree of Disguise

More often, however, children represent themselves and their problems in more or less disguised ways, which offer symbolic protection for the expression and communication of unacceptable thoughts. Just as children may physically hide behind an easel or turn their backs to the worker; so too they may hide symbolically, going as far away from direct communication as abstraction. The careful observation of all behaviors related to the product's making and the sensitive eliciting of associations through creative interviewing thus become an essential aspect of understanding meanings in children's art as they speak through the metaphor (DVD 7.3).

In considering the nature and degree of distortion or disguise, one may look at whether the child's productions are abstract or representational; if figurative, whether realistic or fantastic. Even within these categories it is usually possible to assess the degree of disguise in the kind of representations of self and others employed.

One can probably assume that a child who says "me" through an open self-representation, or even a child of the same age and sex, is using less disguise than one whose self-representation is of a different age or sex, or seems to be an animal, a fantasy creature, or an inanimate object or abstraction. Even the latter, as noted earlier, may become a stepping-stone for projection.

Attitude toward the Product

Whether children are able, in response to questioning, to make connections between themselves and their creations is an index of their capacity for introspection and reflection, of their "observing ego." Especially during the post-creative interviewing phase of the session, a child's ability to step back, look at, and reflect upon process and product is an index of the readiness to use an insight-oriented approach in therapeutic work.

An art product, the form of which has been given to unstructured media by its creator, often feels like a part or extension of the self. Perhaps this is also related to the fact that in an art session, children are symbolically fed with materials, which they then digest with hands or tools, and which finally emerge as their own unique creations, analogous to body products. The sense of ownership and identification varies, but is always present, so that children's feelings about the quality of their products reflects to some extent feelings about themselves, especially their competence (DVD 7.4).

How children feel about their artwork therefore is very useful diagnostically, especially in regard to self-image and self-esteem (7.4A). This is evident in their facial expressions and how they handle the artwork, as well as in any comments they might make about it (7.4B). For many children, especially when they are younger and less likely to be critical of their work, what they produce can be a source of great pride (7.4C).

A satisfied grin is evidence of a good feeling about themselves as well as their art (DVD 7.5). A teenager in a wheelchair working on a sculpture was very proud, calling it a "Beautiful Pot," and recalling how much his grandmother had admired his claywork (7.5A).

In a therapeutic program with multiply-handicapped blind children, a number of them were quite delighted with what they were able to make, which comes through in the film *We'll Show You What We're Gonna Do!* Among those who had discovered that they could make things that they and others admired was partially sighted Greg, who boasted "I can draw things that you can actually see!" (7.5B). Another was totally blind Carl, who was pleased with his wood scrap constructions despite his disabilities (7.5C). Peter loved his art, and gave beautiful titles to his paintings and sculptures, elaborating as he did so his poetic fantasies (see DVD 15.7E).

On the other hand, youngsters referred for therapy often have negative feelings about themselves, reflected in their reaction to their artwork. Many express concern about their skills, like Evan: "I'm no artist. I goofed up already. I got this picture all screwed up . . . I really goofed it, boy! It ain't too good!" Many speak of others whom they perceive as more skillful: "My art teacher can draw better than me. I'd like to be able to draw that well." Or, "I'm a *bad* artist. I'm not as good as my brother. He's a *real* artist!"

Others deal with such feelings of inadequacy by defensively bragging, like Ellen (7.5D), or Jim, who behaved uncertainly, then boasted about his art in school: "I got five paintings up on the wall. *She* thinks they are masterpieces. I did all five paintings in one period, and she wanted them *all* on the board!"

While direct expressions of concern or inadequacy are common in most cases, especially with older children, the degree and intensity as well as the modifiability of these self-assessments are clues to the child's feelings of self-esteem. Some literally destroy what they make as they proceed, identifying it as "no good" or "messed up." During an assessment interview, this is extremely valuable data, and therefore rarely to be interfered with.

However, if the child is so discouraged that they want to tear up and throw away everything, it sometimes seems best for the art therapist to "rescue" something, explaining that she would like to keep the artwork, even if the artist doesn't, with (of course) their permission. The reason for this is that you will be conveying an important message about therapy, which may eventually help them to accept other things about themselves of which they're ashamed. If the child is adamant, but the art seems like an important statement, I confess I have occasionally picked something out of the wastebasket after the child has left, and stored it in a secure location for my own reference.

In addition to the child's response to the task and to the materials, therefore, the art therapist looks at whether the predominant attitude toward the products is one of shame, pride, disgust, pleasure, or ambivalence. As with most things one tries to ascertain in an assessment session, nonverbal communications are at least as significant as those that are put into words.

As described in Chapter 6, a major component of an art assessment, sometimes during and almost always after artwork has been created, is what comes out of the interview about the product(s). Both nonverbal and verbal responses are relevant, and the child's verbal associations are especially useful in trying to learn as much as possible. In addition to the responses themselves, the child's reaction to being interviewed provides useful data. Is he or she exhibitionistic, secretive, hesitant, eager, and so on?

Making Sense

The manner in which the child approaches and structures the hour, plus what is produced and how, add up to a rich storehouse of data that may then be fitted together, like the pieces of a puzzle, to make diagnostic sense. Wolff (1946, p. 113) has articulated the fundamental task facing a clinician following such an interview: "If we have a sequence of [products] and a sequence of associations, our analysis starts in searching for a common denominator to which each element can be related; then, by combining and inter-relating all the elements with each other, we may reconstruct the sentence which was spoken by the child's inner personality in the language of pictured associations."

When the encounter with the child is over, therefore, the assessment is far from done. One then looks over the material for pervasive themes, for patterns, and for interrelationships among all the behavioral and symbolic sources of data. Sometimes one primary theme clearly pervades the hour, being repeated over and over, often with increasing intensity and lessening disguise. At other times several key themes emerge, usually interrelated, one often being the wishful or fearful response to the other.

The different sources of data interrelate and function as checks and balances for one another. Whether what is *said* is synchronous or dissynchronous with what is simultaneously *done* may provide important clues. A child may be tight with words, tight in the body, and tight in their drawings as well. Nonverbal behavior often underlines or confirms what is being said symbolically and/or verbally. The ultimate task for the art therapist is to integrate and interrelate all of the many data sources into some comprehensible notions about the child.

While many kinds of information can be gleaned from an art interview, it is particularly helpful in assessing a child's major concerns and conflicts, their primary coping patterns and defense mechanisms, and their developmental level. The thematic material conveyed through products and behavior may be most relevant in identifying what the child is concerned about, while themes, plus disguise and self-awareness regarding the artwork, are all helpful in defining major defenses (A. Freud, 1936).

Certainly, a child's way of approaching the task and the process are clues to his or her manner of coping in general. Their developmental level, as indicated earlier, is particularly apparent in the formal aspects of the work, for which fairly reliable norms exist (especially in drawing), as well as in the developmental aspects of the core conflicts and major defenses represented (Erikson, 1950; A. Freud, 1965; Levick, 1983).

One area—perhaps less apparent in other diagnostic procedures—is the child's creativity, a capacity made up of various ego functions, including the ability to regress in the service thereof. One thinks not only of originality, but also of flexibility, fluency, and the ability to create order out of unstructured media, especially to create something which conveys an emotional impact, to "give form to feeling" (Langer, 1953).

Another question that is often explicit in an art interview in a treatment setting is whether the child can successfully use this approach in therapy, and if so, how. It is possible that it may be seen as too disorganizing or stimulating, and will therefore be rejected as an option. Or, if it is seen as desirable, it may be suggested primarily for building integrative capacities and self-esteem, rather than as a way of uncovering and establishing insight about unconscious impulses.

It is my own conviction that art is flexible and broad enough that it can be used in different ways by different children, according to their needs. It has been my experience that such individual use rarely needs to be prescribed by others, but will usually emerge quite naturally, as children's own tendencies toward health and integration lead them to use the materials in accord with their own capacities and needs of the moment.

Reporting

Before writing a report, it is helpful to read whatever else is in the child's record, in order to see how the findings from the art evaluation relate to what is known about the youngster. Nevertheless, in writing the report, the art therapist does best to focus on the behaviors and art products from the session itself, continually supporting any formulations with the data that were observed. This not only buttresses your contentions, but also serves to educate others about what can be learned from an art interview. If there is a meeting with others involved in assessment, the artwork itself is extremely important data, and should always be presented. If the information is to be conveyed in writing, it is best to photograph and/or scan the art, including it in the report.

Many art therapists have asked for guidance in how to organize the material from a diagnostic art interview for presentation as a report. I regret not being able to provide a single outline format that is appropriate for all settings, but my own experience has been that the material needs to be organized differently in different contexts; the only principle which makes sense is to try as best you can to answer the questions of those making the referral. In other words, while all of the aspects noted in this chapter are legitimate sources of data and ought to be taken into account in any judgment, there is no single best way to organize a report.

I have experimented with many structures, each designed to meet the needs of a particular setting and staff. It usually makes sense, for example, to emphasize developmental and cognitive factors in an educational situation, and to highlight psychodynamic ones in a psychiatric setting. In either case, it is important to take into account the level of sophistication of the reader(s) of your report, and to try as much as possible to use language which will have meaning for them.

CHAPTER

8

Some Case Studies

While the process of therapy in and through art generally follows the steps outlined in Chapter 4, the precise shape and form is always peculiar, idiosyncratic, and one of the great fascinations of such work. Although goals for and hypotheses about the troubles of a child can be thought out in advance, one can only guess at the particular way in which any youngster will actually use the opportunity for help.

As with development itself, the rhythm of growth and change in treatment varies considerably, and usually cannot be rushed. One must expect not only forward but backward movement as well; not only openness, but also retreat and withdrawal. Sometimes things go smoothly overall, and sometimes they are rocky from the very beginning; generally, there is some of each.

When things get so murky that the therapist feels at an impasse, it is extremely helpful to seek consultation, no matter how many years of experience one may have under one's professional belt. Indeed, it may be an index of maturity to be able to perceive difficulties, acknowledge them, and even to transfer the case—if that seems the best solution, after exploring the roots of the problem.

The degree of success or failure with any particular child is hard, if not impossible, to quantify. When treatment terminates through mutual agreement, one hopes that the child will then be able to go on growing and coping—not that all problems will be gone forever. I was once invited to participate on a panel about "learning from failures in art therapy." I was grateful, for it gave me an opportunity to review for myself, as well as for others, a case which had felt most painful to me at its closure and during most of the work. In reviewing I not only relived the experience, but was able to see, for the first time, that perhaps the failure had not been a total one after all. Since we tend to hear mostly about successes, I think it would be helpful to look at failures as well, as in the case of Ellen.

Ellen: An Elective Mute

What was perhaps most poignant about this failed encounter of two human beings was that it began with a promise of progress, and only gradually became increasingly and consistently painful. We started out, this almost-thirteen elective mute and I, on what seemed like a hopeful note. I knew from the record that in her two initial contacts at the clinic she had not only refused to come into the building, but had turned her silent back on the psychiatrist who had tried to interview her in a parked car. I knew that at the Children's Hospital where she had been sent for observation for the next month, she had talked to no one, had refused to return home upon discharge, and had finally been placed with her grandmother, one of the few people with whom she was still speaking.

I also knew that her hurt, anger, and withdrawal were longstanding, and that she had not spoken to those closest to her for almost two years—first her deaf older sister, then her alcoholic mother, then her father, and most recently her best friends. Though this brilliant girl was still talking to a few friends, her four younger siblings, and her grandmother, she had closed the door to her world on her parents and sister for a very long time.

Knowing her history of rejecting therapists, I was pleasantly surprised when Ellen willingly separated from her grandmother and accompanied me to the office. I was further delighted when she picked up some clay, manipulated it while standing with her back to me, and then sat down at the end of the table facing me. She then proceeded to draw a series of carefully elaborated, tight, complex designs. Between the second and third drawings, she moved her chair a little closer to mine, although she remained tense and silent throughout.

Our first crisis came unexpectedly, when it was time to end. As Ellen picked up her drawings, I asked if she would leave them at the clinic—indicating that she, like the other individuals I see, could have a shelf on which to safely store her creations. I find it useful to save the artwork for the duration of the therapy, and most children acquiesce when assured that they can have anything they want once therapy is finished. When a child is determined to take something home, I ask if I can keep it for a week, in order to make a slide, or—if the urgency is too great—we can photocopy it. In response to my request, Ellen angrily blurted out her first and only words: "You didn't *tell* me!" Then, still visibly upset, she refused the idea of a copy and departed, clutching her drawings tightly to her (DVD 8.1).

So I was relieved when, the following week and thereafter, she not only did not indicate any desire to take her artwork home, but willingly came, and moved within the next hour from a tight checkerboard design to a shield, then to more figurative work—first a lighthouse on a cliff over water, then a pitcher with a cocktail glass, and finally, a looser, more colorful tree, with a warming sun above (8.1A).

Softly, but clearly, she responded with short phrases or single words to my questions about the picture; that she would be swimming near the light-house, but if given the choice, she'd prefer to be near the sun-drenched tree. The pitcher and glass were said to contain tea she would have made, but would not drink. A guitar, drawn last on the other side of the paper, was said to remind her of a friend who plays one. There was a stylistic move-ment from tightness to slightly greater freedom, and a symbolic sequence from isolation to implied possibilities for warmth as well as relationship. These, along with her willingness to answer my questions, albeit mini-mally, filled me with hope for the future of our work together.

And so it went the following week, when, although turning her back to me as she worked, she produced first a painting of a girl playing ball near the street (8.1B), then a headless figure on the other side, to which a head was quickly added by taping a torn corner of the paper above the neck (8.1C). Despite the continued rigidity and tension of her posture and movements, she was indeed using more fluid and more messy media (tem-pera paint and chalk) than the thin markers she had chosen previously.

Probably excited by what seemed to be a loosening on her part, and stimulated by a dance therapist friend who was using mirroring with au-tistic children (Adler, 1970), I impulsively suggested that we do a dyadic drawing. I was thrilled that she was willing to engage with me in this exer-cise. She picked up a blue marker, so I chose to differentiate our lines using red, and attempted to mirror her rhythm and movements and to echo her swirly shapes (8.1D). Though Ellen didn't want to discuss the joint process, she had been intensely involved throughout, and there was a strong feeling of communion.

The following week I painted a picture of her at work (8.1E), in an at-tempt to continue the pictorial dialogue of the preceding session. Mean-while, she drew with markers a girl in brightly colored clothes, then a fat balding man on a stage, with a road in the distance (8.1F). Still respond-ing softly to my questions, she identified the girl as young, going shopping, and not wanting to get married. The man was said to be about 40, carrying an oil can because his car was stalled on the road behind him. She said he was sad, and that he would speak loudly if he were to talk. On the other side of the paper, she drew in the corner a drag race with three differently shaped cars (8.1G). She would be driving the middle one, but did not know if she would win.

The following session was the last prior to an interruption for my vacation, which was to last for 3 weeks. I had told her about my absence the week before, and reminded her at the beginning of the session as well, though she did not visibly respond. Although she was still quiet, and sat with her back at an angle to me, Ellen for the first time filled up a picture space with a single and colorful representation, a stylized female bird (8.1H). The bird was later identified as mean, with few friends, married to a nice kid who's ugly but rich, who has gone to the store to buy provisions. This was followed by a scene of two swans swimming in the sea by a cliff, freer and warmer than her first one (8.1I). And finally, a cartoonish pirate with eyepatch, whom she later described as weak now, having formerly been strong, but having been injured in a sword fight because of his big head (Figure 8.1).

The interruption became a very long 6 weeks, due to scheduling problems in the fall because of changes in her school schedule and transportation difficulties. In retrospect it seems to me that the break may have been more damaging than at first it appeared. Nevertheless, the first session in the fall did not seem to be any cause for alarm. I apologized for my part in the unexpectedly long interruption, and asked if she was distressed by it. She didn't respond, but instead began to draw (Figure 8.2). Beginning with several tight, geometric, linear designs, Ellen continued on the same paper with a fishbowl, a horse's head, then a tree, then a geometric flowerpot, and finally the three creatures in the center, the last with an angry tongue sticking out of a twisted mouth.

I noted with relief that her posture while drawing these latter images seemed more relaxed. She later told me that all three images were female, that the one on the left was older, the one in the middle was younger, and the one on the right was very angry. Asked who she might be in the drawing, she pointed to the fish in the bowl, and then to the horse.

Triumphant at the emergence of aggressive affect and provocative symbolism, I looked forward confidently to progress in the approaching months. Only gradually did I realize that we were grinding to a halt. At her next session Ellen drew, carefully and with absorption, an enlargement of the odd cephalopod of the preceding week (Figure 8.3).

In response to her focus on this strange character, I decided to use watercolors myself, in an attempt to echo the expression of feelings as well as to stimulate the use of other media. I painted an ambiguously sad-angry girl

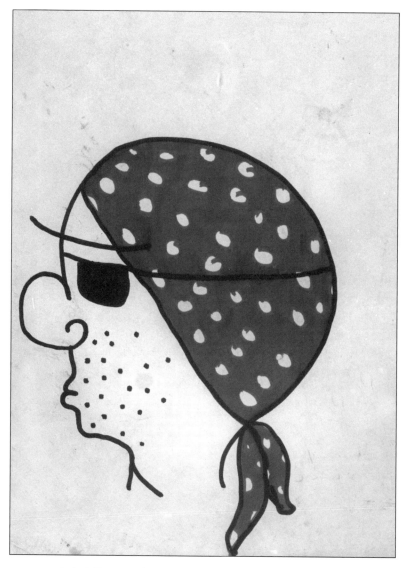

8.1 A Pirate with an Eye Patch, by Ellen. Age 12. Marker

with long nose and prominent eyes, similar to but different from Ellen's creature (8.1J). She called hers a girl who was both happy and sad, and said, about the one I had drawn, that the girl was "sick because she's going to the doctor [who will make her] worse and sicker." She was clearly afraid of this process she had begun, but how frightened I did not yet realize.

Despite my most cautious and conscientious efforts to empathize with her anxieties, to accept whatever she was capable of doing, the process

8.2 *Ellen's First Drawing after a 6-week Interruption. Marker*

from then on was like a stuck phonograph needle. Once in a while, more often in the early months, there would be variations on her single theme—the face divided, the use of different colors, a different treatment of the hair or a shell around the multiply determined body-face.

But Ellen's back turned more and more to me, and though I occasionally

8.3 Ellen's First Enlargement of Her "Creature," 1 Week Later

drew, to contain my own anxiety and frustration as much as anything else, she had tightly shut the door on me. The soft verbalizations to questions disappeared, head-nodding followed for a while, and then my questions, which felt too much like tooth-pulling to me, were discontinued—in favor of silence and my wondering, thinking aloud about what was going on—along with an unspoken hope that she would initiate contact if not pressed.

As the same figure continued to be drawn week after week, and Ellen seemed more and more frozen, I felt more and more helpless—fully a failure, where I had once hoped to be a savior. Week after week—through October, November, and the succeeding winter months—the same tight, silent girl came in, worked for a full hour on her generally-same drawing with only minor variations (8.1K)—and left, when I indicated that the time was up.

I sought consultation from everyone and anyone. They were full of ideas, as was I, about the possible symbolic meanings of her repetitive pictorial statement (8.1L), and were equally full of ideas about how to help her give up her defensive withdrawal. Some suggested being totally quiet, some suggested playing music. Both were tried, for about a month each, with little observable effect.

Frequently I felt like reaching out and touching this frozen girl, yet I always stopped short. In response to suggestions that I interpret directly and openly, all else having failed, I stepped up my comments about mid-February, and it did seem that she was listening, though she did not respond overtly.

In mid-March, though her therapy-hour behavior and drawing had not changed, her grandmother brought in a book Ellen had made, called *From Isolation to Involvement*. This volume, with photographs and poetic text, seemed to be a statement of an intention on her part to move back toward relating to others. Many phrases in the text sounded familiar, like things I had said to her in recent sessions, and I brightened at the thought that perhaps after all there was some positive effect. Ellen continued, however, to draw the same rigid creature (8.1M), to face me with her back, to avoid eye contact, and to shut me out as much as possible in our remaining sessions, which turned out to be five in number.

The last session, in late April, began like all the others—with the making of the same strange figure (8.1N). But at one point in her drawing Ellen stopped, as if immobilized, appearing more openly fearful than usual. Welling up with anguish for her aloneness, I first spoke of, then acted on an impulse to put my hand on her shoulder. It was close to the end of the hour. She did not respond in any observable way, remained tense and frozen, then went on with the picture—and left at the end, walking out more rapidly than usual.

She went back to her grandmother's and, for the first time in almost a year, telephoned her mother. The purpose of the call was to tell her that she did not want to come to the clinic any more, "Because I don't like Mrs. Rubin." A note I sent her the following week remained unopened, though apparently kept, and she returned no more. But she proceeded then to gradually return to her home, first for weekends, then, in a few months, for good. According to her mother, contacted 2½ years later, she returned home warmer and more open than ever in the past, and became a truly solid member of the family, as well as an academic success and a cheerleader in high school.

Despite the family's pleasure at the eventual outcome I felt extremely discouraged, and more like a failure as a therapist than ever before. Because I was so deeply distressed, I was forced to cope, to deal actively with the experience. Fortunately, I was in psychoanalysis during the time I worked with Ellen, and was able to spend many hours on the couch exploring the feelings and fantasies stimulated in me by this difficult, rejecting youngster.

I probably learned the most from probing my countertransference reactions, my exaggerated and distorted responses to her—which stemmed primarily from my own unresolved conflicts. Not only was she thus helpful to me in my personal analytic work; the awareness of how my reactions affected my behavior as her therapist ultimately led to more appropriate interventions with others.

This painful sense of bewilderment as a therapist led to yet another significant kind of learning. What I discovered was that my attempts to find answers from *outside* (as from consultants), were less fruitful in some ways than my efforts to find answers from *inside*—the analytic work on how and why I was responding as I did. I therefore learned that in a situation of puzzlement as a clinician, to look externally for help is only part of the task; to look internally for understanding is equally essential.

Dorothy: A Child with Schizophrenia

Many years ago I worked with Dorothy, a seriously disturbed brain-damaged girl suffering from some loss of vision and hearing, and from childhood schizophrenia. Adjunctive art therapy sessions were made available to Dorothy, as they were to all 10 children on her residential treatment unit. She came every week from November through March for a total of 24 sessions, and usually stayed for about an hour.

At first, her teacher having introduced me as an "art teacher," Dorothy wanted and expected some instruction. Rather quickly, however, she accepted the open-ended nature of the sessions, soon overcame her quiet reserve and initial disappointment, and began to relate in a warm and trusting way. Although she could speak she did so rarely, since her speech was so distorted that it was very hard to understand. She was an articulate draughtsman, however, and from the first was able to express her fantasies and ideas clearly through pencil and paintbrush (DVD 8.2).

During her first three sessions, Dorothy concentrated on the drawing (8.2A) and painting (8.2B) of birds (8.2C), an animal she often pretended to *be*, making birdlike noises and flapping movements with her arms. She seemed stuck on a rather compulsive and careful way of doing this repetitive subject (8.2D), always drawing the birds first in pencil (Figure 8.4).

So, during the fourth session, after her attempt to paint a large bird with tempera, with some frustration due to the lack of small brushes, I suggested that Dorothy try just using the paints without planning in advance. She

8.4 One of Dorothy's Many Bird Drawings. Age 10. Pencil and tempera

did so, and became quite excited and delighted at her new freedom, literally dancing and yelping with glee as she let loose, slopping on one bright color after another. When finished with her first such effort (8.2E), she asked for the largest size of paper (18" × 24") and announced, with some excitement, "I'll make a monster!" She did a rather fanciful and colorful painting of a multilimbed creature (8.2F), and followed this by saying, "I want to make another monster," this time first drawing a birdlike creature saying "Growl!"

The following week Dorothy began with one of her old careful birds, an eagle, first drawn and then painted. She then drew at the right what she

8.5 Dorothy's Pencil Drawing of a Destructive Eagle and Its Victim

later called a "dummy," a crayon figure of a boy with strings like a mari-
onette, standing on a ladder, with his arm in the eagle's mouth (8.2G). "I
want to do another one!" she said, after naming the first "The Dummy and
the Eagle." Her second drawing (Figure 8.5), in pencil, is an even more
graphic picture of the destructive effects of the eagle's rage. The figure
(called both "man" and "dummy") has a chewed-off arm, eyes that are
bandaged, and has been violently hurt. A narrator at the upper left ex-
plains: "Egles. Egles are mad. They want to kill man and eat them."

Perhaps for the first time, the aggressive aspects of Dorothy's bird fantasy
were clarified for those who worked with her—maybe for Dorothy, too.
The following week, emphasizing the flight aspects, she drew a saucy bird,
then covered it over with dark paint, repeating, "Go home!" a commonly
verbalized wish. A girl was then drawn in a cage (the hospital ward as she
experienced it?), saying, "Boo hoo!" with a large monster creature at the
right saying, "Ha ha!"

This was followed by the drawing and painting of a large and a small
bird, along with arm-flapping and repeated rhythmic chanting of the
words, "Go home! Go home! Go home!" Her final product in this emo-
tion-filled session was a rather lovely, carefully painted, large and majestic
bird (8.2H).

At her ninth session Dorothy shifted gears in her imagery, and began a long period of representing the children on the ward, first in rows, later involved in typical activities (8.2I). Her perception of them was so accurate that it was possible for anyone who knew them to identify the figures (8.2J). These drawings were done mostly in marker, along with much verbalization about the children and her relationship to them (8.2K). This subject matter occupied her for the next 6 weeks, with increasing action and drama in the pictures (8.2L). While she was always careful to include each of the others, she never drew herself. In the last one, I asked where Dorothy was, and with a grin she pointed to the bird flying overhead (8.2M).

At her 15th session, Dorothy again shifted symbols, carefully drawing a pictorial list of clothes, later identifying them as all belonging to the youngest child on the unit, a boy of 5 of whom she was jealous. She said she wished she had clothes as pretty as his, and that hers were so ugly. The following week the clothes were drawn first, followed by a picture of an older boy and the younger one, in which the older one has thrown away the little one's doll and he is crying—perhaps her jealous wish as well as her empathic fear (8.2N).

In the next session Dorothy began her "cat phase" (8.2O), and for 7 weeks made pictorial catalogs of cats (8.2P), pictures of cat families (Figure 8.6) and of her fantasy-wish of wearing a cat costume (8.2Q)—a bit more realistic than actually becoming a bird (8.2R). At her 23rd session, the next to the last we were to have, she drew a picture of the young boy and many articles of his clothing, afterward circling those which she also possessed. She was talking much more by then, having improved considerably in intelligibility through intensive speech therapy, and had many questions about "endings."

At the last session, we reviewed the artwork in her folder, a useful way to help a child to get closure. She was very interested, studying the pictures closely, saying little. The most potent images, those dealing openly with hostility, were passed over rapidly, and the greatest amount of time was spent looking at those of the children on the ward.

She looked longingly at her portrait of the "Tortoise Shell Family" (Figure 8.6), remarking that the mommy and daddy weren't there; though previously she had identified the larger ones as parents, saying that the cats want to cuddle up to people. No doubt the perceived loss of parents was related to the impending loss of her art times and art therapist, to whom she had grown attached (8.2S). She did one more drawing of clothing, an item or two belonging to each boy on the ward, then put her arms around me, saying, "I like you," and said a rather clingy goodbye.

Dorothy's therapy was to end prematurely, not because she was ready,

148

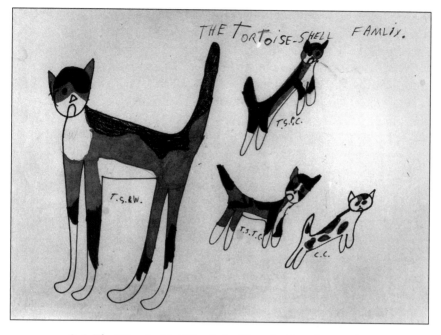

8.6 The "Tortoise Shell Family" of Cats, by Dorothy. Marker

but because I was pregnant (8.2T), and in the early 1960s you couldn't teach or work in a child psychiatric unit for long after a pregnancy was visible. Though she was not able to express her anger at me then for leaving her, when I visited the craft class on the ward a month later, she showed me a drawing of "Mrs. Rubin Attacked for Being Bad" (8.2U).

The experience with Dorothy, as with all the children on that unit, was a powerful one. At the time I had no previous experience in a clinical setting, and was just beginning to read about art and child therapy. I was fearful, cautious, and generally nondirective, except for setting and maintaining reasonable limits. I read the literature on artwork by children who were psychotic, and discovered that Dorothy's use of animal symbols and perseveration of themes were not uncommon (Despert, 1938), and that her productivity, including the speed and fluidity of her work, had also been noted (Montague, 1951).

Perhaps, as some suggest, Dorothy's art was a device used to maintain contact with reality, and her pictures of the children were a way of drawing a map of the world in order to find her place in it. Certainly, even in my naïveté, I could see that there was considerable value in this experience for this child. The opportunity to draw her fantasies and to explore the world in pictures seemed to afford her some relief from inner pressures. Perhaps it was a way of orienting herself and structuring reality, as well as a way of externalizing her fearsome fantasies.

While some worried that Dorothy was using art as an escape, I felt that art became a place for her to feel good because of her competence, to experience some sensory and playful pleasure, and to find her way back to reality through her fantasies, by airing rather than burying them. When I presented her work to Professor Erik Erikson (1950, 1959) at a Grand Rounds in 1964, he felt that art therapy had helped immensely.

Randy: A Boy with Encopresis

A different sequence was found in the art work of Randy, a 12-year-old encopretic from the same ward. Very bright, also diagnosed as schizophrenic, Randy was much more verbal and articulate than Dorothy; superficially more in touch with reality, but inwardly unsure of the distinction between reality and fantasy (DVD 8.3).

In the course of 23 weekly art sessions, Randy began with a variety of fairly realistic topics, using a range of drawing media, working in a casual, rather sloppy way. He drew (8.3A) and painted zebras (8.3B), rockets, school (8.3C), fireworks, an explosive Civil War scene (8.3D), food, rainbows, a series of underwater and cave scenes, and a series of concentric designs (8.3E).

At his seventh session Randy announced that he didn't want to paint that day, although it was usually his first choice. Instead, he drew a picture of outer space, with a red planet (Mars) and yellow pieces—bits of stars which have exploded (8.3F). Some he called "constellations," specifically "the King" and "the Queen."

This drawing led to his decision to create a book, "Our Trip Through Outer Space" on which he worked steadily for the next five sessions, producing a series of pictures about a Martian and the art therapist (me) in outer space (8.3G). During the next four sessions, Randy drew and painted a variety of other topics, generally more realistic, including a castle (8.3H), an ocean scene, a jungle picture, "Darkness in a Mysterious Cave," a painting of his school on fire (8.3I), his "enemies" at school (those who tease him), and a dinosaur near a volcano (8.3J).

At the 17th session he returned to the space series and made a cover (8.3K), including the "new earth," myself with "one of the newest space hairdos," my "old pal, the Martian," and Randy wearing "the newest style in space suits." At his next session he painted an imaginative landscape of the Sierra Nevadas, with "an ice-capped mountain." The following week he initiated another long stretch on the book project, devoting the next four sessions to an "earth series," similar to his space series, but literally more "down to earth" (8.3L).

His oedipal wishes for some kind of romantic relationship with me became clearer in this less-distant and less-disguised sequence. In his drawing of our visit to Egypt (the Martian having dropped out of the story early in the "earth series"), he drew me in fancy clothes, wearing a see-through dress and a fancy hairdo, while he, having dug in the earth for buried treasure, gives me a gift of gems (Figure 8.7). In his picture of Scotland his amorous wishes were even more apparent; he drew himself as an adult-looking Scotsman holding onto my belt so that I "won't trip," and looking very much as though he has me in tow, under his firm control (Figure 8.8).

Randy, like Dorothy, spent his last session reviewing his artwork in sequence, often expressing surprise at things he'd forgotten (suppressed) since doing them. Best-recalled and most-liked were the two series, in which the work had generally been his most careful and best organized. As he reviewed the drawings, his most frequent remarks were to admire the clothes or hairdos he had designed for me.

His final picture was of a woman on the edge of a cliff in the Philippines

8.7 Randy Giving the Art Therapist a Gift. Age 10. Marker

8.8 Randy Holding On to the Art Therapist with a Belt. Marker

(8.3M), for which he made up the following (oedipal) story in the review session: "A sailor from the *Bounty* was trying to kiss one of the island girls, and she backed off and fell down the mountainside, and then there was a war. The island girls fought the men and the men fought the sailors and the sailors fought the island girls. Everyone fought everyone!" I wondered why the island girl had backed away from the sailor, and he replied, "She backed off because she already had a boy friend." His very last drawing, done in the 10 remaining minutes of the session, was, rather appropriately, a battle scene: "The Revolutionary War."

Conclusion

Randy and Dorothy were both schizophrenic, which means that they were very sick children, who lived in a confused world where reality and fantasy were often hard to disentangle. Most children learn to tell the difference between real and make-believe in the course of their early pretend play, gradually developing the ability to discriminate.

Nevertheless, many children have problems in the course of their growing up, sometimes caused by worries and fantasies, wishes and fears, that live within and are kept alive; in part through staying buried—another way of thinking of repression—keeping things out of consciousness. These hidden feelings may also have hidden consequences, so that the youngster becomes inhibited in learning or play through a generalized kind of restriction, which is motivated by a vague sort of anxiety, the causes of which are often not known to the child or to others. One of the tasks of treatment is helping someone to express and articulate those hidden wishes and fears, so that they may then be faced, dealt with, and seen as different from reality.

In the course of art therapy vague, unfocused, and fuzzy images and ideas often become more articulate and clear. When Alschuler and Hattwick (1969, pp. 140–141) compared preschoolers' easel paintings and dramatic play, they concluded that the themes were more explicit in drama, and "that easel painting may be of particular value for expressing generalized emotions, conflicts, and difficulties which are at a non-verbal, non-overt level, i.e., for expressing felt tensions rather than problems and conflicts that have crystallized at the conscious level."

Looking at children's use of easel painting and the similarly unstructured medium of clay, they found that "both media seem to stimulate children to symbolical expression of feelings which they are either not ready or not able to express in more articulate fashion" (1969, p. 137). Even when an idea is beginning to get close to consciousness, it frequently is expressed in art long before it is talked about. "Children, particularly, nibble at communicating ideas graphically and symbolically before entering into the more open verbal arena" (Hammer, 1958, p. 582). Children (and adults) find some things difficult if not impossible to put into words, even with conscious awareness.

I once had the opportunity to work with a young child and her mother, in tandem with a child psychiatric resident. The doctor would see the mother, while I saw the child, for 45 minutes; we would then exchange clients for the same period of time. At our weekly collaborative meetings about the two, my colleague soon dubbed the artwork a *"preview of coming attractions,"* since what was expressed symbolically to me in art was likely to be verbalized to him within the next few weeks. In long-term work with children and parents, individually as well as in families and groups, this phenomenon has been repeated over and over. Even when verbal expressive modalities like drama are part of the treatment, concerns are most often expressed first in art.

Randy's two series, on space and on earth travel, gave him an acceptable and organized framework within which he could explore and symbolically gratify his curiosity and his sexual fantasies regarding his female therapist, who probably symbolized his mother. (He also saw a male psychiatrist for individual and family therapy.)

While it was necessary for Dorothy to loosen up with a free painting experience in order to look at her feared fantasies, Randy needed to get himself together in order to depict his wishful ones. His early work was sloppy, often diffuse, while his work on the series was both thematically and aesthetically more organized.

Different children clearly have different needs, in order to get to a point at which they experience a safe *framework for freedom*. Given support and acceptance, they often provide for such needs on their own, as did Randy. My suggestion to Dorothy, that she try painting without drawing first, was a deliberate intervention. Despite the artificial time limit for the treatment, both children were able to use art therapy to make visible progress. Similarly, Andrew, who had set a fire at his residential school, was successfully treated by British art therapist Roger Arguile (DVD 8.4).

The following chapter describes the treatment over time of one boy, which began with an individual art evaluation. Based on that session and interviews with his mother, he attended a children's art therapy group that also had periodic mother-child art sessions (Chapter 12). This was followed by a family art evaluation (Chapter 10), and then a year of conjoint family art therapy (Chapter 11). In the story of Tim, therefore, you will not only hear about another case; you will also be introduced to procedures that will be described in considerably more detail in the following section of the book: "The Family and the Group."

9

Case Illustration
Understanding and Helping

W hile many clinical illustrations are used throughout this book, it may help to take a relatively long look at one child, and how he and his family were understood and helped through art. The child's name was Tim; his family was educated (both parents had been to college), and was financially comfortable. Tim's primary problem, and the one for which his family had initially sought help, was stuttering.

Tim had been taken to a university speech clinic when he was 5½ by his mother, who stated that he had "had trouble with the beginning syllables of some words and stuttered . . . since he first started speaking." She labeled his problem as "average to moderately severe." Tim was seen at the speech clinic for six sessions and two reevaluations. His parents were seen for several counseling meetings.

Later, he and his mother were referred to the child guidance center for a mother-child art therapy group that was then about to begin. In making the referral, the speech pathologist described Tim's problem as "one of dysfluency which is effortless, and inconsistent over time with . . . no immediate need . . . to receive direct speech therapy."

The clinician stated that Tim was being referred primarily because he was "an anxious youngster, highly dependent upon adult approbation, and reluctant to make decisions on his own." It was implied that the art therapy group would enable Tim to become freer and more independent. It was also suggested in the referral that the proposed occasional mother-child art sessions would be helpful: "It would be to their mutual advantage to engage together in some enjoyable activity without the interference of Tim's intrusive and highly verbal four-year-old sister."

Tim was ultimately seen at the child guidance center over a span of 2½ years, first in the art therapy group with periodic mother-child sessions, and later in conjoint family art therapy. Critical to our understanding of his problems were an initial individual art evaluation, joint mother-child sessions in a group, and a later family art evaluation involving his parents and sister.

Individual Art Evaluation

During his initial 1-hour art evaluation, Tim gave a glimpse of some of his major concerns and ways of dealing with them (DVD 9.1). He was at first hesitant in choosing materials, and finally solved the dilemma by eagerly collecting as many different types of drawing media as he could fit on the table. He was careful to use some of each, making sure that marker tops were put back on immediately, frequently running to the sink to wash his hands.

He had a hard time deciding what to draw, and made a persistent effort to get me to give him a topic. Assured that I understood how hard it was, but that I was certain he could think of something if we could be patient, he finally said he would like to draw a dinosaur. Unable to settle on a theme any more comfortably than on a medium, he soon switched to a monster or Frankenstein. All of these must have been a bit too threatening, however, for he finally chose to make a crane (Figure 9.1).

It is interesting that the form of his crane resembles the shape of a dinosaur—his first idea—and even has "teeth" at the end of a long, thin, extension. The crane was said, while he drew, to have dug a U-shaped hole in the ground; a symbol (hole) which was to appear again in Tim's work. In this case it was quickly filled in, as if to leave it open might entail some risk.

In one of the windows of the house-like crane is the face of a 3-year-old girl, close to the age of his sister. Since the girl is said to be operating or running the crane, with its possibly phallic extension, one wonders if Tim has represented here his feeling that his sister was "running" him. It became quite clear, even in that first hour, that Tim perceived his younger sister as more powerful than himself. He entitled the picture "The Runed (ruined) Work" (9.1A).

He next chose to paint at the easel, selecting the longest-handled (most phallic) brush. Again, he was unable to select from among the array of choices, and took all of the available colors to the easel tray. He began by outlining a square house with a peach flesh-like tone, then drawing two triangular (breast-shaped) roofs, symmetrically placed on either side of the top. He was, as he had been when drawing, quite deliberate and care-

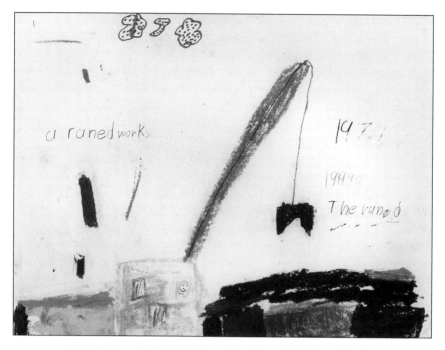

9.1 "A Runed Work" (a Crane), by Tim. Age 5. Mixed media

ful, and painted over the outline of the house several times. He referred to the tempera paint as "temper" paint, and each of the many times he went to the sink to wash, jokingly called the paint on his hands "my temper problem."

Indeed, his unconscious equation of uncontrolled aggression (temper) and regression with fluid media (tempera), became even clearer as he went on with the painting. Though he began by filling in the outlines of the house carefully, he soon started to mix colors within the thick walls, eventually holding his long brush with both hands, and twirling it rhythmically.

While he had been mildly dysfluent and rather tense initially, he seemed to relax both physically and verbally during this regressive mixing and twirling. He covered what he called his "mess" of colors with white paint at the end, saying firmly, "White solves the problem." He finished his hour by manipulating a piece of clay, labeling his painting "The Dinosaur Picture" (9.1B), and telling the following story: "It started at the beginning of time, and there was a big hurricane came, and it blowed down the dinosaur house, and that was the end of the dinosaur."

Thus, considering both the process of his work and the form and content of his products, Tim in his initial interview not only showed how he could relax and become almost fully fluent using an expressive medium; he also outlined some of his primary concerns and ways of coping.

He indicated that his sister represented a powerful threat to his autonomy and potency. He showed that he felt not only weak but dependent and vulnerable, demonstrating a need for help in getting started, and for protection in the form of thick walls (the house), compulsive care (his use of every color and frequent handwashing), and perhaps phallic weapons (choosing the longest, thickest brush).

He hinted at oral-dependent needs and wishes in his "hunger" for materials and advice, as well as oral-aggressive impulses in the dangerous "teeth" of the crane. The hole dug by the teeth had to be quickly filled in, just as the regressive mess in the dinosaur house had to be painted over with white, as if some form of defensive "whitewashing" could solve "the temper problem." He seemed to be expressing behaviorally and symbolically his anxiety that, if he could not contain his messy, angry impulses (especially toward females), he might, like the dinosaur house, get "blown up."

Group Art Therapy

On the basis of this first interview, group art therapy did indeed seem to be an appropriate form of treatment for this constricted child, who needed to move in the direction of greater independence and freedom at his own pace, with peer role models and neutral adults to assist him. The nice thing about art therapy groups for children is that timid ones can be emboldened by children whose controls are less rigid; while the latter can see and emulate models of organization in the former. As it turned out, the art therapy group (of children ages 5 and 6, with a male cotherapist) was very helpful to Tim (DVD 9.2).

When anxious in the group, his symbolic defenses were similar to those hinted at in the diagnostic session. He made numerous thickly bounded, well-defended fortresslike sculptures of clay and wood scraps (Figure 9.2), as well as similar paintings. Often what was inside (the hole or opening) would be prominent, as in his clay "caves" (9.2A).

Tim would sometimes compulsively cover over a whole sheet of paper with chalk (9.2B) or paint, as if his fear of loss of control had been translated into a fear of emptiness or of open spaces and holes. Similarly, he would, when unhappy, sit alone and draw repetitive abstract designs, charts (9.2C), numbers, or checkerboards, or would compulsively cut out small squares of paper.

Such occasions, however, were as rare in the group as the times when he actually stuttered. By and large, Tim was able to move from a timid, watch-

9.2 A House by Tim, Done in Group. Age 5. Wood scraps and glue

ing position to an active one in a short period of time (9.2D). He soon became fluently expressive of ideas, feelings, and speech. He utilized the opportunities in the group to try out regression, aggression, and progression in both interactional and symbolic behavior, using both the two leaders (parent figures) and the other children (surrogate siblings) as well as the art media.

He gained support from the other children, especially those who were more free. With them he safely regressed, mixing "gooshy" finger paint (9.2E) and playing at being a baby. He risked aggression, with ugly paintings of me as a witch, and attacked the male therapist with vigor in several dramas. He risked frightening activities, like being pushed high on a tire swing (9.2F), and worked on cooperative and competitive products with the other children. Most often, Tim's self-portraits done in the group were strong and adequate, just as he was trying out his potency in behavioral and symbolic ways (9.2G).

Parenthetically, it seems clear that the group provided not only materials, but safety, permission, support, stimulation, and protection. A child like Tim might have taken much longer to loosen up in individual art therapy, though this is not an easy thing to predict. There is no question, however, that the group helped him, especially one other boy who was as loose as Tim was tight. It was a lovely "therapeutic alliance" in that both derived mutual benefit from the friendship, each learning from the other the freedom or control he needed (9.2H).

Joint Mother-Child Art Sessions

The first joint art session of the children's and mothers' groups (which met during the same time period) was held following 6 weeks of separate group sessions. It was designed for diagnostic purposes as open-ended, so we could just watch and see how each pair would behave, to learn more about each dyad and how to help them (DVD 9.3).

Tim began by proudly making, then showing his mother, a smeary painting on an oversized piece of paper (9.3A). His mother then did her own huge abstract painting. Tim began to follow her, slavishly imitating her next drawing (9.3B) in medium, color, and style (9.3C), and became noticeably more subdued than at the beginning of the session.

He then drew a second picture of a 3-year-old girl operating an immense crane (9.3D). The girl was immediately identified by his mother as his sister, who was said to be more assertive than Tim. He selected his large smeary painting (9.3A) as the one to share at the end with the group, and called it "The Sun Blowing Up." He explained that the sun blew up "because the moon was in the way of the sun, and the moon touched the sun." When asked what sex they might be, he stated firmly that the sun would be a boy and the moon a girl, and that the story would be the same. This competitive theme was repeated in a puppet drama several weeks later, in which a younger sister kills her older brother, and is so powerful that even lions can't contain her.

During the second joint session attended by Tim and his mother, our goals were still primarily diagnostic in terms of each mother-child dyad, but the approach was structured around authority and control. It was suggested that one member of each dyad direct (or "boss") the other in doing a work of art. Tim directed his mother in a rather structured drawing of a road with cars and houses on either side (9.3E). She often added items he was not specifying, such as lines on the sidewalk, apparently not submitting to his control. Although their second effort also began with Tim bossing her, he became frustrated by his mother's unwillingness to follow his directions accurately, and took over the drawing himself (9.3F). She then assumed the boss role, and instructed him for the remainder of the drawing.

The last joint session of the art therapy group was open-ended. Tim and his mother chose to work jointly on a drawing with some sense of uncertainty about who was in charge. They then created a wood scrap construction on a common base (9.3G). Tim made a garage with diagonal walls, much like his fortresses, while his mother created a tall structure alongside his diagonal barriers (9.3H).

Tim was a member of the children's art therapy group, which met weekly for 1½ hours for 14 months. He attended quite regularly and participated intensively. Despite clear, positive gains, evident in group, at home, and at school—in personality, self-concept, and social skills, the dysfluency continued to be of concern to Tim's parents, though it was highly variable, practically nonexistent in group, and was not heard at home for long periods.

Because of his parents' continuing emphasis on and anxiety about his symptom, and based upon evidence in Tim's artwork, dramatic play, and the joint sessions with his mother, a family art evaluation was conducted, involving both parents, Tim, and his younger sister.

Family Art Evaluation

During this 2-hour session, which was conducted according to the format described in Chapter 10, some hypotheses about the family dynamics and interaction were confirmed (DVD 9.4). Mother emerged as dissatisfied, describing her dull life situation in her scribble drawing, entitled "Basket for Boredom Blues" (9.4A). Father revealed his possible identity conflicts in a scribble drawing of a "Kabuki Actor" (9.4B).

During the second task the family literally spread out all over the room, each one working independently (9.4C). Tim's sister's picture of the family consisted of one member: "Mommy Going to a Party all Dressed Up" (9.4D). Tim had difficulty with this task, made several false starts (9.4E), was quite self-critical, and finally drew "Me and Daddy Playing Ball" (9.4F). Both parents also represented the family in dyads. Mother drew herself with Tim and her husband with her daughter as partners in a square dance (9.4G), while Father drew two sets of parent pairs and child pairs (9.4H). No one showed the whole group interacting as a unit.

While deciding on the topic for their third task, the joint mural, Tim made suggestions which were agreed to, but then not followed. In the execution of the mural, it was not clear which parent was in charge, though there was a sense that the control had shifted from father to mother. Family members stood side by side as they worked on the wall, occasionally working in parent-child pairs, but most often independently (9.4I). While the joint mural represented the seashore where they had shared an enjoyable family vacation (9.4J), the sense of togetherness about which they reminisced was absent from the room during the 2-hour session. When interactions occurred, they were primarily dyadic and generally competitive, no matter who was involved.

It seemed to myself and Dr. Magnussen,[1] who conducted the session with me, that because of Tim's father's own insecurity, he was not consistently able to provide an effective role model for his son. The females were dominant, the males interacting with them in a conflicted manner. Tim seemed to bear the brunt of the negative attention in the family, being critically teased by both sister and parents, thus effectively absorbing and neutralizing areas of conflict between the adults. Both parents were bright and articulate, able to rationalize effectively. They reacted strongly and perceptively to some things they felt they discovered about themselves and the family through the art session.

Combining impressions from this session with additional data from a history-taking interview by a psychiatrist with Tim's mother, the assessment team became further convinced that the persistence of his symptom was rooted in its function within the family system. In a diagnostic conference, the team felt it was necessary to induce change, which would permit both the family and the child to give up the stuttering.

Conjoint family art therapy was recommended for additional reasons. First, it was necessary to work with the entire family unit in order to shift the focus of concern from Tim's speech to the intrafamilial dysfunction. Second, it was decided to utilize a modality which had a chance of cutting through the very adequate verbal defenses of all members, especially the parents. It was because of the evidence gathered during the evaluation session, as well as the fact that the family liked it and found it both fun and thought-provoking, that conjoint family art therapy was the treatment modality finally recommended. Indeed, it was both appealing and appropriate for this group.

Family Art Therapy

The family came for weekly conjoint art therapy for a total of 32 sessions, half lasting 1 hour, half 1½ hours. In the course of this work, through the use of art and discussion, the family's definition of the problem, as well

---

[1] Max Magnussen, PhD, was Chief of Child Psychology at the clinic, and was the person with whom I had developed the Family Art Evaluation (FAE) described in the next chapter. We had visited the National Institutes of Mental Health (NIMH), consulted with the creator of the FAE, Hanna Kwiatkowska and her colleagues, and had then developed a format that worked in our center.

as their attention, shifted from Tim's speech to his personality, to his sister's personality, to marital difficulties, and eventually to individual problems of both parents (DVD 9.5).

Tim's artwork during the year of family art therapy was sometimes an indicator of the internal changes that were slowly taking place. His formal pictorial defenses, such as covering-over or compulsively numbering and organizing, continued to come into play when he was anxious, particularly about competition and aggression. At first his sister, even in her abstract work, was more intense in color and tone than he. As time wore on, however, he became the leader and she the follower. He drew birthday cakes for her (9.5A) at her request, showing her the "right" way to do it (9.5B), and she was grateful.

Tim continued to mess and regress when anxious or angry, though less often in the family than he had in group. His interest in holes and in openings persisted, but he was increasingly able to leave them open and to explore beginnings and endings, as in a maze. At the end of the year, he proudly made a completely open, undefended clay "Fort" (9.5C) and a "Pool Table" (9.5D), discussing with pleasure how the balls fall into the holes. His houses also had more windows (9.5E), suggesting that his feelings and curiosity had been freed to function in a more normal way.

Although his projected images of himself in the group had usually been strong, Tim was often criticized and pressured to achieve more in the family, and was frequently dominated by one of the other members. It is thus not surprising that he sometimes drew himself, at least in the first 6 months, as vulnerable to rejection or injury, in pictures showing: himself alone in the rain (9.5F), a faceless boy about to crash on a sled (9.5G), a snowman who Tim said might melt in the sun (9.5H), a creature yelling, "Help!" and perhaps most poignant, a boy with no mouth, holding on to a pet snake, whose tail he decided needed to be further extended after the drawing was finished (Figure 9.3).

Conversely, both his sister and his mother usually pictured themselves as central figures, usually pretty and desirable, often rich and brilliant, always powerful (9.5I). In a spontaneous family puppet drama, which happened during one session, mother was the star, "The Beautiful Gisela" (9.5J), over whom there was a struggle between two men, "Handsome Harry" (handsome but poor) and "Dopey" (9.5K), (dumb but rich). Mother often pictured her own dilemma in the family sessions as lack of fulfillment, with occasional pictorial implications that there was no way out.

Although Tim had gradually expressed anger more and more freely in the group, aggression was slow to be expressed directly in the family context. Tim's picture of his sister's "Tummy" (9.5L), with an aggressive arrow

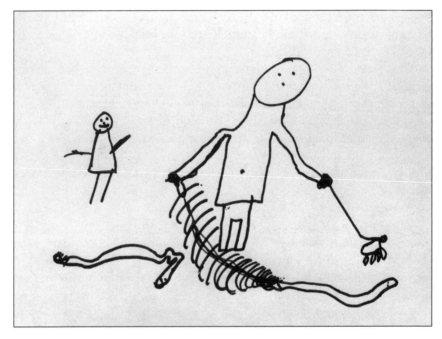

9.3 A Boy Holding On to a Pet Snake, by Tim. Age 6. Marker

pointing at it, was done in the family art evaluation; her drawing of him punching her in the stomach 6 months later (9.5M), and his own representation of a dyadic aggressive interchange, 3 months after that.

Two months later, Tim drew a series of 15 "Meanies" (9.5N); most of them represented his own rage, and a few seemed to be symbolic attacks aimed at other family members. He drew "Meanies" furiously, then drew a "Fire-Breathing Dinosaur" (Figure 9.4), and finally proceeded to verbalize his anger, for the first time shouting assertively in the family, as he had done in the group, "You don't care! You just don't respect me like I respect you!"

His frequent representations of himself and his father in dyadic relationships, while at times competitive, were usually mutually supportive. Indeed, the two males needed to stop competing and start helping one another, in order to gain equal status with the females in the family. Tim's picture of "Me and Dad Playing Tennis" on one side of the paper, with "Mom Divin' Down" (9.5O) on the other, was a graphic statement of such a wish. His drawing of two serpent-like phallic dinosaurs about to destroy a house drawn by his mother suggested a similar impulse to achieve dominance (9.5P).

As with individuals, it often seems that families develop a preferred symbolic idiom, which may communicate complex ideas within the group

9.4 A Fire-Breathing Dinosaur, by Tim. Age 6. Marker

in a condensed and emotionally loaded manner (DVD 9.6). Some *family themes and symbols* became evident with Tim's family, both in free drawings and in those suggested by myself and Dr. Magnussen, who worked with them as co-therapists.

One such symbol was the house or "home." In the second month of family sessions, Tim carefully drew four houses (9.6A), similar to a configuration done previously in a joint session by his mother (see DVD 9.3E). One month later, his house drawing had many windows, and he drew a "Motel" with two pointed towers and even more openings (9.6B). His mother drew a picture of the family outside the new house they were hoping to buy (9.6C). There was a shared fantasy that this house would be the antidote to family tensions; an idealized memory treasured by both parents was of a "perfect family" they had once met, whose home was "a haven from the world's pressures."

All of the pictures drawn in response to two themes suggested in the early weeks of treatment took place inside the home. The first topic was "the Main Problem in the Family that you Would like to Work on." Father drew mother abandoning him with the two screaming kids at the supper table, complaining that, "She never joins us" (9.6D). Mother, meanwhile, drew him reading while the kids argue and she wearily does the dishes, begging him to intervene in the fight between the children (9.6E). Not seeing the other's drawing until it was completed, each was astounded at the similarity between their feelings of abandonment and resentment. They were then able to be more understanding of each other, rather than so defensive.

Another shared, wished-for romantic solution was to be "somewhere else." Father's solution to family problems was a drawing of the group walking in a line in an idyllic autumn forest setting (9.6F). In addition to the group mural of the seashore done in the family evaluation, Tim had done a free construction of "Me and Dad on the Boat Vacation" (9.6G), and there was much talk about how good things had been when they had all gone away together.

In response to a suggestion several months later to "Draw Things the Way you Wish they Were," mother made a picture in which a maid is cooking a meal in the kitchen, while she and her husband have a drink on the sofa, romantically planning a trip to Africa, as she thanks him for the beautiful flowers he has sent her. The children are notably absent (9.6H).

Father, however, had a very different wishful image. In his picture, his wife is happily cooking the meal, both children at her side; on the other side of his drawing she is sending him to work with a kiss, while the angelic youngsters (complete with halos) wave goodbye from their windows (9.6I). Their conflicting images of perfection and their mutual dissatisfaction were poignantly evident in these drawings, and became an increasingly open topic of discussion.

Before father left on a trip, he drew himself calling home from overseas, complaining that no one ever answered his letters, and that they had even argued on the telephone the last time he had called from far away (9.6J). A month later mother drew about her loneliness while he was gone (9.6K); but when father returned, 2 weeks later, he drew himself on a lounge chair "on the beach" with two unidentified companions, ruefully labeled as him with "two ladies" by mother (9.6L). Three months later, the adults' mutual feelings of hurt became such an intense focus of their discussion that the children, no longer involved in or playing out the parental battle, worked quietly and cooperatively, producing some impressive joint constructions (9.6M).

Two other interesting family symbols in their art were the roller coaster and the seesaw, each appearing on some group and individual drawings. The *roller coaster* was a symbol for the excitement and thrill of activity, and of a scary sense of helplessness, with an attempt at mastery (9.6N). The family lifestyle was indeed rushed and hectic, and anxiety-provoking to Tim in particular. His natural tempo was slow and deliberate, quite out of synch with that of the other members.

The *seesaw* symbol was most useful to us in dealing with the theme of competition (9.6O). As with a roller coaster, it is possible to be up or down, but not both simultaneously. As with so many images of the family by all members, the functional unit is a competitive dyad—one wins while the other loses, one must be down in order for the other to be up. Somehow, the notion of a balance position had rarely occurred to them, as both mother and father needed so badly to achieve, to get what they deserved, and not to be in a submissive, helpless position.

Tim's sister could be quite aggressive, identifying alternately with her mother and father. Tim, on the other hand, with his slow, deliberate pace, was left out of the family rush, and usually lost the family competitive game. They all needed a loser, someone who was down on the seesaw, and that was Tim. His main defense in the family was often to move away from the circle, to work alone, quietly and self-sufficiently, in sharp contrast to the dependency seen in his initial interview.

Most of the sessions were conducted in a free-choice fashion, with a variety of materials and working surfaces available. Occasionally, however, we would find ourselves suggesting working in a particular way or on a theme, as described earlier. While such structured approaches were rare, they were usually stimulated by our feeling that the family was just on the edge of some awareness that we could help to illuminate through a creative intervention.

Joint Nonverbal Drawing

One day, frustrated by how cleverly and effectively the adult family members could intellectualize, we suggested that they try to work together on the same sheet of paper (18″ × 24″) without talking (DVD 9.7). They drew silently for a surprising 45 minutes, each using different amounts of space, mother moving around and eventually drawing in everyone's area. Tim began by drawing a house in the center, but was soon surrounded tightly on both sides, and left to work alone with clay at another table (9.7A). He tried to get his father to join him, and his father did so for a while (9.7B), but then rejoined the females, still at work on the nonverbal group drawing (9.7C).

When all were seated, discussing the picture, which was most useful in helping mother to perceive and acknowledge her intrusiveness, Tim felt safe enough to go up to the drawing and add some more details to his house (9.7D). While working with the clay, he had dug a very large hole for what he called a "Bank," something strong in which he could safely store and protect what was valuable to him (9.7E).

During one of the last few family sessions, Tim created a clay pool table with open holes (see DVD 9.5D), and his first open fort (see DVD 9.5E), after many closed-in structures. While his parents had refocused on the boy's dysfluency at a point of tension in their marital relationship, and had suggested another speech evaluation, they had finally decided not to do that. When the adults began to deal seriously with their interpersonal difficulties, Tim's speech noticeably improved, as did his mood, and particularly his ability to relate productively to other family members.

The last two sessions were devoted to *evaluation*, in which parents and children reviewed the art and the therapy; the consensus was that there had been positive changes within the family. Our final meeting was with the parents alone, in which they first spoke with pride of the improvement in their children, particularly Tim.

They then turned to each other, and plunged into the most open and intense confrontation we had seen in the clinic. Each angrily identified the other as "needing psychiatric help." In spite of such anxiety-provoking attacks, it was clear that they were ready to deal with both marital and individual issues. Each was more open to the idea of therapy for themselves, and it was our recommendation that they seek help, as individuals and/or as a couple. Perhaps most important, the spotlight was no longer on Tim's almost-absent *symptom*, but rather now on the family *system*, resulting largely from work through the *symbol*-art.

Tim's speech behavior in the course of his work at the clinic, in the group and with his family, had changed from stuttering to fluency. A follow-up contact a year after termination revealed that Tim had not stuttered for the past 6 months. Stuttering for Tim may have been an indirect means of expressing anger, of fighting back—"talking back" to his parents. Although his parents wished to eliminate this annoying symptom, this was not possible without changes—both in Tim and in the family system. Family art therapy made it possible to focus on the conflicts within and between all members, and allowed Tim space and support to compete openly and to be verbally aggressive without fear of losing or of punishment. Such work would not be possible without the involvement, investment, and sincere hard work of everyone in the pleasurable/painful task of family art therapy.

During high school Tim returned for some individual sessions, in which he used clay and told me how he felt close to stuttering when anxious, usually before a test. We talked about cognitive strategies he could use at such times, which he later reported worked well. My next contact with him was informal, when he was a successful college student.

Over the years since then I've often run into his parents. At such times I have heard about his sister's academic success, and about Tim's two advanced degrees, his successful professional career, his wife, and his happy life. Both parents, still happily married, credit the family's experience at the clinic as having had a positive impact on everyone. Of course, I would like to believe the same.

PART III

THE FAMILY
AND THE GROUP

A Family Art Evaluation

Young children are realistically dependent on the adults who care for them. They are still "becoming" as human beings in interaction with those adults. It is, therefore, especially important in working with children to know about, and sometimes to work with, their families. As Joan Phillips said so eloquently in her review for this 25th anniversary edition, "the family is the crucible for the developing child."

Even if the primary mode of treatment is individual, it is often helpful at the beginning or in the middle of the process to meet with the entire family, as in Tim's therapy, which was only partially successful until the family was involved. In getting to know other members, and in understanding how they relate to one another, the *family art evaluation* has proved extremely useful, and has been a diagnostic option at the Western Psychiatric Institute & Clinic, and before that at the Pittsburgh Child Guidance Center, since 1970.

I was inspired by the pioneering work of others with families (Kwiatkowska, 1962, 1967, 1978) but found it necessary to develop a session appropriate to the needs and capacities of our young clinic population and their parents. I was also fortunate to have the interest and support of the Chief of Clinical Child Psychology (Max Magnussen, PhD), who collaborated in the design, development, and implementation of the technique, as well as on the paper on which this chapter is based (Rubin & Magnussen, 1974).[1]

---

[1] Since the last edition, others have described additional ways of evaluating families through art that are inventive and clinically useful (cf. Landgarten, 1987; Linesch, 1993; Riley & Malchiodi, 2004; Sobol & Williams, 2001).

We tried various formats, including an open-ended one like the individual art interview described earlier. We found, however, that such an approach is more threatening to families, especially for the older members, perhaps because people were exposing themselves to one another as well as to a therapist. Lack of structure also seemed less fruitful in getting the kind of data wanted, that is, how individuals in a family perceive and relate to one another. After experimentation with many possible tasks and sequences, we arrived at a series of three, best done in a 2-hour time span (though possible in less), which seemed most productive under most circumstances.

We usually conducted these sessions in a large group room that had a large round table, two smaller tables, two easels, a supply table, and a big wall for the mural. However, that is the ideal, which is rarely found, and the setting can be any space big enough for all family members to be able to draw separately and together. In my private office, there were no choices of where to work in my small playroom, yet many families went through the sequence (often in less time with fewer media options), and we were still able to learn a great deal in a short time (DVD 10.1).

The whole family may be seen at any point in the diagnostic evaluation or during treatment. Although shorter time periods are feasible, 2 hours is a comfortable span of time for most families. It seems best to invite all members of the family living at home to attend if that is possible, with the exception of infants and toddlers who could not realistically participate. Three- and 4-year-olds who are able to sit still and use art media, however, have often been involved. The only exception to the format for a child at a pre-figurative level is that the projection of an image onto a scribble is not possible (see Task 1). It is no problem, however, for a youngster to "scribble" a free drawing.

I prefer to have minimal information about the family prior to the evaluation, and feel that this enables me to be more free and objective in my observations. As noted earlier, I find the same to be true with the individual art interview, though reading the record after the session can help to put initial diagnostic hunches in perspective.

Format

Through experimentation with possible modifications, Dr. Magnussen and I arrived at the following sequence of tasks (DVD 10.2):

Individual picture from a scribble

Seated around a table (circular is ideal), each member chooses from the drawing tools in the center (colored pencils, craypas, markers, pastels) and on the small (9″ × 12″) white drawing paper, draws a continuous line scribble with eyes open or closed, whichever is preferred (10.2A).

When finished, they are encouraged to examine their scribbles from all possible points of view, in order to see pictures in them. Each is encouraged to select one or more images, elaborating them into a picture to which they then give a title (10.2B).

When all are done, they take turns placing their developed scribble drawings on the easel or wall, the creator of the picture first describing it. The others are then invited to respond. The artist, as the expert on their own creation, is encouraged to react to their comments and to answer any questions they might ask (10.2C).

Family portraits

Each individual is asked to create an abstract or realistic portrait of the family in two or three dimensions. All are shown the range of media available (any of the following: drawing materials as in Task 1, watercolors, tempera markers and paints, plasticine, clay, wood scraps, glue, assorted sizes and colors of construction paper). When there are options, potential work spaces are pointed out, and each person is encouraged to work wherever they wish (see DVD 2.4H).

When everyone has completed a representation of the family, the works are taped on the wall or placed on the table so that all portraits are simultaneously visible. Members first react spontaneously to the array of renditions, each person eventually being asked to describe their work, the others commenting and questioning as they wish.

Joint mural

The family is asked to create something together on a large (3′ × 6′) paper taped on the wall, using thick poster chalks. It is suggested that they first decide together what they will do, and then work on the paper.

Like the other tasks, this can be done differently. The important part is planning and then working together, so the picture can be done on 18″ × 24″ paper on a table as well. When the mural is finished, all look at it and are encouraged to discuss the group experience, as well as the product which emerged.

Free products

If anyone completes either of the first two tasks before all members are done, they are encouraged to create art products using any medium and topic.

Whether referred by someone else or invited by the art therapist, even with prior preparation, most family members, especially adolescents and adults, are apt to be self-conscious about their lack of ability in art. As they first enter and are seated around the table, an attempt is made to explain the purpose and nature of the interview, which is for the therapist and the family to learn more about them as individuals and as a group.

They are invited to ask any questions and to express any concerns they may have before beginning. Exploring aloud such worries, anxieties, and confusions as may exist is often essential, and always helpful in overcoming normal resistances to exposure. It is emphasized that artistic skill is irrelevant, that individuals are encouraged to explain and explore the meanings of what they produce, and that the evaluation is meant to be a learning experience for both family and clinicians.

People are naturally fearful of being seen through, of exposing something to others of which they themselves may not be aware. While there is some justification for this anxiety, it is my sincere belief that the meaning of anyone's symbol must ultimately depend on their own associations to it, and that the expert in the interpretation of anyone's artwork must be the person who did it, at least as much as the observer. Ideally, understanding of meanings emerges out of a joint consideration of the work and associations thereto. It is, therefore, possible to present the session to the family as a collaborative undertaking.

Prior to the termination of the interview the family is encouraged to explore any concerns, questions, or issues that may have arisen in the course of the session. Questions such as, "How was this experience for you?" "What happened that you did not expect?" or, "How typical or atypical was your family today?" are helpful for engaging members in the learning process. Most families, in fact, do find a way to use the session as a means of self-understanding, something which I have now observed for 30 years.

Despite early concerns on the part of colleagues about the threatening possibilities of a family art evaluation, my experience is that most families can handle the session quite comfortably. The atmosphere typically becomes increasingly informal and relaxed during the session. My impression is that this is due in part to the opportunity for selection of an ego-syntonic medium, style, and location during the second task. In addition, the presence of younger children in many families is an asset to their more self-conscious parents and older siblings, for they tend to enjoy the procedure, often request more such sessions, and clearly help the others by their natural, spontaneous behavior.

Scribble Drawing

The sequence of tasks is designed to provide a maximum of information about individual and family characteristics with minimal stress. Thus, the making of a *scribble* as the first task puts the non-artist at ease, despite the fact that it is a powerful assessment tool. Sitting together around a table is conducive to informal communication among family members, and since the paper is provided at each seat, the only choice required is the drawing medium. The scribble technique is drawn from previous work in education (Cane, 1951), therapy (Naumburg, 1966), and diagnosis with both individuals (Ulman, 1965; DVD 10.2D) and families (Kwiatkowska, 1967).

The request to develop a picture from an image or images perceived in a scribble presents each family member with the task of structuring their own self-created, ambiguous stimulus. Like the Rorschach, the projective content and associations are idiosyncratically valid, as are the formal aspects of how the person performs the task.

Further projective and interactional data on each individual is available as they respond to other members' drawings during the doing and discussion phases. For example, one thinks of a 6 year old's response to his mother's picture of "A Smiling Doggie," "Maybe they chopped his tail off!" Who sits next to whom, who interacts with whom, and the nature of the interaction all provide further useful data.

Mrs. I., for example, was at first unable to see anything in her line, but when encouraged to look again, finally said it reminded her of "a Barbed Wire Fence, like in a concentration camp" (10.2E). She thus let us know how she felt about being cooped up alone with five active children, and perhaps about the art evaluation itself, during which her youngsters were getting quite rambunctious as she sat passive, helpless to control them.

Mr. F. at first said that his scribble drawing "might as well be a Bum as a Clown," but finally entitled it "Clown," emphasizing the lighthearted elements (Figure 10.1). He thus suggested some ambivalence in his self-image, and reinforced our impression that he used humor as a defense against strong feelings, especially of depression.

Carl and Carol I., 8-year-old twins, each saw monsters in their scribbles. Carl, the initial referral, said his monster (10.2F) was a boy of 6 who was "stupid, eating everything, eating people. People call him names like big-head or stupid." Carol described hers as a girl monster (10.2G) who "likes to go and eat people's guts and eat people when they bother her sometimes." The disorganization of her drawing, its oral aggression, and her critical attacks on others' pictures led to her being seen as a patient at the clinic, as well as her brother.

Family Representations

The second task requires not only the production of a family portrait, a very common procedure, but also provides a free choice of materials and working location (DVD 10.3). The *Abstract Family Portrait* described by Kwiatkowska (1967) is suggested as an alternative possibility (10.3A), and no specific instructions are given beyond the initial request to create the family using any media.

10.1 Mr. F.'s Scribble Drawing: A Bum or a Clown. Chalk

The products range from static to active, from heads (10.3B) to full, realistic drawings or paintings, or sculptures of clay or wood scraps (10.3C). It is not unusual for diagnostically significant omissions, condensations, and elaborations to occur; nor is it infrequent that an individual will create a second representation of the family in another medium, often revealing even more than the first.

In addition to the possible projective significance of such factors as sequence of figures drawn, relative size, and position, there are additional data concerning family relationships, from the way in which the members position themselves in the room and interact spontaneously in the course of this second task. For example, Mr. and Mrs. F. and their 16-year-old biological daughter stayed together, verbally interacting, at the round table at which they had developed their scribbles. The two adopted youngsters, Jack (10.3D) and Jody—the 11-year-old identified patient—each isolated him- or herself at separate tables away from the trio and worked silently at the task (Figure 10.2). As with the scribble drawings, much is also learned from responses to others' productions, as well as from each individual's projected image of the family.

Mr. F. said he was "trying to get a feeling of closeness" (10.3E). Actually, he drew himself, his wife, and his two biological children in a tight group, then subtly isolated his two adopted children (Jack and Jody). They are placed slightly apart from the others and were drawn last, even though he had said that he drew the family "in the order of the ages of the children."

Jack, Mr. F.'s 8-year-old adopted son, chose for his family picture to represent only his baby brother in their shared bedroom, describing himself as "outside trying to get in" (10.3F). Further evidence of sibling rivalry was found in his response to his mother's family drawing (10.3G). He said with irritation that her picture of the baby, not physically but psychologically present during the evaluation, was "too big!"

Mrs. F. said she drew the family "holding hands—a happy, close family." Her picture helped to confirm our feeling that Jody and Jack were being subtly excluded from the family circle, or at least put on the periphery. A similar impression was gained from Mr. F.'s family drawing, Jack's family portrait, and the way in which the members positioned themselves during the second task. Though both parents denied conflicts within the family, these signs suggested that the task of emotionally including the two adopted children had not yet been fully accomplished.

During the second task, the range of media available makes it possible to observe individual styles and modes of decision-making and working. Flexibility or rigidity of response to such possible variables as the running together of watercolor paints can also be observed. Not only may the indi-

10.2 F. Family Creating Family Portraits

vidual's selection and handling of the medium be significant, but equally revealing are the responses of other family members, as when a mother becomes upset at a child's messing with finger paint or clay.

The discussion period is at least as valuable as the working time, and can be introduced in a variety of ways. Family members can be invited to look at all of the representations together (10.3H), and to respond in an unstructured way as they compare them (10.3I). They can also take turns presenting their images to each other, inviting the reactions of the rest of the family (10.3J); and a combination of the two is feasible as well.

Family Mural

The last procedure requires the family to make (sometimes to abdicate) a joint decision and implement it, in regard to a common task (DVD 10.4).

10.3 F. Family Working on Their Dinosaur Mural. Poster chalk

In format it is not unlike other group mural techniques, and as a group task it is related to the joint projects used by others in family art evaluations (10.4A). In the open-ended, free-choice decision-making around content, with not even a beginning like a scribble or a topic to focus upon, individually significant themes quickly emerge, as does the family's habitual problem-solving strategy. It seems that the degree and kind of organization in the final product reflect the family's ability to function as a unit, though they don't necessarily experience the process as comfortable (10.4B).

The manner in which members participate in both the decision-making and the execution phases of this task (10.4C) gives further evidence of family characteristics and interaction patterns (10.4D). In the open-ended discussion following the group task, further information is gathered, such as who the members felt to be in charge, how typical the interaction seemed, and so on (10.4E).

The F. family considered several options and was able, with little friction, to come to a joint decision to draw a dinosaur (Figure 10.3). Although 8-year-old Jack did not participate initially, annoyed that his idea had not been chosen, he finally joined the others, who were working together smoothly, efficiently, and with evident pleasure in the joint endeavor. The bright, playful fantasy and overall organization of the mural reflect the imaginative strengths and cohesive potential of the family that created it (10.4F).

The I. family, however, unable to engage in any group discussion prior to drawing, impulsively began to work independently and somewhat competitively, as reflected in the scribbled attacks on several portions (10.4G). A shared sense of family identity and wishes may be reflected in the common theme (houses), while the disorganization and confusion apparent throughout the hectic, 2-hour session are mirrored in the disjointed, isolated, patchwork quality of the family's joint effort.

Free Products

Free products, though not assigned, usually occur for at least one or more individuals for the simple reason that people work at different speeds (DVD 10.5). It is not surprising that Tim, whose story you read in the last chapter, sent out a cry for "Help" in a free drawing done during the Family Art Evaluation (10.5A).

A crayon drawing by Glen, done while the others were finishing family portraits, was also a graphic appeal for "help"—the word shouted by the boy in the parachute who is being shot at from below by an older boy in a dragster (10.5B). Glen, age 6, attempted to both emulate and challenge his older brother throughout the session, while his mother effectively withdrew from any kind of interaction with either boy. He seemed to feel unprotected and vulnerable, and the story about his drawing was that the two therapists would rescue the parachuting boy, clearly a projection of himself.

Mrs. Y. was tense, constricted, and withdrawn throughout the Family Art Evaluation; her pictures were tight, compulsive, and unelaborated, her verbalization sparse. Her drawing of a teepee (Figure 10.4), made while waiting for the others to finish family portraits, was somewhat looser than her other products. Her association was that the Indian inside was sending smoke signals, asking for help for an unspecified problem, much as she herself, hiding behind an anxious silence, was mutely asking for assistance at the clinic.

Making Sense

To illustrate the procedure of putting together the various sources of data, it may help to look again at the F. family. Both parents thought they had successfully handled their own feelings regarding their two adopted youngsters, and had integrated them into the family unit.

10.4 Mrs. Y.'s Teepee. Free Drawing. Marker

However, there was ample evidence of the children's subtle exclusion: their vocal concern that their artwork would not be acceptable to their parents, their sitting apart from the others during the second task, Jack drawing the family as consisting only of the baby shown as displacing him from his bedroom, father's unconscious sequencing and placement of figures in his family drawing, and mother's placement of the two adoptees on the edges of the group in her family portrait. Although the referral had been made because of Jody's underachievement and possible learning disability, it was clear that her position in the family could well be one source of her problem, and that intervention efforts needed to involve the whole group (see Betts, 2003).

Characteristics

Like any assessment involving the whole family, an art session provides an opportunity for direct observation of their interaction. Like any activity approach to family evaluation, the art session provides an event in the present that can be observed as it occurs, and can be a focus for discussion in the group. Because more than one person is active at one time, multiple observational opportunities are also available.

And, in common with any assessment using art and nonverbal communication, defenses are frequently bypassed. As in group art therapy, communication through shared focus on products is often easier for family members in regard to each other, as well as the clinicians. A Family Puppet Interview is perhaps the most similar of other activity assessments with families, because of its projective qualities (Irwin & Malloy, 1975).

There seems to be no question that "the family art evaluation session gives an unusually rich amount of information with a minimal expenditure of the family's and the therapist's time" (Kwiatkowska, 1967, p. 54). Those who have systematically compared family art evaluations with verbal family interviews have consistently noted the additional understandings obtained through art (Kwiatkowska, 1967, 1978).

Since this interview was adjunctive to the more traditional diagnostic procedures of the early 1970s at our clinic—multiple interviews, psychological testing, and reviewing patient records—it was possible to informally compare and contrast the findings from it with those of other assessment approaches. On a small sample of cases Dr. Magnussen and I tried to arrive at diagnostic formulations, independent of other approaches to the same family within the Center. We were surprised and pleased at how similar were our findings.

A family art evaluation elicits a number of different kinds of diagnostic data, which provide a built-in system of checks and balances for assessment. In the course of the three tasks and discussions, one observes a great deal of behavior—verbal and nonverbal, independent and interactional—on the part of each individual family member. There is much symbolic data in the products produced—in their form, content, process, and style of execution—and in associations to them by each individual, to his own works and to those of others.

By systematically varying the specificity and degree of choice (in topic, medium, location) inherent in each task, as well as the degree of closeness or interaction necessary for its completion, it is possible to gather extensive data on individual as well as family dynamics. Because there is so much activity to be observed, it is helpful (though not essential) to have two clinicians involved, just as it is helpful to make videotape recordings whenever possible.

One advantage of the combination of multiple sources of data is the possibility of finding degrees of commonality. For example, if symbolic art content parallels observed behavior, the diagnostic impression is reinforced. To verify or refute such an impression the interviewer(s) might point out to the family the consistency or inconsistency of their findings, to get further reactions from them. In this way, the family is involved directly and openly in determining the significance of their productions, interactions, and verbalizations. The family can actively assist in analyzing the data, interpreting it, and rejecting or accepting the therapists' impressions.

When Dr. Magnussen and I first developed our family art evaluation we were surprised at the amount of resistance among our colleagues. Despite our assurances that Kwiatkowska's pioneering work at NIMH had resulted in the routine use of a similar tool there, many expressed concern and uneasiness, though often interest as well. It naturally takes time for clinicians to become familiar with and to utilize a new technique. With an increasing emphasis on family approaches to diagnosis and therapy, the popularity of art-centered family tasks grew steadily after they were first introduced.

It is my feeling that the clinician's own comfort in presenting and conducting such an interview is the primary factor in the patients' ability to handle the stress. As noted earlier, most families tend to accept the procedures quite readily, and even to enjoy the session to some extent. Here, as in any use of art in a clinical setting, a vital variable in the comfort equation for the client is the therapist's own feelings about the activity.

Modifications

Thus, when workers are comfortable things tend to go well, even under conditions which might conceivably produce stress. A good example of clinicians' positive expectancy effects was the experience of a child psychiatrist and a social worker, co-therapists for a parents' group. After one month of weekly meetings, the couples were told that each entire family was to come in for an art session, and that it would be videotaped and later reviewed in the group.

All five families were seen for a family art evaluation within the next few weeks, each session lasting for an hour and involving the third and fourth tasks. The cotherapists proceeded to review the tapes and artwork with the couples' group, taking 2 weeks for each family. The group discussed them in detail, attempting in the process to learn more about themselves and to promote constructive change.

The group leaders were so pleased with the results of their innovative approach that they later wrote and presented a paper describing it (Henderson & Lowe, 1972). My experience with them and with others has confirmed Kwiatkowska's observations that such procedures are eminently teachable, requiring minimal art background (1967, 1978).

The work of these two colleagues with the couples' group also exemplified the possibility of modifications for different purposes. Because of their plan to review the entire procedure in the group, 1 hour was the maximum amount of time. A more limited space was utilized, so that the videotape would include all members at all moments. A rug on the floor necessitated some limitation of media (for example, no paints or wet clay), though the principle of choice of materials and location was retained. Because of less time, it was decided to use only the second and third tasks, to omit the largest size paper for Task 2, and to present a more limited and quickly usable selection of two-dimensional media. What was learned was not only that the whole conception was feasible, but also that the necessary limitations and modifications did not seem to inhibit the emergence of useful and relevant data.

Modifying the evaluation is often useful, and at times extremely helpful. In no way do I think of the family art evaluation described here as a fixed, invariant, rigid procedure from which no deviation is possible. Instead, it represents the three tasks and the sequence which so far have proved most comfortable and productive with families, if enough time is available. With less time, one must choose, as did a former psychology intern, who in her first job at a California clinic used a 5-minute group mural (a time-limited version of Task 3) as part of a brief family evaluation (Goldstein, Deeton & Barasch, 1975).

In the course of developing the evaluation, Dr. Magnussen and I experimented with a variety of times, sequences, tasks, and settings. There are pros and cons to all possibilities, and a carefully controlled study would be necessary to truly define which portions or aspects of the procedure are most revealing. Often, if much time is spent on the first two tasks (or if the family comes late), I have found it necessary to suggest a time limit for the third, which seems, if anything, to help people get started, although it may obscure the conflicts which might become apparent if more time were available for the planning discussion.

It should be noted that caution is as important in reading meanings from pictures by or about families as it is in work by individuals. While there are many suggestions in the literature about the meaning of such things as omission, size distortions, or placement in family drawings, for example, these have never been experimentally validated, and probably ought to be regarded as hunches, to be confirmed or refuted by additional data.

In the early 1980s a child psychiatrist and I designed an elaborate study in which we developed a checklist for features in family drawings by mothers and children, as well as a questionnaire about their families. We looked at things like relative size and placement in the drawings, and asked questions like, "Who do you go to when you're scared?" and, "Who do you get angry at the most?" After doing a computerized analysis of correlations between judges' ratings on the drawings (they agreed at a high level) and responses to the questionnaires, we ended up deciding not to publish the results. The reason was that they were so inconclusive that we feared we would simply add to the already great confusion in this area.

The only conclusion we could comfortably reach was that our original feeling of caution was appropriate; that one should not make any assumptions about features in family drawings without a good deal of additional information. Nevertheless, like individual art evaluations, family art assessments can be amazingly rich sources of information, which are efficient and often remarkably pleasant for the participants.

CHAPTER

11

Family Art Therapy

Although family art therapy can and usually does involve the entire nuclear family, as in the family art evaluation and the case study of Tim, it is also helpful to work with smaller components of the larger unit. Before describing more conjoint family art therapy, I should therefore like to describe art sessions with family member dyads.

Family Member Dyads

The most important and influential person in a child's life is usually the mother. It is often useful to have occasional mother-child sessions both early and late in treatment, for a variety of purposes. The following examples illustrate just what can occur and how it can be used to facilitate the work of child art therapy.

A Little Girl and Her Mother

Mrs. Lord and Lori, her 4½-year-old daughter, were seen weekly by myself and a psychiatrist, each client spending 45 minutes with each worker. Both were depressed following the sudden departure of Mr. Lord and his disclosure of an affair. Following the first 5 weeks of such sessions, the psychiatrist was to be away for a week. We agreed in our collaboration session that a joint art session for mother and child might serve useful diagnostic and treatment purposes. Both clients agreed to the procedure, though each expressed some ambivalence about sharing their hitherto private time, place, and helping person.

In the course of five art sessions, Lori had moved from careful, compulsive drawing and painting to the mixing, then tentative use, and finally free smearing of finger paint. While she was mixing she had verbalized concern about her mother's probable negative reaction: "My mom will be real mad. . . . I ain't gonna paint 'cause I'm not allowed. . . . My mom says so. I ain't gonna finger paint."

In the session preceding the joint one, she had involved me in finger painting alongside her, perhaps to provide concrete adult approval for such messy activity, taking a bossy teacher role: "You start here. . . . You *have* to put your fingers in it." In anticipation of the joint session, she had announced, "I can show my mom how I mix the paint, how I do all the things. We can stay a long time and have fun together. We need lots of water to mix and mix and mix and mix!"

Mrs. Lord, during her first five art sessions, had expressed much concern about her poor artistic ability, and guilt over limits she had placed on the children since she became a single parent, such as fencing them in the backyard. While she knew it was "good for kids to get messy," she said she was "a real bug on neatness," and that, "once you give them an inch, they do everything."

She had symbolically expressed her own fears of loss of control, as well as her covert rejection of the children and wish to escape from them. Once she had pictured Lori and herself as scribbles of strikingly similar shape, with a line around both because it was "so important that we be together." She saw her daughter as "a carbon copy of me," while projecting the depth of her own depression onto the girl and over-identifying with her: "She and I are the same."

Although Lori had said at the end of her first tentative fingertip exploration of a paint mixture during her third session, "It's fun to finger paint," during the joint session she stated, "I hate it . . . because it is sloppy." She nevertheless mixed and used finger paint, working on the table surface next to her mother, who refused Lori's request to join her in the activity and did a neat drawing instead.

The child next invited her mother to join her in using clay. Reluctantly, Mrs. Lord agreed, and proceeded to imitate her daughter, who made a snowman figure like one she had modeled the previous week. At that time, she had made two "little girl snowmen," who had engaged in a dialogue like puppets, Lori crouched under the table manipulating them. Although she asked her mom to join her for such a drama in the joint session, Mrs. Lord refused, with evident discomfort. Lori then manipulated both snowmen. Speaking for both, she directed the drama more to me than to her mom.

She identified her snowman as "a little girl, almost five," and the larger one as "the mother," who gradually became more and more punitive towards the "messy," "bad" little girl.

Although painful for Mrs. Lord, the joint session illuminated for her the intensity of the pressure experienced by Lori over messiness, and helped her to recognize her own fears of loss of control. Moreover, in her attempt to duplicate Lori's snowman, she realized in our subsequent discussions that she was perceiving a false identity between herself and Lori. She commented many times throughout the joint session and in later ones about what she saw as Lori's greater ease and freedom in the same art room where both had been for five previous sessions: "*She* really knows her way around here. . . . *She* really makes herself at home."

A Teenage Boy and His Mother

Billy was a 13-year-old whose mother was concerned about his rebelliousness. His father had died, and an older sister no longer lived at home. He was seen for a series of assessment sessions, which included not only individual art sessions for Bill and interviews with his mom, but also some joint art experiences (DVD 11.1).

In the first, because both mother and son had each talked about problems between them, I asked them to *draw a picture together* in order to observe them interact. Although they discussed it and tried to create a joint picture, they ended up dividing the paper in half, working on opposite sides, each drawing his own version of their jointly-selected theme: "Our House" (11.1A). They were astounded at the end to discover how different were their representations.

Billy's house had "dark clouds over it," while his mother's looked more cheerful. They agreed that they often perceived the same thing quite differently, and that this was one of their main problems, both in communicating and in getting along. Billy became openly tearful about how he felt his mom not only misunderstood but also rejected him. His mother had as much difficulty hearing what he was saying as she had had in noticing his drawing while working on her own during the joint picture.

At the second joint art session, I used a reversal of Harriet Wadeson's (1973, 1980) task for couples. I asked each to draw a portrait of the other on opposite sides of a table easel (Figure 11.1). Each then "corrected" the other's artwork, modifying it as he or she wished. Billy felt that his mother had portrayed him as bigger than he really was (11.1B), sensing her covert wish to have him replace his recently dead father—to be the man of the house—while at the same time she complained about his assuming that role.

190

11.1 Billy and Mrs. K. Drawing Each Other at the Easel

Mother saw Billy's drawing of her (11.1C) as having both mouth and eyes that were too large. She modified these features, and then added what she felt was a "more attractive" hairstyle and earrings. In fact, she made the portrait more seductive, while at the same time speaking of it in a critical, distancing fashion. This ambivalent message was confusing to Billy, because it echoed his own adolescent revival of oedipal wishes, complicating his need to separate.

Mother described Billy as "putting up a wall" between them, while Billy felt that his mom was "holding me on a leash." The intense ambivalence on both sides of this mother-son relationship, apparent in their drawings and responses, as well as in their behavior, became clearer to me as well as to the participants through their graphic representations.

A Girl and Her Father

While mother and child are the most common and often most conflicted dyad within the family, there may be reasons for inviting other family members to an occasional joint session with a child. Laura's parents had recently been divorced, and it was very important to Laura to have her dad come to the clinic for a session with her, especially since he had not participated in her therapy (except financially) since the assessment.

The joint session was dramatic—father came a half hour late, and was demanding and critical of Laura's productions. She worked hard to please him, but it was clear that gaining his approval was a difficult, if not impossible, task. She was glad that he had come at all, though deeply hurt and angered at his lateness. This single brief experience with her dad was helpful to both of us throughout her 4 years of treatment, because it was possible not only to look at what had happened but also to use it as a reference point for subsequent events and feelings about her father.

A Boy and His Brother

Danny was eager to have his older brother join him, and Ross finally agreed (DVD 11.2). During the session, Danny, usually quite inventive, spent all of his energies either trying to get Ross to do what he wished, or imitating Ross's efforts. He attempted to get his brother to do a joint drawing, but Ross, quite independent, refused. Danny finally tried to copy Ross's picture, but he felt discouraged about the outcome.

A year later he again wanted Ross to come, and I thought it would be useful to see if things were different. Indeed, they were—Danny went about his own business quite autonomously, only occasionally asking for Ross's attention, to show his brother what he was making. Much to my surprise, and Danny's evident delight, Ross ended up imitating Dan, using the same materials and process (pounded soldering wire) to create abstract metal sculptures and candleholders.

A Boy and His Mother with Both Individual Therapists

After almost a year of separate individual work with 8-year-old David and his mother, both her therapist and I were discouraged, feeling that we had progressed little in loosening their close ties to one another. We decided on a joint half hour, to be followed by separate half hours with each (DVD 11.3). During their together time, David and his mom were asked to work together, which they did with hardly a word. Using watercolors, they created a picture of Lake Erie, where they had been on vacation, a peaceful image of water and land with a common linear boundary (11.3A).

While there are certain elements in the picture itself suggestive of wishes for a kind of symbiotic fusion on the part of both, this was even more evident in their almost mystical nonverbal communication during the process of painting it. At the end each said they had known what the other one was thinking, revealing a joint belief in their ability to read each other's mind. As mother put it, "I always know what he's thinkin,' sometimes before he does," while David nodded his head in agreement.

After doing and discussing the peaceful scene, David's mother took advantage of the remaining minutes to complain angrily about his messiness, as well as his strange and bothersome interest in collecting junk. After she and her therapist had left for some individual discussion of what had occurred, David worked on one of his "Beautiful Mess" paintings (11.3B) using a swirling technique with bright enamel paint (11.3C) and spoke of how hard it was to feel mad at a mother to whom he also felt so close, interdependent, and with whom he identified.

Aside from learning more about specific intrafamilial interactions, such dyadic sessions may also be useful in helping the child to feel and see things, like competitive strivings. Lynn, for example, thought she wanted her younger brother to join her toward the end of her therapy, perhaps to dilute the intensity of feelings she was having toward me regarding termination. But after about 10 minutes in the playroom she decided that Tommy had been there long enough, and told him that his time was up for the day. After taking him back down to the waiting room she returned, and informed me that it was making her "too jealous," and it was making her mad like it did at home, when she had to share her mother with Tommy. The experience was helpful to both of us in looking at her envy of her siblings at home and of the other children who came to see me at the clinic.

As in other contexts, joint work in the course of individual, group, or family sessions can be approached in an open-ended fashion or with some direction by the therapist. Deciding how to proceed here, as elsewhere, is primarily a function of the goals of the particular session.

Conjoint Family Art Therapy

Ironically, it seems that the two kinds of families that benefit most from art therapy are those for whom talk is a way to escape and to hide (like Tim's family), and those who talk little, distrust words, and fear that therapists will "play with their minds."

The W. family was recommended for conjoint family art therapy, in part because of the parents' poor history of relating to helping agencies. Three of the four children (ages 5 to 12) they had adopted had already been referred for help at various points in time; the two boys who were sent to our clinic had received some short-term intervention at other places in the community (see Betts, 2003).

The parents had typically been seen as resistant, had not come in for their own interviews, and by the time we met them were openly distrustful of mental health facilities. An older, uneducated couple, who had taken in foster children and then adopted them, were vulnerable, frightened of being exposed as poor parents, and of having their already shaky defenses further undermined. Yet it was clear that without some change in the family structure, neither of the boys had much of a chance for healthful growth himself.

Much to our surprise they enjoyed the family art evaluation, to which they had come with all the children. During the session itself and in subsequent contacts with other clinicians they spoke of how much fun it was, how much nicer than what usually went on in such places. They were not such confident artists, but they were less confident articulators, so they were offered weekly conjoint family art therapy, in addition to individual psychotherapy for each boy, in the hope that this time they might find treatment more tolerable, and not run, as in the past.

The family did come regularly for 6 months, working in art as a group for an hour (following the two boys' individual therapy hours) with myself and a child psychiatrist, Juergen Homann, MD, MPH. Although they still terminated treatment before we thought they were ready, they did come for longer than they ever had before, and participated intensely while they were engaged (DVD 11.4).

Most of the time, the simple provision of materials and an open invitation to use them as they wished was enough to allow important themes and issues to emerge (11.4A). The only structure Dr. Homann and I usually provided, therefore, was to suggest that we spend some time at the end talking together about what people had made that day, and organizing the 5 to 20-minute discussion time so as to make sure each person had a chance to tell about what they made (11.4B).

Occasionally, we would find ourselves suggesting working in a particular way (e.g., dyads) or on a theme (e.g., wishes), but that was very rare. With this family, as with most, the open-ended approach seemed to be most fruitful over time (with some variations), as we therapists sensed a particular need for focus.

In the beginning, each parent tended to work with one of the children, usually seeming more comfortable, perhaps less exposed, than if he or she had worked alone. We were able thereby to focus their attention on some of the child-parent issues causing stress in the family, especially those around limits and authority. When Bill and his Dad, for example, worked together on their "Smoking Picture" (11.4C), they talked about who was in charge on the picture, as well as on issues like whether or not to smoke (11.4D).

When Josh and his mom, on the other hand, made a three-dimensional farm together, Josh remarked with a surprised smile that he didn't know that she liked him well enough to work with him for so many weeks, since she openly favored his brother most of the time (Figure 11.2). The two younger children, who did not have behavioral problems, provided a stabilizing presence for the others (see 11.4A and 11.4B).

Much to our surprise, the parents actually requested couple sessions (for 1 hour prior to the family meetings) for the last 2 months, in order to deal with some marital problems of which they had become aware during family art therapy. Although it was our feeling that they terminated prematurely, there had indeed been some important learning and changes during their treatment. While they came and worked, conjoint family art therapy did seem to be the treatment of choice for this generally resistant group.

It should be clear from the preceding examples that there are many possible ways of working on intrafamilial problems through art therapy. The potential groupings and ways of structuring the transaction are varied. Work with all or part of the family unit may be the primary treatment method, or may be introduced periodically as seems indicated. Just

11.2 Josh and Mrs. W. Working Together on a Clay Sculpture

as occasional joint parent-child art sessions seem useful, so it also happens that an occasional session with all family members serves to provide information or to facilitate communication in the course of other forms of treatment.

Occasional Conjoint Family Art Sessions

Laura was seen primarily in individual art therapy, while her mother was seen mostly individually, and for a 6-month period in a single parent's group. In addition to some mother-child meetings, several sessions involved the entire family. In one family session, I decided it was important to help the mother see how she had insulated herself, withdrawing from her four young children and their needs, which she felt as incessant demands. I therefore suggested a game that all could play, which I thought might clarify this situation (DVD 11.5).

Each family member was first invited to make a small plasticine self-representation. Then, without talking, they were asked to move them around on a shared territory—a large piece of posterboard—until each found a place he wanted to settle on (11.5A). When that was done, each was asked to further define his space using felt-tip markers, still without talking to each other.

Although mother placed herself in the center, her territory seemed closed in, with only minimal indications that her space was reachable by the others. Each child isolated him- or herself in a corner, providing protection through a large house, a big fence, or a powerful pet (11.5B). The children were then able to talk about how they felt they had to fend for themselves, and of how uncertain they were about support from each other, as well as from mother.

She, responding empathically, revised her original description of her space, saying that the paths she had drawn were meant to lead *into* it; that, although it was hard, she really wanted to be available to her children. While the session did not solve the problem, the experience served to get it out in the open, where it could be dealt with more easily by all family members.

Sometimes a joint session happens informally, as when Andy agreed to invite his mother in after his individual art evaluation (DVD 6.5C). Similarly, Sloane brought her painting to show her mother (DVD 11.6) after each of them had an individual art therapy session (11.6A). They then worked together on a picture, another kind of family art therapeutic opportunity (11.6B).

In the years since this chapter was first written a number of other art therapists have developed a variety of ways to work with children and their families. Among them are Helen Landgarten (1981, 1987), Deborah Linesch (1993), Gussie Klorer (2000), Barbara Sobol (1982; Sobol & Williams, 2001), Doris Arrington (2001), and Shirley Riley (2001a, 2003; Riley & Malchiodi, 2003, 2004).

In 1980 I moved from the child guidance center to a psychiatric hospital that had a Family Therapy Clinic, where most of the staff wanted to learn how to do family art evaluations, and some wanted to do ongoing family art therapy. They also requested family drawings, along with commentaries, for their monthly newsletter—a way to educate other clinicians about the value of art in family therapy.

Meanwhile, I ended up seeing youngsters of all ages in private practice, both in my hospital office and, later, in a private office. Since I had never been trained in family therapy myself, I didn't feel competent to conduct it in an ongoing fashion, except when I had a co-therapist who knew how to work with the family system.

But I was surprised at how often I found myself initiating dyadic or conjoint family art sessions, for both evaluation and in the course of therapy. Even when the space was much more cramped than what had been available at the clinic, it never ceased to amaze me how much I and the patient(s) could learn from family art interviews.

And of course there was no limit to the kinds of family problems that could be helpfully addressed through art sessions involving some or all members. These included court-ordered custody and abuse evaluations, issues related to foster or adoptive parents, crises caused by adolescent acting-out (such as alcohol and drug abuse), tensions related to eating disorders, suicidal impulses, dissociative identity disorder and other post-traumatic stress disorders, and so on.

Multimodal Family Art Sessions

While codirecting a Creative and Expressive Arts Therapy Department in the psychiatric hospital that served the child and adolescent units, as well as all of the others, my drama therapist colleague and I developed a multimodality family evaluation (DVD 11.7). We based it on her work with families using puppets (Irwin & Malloy, 1975) and the family art evaluation described in the preceding chapter.

The procedure included both art and drama tasks: a group mural, representations of the family, and a family puppet story, in varying order, depending on the family. Although the multimodal family evaluation is, like the art evaluation, quite useful during assessment, we also found that it was helpful during ongoing therapy (11.7A).

Since we ended up sharing an office (after leaving the hospital for full-time private practice), and one of us often saw the parents while the other treated the child, it was easy to schedule family sessions as needed. Sometimes we each treated a sibling, with only occasional parent counseling sessions, and again, family sessions were most useful. By the time we had worked together for many years we freely chose art or drama activities, or a combination of the two, for such sessions.

For example, one involved the family of Lila, a young girl with anorexia who I had seen in group and individual art therapy while she was hospitalized to stabilize her weight. After Lila was discharged, and I'd left the hospital for private practice, she asked to continue in art therapy. We met twice a week for almost a year (DVD 11.8).

Like many patients with eating disorders, Lila had found that her old symptoms began to return as soon as she left the controlled environment of the hospital. Unlike some, however, she was eager to overcome them. She expressed her feeling of emptiness (11.8A) and her longing for nurturance in a series of agonized and eloquent drawings and paintings (11.8B).

11.3 *Family Drawing by Girl with Anorexia*

Despite her excellent intellect, she could articulate her pain in pictures far better than in words (11.8C). Using her own images as springboards for associations, she began to name her vague feelings (11.8D).

I had referred her parents to my officemate, Dr. Irwin; at about the middle of the year of treatment, we agreed that a session with the whole family would help both of us to assist our clients. In an hour and a half of observing them create scribbles, family representations, and a joint mural, Dr. Irwin and I were able for the first time to understand how painfully enmeshed the family really was (Figure 11.3).

The really delightful thing is that art itself is so flexible that it can be adapted to many different theoretical orientations in individual therapy, as is evident in *Approaches to Art Therapy* (Rubin, 2001). Similarly, art can be utilized in either family or group therapy from virtually any theoretical point of view (Arrington, 2001; Riley, 2001a, 2001b; Riley & Malchiodi, 2004; Sobol & Williams, 2001).

CHAPTER

12

Art Therapy with Parents

Individual Art Therapy

Although mothers and fathers in a child guidance center were typically seen not for their own therapy but for child-centered counseling, in truth it was often necessary to help them with their issues, in order for them to better parent their children.

Mrs. Braver

Mrs. Braver had suffered both emotional and physical abuse when she was young. Despite having needed radical surgery because of her body's response to all of the stress, she was determined to get her daughter the help she never had, and to turn her own life around too (DVD 12.1). Working as much on her own issues as on those involving her parenting, she became involved in exploring her identity not only verbally, but artistically as well.

First she made a Pariscraft head (DVD 12.1A) which she carefully painted, explaining that it was a self-portrait. When she was done, she was so pleased that she took it home (12.1B) She then did a painting about how split she felt at that point in her life about her identity (12.1C). By then doing art at home as well as in her sessions, Mrs. Braver worked for about a month on a Self Collage, which she proudly brought in to show me when it was completed (12.1D) as well as framed (12.1E).

Mrs. Silver

Another such woman was a young widow, Mrs. Silver. She and her daughter had participated in the mother-child art therapy group described later in this chapter. When the group ended, the treatment team recommended that each be seen individually (DVD 12.2). She too was able to use art therapy (12.2A), developing a way of working things out on paper that was truly unique (12.2B).

Mrs. Silver had frequently expressed her disgust at the finger paints, often noticing but never using them. I had asked if she could describe her feelings of revulsion, but she found it hard to define them. I then wondered if we might not find out more if she were to *try* the paints, despite her negative response. She was willing to do so in an openly experimental fashion, and it was quite a powerful session, referred to many times in succeeding months.

Mrs. Silver began by feeling and expressing disgust, but gradually got more and more into it, exclaiming with glee, "Ooh! What a pretty mess!" After a tentative beginning, she took large gobs of paint, and eventually used both hands and fingers with a high degree of freedom. Her unexpected discovery was that she liked it, that it was not unpleasant, as she had anticipated, but that it was actually fun. She related this surprise to her initial anxiety about getting her daughter out of school for morning appointments, and her discovery that it was neither uncomfortable nor harmful, as she had feared.

Mrs. Silver's associations to the first painting (12.2C) were that it was a series of "Roads" which led to various places, and that she had to decide where she was going, a fairly accurate description of where she was in her life at that time. The second (12.2D) she described as "like Hell, a Storm with Lightning and Turmoil." She ended up talking about her own feelings of sinfulness and guilt over sleeping with a man to whom she was not married. The shame she felt about being "dirty" was stimulated by the medium itself, as well as by the images she "saw" in her abstract finger paintings.

Mrs. Lord

Although she had come to the clinic because her formerly cheerful daughter Lori was sad, Mrs. Lord was also depressed. Both were reacting to Mr. Lord's recent announcement that he wanted a separation, and his subsequent move out of their home. Although Lori cried a lot, Mrs. Lord was generally able to hide her depression behind a cheerful facade.

After 5 months of weekly art therapy (DVD 12.3), she usually began a session by telling me what was going on in her life, while painting or drawing (12.3A). Then, we would look at what she had made on the easel (12.3B), allowing her to feel less self-conscious than if she had to make eye contact with me—one of the reasons art therapy is so effective (12.3C). Mrs. Lord had also learned by then to associate freely to her images, saying whatever came to mind as she looked at her pictures. After she reflected on her verbal associations, we would attempt to figure out their relevance to her life.

One day Mrs. Lord arrived looking uncharacteristically somber. She said she had almost not come, and was so upset that she wondered if she would be able to talk about anything at all. I asked if she could *draw her feelings*, rather than trying to put them into words (12.3D).

She quickly selected a piece of black construction paper ($12'' \times 18''$) and large poster chalks, by then her favorite medium. She furiously scribbled a series of color masses whose brightness screamed out against the black—red, yellow, orange, magenta, and white. Mrs. Lord then grabbed another piece of black paper, and quickly drew a series of multicolored lines which met, but did not intersect.

Putting both on the easel, she regarded them as if seeing them for the first time. She entitled the first drawing (12.3E) "Shock," and then, much to her surprise and embarrassment, this usually well-controlled woman began to sob. "All I have to do is break down and start crying," she said, "and everyone will think I am crazy! . . . He's the one who should be here!" She then said she had just discovered that her husband had a girlfriend, and that the affair had been going on for quite a while. Still agitated and tearful, Mrs. Lord went on to say how painful the *shock* had been.

The title for the second picture (12.3F) was less clear to her than the first. She groped for words, finally settling on "Ambivalent, Dilemma, Uncertainty, and Confusion." She was unable to say much more, except that the image described as best she could her tangled emotions. By the end of the session, Mrs. Lord had regained her composure. While still visibly sad, she was no longer as tense as when she arrived.

The art activity allowed Mrs. Lord to release some of the feelings that were flooding her. The drawings, which expressed her anguish and confusion better than any words, also helped her to sort out what was happening, both internally and externally. She was then able to begin to consider how she might cope with the unwelcome news. In other words, articulating her inner world helped her to cope with the outer one.

Mother-Child Art Therapy Group

There are many possible ways to group people in art therapy. One is to work with the nuclear family or with portions of it, as described in the preceding chapter. Another is to work with more homogeneous sets of people, such as single mothers, or same-age children, or patients with a common problem. I have found a particular hybrid approach to be quite useful in a variety of settings, one that involves groups of mothers and their children meeting together, all or part of the time. This model is midway between family art therapy and group art therapy, involving elements of both.

The first mother-child art therapy group in the clinic was proposed after noting the interactional problems between mothers and their young disturbed children, the difficulty of getting from many an undistorted picture of the parent-child relationship, and the problems for both in trying out new ways of relating. In a memo to the staff, the criteria for referral to the group were: a primary problem in the mother-child relationship, the absence of serious pathology contraindicating either peer or joint group treatment, and the ability of each to profit from the proposed format of weekly group art therapy for the child and a discussion group for the mother, with occasional joint sessions.

Prior to final selection, the social worker who was to lead the parent group screened the mothers in individual interviews, and I saw each child for an art interview. All had previously been seen, in most cases by other clinic personnel, in a routine intake procedure, culminating in a diagnostic conference. Two of the mothers and their children had been receiving individual therapy prior to entry into the group; four began treatment with the group.

All six children (four boys and two girls, ages 5 and 6) received no other form of treatment during their involvement in the group. Four of the six had no father in the home (two through death, two through divorce); of the other two, one had a father whose work kept him away from home except on weekends, and the other's mother was on the verge of separating from her alcoholic husband. The autistic 5-year-old son of a seventh mother was judged unable to participate in the children's art group, but was able to attend the second joint art session.

Mothers' Art Therapy Session

The mothers first met with their leader for 3 weeks; I attended their third session. The fourth week, the mothers came to the room where both child and joint groups were to be held and had an art therapy session, in which the assigned topics were "Family Drawings" and pictures of each one's "Life Space." The instructions were to choose paper of a size and color that seemed right, and to make a picture of their life space at the present time, including the most important elements, both positive and negative. The activity was followed by discussion, centered around the sharing of each mother's artwork with the group. Both topics were selected as ways of assessing where and how the child client stood in the mother's current perception of her family and herself.

As might be expected, these drawings revealed many aspects of each woman's self-perception as well. Mrs. J. first drew her husband, then herself, then her autistic 5-year-old son, and finally her two sons from a previous marriage (Figure 12.1).

Another woman asked if her husband was shorter than she in reality, as she had pictured him. She replied hesitantly and with agitation, "I don't know *why* I made him that way. He *is* taller, but when I'm with him, I feel in this respect that I'm—I feel *bigger* than he does. Now I don't know *why*, but I *do*. I mean, I always—my father and my brothers and the other two boys are exceptionally tall, and I know, and I feel—well, he's thin, too, thin built, and I feel like, I—like if I *fell* on him, I'd *crush* him! I don't know why, but I do. . . . Yeah, there's somethin' about, uh—I guess I feel like a *massive* person. I don't know, I feel like a man or somethin'. My husband is more strong, but I get the feelin' that—uh—I always *have*." The discrepancy between fact and feeling, so clear in this drawing, helped the others to read their own productions more symbolically.

Mrs. J. told even more about herself in her life-space picture, which, unlike others, was mostly of significant people. She put herself in the center, explaining, "I'm middle-aged, and in the center or middle of life. I've lived half as long as I'm gonna. I'm red." Her husband, also red, is above her, with lines pointing to him. Lines also lead left from her figure to her brother ("in and out of my life"), to her 16-year-old son ("green, the color of hope"), and right to her 19-year-old son ("blue, he's okay").

12.1 Mrs. J.'s Family Drawing. Marker

From her head a line leads right to a small black figure, her autistic child, the color representing "my worries about him." A dotted line leads to her sister-in-law, in pink ("she's like a sister to me. She lives in California, but I feel very close to her"). Below are three boxes of activities; the left one depicts housework, which she "hates," the center and right boxes show "talking to my boss" and "talking to my friends," both of which she enjoys. She elaborated verbally on her worries about her youngest child and on her feeling of having few sources of emotional support.

Many of the women felt equally alone emotionally, including one who had represented herself and her children as flowers (Figure 12.2). Mrs. K. had incorporated the children's colors into her self-flower, saying, "My children are just a part of me."

One of the largest items in her picture was a flower representing, she said, "My mother. This ugly little daisy. It's big and it's ugly. I love her, but I don't *like* her too much. She'd love to have my children. She's overbearing. She keeps the kids, and there's a conflict between my mom and me about raising the children. I intend to go to California and find a guy, and get away from her."

12.2 Mrs. K.'s "Life Space" Picture. Marker

Another woman, Mrs. R., also expressed ambivalent feelings about her mother while regarding her drawing: "I love my mom, but there's things she does that I dislike." While it took all of them many months to acknowledge as freely their mixed feelings toward their children, this sharing of such thoughts about their own mothers made that later step easier.

Joint Art Sessions: Mothers and Children

The children's art therapy group began the following week, meeting for the same 1½-hour period as the mothers' group. Joint sessions were held at varying intervals, the specific dates mutually decided upon by myself and the mothers' group leader during our weekly collaborations. My co-therapist was a male clinical child psychologist, who joined the children's group during the fourth session and who also participated in the decisions about the timing and format of joint sessions.

First Joint Art Session: Unstructured

The first mother-child art session took place after the children had met as a group for 4 weeks, and was conducted in an open-ended fashion. A wide range of art materials was available, as well as a variety of possible working surfaces in the large group room. As the mothers and children entered, they were told they could work with anything they liked, anywhere they wished, and could make whatever they desired.

There were, therefore, many opportunities for observation of dyadic interaction patterns. From the moment of entry through each decision demanded by the unstructured activity period, we were able to get a rich picture of each pair in a busy, pleasant, only mildly self-conscious situation. As with the naturalistic observation described in a therapeutic nursery school, "there is little doubt that . . . direct observations of the child and of his interaction with his mother add considerably to the overall understanding of his personality and specific pathology" (Furman, 1969, p. 98).

With further joint sessions over time, we too found that "the observational advantage extends beyond the diagnostic stage," and could verify "the obvious usefulness of these observations for the therapist in enabling him at all times to obtain a total picture of the child and to pinpoint the mother's changing areas of strength and weakness" (p. 98).

These joint sessions were particularly helpful in planning and managing the treatment program for each mother and child in the groups. In addition, videotape records of some provided us with an additional chance to study those subtle behaviors that often escaped attention in the busy working atmosphere.

We tried to observe as closely as possible, and to tune in to all of the rich behavioral and symbolic data available in the situation. One pair, for example, isolated themselves at an easel, their backs to the group, the girl sharing her mother's discomfort in being exposed to so many people. These two stayed close to each other and worked jointly throughout the session.

Another pair, in contrast, behaved as if the other was not present, each doing their own thing in separate parts of the room. This behavior was followed by the mother's laughing ridicule of her son's chosen product during the later sharing time, as well as by a competitive, peerlike interaction during the snack. When their separate-but-equal behavior was noted by another mother during the following week's adult group discussion, this woman spoke of her intense discomfort, feelings of inadequacy, and jealousy of her son's greater ease in the art room.

With another dyad, there was considerable evidence of covert maternal rejection, of which we had not been aware. The woman watched in what appeared to be a kind of icy horror, while her child thoroughly enjoyed smearing with powder paint, water, and brush on an extra-large piece of paper. Her cold, disapproving glance was probably harder for the boy to cope with than if she had expressed her anger more directly. Although she sat next to him throughout the session, there was hardly any verbal interaction. When she spoke of her feelings in the mothers' group the following week, she stated angrily, "I had no interaction with my son. He was very wound up. He ran like a *wild* man. . . . It's not typical of him. He's very neat at home."

Another mother, whose son had engaged in a similar kind of exploration with paint prior to more structured products, was able to share with the first her own joy and pleasure in her son's unexpected freedom. Since other mothers also let the first woman know how they admired her child's control of his potentially explosive medium, she began to see some of the irrational aspects of her anger. Having expressed that anger openly with the group for the first time, she was then able to perceive and discuss her own fears of loss of control.

The mothers were able to help each other, not only in the discussion the following week, but during the joint art session itself. For example, one woman had effectively isolated herself and her daughter from the rest of the group by choosing to work at the smallest table in the room. She sat stiffly, looking tensely and anxiously around, while the child proceeded to draw. When the girl sought her mother's attention, there was at first no response, eventually stimulating a whiney pleading, which succeeded in producing an irritated glance at the child.

The one lone mother (whose autistic child was not present), sat down at the table with this pair, effectively intruding upon their self-imposed isolation (DVD 12.4). The child, who had been asking vainly for a warm maternal response, immediately began a pictorial dialogue with the other mother, drawing a "Baby Kitten" next to that woman's larger animal, which the girl had named "a Mother Cat" (12.4A). Thus reinforced in her attempts to relate positively to an adult, she proceeded to draw a mother cat of her own (12.4B), and then another, which she identified as her own beloved pet, "Twiggy" (12.4C). Having been unable to involve her own mother in artwork, the child experienced through her interactions with another mother the satisfactions of a shared creative experience. Her mother, meanwhile, was able to observe the other woman's pleasure as well as the girl's happy responses.

When the other mother left the pair to engage in a lengthy period of finger painting, the girl and her mother began what became a truly interactive effort, in which each made parts of a bird nest scene with clay. They even tried their own joint finger painting at an easel, with surprising mutual pleasure. While this mother's involvement with her child was stimulated in part by the feelings of rivalry aroused by the other woman, she eventually allowed herself to relax and even to enjoy the finger painting, her earlier tension lessening noticeably.

Second Joint Art Session: Working Together

The second joint art session, held 6 weeks after the first, was more structured. Based on suggestions from the mothers and our collaborations, each pair was asked as they entered to engage in at least one project together (12.4D). The media and working surfaces were the same as in the first session, but this time there was the explicit task of deciding together what to use, where to work, and what to make. As in the first session, the working period was followed by a snack, and the sharing with the group of one jointly chosen collaborative product from each mother-child pair, with mother (not therapist, as in the first session) as interviewer (12.4E).

Since 6 weeks had elapsed between the first and second joint art sessions, we were able to observe any changes in individual and interactional behavior. One mother and daughter, who had shyly isolated themselves during the first joint session, now sat at a table with others, worked independently most of the time, and actively joined into the conversation.

Both partners, previously locked into an interdependent relationship, seemed to be readjusting—in response to the girl's newfound self-assertion and drive for autonomy, along with her mother's growing self-confidence. This was particularly apparent during the post-product interview of the child by the mother, as well as in the subsequent spontaneous interview of

12.3 A Mother and Son Working Together on a Drawing

the mother by the child, who was teasingly provocative about her mother's clay ice cream cone.

Another pair, who had worked at opposite ends of the room with little awareness of each other during the first session, now not only worked together as required, but did so in a comfortable, cooperative manner (Figure 12.3). Although their three joint drawings reflected the dominance of the mother in style and conception, as opposed to others in which a child had clearly been in charge, they were deeply and happily involved in the working process. Most impressive was the mother's unanticipated sensitivity in her role as interviewer (see DVD 12.4E).

Of course, the persistence of maladaptive behaviors or attitudes was equally visible, as with the mother who had been so angry at her child for being sloppy and wild during the first session. While slightly less tense during the second joint group, she seemed to derive little pleasure from the process. A therapist sitting nearby observed that nearly all of her spontaneous conversation with the boy was critical, although they created three joint felt pen drawings. Her sparse verbalization was restricted to telling him what *not* to do, or what he had done *wrong*, an attitude also reflected in the brusque, irritated tone of her later interviewing of her son about their chosen product.

While the diagnostic value of joint art sessions for the treatment team is obvious, what is less apparent, but perhaps more important for therapy, is the educational potential of such meetings for both mother and child. Each is able to observe other modes of response to the same situation, to know and to see alternatives. Both the girl who made the cats and her mother were able to learn from the other mother who drew along with the child.

Perhaps some of the greater freedom and lesser self-consciousness of the previously isolated and interdependent mother-daughter pair was, at least in part, due to their interaction with two other teams around a shared table during the second joint session. It is also possible that the mother-son pair who stayed far apart during the first session were able to collaborate so well during the second because each had observed other mother-child pairs doing so with pleasure.

A mother might also perceive her child in a new light from his or her behavior in a joint art session. This usually involves a comparison of the child's behavior in the session with behavior in the past, with that of peers in the group, or with the mother's own anticipation. The powerful effect of an adult's expectations on a child's behavior, evident in infancy (Broussard, 2003) has been forcefully demonstrated in a study of teachers about "interpersonal self-fulfilling prophecies" (Rosenthal & Jacobson, 1968).

One mother, for example, stated in the mothers' group meeting the week after the first joint session that she had been "pleasantly surprised" by her son's behavior during the art activities. She had expected him to be what he had been when he first came to the clinic, a tense, anxious, compulsive little boy. Instead, she discovered an unanticipated degree of freedom in his work and his interaction with her.

The mother of the autistic child nervously brought him to the second joint art experience, and was relieved and pleased by her son's ability to handle himself appropriately in the very stimulating environment. They completed two joint paintings with tempera markers, the process thoroughly enjoyed by both.

Even more valuable for her were the comments of the other mothers, for when they met for a half hour of discussion following the joint session the group told her she had been drawing for them a grossly distorted picture of her boy. Since their assertions were based on a full hour of observing his behavior, and since they had by then been meeting for 15 weeks, she was able to trust and to accept their feedback.

The mothers seemed gradually to be learning to sense, if not to translate, the symbolic meanings of their children's creative expression, and in the interviews as well as their discussions, gained new insights into their children's inner lives. They were learning, in effect, that "your child makes sense" (Buxbaum, 1949, p. 51).

For example, while I was interviewing one little girl in the first session about her two clay turtles, her mother was able to see the relationship between the story of the 5-year-old girl turtle's victory over her baby brother turtle, and the child's wish to win out over her own younger sibling. This same mother, interviewing her child during the second joint session, smiled knowingly when the girl identified the larger of two clay baskets as hers, and the smaller one as her younger brother's.

Later in the interview, a "little boy mask" made by the child "opened his mouth up" and was "screamin' because he can't find his basket." Again, the mother nodded with understanding when told that the sister had stolen it. Over the succeeding months, this woman often brought in artwork created by her daughter at home or in school, along with useful and perceptive ideas about its possible meanings to the child.

Another mother, who was becoming aware of her son's wish to replace her divorced husband, seemed to understand the meaning of the following interchange about their picture:

Boy: The tree is tryin' to reach over to kiss the airplane.
Mother: Is he gonna reach the airplane?
Boy: If he tries harder, he's gonna bust!
Mother: Do you think the airplane *wants* him to reach her?
Boy: Yeah! He does!
Mother: He does?
Boy: They wanna get *married*.

The mother raised this story in the parent group discussion following the shared experience, and wondered aloud what her own role and wishes might be in stimulating and reinforcing his fantasy. Her ambivalent (seductive/rejecting) behavior had been observed by the therapists, but this was the first time that she became aware of her role in inhibiting her son's resolution of his internal (oedipal) conflict about winning his mom.

The joint art sessions were also found to be particularly useful reference points for a series of parent conferences on each child's progress in treatment, held 5 months after the groups had started. For example, one mother, unable to see the extent of her own role in her daughter's problems, began to discuss her own difficulty in identifying and expressing angry feelings. She could perceive her child's surface compliance, but was helped to see the girl's need to deny her hostile impulses by recalling the following excerpt from her interview of her daughter about the child's picture, entitled "That's Me with Some Dots."

Mother: What do the big dots mean?
Girl: Happiness.
Mother: What makes you happy?
Girl: That you're near me.
Mother: They mean happiness too? You told me before they meant anger.
Girl: They mean happiness now.
Mother: You changed your mind.
Therapist: Can you feel angry sometimes at somebody, and then sometimes feel happy with them?
Girl: No!

When the mother connected the meaning of this interchange with her own hunch about why the girl had profusely praised everyone else's picture, she could see the relationship of the child's problem to her own. This interview with her also marked the beginning of her own real commitment to the group.

Later joint sessions made possible the assessment of change over time in dyadic interactions, as well as any differences between individuals' behavior in the joint group versus the homogeneous groups. Over time, the differential between the two situations decreased, with the children tending to make more blatant their pictured conflicts.

In a later joint art group, for example, Joey, a child with severe castration anxiety, drew at the easel, in front of his mother, a picture of "A Lady with a Weiner" and a missing, injured eye (12.4F). He openly stated his assumption that girls have penises, and his conviction that they once had them but lost them, which caused him to fear that he, too, could potentially lose his.

Joey followed his initial drawing of the "Lady," accompanied by much anal humor (in response to which his mother alternately laughed and scolded severely), with an undisguised portrayal of feces emerging from rectums (12.4G). His mother wondered aloud why he had been so "vulgar," and was helped by the other mothers to see how often her laughter and attention had reinforced this behavior. Although Joey's mother was acutely uncomfortable during this display of his anxiety, his picture and comments

212

became the focal point for a mothers' group discussion following the joint art time, about the reality of young children's concerns about bodily integrity. The leader also explained that, since feces come out of the body, this natural process of elimination reinforces the normal anxiety about loss of body parts.

Possible Formats: The Boss-Slave Game

Any number of possible formats could be employed for such joint sessions, depending on the goals of the team for group members at the time they occur. One structure we used was to suggest that perhaps the children would like to tell the mothers what to draw. Of the three pairs present at that session, two boys thoroughly enjoyed being in charge, though neither was completely satisfied with his mother's performance.

In the children's subsequent discussion of the experience, one boy, who had vigorously complained of his mother's "mistakes" right after she left the room, within 10 minutes was denying any disappointment in her. He was helped by hearing another boy's irritation that his mom did not draw the building he had in mind: "I wonder if *you're* thinkin' about one thing, could the *other* person think about yours, that you're thinkin' about? . . . I was thinkin' about if the building isn't *exactly* the same as you thought—as you're thinkin' about." A productive discussion ensued, about the difficulty of communicating to grownups, especially when you have an image to translate into words.

The third boy, who felt quite weak and incompetent to direct his strong, critical mother, refused to be in charge, requesting that she tell him what to do. Interestingly, one of her chief complaints about her son had been his inability to do anything well or to follow directions. She gave him enough instructions to fill up several papers, but he carefully persisted in attempting to draw, in the eventually crowded picture space, everything she suggested. When there was not an inch left on the paper, the mother stopped, and the child's pride in his mastery of the difficult task she had set him was clear to all.

In the later parental discussion, she was helped to see how much pressure she had put on him, yet how well he had handled her demands. He, on the other hand, stimulated a discussion among the children after the parents had left, about mothers and teachers always telling kids what to do, never seeming satisfied, demanding more and more. The boy who had drawn the feces excitedly joined in, helping us to better understand some of the meanings in that picture: "You know what my mom says? She always says, 'Go to the bathroom! Unless I *make* you go to the bathroom! And fast, too! I'll *make* you go! It'll probably *hurt*!'"

We had anticipated that while the mothers would feel somewhat uneasy and self-conscious during joint art sessions, the children might resent the adults' intrusion into their room, and could be less than willing to share their space, materials, or their group leaders with their parents. They surprised us, however, by looking forward to and clearly enjoying the joint sessions. As one boy put it after the mothers had left, and all had agreed that they liked it better "with the mommies," "It was fun. . . . A good, fine time."

When asked the week before Christmas what they would like to have for a party, most responded with "candy canes" and such; but one boy answered, "the mothers," to which the others quickly agreed. They worked hard decorating the group room before their mother's arrival, complete with a sign saying "Love to all the Kids and the People . . . Welcome to the Mothers."

The use of joint mother-child group art sessions at intermittent intervals seemed to provide useful assessment and therapeutic opportunities for all involved. Like any other treatment format, this one is potentially quite flexible and can take many forms.

Short-Term Parent-Child Art Therapy Groups

Over the years, I have often led short-term weekly joint groups for parents and children in a variety of settings, both in clinics and in the community. Most met jointly for 45 minutes, followed by separate activities—usually a 45 minute discussion time for parents and snack and activity for children. Although time-limited (1 to 6 sessions), the same kinds of learning and growing opportunities were available and were utilized by the participants.

Chapter 16 (pp. 305–308) describes a mother-child art session which was part of a 6-week group for parents of blind children. Chapter 18 (pp. 330–344) describes several such experiences for parents of normal children in various community settings. Since art activities are among the few in which adults and children can participate simultaneously, each at their own level, yet can work together on joint projects, they are particularly appropriate for activity therapy or educational approaches involving parents and children.

In Vancouver, British Columbia, art therapist Lucille Proulx (2002) has utilized a similar approach to work with infants and preschoolers, often involving fathers as well as mothers (DVD 12.5). For parent and child, such a shared experience may indeed help them to develop "a new code of communication" (Ginott, 1965, p. 25).

Mothers' Art Therapy Groups

Single Mothers

Although this group took place in a local community center, and was labeled as parent education, what occurred was indeed therapeutic for the participants (DVD 12.6). They were first asked to do life-space pictures. One young widow explained that her picture (Figure 12.4) showed schematically her feelings of concern and confusion about the burdens of homemaking, bill-paying, and child-rearing on her own. Although she saw her hobbies and the church as sources of recreation and renewal, her view of the future was dominated by thoughts of deterioration (air pollution) which she felt powerless to halt. Other single parents in the group empathized with her feelings of being overwhelmed by responsibilities, and many were helpful, as they shared with her their own ways of coping and managing without a partner.

Head Start Mothers

The Pittsburgh Child Guidance Center included a special Head Start classroom for seriously disturbed youngsters. A social worker and a child psychiatrist first met with the mothers in an attempt to conduct a verbal psychotherapy group. These women were not especially articulate, and

12.4 A Young Widow's "Life-Space" Drawing of Her Many Concerns

were suspicious of the clinic; although they were genuinely grateful that their children, who had failed in regular Head Start classrooms, were able to come.

The drama therapist and I consulted regularly with the classroom teachers, and in the course of one meeting they asked if we would like to try doing an expressive arts therapy group with the women. We said we'd be happy to try, and it turned out to be a success (DVD 12.7). It was our feeling that one reason was that these mothers were themselves so hungry for attention, approval, and help that it was virtually impossible for them to give much to their children—one reason for their youngsters' problems.

We not only fed them snacks, in order to help them to be more relaxed around the table in the group room; we also fed them materials and supplies. These they gobbled up as eagerly as the soda and pretzels, energetically creating things for themselves, like hats (12.7A), purses, and jewelry (12.7B). In the course of these playful sessions we were able to encourage and evoke a considerable amount of casual discussion of their children and the difficulties they were having in raising them (12.7C).

Because the atmosphere was so informal, it was probably possible for the mothers to communicate with us and with each other in a more natural and open way than they had been able to in the more formal therapy/ discussion group previously offered. And because they were being fed themselves, on all levels—including information about child development and ways to manage little ones, they gained greater reserves to offer their children.

Mothers with Substance Abuse Problems

Some years later, the drama therapist led a group for women fighting substance abuse, who were in a residential program that included their children and a considerable amount of parent education (DVD 12.8). Although the focus of the group was not on parenting per se, the children came up frequently in discussion. As with the Head Start mothers, this was a needy group of women, as one might imagine from their symptoms. Here, too, they were eager to consume the food and drink, and to metabolize the art supplies into lovely artwork of their own creation (12.8A).

Their pleasure in discovering things about themselves was evident (12.8B) and was articulated fairly often (12.8C). Despite the fact that much of what came out visually and verbally was distressing, they grew from it and were pleased (12.8D). The social worker from the agency, who also attended the weekly group, reported that they seemed more understanding of their youngsters after the art sessions, an observation which confirmed our hypothesis that nurturing the parents enables them to be able to better nurture their children (12.8E).

A month after the mothers' group had ended, we were asked to conduct a joint art session with their children, which was followed by a series of art sessions for the youngsters. Instead of being held like the adult group at a community arts center, these were conducted in the residence where the parents and their children were living, as the women went through rehabilitation.

Conclusion

It is no surprise that art therapy can be helpful to adults who are parents—as individuals, as couples, and in a group—when their children are being seen for psychotherapy, with or without art. It is also no surprise that joint sessions with their children, or group sessions for mothers and children, should be helpful as well. Similarly, parent groups, which can include or be restricted to fathers, can also be facilitated through the addition of art activities.

In the following chapter the focus is on children's art therapy groups, one of the most common treatment formats when this book was first written, and today as well—almost 30 years later. Group therapy is not only cost-effective, it is also a powerful modality in its own right. When art is added, it further enhances the effectiveness of this form of treatment.

CHAPTER

13

Group Art Therapy

History and Development

A family, of course, is a particular kind of interdependent group, so it is not surprising that procedures utilized to assess families can also be used productively with groups. Asking group members, perhaps at varying points in time, to represent the group (Denny, 1972; Hare & Hare, 1956; Rubin & Levy, 1975) may be extremely helpful in getting a sense of how individuals perceive the unit. Similarly, group members may work together on a joint project, such as a mural, in which therapists can observe their decision-making and interaction processes.

The early years of group art therapy with youngsters, as with adults, featured an emphasis on work by individuals done in a group context, usually (though not always) followed by some discussion of each person's product (Dunn & Semple, 1956). While there was some awareness of the communicative function served by the artwork among group members (Kramer, 1958; Sinrod, 1964), the emphasis was on individuals rather than on the group as an entity. With the growth of group psychotherapy, and the concomitant emphasis on the understanding and utilization of group process as a tool for change, group art therapy has increasingly looked at group dynamics (Riley, 2001b; Sobol & Williams, 2001; Waller, 1993).

Sometimes this is accomplished through joint projects, which are particularly useful as ways of helping individuals to experience and examine their relationships with others. While these usually involve discussion, some have described working together silently, as couples (Wadeson, 1973) and in a group (Rhyne, 1995). Work with groups in art has been reported within a variety of theoretical frameworks, including Gestalt (Oaklander,

1988), Humanistic (Denny, 1972), Freudian (Kramer, 1958), and Narrative (Riley, 2001b). As with representations of the family, pictures of the group have been utilized as a way of looking at members' perceptions of the unit (Hare & Hare, 1956).

Sometimes representations of the group emerge spontaneously or in projected associations. In the 6th month of a weekly adolescent group, for example, Hannah first labeled her vibrant-colored abstract acrylic painting "Hate, Hate, Hate!" Looking at it during the snack-discussion time at the end of group, she pointed to the areas of color, identifying each one as a member of the group, with herself next to the leaders in the center. Pointing to a strip of gray at the left-hand corner of her painting, she said, "There's Matt, trying to squeeze in, and this is Jim next to him."

It is significant that both boys were the only black members of the group and that Hannah's projective comments had been preceded by a discussion about discrimination, in which she had made a slip: "I don't think people should show discrimination *for* the colored people. . . ." Jim had reacted angrily, correcting her: "You shouldn't say discrimination *for* black people. You should say discrimination *against* black people." It was indeed true that the two boys had not yet been accepted or trusted by the others. Her perception of herself as close to the leaders reflected a wished-for intimacy, evident from her demanding behavior.

While most publications on group art therapy have dealt with adults, some have described work with children and adolescents in a variety of settings (Bender, 1952; Dunn & Semple, 1956; Kramer, 1958, 1971, 1979; Landgarten, 1981; Linesch, 1988; Namer & Martinez, 1967; Oaklander, 1978; Riley, 1999; Safran, 2002; Sinrod, 1964). The literature on play therapy groups (Axline, 1947; Ginott, 1961; M. Lowenfeld, 1971; Schiffer, 1969) and on activity and activity-interview groups (Konopka, 1963; Slavson & Schiffer, 1975) is also closely related to work with children in group art therapy (see also Hanes, 1982).

Group art therapy takes advantage of the potency of both art and the group. Describing a self-awareness group with adults, Vich and Rhyne explain how their previous work had made them "aware of the power of the small group process to expand the usual range of human awareness. [They] believed that adding visual, tactile, and kinesthetic means of expression and communication to verbal methods could further extend this range for individuals and the group" (1967, p. 1).

From a similar but different point of view, having a therapeutic art experience within a group adds another dimension which, though it may be inhibiting for some, may be facilitating for others. Some children, for example, are painfully self-conscious when alone with an adult; often they have lost faith in grownups, but are still optimistic about trusting peers. For such youngsters, the group is a much safer, more dependable, and more comfortable context within which to explore themselves.

Deciding What to Do

I believe the most useful way to approach group art therapy is in an open-ended fashion. As with individuals, a "framework for freedom" allows unique and common concerns to emerge organically in a natural and comfortable way (DVD 13.1). Because an art therapy group, when unstructured, allows for individual freedom of movement and activity, a member can either choose to observe or to participate, to talk or to remain silent, to be alone or with others, to work independently or jointly, to relate actively or to distance from others (13.1A). As children begin to relate to one another, they are stimulated, get ideas, gain courage, help one another, and sometimes decide spontaneously to work together on joint projects (13.1B). There are times, however, when some structure or direction from the leader seems appropriate.

It is possible to provide varying degrees and kinds of structure, depending on the goals for any particular group at any particular moment in time. Thus, in early meetings it is important to set the stage for later work by clarifying the nature of the contract between members and leader(s), and enabling people to feel secure and comfortable in the environment, as well as with each other. For very young children, the most comfortable beginning format is probably an open one, where a free choice of media and activities is provided, and individuals are encouraged to explore, select, and get to work on whatever interests them.

Warming Up or "Unfreezing"[1]

For older children, however, some initial warmup activities or a specific task may ease their adjustment to the unfamiliar space and people. Thus, a group of 5- and 6-year-olds began around a table, exploring in turn a "Feely-Meely Box," a game in which one feels what is inside the box without seeing it and describes and guesses what it is, mirroring some of the mystery of the new group. After telling each other their names and grades, they were ready to explore the art media, to choose and to work on one or more projects for an hour, returning to the table for a snack and sharing time at the end of the 90-minute session.

Finding ways of overcoming learned inhibitions about work in art is

[1] "Unfreezing" is a term coined by Aina Nucho (2003) for warmup activities.

especially essential with adolescents and adults, for whom one must often "unblock the natural impulse to draw" (McKim, 1972, p. 49). Warmup techniques all have in common the dual goals of reducing self-consciousness and freeing personal creativity (DVD 13.2). Some involve an explicit de-emphasis on representation, like making an abstract color picture of feelings (Culbert & Fisher, 1969). A time limit for exercises facilitates spontaneity, and reduces anxiety about the finished product.

Sometimes it helps to suggest closed eyes, enabling individuals to work freely without judging the product (13.2A). It also helps to use visual starters, like beginning a picture with a scribble, a line, a piece of paper, a photograph, or a blob of paint on wet paper. Such exercises not only help individuals overcome blocks, but enable them to get in touch with more personal imagery. Linda Gantt, following in the footsteps of her teacher, Hanna Kwiatkowska, asks group members to begin with a "clay scribble," analogous to a linear scribble, working the clay until it suggests an image that they can then develop (13.2B).

A playful approach to the activities can also reduce self-consciousness, and can be accomplished in a variety of ways. Another is by asking participants to "fool around," especially with a contact medium like plasticine, in order to get to know it better.

Sometimes a group is helped to reduce concern about the finished product, and to get to know each other, by working together and sharing responsibility (13.2C). In some groups, a simultaneous nonverbal mural, done with poster chalks on a large sheet of paper on floor (13.2D), or table (13.2E), or wall, can be a powerful experience of "letting go." As with round-robin activities (taking turns molding a chunk of clay [13.2F] or drawing on a sheet of paper passed around the group [13.2G]), such shared involvements carry both risks and opportunities. If managed insensitively, they can unleash potentially threatening hostility; if handled carefully, they can enable group members to feel an instant sense of community.

Getting to Know Each Other

In addition to warming up in a way that enhances comfort, an early need of group members is to get to know one another (DVD 13.3). While this will occur in time, and may indeed be best left undirected, there are times where it may facilitate the process to give specific tasks. A game where teenagers introduced themselves by making a clay symbol, then sharing it with the others, helped them to meet each other (13.3A). They were then asked to work together to make a bridge, thus fostering interaction (13.3B).

Another group of adolescents was asked to describe with any medium what they wanted to gain from the group; their pictures and sculptures had

221

astounding communicative as well as expressive power. Yet another kind of introduction is to use initials as a "starter" to tell others about themselves (13.3C).

Just as the range of productive tasks is infinite, there are also endless possibilities for beginning with responses to artistic stimuli. For example, mothers of children with disabilities were asked to select from among a series of photographs the one that most reminded them of their youngster. A group of elementary-age children was asked to choose the picture they liked best and the one they liked least, from among a selection of reproductions of paintings.

As with productive activities, the subsequent discussion may focus on process, product, or both. The group members can be led to examine *how* they made their choice and *why* they chose a particular item, as well as to look at and further associate to the product selected, perhaps by telling a story about a picture or imagining why a person in it is feeling the way he looks to the group members.

Activities in Art Therapy Groups

Some kinds of groups, focused around a particular topic or problem, perhaps short-term and limited in scope, may do best to proceed in a "theme-centered" manner (DVD 13.4) (Cohn, 1969–70), like the groups for children with ADHD run by Diane Safran (DVD 13.4A; Safran, 2002). In a series of "art-awareness" groups for adolescents in various settings, it proved productive to focus on a particular theme or task at each session, with only occasional free-choice meetings (Rubin & Levy, 1975). Since the explicit purpose of the groups was to help teenagers to express, define, understand, and accept themselves, topics centered on identity issues. These included thinking of their real selves in terms of time, as in a life-space drawing, a picture of their future goals, or a life-line pictorially representing their past. They were also asked to think of their inner selves, in terms of fantasies, wishes, dreams, or fears, with such explicit topics as "My Worst Fear" or "Myself as I Wish to Be."

Similarly, youngsters might be asked to do the same task, like the Ukrainian orphans who were invited to make masks with feelings on the inside (13.4B). Or they might be invited to work together in some fashion (13.4C). Sometimes the group task is to create something specific, like an island (13.4D). On the other hand, the sharing of a pictorial space can also happen without planning (13.4E).

And of course, members can also be free to decide what to use and what to make in all kinds of groups, including those with multiple families (13.4F).

Conversely, the topic might be the same with a choice of drawing media (13.4G), or the medium might be the same with a choice of topic (13.4H). In much group art therapy, there is a combination of structured and unstructured activities, like the program at RAW Art Works (13.4I).

Interpersonal issues of territoriality, authority, and control are always present whenever two or more people work together. In a nonverbal pictorial exercise, in which two people work together silently on a shared picture space without prior discussion, such issues come to the fore, and can be discussed following the activity (Figure 13.1).

Transactional themes can also be the explicit subject matter of an assignment, as in a boss-slave game, like that done with mothers and children. In a group, one member of a dyad tells the other what art materials to use and how to use them. They then switch roles and do it again. Later they discuss their experiences together. Not only can dyads or triads discuss such events, but later they can join with others who have done the same activity, and can then learn about other small-group perceptions of the issues involved (see DVD 13.4C).

In order to clarify and to enact finding one's place in a group, each person in a small group can make his or her own three-dimensional self-image (of clay, plasticine, or wood scraps), and then move it silently, along with others, on a large paper representing a shared "world space." A nonverbal movement-drama ensues, at times going on for many minutes with great intensity, until each person has finally found his spot (see DVD 11.5A).

When all are settled into their places on the shared territory, it is suggested that they further define the space through line drawings on the surface. They are then asked to discuss the entire transaction, sometimes assuming the relative positions of their self-symbols for the discussion, whether huddled together in a bunch or separated in some way. Such an exercise is extremely helpful in enabling individuals to clarify the roles they assume in groups, such as intruder, compromiser, outsider, facilitator, disruptor, and so on (see DVD 11.5B).

The specific technique or format of an exercise—media, theme, instructions, number of people involved, spatial relationship, time available, focus of the discussion, leader involvement, and so forth—should relate to the goals of that particular exercise, in the context of the comfort level of that particular group. There are always variations among group members in openness. For some, the risks are primarily interpersonal—revealing too much about oneself, being judged and evaluated, excessively dominating a group, and so on. For others, the risks are more often of an intrapsychic nature—among others, fear of loss of control or disorganization, or worry that unacceptable impulses will emerge.

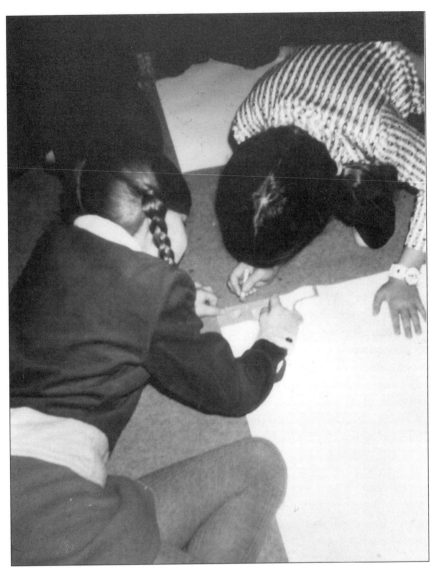

13.1 Two Girls Working Together on the Same Space without Talking

One way to help individuals to protect themselves against undue risk-taking is to provide options. Thus, whether a group is structured or open-ended, the decision about whether to participate is best if left up to each member. Similarly, some degree of choice, even within a structured task, should always be present (for example, paper size, medium, position in space, and so on).

In a group, an explicit limit on negative judgmental evaluation of others' productions may be necessary, to reduce the degree of threat involved in opening up, both symbolically and verbally. It is also made clear that each individual is their own expert, the sole recognized authority on the meaning of their own art. If they choose to respond to another's work, they are seen as using it as a projective stimulus for themselves, but not as being able to validly interpret someone else's creative expression.

Within a framework of constant respect for and protection of individuals, one may use all of the tools at one's disposal: leader(s), space, time, materials, degree of structure, nature of the task, and so forth. Given these tools, it is possible to creatively design activities which meet the needs of any particular group at any moment in time. The role of the leader may vary in the course of a session, from instructor to passive observer, to active participant, or discussion leader.

The preceding activities are examples of ways of manipulating the many variables at one's disposal in order to achieve a particular goal. Nevertheless, even in a group with a central theme, like "art for self-awareness," it seems vital that some time be spent in a free-choice situation, in which each person follows his or her own creative self-defining bent.

It is my feeling that the question is never one of either-or, of structure versus no structure—but rather is an ongoing task with every group, of planning, or picking up on, ways of enhancing therapeutic movement at any moment. In most cases, a combination of open and more structured activities seems to be appropriate, enabling participants to experience a greater variety of media and roles than they might otherwise explore (see 13.4I).

Groups and How They Grow

A group is both a collection of individuals, and a becoming entity made up of those individuals, yet qualitatively different from the sum of its members. It is not unlike a collage or construction, where the final product includes each component part in its original form. And, like a collage, a group represents the creation of a new gestalt, wherein each component appears differently than when it is seen in isolation from the total work.

Unlike a collage or construction, a group changes its shape and form over time in an organic fashion, as the members deal with each other and the leader(s) around the critical issues of each phase. Some of the key issues in groups are intimacy, trust, rivalry, peer pressure, and authority (DVD 13.5). While these are all present to some degree in individual therapy, those related to the power and danger of alliances between members are unique to the group and are part of what give it therapeutic potency. Each new group is a new adventure, and part of what makes group art therapy exciting is that it is impossible to know its path in advance.

Nevertheless, there appears to be a fairly uniform pattern of growth in groups which, like graphic development, varies in tempo, but is quite predictable in sequence, whatever the age of the members. Groups usually begin as collections of individuals, each relating separately to the leader, often with rapidly increasing rivalry for the leader's attention and approval.

Over time, usually after some testing of each other and the leader, members begin to form alliances among themselves. These tend to be primarily dyadic, though occasionally include more than two members, and might reflect subgroups related to sex, age, psychopathology, and so forth. The dynamics of small groups have been fairly well studied, and seem to be quite ubiquitous (Cartwright & Zander, 1981; Freud, 1922; Yalom, 1995), including what goes on in art therapy groups of any age level.

An art therapy group, like any kind of activity group, makes possible a kind of natural, simultaneous interaction of individuals, in a way that is both informal and relatively unthreatening (DVD 13.6). Members can talk about their artwork to each other or the leader while working (13.6A), or can choose to tell everybody about it in a sharing time, usually provided at the end of group session (13.6B). Members can learn by watching others, gaining confidence and participating vicariously, and by working with others, thereby practicing sharing and cooperation, as well as mutual respect for individual differences.

For the therapist, being able to observe youngsters in live interaction with peers affords a much richer understanding of the reality as well as the distortions of their social behavior. While the presence of peers may make it harder for some to talk about their art, for others the desire to be accepted, or even natural competition, may enable them to overcome inhibitions in telling stories or associating to their products.

Not only can individuals in a group explore their own ideas in relation to their art, they can also utilize the work of others as a stimulus for projection and imagination (13.6C). Sherry, age 17, had spent most of one session working hard on a life-size Pariscraft sculpture of her father, explaining that then she could tell him off without having to hear his reactions. Sam, looking at her unfinished figure, commented that he looked "like a person fighting in order to bring out his emotions," and that he had an "expression of frustration," reflecting how Sam himself was feeling at the time. Yet another member playfully kissed the ambiguous sculpture.

A year later, when Sam was getting close to an awareness of his repressed anger in a negative transference to me, he projected a destructive wish as he—calling himself "Dr. Fraud"—analyzed my ambiguous, abstract water-color painting: "The picture shows that she's afraid she's going to die. There's going to be a great storm that comes up, and it's going to cast her over a big cliff. . . . She will break her neck when she falls face down on a carving bush, and no one will ever remember her. They won't even find her after she's eaten. Everyone will forget about her, and no one will remember her. Nothing will be left behind, and there will be nothing good that would have been done in her lifetime. Her good spirit will drown in the sea."

Sherry, looking at the same picture, expressed her own anxiety as she de-scribed what it said about the artist: "She likes adventure, but she's afraid of it. She gets lost easily, and she's afraid to be by herself. She has a deep fear of being in the woods, 'cause some lion is going to attack her."

Sam, unable to stop, had to say more about what would happen to me: "There's going to be a stoneless plot for her, so no one will ever know where she is. Every once in a while we will throw a worm on her and hope that her body gets eaten up. When she lands in the bush, she will get buried, and everyone else will throw up on her. Cow dung will be thrown on her grave, and then everyone else will live happily ever after. No one will ever notice that she's missing, but everyone will be cheerful." Sam told the story with great relish, and denied vehemently the suggestion that it might have something to do with his anger that I was about to be away from the group for almost a month (for a long vacation). Nevertheless, he had an espe-cially hard time leaving the group room that day, as if to confirm the inter-pretation through his behavior.

As time goes on, children with common or complementary problems tend to form subgroups, sometimes sharing such concerns openly as well as symbolically. In the ninth session of a group of 5- and 6-year-olds, instead of working independently and relating primarily to me, for the first time four members formed two pairs. Jenny and Lisa worked side by side at a table with clay, while the boys mutually created and painted a large city of wood scraps, after some competitive but cooperative block building.

When I asked Jenny to tell me about her "Skyscraper Building" she said, "You live there and so does Lisa. You used to have a father, but he died." (Both girls' fathers were dead, Jenny's through suicide.) When I asked how the father had died, Jenny replied, "He took too much medicine . . . 'cause he was sick, and then he thought that would make him better." She then added, with excitement, "You can have another father. . . . You get one at the store. You have to try to catch one. . . . When you see a pretty man, then you catch him. . . . A handsome man."

Lisa had listened to this interchange silently, and when I asked her what she thought of Jenny's idea, said, "I don't want to." She went on to explain that she liked the idea of living with me in a skyscraper, but not of catching a father. I tried to clarify for Jenny: "Lisa says she'd just as soon not. She'd rather just stay there with me, and you're saying you'd rather find a father. Do you think sometimes when you had a father, and then he's gone. . . ." At this point Jenny interrupted me, saying, "He died!" Lisa also quickly stated, "He died." "Yes," I said, "That happened to both of you, didn't it? You both had fathers and they died, and Lisa's not so sure she wants another one, and Jenny, you're saying that you think you *do* want another one. So you feel differently." Lisa, who was feeling quite angry at her father for dying, spent most of the time making "little monster faces" out of clay, who had nothing to say, except that they were "mad."

The Use of Structure in Unstructured Groups

There are times in an ongoing group where most sessions are open-ended, when a suggested structure may help members deal with particular emerging concerns. During the 6th month of weekly group meetings with the same young children, and stimulated by their increasingly vocal worries about what they saw in the dark, I decided to introduce a spotlight and shadows. A filmstrip projector in a darkened room threw a large spot of bright light on the wall.

I suggested first that the children move freely in the light and look at their shadows. Next, they took turns if they wished, finding a pose, freezing in that pose, and standing in front of the large sheet of white paper taped on the wall, while one of the leaders traced their shadow on the paper. Those waiting their turn sat at the table and worked with clay, using the light from the back of the projector, enjoying the excitement of the scary atmosphere. Some chose to finish the shadow-tracings by filling in with paint or other media, others left the outlines untouched. What seemed most important was the experience of being in the dark with shadows that you could look at, know about, and even capture on paper, further defining them if you wished.

With a group of inpatient psychotic children (ages 9 to 12), a predominant theme of the artwork and discussion had been their unhappiness about being hospitalized, and their often mixed feelings about returning home after what they knew to be time-limited treatment. Following several open-ended sessions, therefore, I suggested that perhaps they might like to think about a theme, specifically, "Where I Would Like to Be Right Now."

Essie wishfully painted a peaceful house by a lake and mountain out in the country, with only animals inside. Ben, whose mother had abandoned him, was even more wishful, as he painted a huge castle, a tree whose limbs reach toward it, and a vibrant sun, in bright colors. Rob constructed a wood scrap complex of houses and buildings, first naming it as the hospital (where indeed he did feel safe), then saying it was a graveyard (perhaps the more fearful aspect of interment).

Glen drew an elaborate picture on oversize paper of a wishfully intact family, with a nice house and a yard with swings; radically different from the chaotic, broken home to which he could not return, instead being confined to a state institution for the retarded. The children were able to share, in both the doing and the discussion, their intense wishes for a better place to go than reality held in store for any of them.

Individuals can easily use a common task or theme to deal with their own concerns, as long as it is sufficiently flexible. Thus, each child in the group of 5- and 6-year-olds made a bendable doll with elasticlay, and a wood scrap house for it to live in; yet each doll and house and associated story was as individual as the child who created them. Lisa's doll, for example, was "a little girl" who has "a bad boy and a bad sister. The bad boy hits me and the bad sister hits me too," Lisa said, talking for the doll and paralleling her own sibling rivalry situation. Steve's "boy" doll lived in "a new house, and we're gonna move into it. . . . It's very beautiful in the new house," just as Steve's mom was constantly promising a new lifestyle, which never happened.

Jamie's doll was called "my man, Smokey the Bear," and as he was then developing intense affectionate (oedipal) feelings toward his female therapist, Jamie explained that "Mrs. Rubin lives with Smokey the Bear." Jenny's house was small and, like Jenny, a bit disorganized. In it, Jenny said, lived a dog doll who needed to have his temperature taken repeatedly, a subject of intense interest to all of the children.

Group Themes and Concerns

This same group of children often shared other concerns as well, and became especially involved over time in the playing out and reworking of dramas involving the male therapist as a monster who scares, captures, or threatens them, and is eventually robbed or killed off by the children. This theme was introduced quite spontaneously when one of the children during the snack made a monster with the gumdrops and toothpicks provided, and the others suggested they play monster afterward.

The two girls went with the monster (father) as assistants, while the four boys chose to go with me (mother), suggesting that we hide under a large workbench, which they dubbed "the safe place." They gave the monster a bag of clay, which they called "gold," then told him to "be asleep" so they could steal his treasure. The excitement and challenge of venturing forth against the powerful father-monster was great for the boys, while the private assistantship was satisfying to the equally oedipal girls. As an index of the intensity and seriousness for the children of this make-believe, Tim arrived the following week wearing an outfit with many pockets, in each a paper knife with which he planned to kill the monster.

Over time, they demanded repetitions of the drama after snack time, often putting on paint makeup in order to scare the monster or to be a better monster assistant, depending on which role each wanted to take that day. They introduced variations and modifications, and eventually were able to find a way to reform the monster and make friends, neither killing him off nor punishing themselves by being jailed or killed off in retaliation. While the theme may have touched on separate issues for each child, it carried enough meaning for all of them that it was requested almost weekly for about 6 months. One might hypothesize that it enabled them to deal with numerous issues around oedipal wishes and conflicts over aggression, with which each one was coping in his or her own way.

Creative Play with Food

Using gumdrops and toothpicks as a snack with dramatic potential is only one of many ways to extend the possibilities for creative fantasy. In a group of 9- to 11-year-old boys, for example, small multicolored marshmallows were made into objects or figures with toothpick connectors. Matt created an airplane, happily suggesting that he, as the "bombardier," would hit all the schools, so there would be no more school. Tommy's marshmallow man was described as "big and mean," and was then toasted and eaten. Similarly, using icing dispensers, the boys created faces on large round cookies, then used them as puppets who talked with each other, before eating them up.

In the group of 5- and 6-year-olds described earlier, the children one day made creatures of marshmallows and toothpicks and then used them dramatically. Jack, whose brother had died of a cerebral hemorrhage, was able for the first time to express some of his mixed feelings, about which he had only giggled nervously in the past. He said that both of his figures were boys, then put one down and said sadly, "His brother died." When I asked what "he" did, Jack replied, "Then his father cried. And he felt sad, and he laughed." I wondered how it happened, and Jack said, "An accident. His mother was in the accident too, but she didn't die. . . . His father said, 'Don't die.'"

I asked if the brother died anyway, to which he replied, "Yeah, he died." Then I asked how the little boy felt, to which Jack replied seriously and with feeling, "Sad, sad, sad. . . . Yeah! I was sad when *my* brother died." "I bet you were," I commented, after which Jack went on with material he had until then been unable to verbalize: "Yeah. My brother died, and the veins in his head broke, and all the blood came out from his veins. But my brother didn't have an accident when he died. His veins broke."

Role-Taking in Interviews

In the above illustration, it seemed easier for Jack to gain psychic distance by talking *about*, rather than *for*, his creation. Sometimes it is more comfortable for a child to express himself by taking a role—either as what he has created, or in relation to it. Twelve-year-old Fred, for example, was being asked lots of questions by others in his group about his drawing of "Joe Frazier" (Figure 13.2), also called "The Stupid Man"—a boxer who had challenged Cassius Clay to a duel and gotten badly beaten.

At one point Fred responded to a question with "Ask Cassius Clay!" and I suggested that he might speak for Cassius Clay himself. Using a deep voice, he described quite vividly his worries about the dangers of aggression: "Well, he tried to get smart with me in the first round. He punched me on my nose, so I just had to yoke him up. He got me mad. . . . I just kicked a few teeth out. He was so scared that his teeth turned orange, and all the rest of his body turned all colors. Boy, the hospital says they can't even put him in critical condition!"

I asked, "Are you worried that you might have hurt him in a way that they can't fix him up, Cassius?" to which Fred replied, "You better believe it!" I reminded him that there were rules in boxing, and that a referee could stop a fight so a man couldn't get too badly hurt, but Fred shook his head, saying sadly, "The referee was his mother-in-law." It was my feeling that Fred was telling us of his own worries; that his mother would not be able to prevent him from carrying out his aggressive wishes toward his abusive father—indeed, that his impulses were murderously dangerous.

Interviewing Each Other

In a group, children can and do interview one another regarding their artwork, learning further to develop an "observing ego" by helping someone else to do so (13.6D). In the following excerpt from a taped interview

13.2 "Joe Frazier" or "The Stupid Man," a Boxer Who Got Beaten Up. Marker

with a group of 10-year-old boys, Victor helped Jerry to define his product, as well as expressing some of his own curiosity:

> Jerry: I made a sculpture of this mountain with a pond on it, and with a stream running down. It's made out of clay, and it's on a piece of cardboard. At the top, in the pond, I have glue around it . . . and I have water in it, real water. Are there any questions?
> Victor: Does anybody live on it?

Jerry: It's a deserted island.

Victor: Can the water run away?

Jerry: Not right now, but it's supposed to. I have to put a drainage system in it. Actually, it's sort of like a circulating system.

Victor: Do you have any living animals there?

Jerry: No, there aren't any, but there's mice thrown into it, by sea or else by land. It's a lake with a stream running down.

Victor: Does the lake run into a river or an ocean?

Jerry: It runs into the ocean. It's an underground spring. Any other questions? Thank you very much.

Until this session, Victor had been very inhibited during the discussion time, despite his interest in holding and using the tape recorder microphone. Indeed, he asked questions of others for some weeks before he was able to eventually talk freely about his own creations.

Reviewing in a Group

Reviewing what has gone on over time in a group, as with a family or individuals, is often possible through looking back over art productions. In addition, slides of products or activities, and films or videotapes of sessions can enable the group to relive and review what has gone before (13.6E).

With the 5- and 6-year-olds described earlier, one discussion session was organized around viewing slides of wood scrap houses they had made, eliciting a whole new set of projections about these constructions. Another focused on slides from a recent joint session with their mothers, enabling them to talk about some of the feelings they had experienced that could not be easily shared during the joint discussion time.

Over a year after an adolescent group had been meeting, an hour was spent reviewing all of the Super 8mm film shot, most of it taken by the group members. While no one was able to talk about changes in her- or himself, many were able to see positive changes in each other, pointing them out with delight. Most dramatic were their changed perceptions of the leaders, who were seen as having been nicer in the past, relative to their present disillusionment with formerly idealized parent figures.

Individual Growth in a Group: Don

Change in a group can be seen as members develop trust and the group takes on shape and definition as an entity in its own right, becoming more cohesive. In this context, the individuals in group treatment also change, as they utilize the resources in art and each other to work on and resolve their conflicts.

Don, for example, began by working alone, making compulsive abstract designs (Figure 13.3a), but gradually moved toward more communication with the other boys and in his art. At first he sat closer to others, still silent, and became somewhat freer in his abstractions, needing fewer boundaries and allowing himself more range within them.

He then turned to work with more tactile media like clay, perhaps stimulated by the others. At first he made tame animals (dogs and cats), then larger, more aggressive ones (lions and dinosaurs). Eventually, he was able to model and paint a boy who had been violently wounded, with red blood streaming out of his maimed body (Figure 13.3b).

While he declined to say who it might be the week he made it, the following week he whispered to me that he knew who it was, but was afraid to tell the others. I asked if he could tell me, and Don whispered, "My brother." I then suggested that it might help the other boys in the group, many of whom had similar angry feelings and wishes toward siblings, to know that they were not alone.

During group discussion time at the end of the session he tentatively whispered that it was "somebody younger," then, "somebody I'd like to throw something at," and finally, "my brother." The others responded with relief, and with an outpouring of their own hostile impulses to hurt younger siblings—along with fears of their strength and potential dangerousness.

Don was delighted, and responded the following week by becoming very messy, smearing and mixing lots of tempera paint colors with another boy, for the first time allowing himself to regress and to interact freely with other group members. His products for the next 2 weeks were not much to look at, but the process he engaged in was vital to his own eventual recovery.

He followed this aggressive/regressive phase with a freer kind of order in his work, selecting a tempera painting with movement, color mixing, and clear but not rigid boundaries, as a gift for his individual therapist when he terminated treatment several months later (Figure 13.3c).

Group Growth: New Members and Endings

While the most effective ongoing therapy groups in my experience are those with a fairly stable membership, it is often necessary to admit new members when others leave the group. The introduction of a new member is like the coming of a new baby, for in many ways a group comes to represent for its members a symbolic family, the leaders seen as parent figures

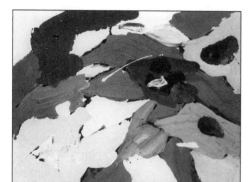

13.3 Three Works by Don
(a) A Tight Drawing; (b) A Bloody Sculpture; (c) A Free Painting

and the other members as siblings. Not only do the members need preparation for such an event, but their ways of dealing with it may be indicative of how they feel about other family members at home.

Jamie, for example, was very upset on the day that Sally entered his group for the first time, making many silly aggressive remarks, even "attacking" the paper on which she was drawing by writing his own first initial. Jenny, on the other hand, was delighted to have another girl in the group, and quickly latched on to Sally, asking her to draw next to her on mural paper, eventually trying to copy Sally's picture.

Endings with groups are much like terminations with individuals—no matter how long or short, there are feelings about ending that are related to separation issues for all members. These can be stormy as well as sad, and often require much time, if a group can be open about a termination date, for adequate working-through.

In most long-term groups, the introduction of the idea of termination is followed by both regression and aggression. In two groups, dramas of capturing and killing off the leaders expressed the intensity of the members' rage at being abandoned. These were followed, as in most termination processes, by expressions of sadness—of mourning—for ending a therapeutic relationship is a real as well as a symbolic loss. If there is sufficient time and all goes well the loss is accepted, along with all of the feelings involved in saying goodbye.

Conclusion

Art in a group is in some ways different from other group approaches, especially in comparison to discussion formats with adolescents and adults. Like play or activity approaches, it makes possible simultaneous communication between and among group members throughout the working period. Art also allows for more informal, non-spotlighted communications, as preparation for those inhibited about speaking openly to the whole group.

Unlike games or crafts, the art activity provides not only for mastery of skills but also for symbolic expression of conflicted inner feelings, fantasies, and fears. Because of the range of possible media, individuals can discover their own preferred materials and processes and thus work on individual identity and mutual respect within a group context. As in individual art therapy, both expression and reflection are possible, and each may sometimes be enhanced, stimulated, and facilitated in a group setting.

CHAPTER

14

Multimodality
Group Therapy

Relationships among the Arts

For a long time, as an art teacher and as an art therapist, I never realized that what I did with visual and plastic media was related in any but a semantic way to work in other art forms. I had always loved literature, film, music, dance, and drama, but had thought of them as essentially different and unique creative modalities. I have since discovered that, while in many ways they are indeed distinct, in other ways they are not. This paradox derives from what I have come to perceive as their organic interrelatedness—as forms of thinking, and as ways of sending and receiving messages.

This first was apparent to me when I became a mother, and watched my infants explore the world with all of their senses. It was even more evident as they grew older, and began to express themselves in rapidly shifting but closely related ways. They cooed, they rocked, they touched, and they moved, all in ways that conveyed meaning. These expressions were often combined—the coo and the gesture, or the manipulation and the body rhythm.

As I related to them, I too used various forms of communication in my maternal efforts at contact. I would touch, I would rock, I would make sounds and gestures, I would use words, and sometimes I would direct their attention to visual phenomena. Thus, very early, we were each using all of the precursors of those forms of expression that, in their later development, we call the arts.

By the time they were preschoolers my children would play in a similarly multimodal fashion—swaying while they made sand castles, growling as they pretended to be giants, or singing while they drew (DVD 14.1). In nursery school this fluid interweaving of expressive modalities happens all the time. Anyone who has observed little ones knows that spontaneous drama will emerge almost as often during their play with blocks, sand, or chalk as it will when they are engaged with dolls, puppets, or dress-ups.

Similarly, music is not confined to the time spent using rhythm instruments, but erupts spontaneously in hums and tunes, often self-created, while they are also engaged with crayon (14.1A), paint or clay (14.1B). One of my favorite children with schizophrenia used to dance whenever she would paint, so that to be with her was to witness a genuine multimedia "happening." Another would rock and hum while he moved his paint-filled brush up and down on the easel paper, as gracefully as if he were in a meditative trance.

Although I started out using only art materials in my clinical work, I soon began to perceive what was happening in dramatic terms (DVD 14.2). Sometimes it was unfocused—the gestural drama of a rhythmic scribble, the sweep of a brush, the caress of clay. At other times it was the narrative quality of the story told while smearing finger paint, or the explicit drama of the pictured or sculpted scene. A child might pick up a sculpture and transform it into a puppet, speaking *for* it in a way that was qualitatively distinct from speaking *about* it (14.2A). Or they would make sound effects for the explosions they were drawing, enlivening the represented action (14.2B).

A face would be transformed by soap crayons or finger paint (14.2C), or a child would spontaneously make a mask and use it dramatically. The chopping up of clay while describing it as the destruction of someone (14.2D), or the literal wiping out of something drawn into finger paint, was clearly as much a dramatic as an artistic event, and the familiar telling of a story about an art product could only be perceived as containing powerful narrative elements.

I learned, therefore, from my own children and my young patients, that at their source in the human being, expressive modalities are not separated by hard and fast lines, but may instead be seen as points on a continuum: from the body to the sound to the image to the word—dance, music, art, and drama. My patients also taught me to be flexible, to be ready to follow a person into another creative modality, if that is where his spirit leads him. Natalie Rogers (1993) calls this "the Creative Connection."

Carla, for example, went from drawing her nightmare monsters to cutting them out, putting them in cages and locking them up. The next step in her working-through process required an even greater use of dramatization, as the two of us enacted the roles of scary monster and frightened child (see Chapter 4; DVD 4.1 and 4.4).

On the basis of such child-initiated experiences, I became convinced that art alone may not always be enough, and that it is often essential to expand the therapy in other directions. This has occurred spontaneously so often in my own work that I am sure it is a natural thing for children to search for congenial forms of expression, and is unnatural to restrict them to any one creative modality. Had Carla stopped at the representation and even the locking up of her nightmare monsters, I think she would not have been so well able to recognize that much of the aggression she feared was her own (projected). By taking the role of the monster in a drama she was able to experience her own angry feelings. She was, therefore, ready to see later on how those angry monsters in dreams and drawings were also scary, mad wishes in herself.

Such experiences suggest that even though an art therapist's primary tool is art, it is essential to be able to permit the use of other expressive modalities, especially when they spring from the child himself. The spontaneous emergence of drama in the course of art therapy has occurred many times, in work with individuals of all ages and with all kinds of disabilities, in all kinds of settings.

Sometimes it is stimulated by the media themselves, as when Larry, who was blind, was reminded of candles by the swabs he was using, and pretended to have a birthday party (14.2E). At other times, the flow from art to drama is stimulated by the identity given the medium, as when Karen pounded and yelled at her clay blobs, as a punitive mother scolding and spanking her naughty children (14.2F). At such times, it seemed that what the child needed to communicate required the action that only drama could provide.

Such an evolution from art to drama happened as many times with groups as with individuals. One day I came to work with an art therapy group having gotten a cut, stitches, and a bandage on my leg the night before. Thinking my accident might stimulate concern about bodily injury in the children, I had brought along a new sculpture material—Pariscraft— gauze impregnated with plaster of Paris.

Almost all of the boys in the group of 12-year-olds not only modeled forms with the Pariscraft (DVD 14.3), they also experimented with casts (14.3A) on arms (14.3B), wrists, fingers, and so on (14.3C). One boy had wrapped some around both an arm and a leg, and came to the discussion time limping, saying that he had had a serious accident. I interviewed this "victim," who explained, "I got all broken up with blood."

At this point, another group member announced that he was the doctor, saying, "This is my patient. Well see, he got hit by a car, and broke his leg and arm. Up here, he got a hole in his arm, and through it you can see his veins and stuff. His leg—I gotta fix his leg up some more. You see, it's bad." After the doctor assured all of us that he would be repairing the patient, the victim dramatically unrolled his bandages and triumphantly announced, "I'm cured!"

At times the sequence is reversed and a story emerges first, to be followed by its enactment, using art media to help in the telling. Chip, a boy concerned about castration after an operation for an undescended testicle, joined a group of 6-year-olds and told a story about a baby with a broken leg whose mother was very upset. In order to play out the story, Chip made a life-size baby of brown clay with one leg missing.

Asking that I play the mother, Chip as the doctor explained, "All babies are born without another leg! You dummy!" As I and my "husband" (another group member) said how sad we were, Doctor Chip tried to restore what was missing, adding another leg to the clay baby. My "husband," who had his own castration anxieties, playfully knocked off the new clay leg each time it was attached, to which Chip responded as if immobilized, saying there was nothing he could do to help.

Finally, the male cotherapist entered the drama as another physician. He helped Chip to repair the baby and prevent the father's aggressive attacks, so that the mother was able to take a whole baby home. While the clay infant was powerfully formed, by itself it could not carry the affective impact of the drama built around its missing or damaged part.

The First Art–Drama Therapy Group: Latency-Age Boys

Experiences like those described above led to a proposal for an art-drama therapy group with Ellen Irwin, my drama therapist colleague (Irwin, Rubin, & Shapiro, 1975). As we considered working together (which was rare in those days), we worried about Susanne Langer's statement that "there are no happy marriages in art—only successful rape" (1957, p. 86). Neither of us wished to lose our still-fragile professional identity, much less to rape or be raped. We were each committed to our particular art form, and had some trepidation about the proposed union. We also feared the potential competition in working together, as well as the loss of integrity possible in each modality.

We began our work with six boys, ages 9 to 11, previously referred for art or drama therapy. Prior to beginning the group, we each met the boys for individual art and drama assessments. The art sessions were unstructured,

240

as described in Chapter 6. The drama interviews were similarly open, with puppets provided as primary projective materials, along with costume pieces and props (Irwin & Shapiro, 1975). The child was invited to make up and play out a story.

Analysis of the data from these interviews helped us to make up a behaviorally balanced group of boys who could tolerate regression and who could use creative modalities as media for change. In these assessment sessions we got to know the boys, and they got to know each of us. They also had an opportunity to try out in private the tools of the trade, which they were later to put into practice in the group.

Initially we thought we would have alternate sessions, with art activities one week and drama the next. However, it quickly became apparent that the boys would not adhere to such artificial boundaries. Each meeting, in fact, verified their need to express themselves freely in both modalities. This was clearly demonstrated in the very first session, and proved to be a recurring pattern in the life of the group, which met once a week for an hour and a half (DVD 14.4).

In the first meeting, the boys soon expressed their anxiety over the newness of the situation. As they finger painted around a table (14.4A), they shared stories of witches and vampires who really suck blood, of boats that capsize when one is unprepared, and of bombs that suddenly appear and explode without warning. At that point, one boy angrily left the group, and went off in a corner to paint an "ugly picture" of me. Unable to finish, he returned a few minutes later, held out his forefinger, which was covered with red paint, and said, "I need a doctor. I'm cut."

As the drama therapist entered the fantasy as the doctor, he elaborated, "I was cutting open my cat and got blood all over my hands." This stimulated the others, and soon the air was filled with dramatized fantasies of hurts and injuries. Another boy, who had previously drawn himself in a grave with a scary monster standing over him, immediately imitated the first and covered his hand with red paint, too. That, he said, was "my brother's blood, because I just killed him, and he's lying in a coffin."

Perhaps meeting each of us earlier in an intense evaluation session facilitated this rapid involvement in dramatic and pictorial fantasy, and the high degree of trust that made it possible to share and to verbalize anxieties. Perhaps, too, the alternation of picturing and wiping out, possible in the regressive medium of finger paint, and the mutual discussion of fantasies, induced a state of readiness for the castration-murder-doctor drama.

So intertwined were the two modalities that it became impossible to state that a session was pure art or pure drama. From that point on, therefore, materials for expression in both forms were available every week, to extend the range of possibilities for symbolic expression. In art, there were various drawing, painting, modeling, and construction materials; in drama, there were puppets, plain gauze masks, simple costume pieces, props, cloths of various sizes and textures, stage lights, and so on.

A further expectation related to the need for planned versus spontaneous activities. We had planned, and deliberately introduced, a number of combined art-and-drama techniques into the early sessions, in order to help the children learn to use them together.

The simplest was to suggest telling a story about a picture. During the first session Tommy made a peace symbol with yellow finger paint. In associating to the picture, Tommy began to talk about the problem of aggression, and his concern about war and killing. When asked what peace meant to him, he answered, "Peace means a lot to me. . . . I think peace means people talking together and children playing together instead of fighting . . . fighting with their fists." Trying to be peaceful by managing aggression reminded me of Danny, a boy with spina bifida, who had similar concerns (14.4B).

Conversely, we would sometimes suggest that someone dramatize his artwork, as when Matt was encouraged to act out the story he had told about his tempera painting of "A French Soldier Going to an American Fort." He said that the soldier had gone to George Washington to ask for reinforcements in a battle with the Indians; but he puzzled over the outcome, explaining that General Washington "sometimes says yes, and sometimes says no." In order to solve the dilemma, Matt took the role of George Washington, and acted out the story with Dick who, as the French soldier, came to see the general. Matt, as Washington, finally agreed to the Frenchman's request for 200 soldiers who, he explained, would win the war using cannons against the Indians' arrows, but would be badly wounded in the process.

Yet another combined approach was to suggest doing artwork based on a drama. In a later session, for example, following the spontaneous dramatization of a spy story, we suggested that the boys picture some of their feelings about the events they had just played out. Matt quickly produced a drawing of a man attempting to shoot a woman (Figure 14.1), describing pictorially his impulse to attack the therapist. This hypothesis was confirmed when he grinned and said to me, "That lady in the picture looks like you!"

Art materials were often used to make puppets, masks (14.4C), costumes, and props, which the boys were then encouraged to use in dramatizations—or more simply, to be interviewed as the character they had created (14.4D). Jerry, for example, was quite proud of his vampire mask, to

242

14.1 Matt's Drawing of a Man Trying to Shoot a Woman. Age 9. Marker

which he later added a self-made costume and, as Dracula, intoned, "I suck ze blood. Some blood eez better zan others." When he needed a stake to complete his vampire attire, he carefully made it himself, from cardboard.

In retrospect, it may have helped to introduce these combined art-and-drama techniques to the boys in the early sessions. But it was soon apparent that they were capable of creating their own imaginative combinations, quite independently of the leaders. In fact, in time it became clear that the boys' ingenious uses of unstructured art materials often led spontaneously into drama, promoting a natural and dynamic flow.

Thus, a cardboard carton was not only used for the suggested box sculpture, but also became a boat for Ben, a house for Matt, and a puppet stage for Dick. Similarly, soap crayons became makeup, as the boys painted their faces, externalizing their specific inner fantasies (Figure 14.2). Jack, for example, streaked his face and hands to become Frankenstein, acting out the role of a monster who wanted to chase me in order to devour me. Cotton and yarn, provided for collage, also became beards, moustaches, and wigs.

A natural merging of art and drama often occurred, as associations to the boys' creations were spontaneously dramatized. Thus, using styrofoam, papers, and colorful pipe cleaners, several boys one day made magnificent "king" and "queen" boats. It was only logical to sail the boats (in an empty portable sandbox), relating action-filled stories of races, battles, attacks, wins, and losses.

14.2 Soap Crayon "Makeup" Turns Jack into Frankenstein. Age 9

To extend and clarify each child's fantasy, one of us interviewed each boy at the scene of the event, as though for a radio or television program. The same interviewing procedure was often used after a drama, to help the child achieve some distance from the play, and to build bridges and strengthen boundaries between reality and fantasy.

We had expected the children to show individual preferences for either art or drama. Although this was so at first for some, by the end of several months it became much more difficult, if not impossible, to select a preferred art form for each child. Two of the boys engaged solitary or dyadic play with puppets as a way of expressing feelings before they could com-

244

fortably make and keep artistic products. The others began with art and moved to drama, but as each boy's confidence and curiosity increased, he would explore and try out new ways of expressing himself, especially if another group member was doing so. In general, a dynamic interaction took place, with individuals using both modalities to express and to work through conflicts.

Matt, for example, at first went off to work alone at the easel, painting pictures of George Washington, "the father of our country," an idealized parent symbol. His other favored symbol was a pirate—Black Hook or Bluebeard—who represented evil, aggressive impulses toward authority figures, always shown as damaged in an eye and/or leg (see 14.4D). Two of Matt's paintings in his art evaluation were of Washington's house, Valley Forge, with a quiet cannon outside, and Black Hook's boat. Matt had told a story in which Black Hook "almost" had his leg bitten off by a shark.

In the third month of group Matt painted a burning church, in which the steeple is destroyed. Soon after, he painted his first picture of two airplanes, a big and a little one, locked in a fierce battle. In these pictures and stories, one could see Matt's anger at his all-powerful parents, his ambivalent wish to attack and to identify with his policeman-father, and his fear of his father's retaliatory superpowers, and of his being punished (and possibly damaged).

In time, however, this conflict moved from solitary art at the easel to more direct avenues of expression, as Matt repeatedly, symbolically, attacked and destroyed the powerful parent forces. He would tease both therapists, calling us "witches," verbalizing his wish to make us his "slaves," and taking an imperious and authoritarian role. Gradually, he gained the courage to argue with the other boys, and one day a verbal fight actually escalated into a physical battle.

When it was suggested that perhaps the combatants could fight it out on paper, the two made a large mural (14.4E), intently drawing and painting Japanese, German, and American planes in an air war (14.4F). As they worked side by side, the air was filled with accompanying shouts and sounds of battle. After the mural (14.4G) was finished, all of the boys prepared plasticine "bullets" and, yelling out their fantasies about the war being fought, they let loose with a hail of bullets, directed at the mural in barrage after barrage.

When the battle was over they returned to the refreshment table, to replenish their bodies with food. Still excited by the drama, the boys were interviewed as the "sole survivors" of the terrible battle. Matt, of course, identified himself as George Washington, and related his version of the conflict. Suddenly, in response to an unrelated noise outside the room, the boys spontaneously dived under the table for cover, yelling "Duck! There's one plane left, and it's bombing us!" In a fantasy of retaliation for their aggression, one boy lost his leg, another his head, and another (Matt) his arm.

The drama therapist quickly became a medic who magically restored damaged body parts. The boys then returned to the battle, and putting up the last few pieces of the mural, they bombed the enemy again, saying that they had to "get that last enemy plane." After the war, we decorated the boys with quickly made "medals" for their bravery in battle, as they talked and shared their feelings about what had just transpired.

Such an interweaving of art and drama occurred many times. In a sense, the preceding drama and its variations were preparation for a later hospital scene, in which themes were more clearly played out by the group. Just as each child used the media in his own way, so each boy used the dramatic structure of the hospital to enact his own conflicts.

One, for example, was "dying of thirst," afraid of abandonment; while another played a wild, "crazy" patient "falling apart inside" from his inner confusion. Matt, who by this time had started to work through some of the anger at both parents, lessening both his rage and his fear of injury, was able to be a kind and helpful doctor in this hospital drama, repairing injuries and replacing missing parts. For him, as for others, the group experience provided multiple opportunities to express, understand, and work through both intrapsychic and interpersonal conflicts.

It was possible within the group structure for individual members to work on their particular areas of difficulty, as well as for the group to work together on shared concerns. Because of the unstructured nature of the 90-minute sessions, a child could work alone on a particular problem area, or, if he chose, could join in dyadic or group interaction. The flexible setting encouraged the exploration of multiple alternatives in time, space, and support, as the children worked toward clarification and resolution of their conflicts.

Because of the essentially individual nature of art and the group nature of drama, we had expected that the boys would generally work independently in art and together in drama. Much to our surprise, and perhaps because of the simultaneous availability of materials and space for work in both modalities, it soon became apparent that individual, dyadic, and group involvement were possible in each area.

There were often times when children worked alone in art, thoroughly engrossed in their activity; but there were also times when individuals engaged in solitary dramatic play, particularly with puppets. Children would

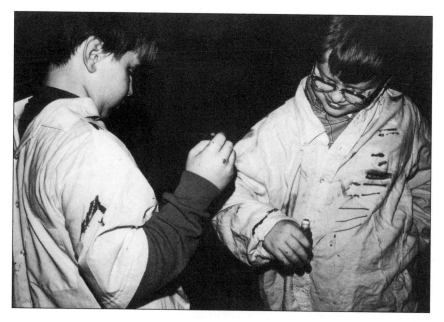

14.3 Two Boys Help Each Other Use Paint to Become "Generals"

frequently work in parallel or cooperative dyads in art, or in dramatic play, and at times all members of the group ended up working together on some cooperative productive task, like making a mural or decorating each other (Figure 14.3). Spontaneous dramas also evolved in which every group member took part in a way that truly reflected individual as well as group needs and concerns.

A similar range of interactions occurred with the boys' use of other human beings in the group. Just as they seemed able to use each other as companions, helpers, observers, or protagonists, so they were able to use the adults in multiple ways. We were intrigued by the range of roles in which the boys put us, including observer, teacher, co-worker, role-player, limit-setter, and commentator. The nature of the group served to stimulate various projections on the two therapists, and the enacting of transference wishes and fears. As the children relived and explored feelings and impulses, they were often inclined to dramatize the transference relationship, prolonging and further exploring the fantasy through enactment.

Thus, for example, when Matt had begun to taste the sweetness of power in dramatic play as a general, he pretended to be omnipotent, and ordered me about, saying peremptorily, "Slave, get me the tape!" or, "Come here, missy!" Later, playing Santa Claus in a spontaneous drama, he told me I was his doll, under his power, and must act in whatever way he commanded. It is evident that Matt's transference (distorted perceptions of the therapist meeting internal needs), required me to be a helpless parent whom he could order around. This seemed to be a compensation for his feelings of helplessness in regard to his mildly abusive father.

Once the children learned to take roles and to pretend, they often elected to relate to us in this dramatic way, because it served their needs so well. It made possible, of course, a greater flexibility for us too, since one could play out the assigned role and discuss it later, or could respond therapeutically in character, for example, "You like to boss me around don't you?" or as one's real self, "If you could really be such a powerful boss, what else would you order me to do?" This dramatized way of working enriched the experience for the child and offered multiple opportunities to explore emotional conflicts, as the child turned from one art form to another, from one adult to another, "working through" using all available resources.

The therapeutic utility of the activity was enhanced by the post-play discussion. These end-of-group round-table talks over refreshments were essential in helping the children to integrate the preceding activity. While a great deal of sharing of feelings went on during the "doing time," the last half hour of each session was used to help the boys focus on the meaning of what had occurred and to verbalize feelings and understandings.

The regressive potential of groups, as in mob behavior, may be amplified when using art. While useful for children who are constricted, like Don or Tim, it can be disorganizing for children whose controls are weak, like Joey or Pete. The arts are powerful tools which stimulate regression, the rate of which sometimes has to be controlled by the therapist—by stepping in, for example, with a suggestion to stop for a moment, step back, and look at what has just transpired.

Because the arts greatly aid in the uncovering and expressing of conflict, the post-activity discussions were an integral part of the therapeutic process; during these, the children were helped to use what they had made (art) or done (drama) as a vehicle for verbal expression, insight, and change. Thus, the making and doing that served to complement each other as expressive tools were themselves enhanced by talking. The suspension of the reality principle, which occurred during the time of artistic or dramatic creativity, was replaced by a consideration of that activity in the light of the child's past, current, or future realities. Not only did such sharing of anxieties, wishes, and fears help to dispel each boy's "delusion of uniqueness," but the differentiation of real and fantasied actions enabled the children to gain mastery over their impulses, just as they gained increasing mastery over the media and tools of the two art forms.

The Second Art–Drama Therapy Group: Adolescents

Dr. Irwin and I worked with the boys in this group in the way described for a year, at which time termination seemed appropriate (Irwin, Rubin, & Shapiro, 1975). Later, we worked for 2 years with a male child psychiatrist, Dr. Guillermo Borrero, and a group of adolescent boys and girls, ages 15 to 18 (Rubin & Irwin, 1984). They came for 2 hours a week, each with a different diagnostic label, each in some kind of psychological pain (DVD 14.5).

A wide range of flexible, unstructured materials that could be used in a variety of ways—for art, drama, poetry, music, movement, and photography—were made available to them (14.5A). As in the earlier group, different things often happened simultaneously, and the members were able to use all of the modalities as ways of communicating with us and with each other (14.5B).

Paula sat at the table one day with the others, yet quiet and apart. She was obviously depressed, but could not talk about it. She wrote slowly on a piece of paper, then showed it to the group: "I sit here wondering why there is so much sadness in this lonely room. Although it is filled with people, I feel like the world is falling in on me, which I really don't understand—this feeling of sadness is hurting me in a way no one understands. It's like the world is against me, like I'm in a world of my own. . . . It is a lonely feeling, which hurts. O God help me!" Her anguished cry on paper was heard by the others, who then responded warmly to her distress with support and affection.

On another day, when Paula was working actively on her Black identity, she proudly wrote and read aloud her poem, "Who Am I?"

"I'm the child of the man.
The child of the man
Who no longer wants to live.
The child of the man
Who wonders why he is the man
And I'm the child.
I'm the child of the man's Pride.
I'm the child of the Black man's Pride.
I'm the child who fights for freedom.
I'm the child who lives for freedom.
I'm the child who does not have any freedom.
I'm the child who lives in a world of Poverty.
I'm the child who lives under the (white) man's laws.
I'm the child who has gone out to see what life is all about, and has gotten
    her mind together. . . ."

Another girl, also not very comfortable with speech, quoted a poem following a sexual assault, reflecting both her anger and her wishes about being a woman:

Woman was created from the rib of man.
She was not created from his head to be above him.
Nor from his feet to be trampled upon—
She was created from his side to be equal to him,
And close to his heart to be loved by him.

Matthew, even less verbal, often found music and movement to be his most congenial modalities for expression and communication. Sam, although quite articulate, was most comfortable with art. Thus, on a day when Jim was depressed and uncommunicative, Sam was able to let him know he cared by drawing a portrait of him, rather than by saying anything in words.

In one session (unusual because the other two leaders were out of town), I sat with three boys and one girl around a table. Matthew focused on playing a record he had brought in, asking me to write down, and all of us to listen to, the lyrics, which he felt related to him; "I need to belong to someone. . . . I feel like a motherless child." (His mother had indeed abandoned him.) Another song, which he played and replayed, ended, "I guess it goes all the way back to my mom and dad—two people I never chanced to know. I wonder why I miss them so. I never had a mother's touch or a father's hand."

Sam, sitting next to Matt, first wrote private messages to me in German and Russian, then worked with clay, making a figure he called "Need," a sad, large-headed, abstract-looking man (DVD 14.5C). Jim was relatively quiet, doodled for a while, and finally drew a man with a strong head and over-elaborated neck, during a discussion of getting high on drugs. Sherry drew a childlike scene of "a place with kids," explaining that it showed how she pictured the Child Welfare Shelter, where her younger brother had been placed when he had run away from home the previous week. She related her idyllic image of the shelter to her own wishes to "get away," a move she was able to make several months later.

At one point all four became quite demanding of attention and of supplies, as if to highlight the absence of the other two leaders. To help them understand their wishes, I pretended to be a waitress, taking orders, before going to my office to get the art supplies. Their orders were for extravagant quantities of money and food, and reflected the hunger and competitiveness which was intensified with only one leader. They were also mutually supportive and helpful in many ways during this session, as if they were banding together in the absence of two of the parent figures.

Most often, members would not remain clustered at any one place throughout the 2 hours, but would move around as their needs and wishes dictated. Spontaneous musical and dramatic happenings thus occurred quite often, making the situation unpredictable and exciting for all of us. The dramas often began with one member but were flexible and sponta-neous enough for others to participate in both the planning of the story and the expression of different roles. In one round-robin story which grew out of Sherry's telling of a dream, the plot was fluid enough for each one to add their own unique touches, as in this excerpt from the discussion:

> Sherry: This could make a good movie, maybe a cartoon. . . . I'm goin' on a boat across the ocean. Someone pushes me off, and I find myself in the cellar of a mysterious friend. . . .
>
> Sam: And your friend was this penguin, this really huge thing—a glan-dular case—and then the penguin says, "Come and help me. We must fight together. . . ."
>
> Cindy: And then the penguin grew wings, and flew away. Then it made do-do's all over everything. . . .
>
> Jim: And then I grab one of those birds, and carry him home, and use it as a flapjack!

Thus, they were able to work together, not only sequentially and side by side, but often in mutually supportive interaction. Many times one person would teach another a skill, and often two or more members would work together on a sculpture, a painting, or a construction. Their artistic sym-bols evolved over time, as we tried to help them to find meaning in their creations (14.5D). Dramas with puppets, masks, and themselves evolved fairly often, with members taking different roles, usually around a mutually meaningful theme (14.5E).

The Story of Sam

Sam, oversized (6′9″), overweight, and extremely bright, had dropped out of school and had literally locked himself in his room before coming to the clinic. He had been in individual and family therapy for several months, and was referred to the group, partly because he was talented in art, but particularly because he had withdrawn completely (DVD 14.6). His progress over time was both visible and moving (14.6A).

In the group, he began by isolating himself behind an easel in a corner and working on a series of brightly colored, organic, curvy, voluptuous paintings. During those early months, his work in clay was equally soft, undulating, and fluid (Figure 14.4a). But in the 4th month, for the first time he played a role in a drama, that of a defense attorney, where his debating experience enabled him to be verbally aggressive and competitive.

His artwork around this time started to gradually change, extensions emerging from the clay, projections thrusting out from the flowing masses. In his paintings too, there were more often clearly separated parts, shapes, and colors, becoming more varied and differentiated. Gradually he began to try other media, like wood, which gave his creations even more form, stability, and power. As though a structure was forming internally as well, Sam began in minute, playful ways to display some of the anger he had always repressed. After about a year of group therapy, he spontaneously created a vivid, powerful drama that seemed to represent the psychic awakening he was experiencing.

Saying he was playing a crazy person, he cowered fearfully, retreated inside a womblike enclosure (a large wooden box), and pulled it out the door. Opening the door brusquely, he walked back in, appearing to be a totally different person, stamping and speaking loudly, angrily, and strongly: "Where is that fellow? That other fellow who is so scared all the time? If you see him again, tell him to get out of here!"

He repeated the drama the following week, after proudly reporting the sale of one of his paintings for $25 to a local bank. This time he involved the other two leaders in the drama but had some difficulty being assertive with them. He dressed Dr. Irwin as a witch and Dr. Borrero as a king, and then struggled in pantomime with these powerful parent figures. He was able to win out with the witch-mother, but often weakened with the king-father. Unable to use words to express his anger at the male leader, we suggested that he try numbers, and he then carried on an intense, angry dialogue using numbers, with dramatic intonation and affect. The outcome was a compromise, in which a third Sam finally emerged—not the violently angry one or the fearful cowering one, but a strong, reasonable (integrated) Self.

Simultaneously, Sam's artwork began to change. He began to move from abstraction to representation (Figure 14.4b), sometimes even making people—faces that were often distorted and grotesque (14.6B), perhaps representing some of those long-repressed inner feelings (Figure 14.5). The same damaged Self had been in a story he told several months earlier, following a hospitalization and some regression. Sam described a Martian invasion and an Earthling, clearly self-projection, about whom he then felt almost hopeless:

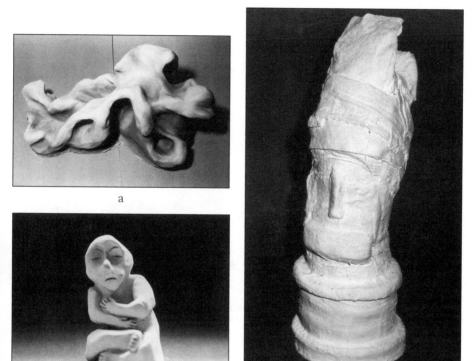

14.4 Three Sculptures by Sam
(a) An Early Undulating Mass; (b) "Need"; (c) A Late Head of a King

"About this time, one of the most primitive of the Earthling creatures wan-
ders to the far side of the ship, and is immediately stranded, and can't get
back. The Martian scanner analyzer at this time determines that the earth
creature doesn't have enough life support system. The Earthling creature
will die. The Martians will have to intervene to save his life. . . . The elevator hydraulic on the lift is raised, and three Martians go out to rescue the
primitive Earthling, who is now dying. This is a great victory for the Martians, as they can now examine an Earthling, and now they can condition it,
and can observe very closely its behavior patterns. The only disadvantage
for the Earthling is that he'll find out. . . . The disadvantage for the Earthling is that there is intense physical pain in the cranial brain area. . . . The
Earthlings are very weak creatures. The Earthlings must realize that the
Martians are omnipotent. They are not only superior but omnipotent. However, the Martians respect the Earthlings for their ability to grasp *some* information, and find that the Earthlings could no doubt be developed into an
intelligent-like life form. The end."

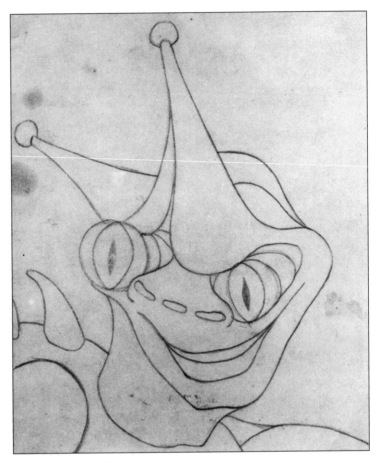

14.5 A Head with Distorted Features, by Sam. Age 16. Pencil

Dr. Irwin, to whom he had told the story, asked, "You mean there's some hope for the Earthlings?" Sam replied slowly, "Well, some hope . . . rather remote. At times it seems nonexistent, but there is *some* hope." His characterizations of himself and the leaders reflected both his fears and his hopes for change through therapy.

Change for Sam, as for all, was often slow, with regression as well as progression over time. Becoming aware of all of his feelings, happy as well as sad ones, he struggled to integrate this newfound awareness of his inner life. As he became stronger, he related more and more to the others, developing genuine friendships, like those he later formed in college. One of his favorite creations was a powerful phallic head of a king, symbolizing perhaps the strength he was beginning to realize without fear in himself (Figure 14.4c). Later, his letters from college were full of humor, and some-

14.6 Sam's Drawing of the View from His College Window. Pencil

times included drawings, like a view from his window (Figure 14.6), that were far more realistic and healthy than those he had done in the past.

The Story of Jim

Jim, often depressed, had a hard time expressing himself in the group (DVD 14.7), except through his art (14.7A). His first drawings were of heroes, but they were usually incomplete (Figure 14.7a). Almost all of the powerful athletes were missing parts of their bodies—sometimes an arm, sometimes a leg—and were often subtly cut off by the edge of the paper. For many sessions, he worked on an elaborate picture of superheroes, like the Green Lantern and the Green Arrow, perhaps triggered by his feelings of vulnerability in the group.

This same sense of helplessness seemed evident in his spontaneous dramatizations; no matter how his role began, he almost always ended up as a victim, hurt and injured.

As a dental patient, for example, he was so passive and wobbly that he kept tumbling to the floor, as though—like a baby—he could not sit up without support. He had actually begun as the dentist in the drama, but was unable to maintain the assertive role and soon switched to the weak patient, who finally had to be tied in the chair to keep from falling on the floor.

In the same way, he volunteered to be a tough cop, driving his police car, when all of a sudden he changed the script, and was hurt and injured in an accident. Rescued by a doctor, he seemed to enjoy the idea of being a passive patient, even when put on the table for an operation. Without a whimper, he masochistically submitted to the doctor's primitive brand of anesthesia—a hit on the head with a wooden spoon. In a later drama, he played a boss who was able to give orders and be a big shot with his secretary but could not confront the angry male employee who he was supposed to fire, cowering and able to gesture assertively only after the man left the room. However, like Sam, Jim made significant progress in the group (14.7B).

As he was taking his first tentative steps to express anger in dramas, his drawings began to change. More often, the sports figures were more complete, with few, if any, body parts missing (Figure 14.7b). Trying other media, Jim made a tall (phallic) three-dimensional plastic construction, and later a huge sword and a clay dagger. One day he playfully pretended to be super-powerful and slowly lifted up a "heavy" chair, said to weigh "at least fifty thousand pounds."

Becoming more comfortable with aggression, he played the role of a domineering husband, bossing his wife around. He demanded special food, insisted that she slavishly follow his commands, and indeed was quite authoritarian. Having learned to express his aggression outward instead of inward, Jim experimented with many roles, sometimes using a toy gun to attack or protect himself from his enemies.

Full of courage, he challenged the male leader to a mock pantomime battle. When Dr. Borrero showed him how to fight in slow motion, he was able to exert the necessary control, yet still win the contest. He kept coming back for more, repeating his slow-motion knockouts, thus mastering his anxiety about the once-feared effects of his own aggression. And,

14.7a An Early Athlete, by Jim   *14.7b A Later Athlete, by Jim*

equally important, he was able to sit down and talk with the leader about the experience when it was over (14.7C).

Role of the Leader

As is clear from these examples, leaders in such groups must be prepared to play many different kinds of roles (DVD 4.8). Most of the time, this means setting the stage, then observing, listening, and responding empathically. There are times, however, that it may mean helping a group member make something, teaching an art process, playing an instrument, or moving alongside someone.

It may also mean taking a role, narrating a drama, or making organizing interventions—like helping members to think through and plan a drama by listing the scenes. A leader might suggest particular techniques, such as role reversal, doubling, or using a specific method, like talking to an empty chair as if someone were in it. Always it means having flexible antennae out, and quickly responding to an emerging theme or activity, facilitating it as well as possible.

In one improvisation, for example, Jim started to frantically gobble up bunches of french fries, saying that they were thermometers and would make him strong. Drs. Irwin and Borrero became MD's who tried to figure out the best course of treatment for such a fantasy, drawing X-rays that showed the thermometers, and measuring him with a yardstick to confirm that he was growing stronger. It was probably helpful to Jim that the leaders were able to join into the spirit of his zany drama, and to use their own creative resourcefulness to help him deal with his wild fantasies. In this group, as in the earlier one, there was a pervasive feeling of excitement, fun, playfulness, and shared community, in which each member helped each other member to become himself.

Conclusion

Experience with these and other multimodality groups suggests that a successful union between two or more expressive art forms is possible, and in fact results in enrichment for workers and youngsters. I know I learned a great deal from working so closely with a drama therapist, and value that as much as any other outcome.

Enlarging the range of possibilities for the group members made possible "different strokes for different folks," as well as different modalities for different expressive purposes. It now seems artificial to make distinctions or to create boundaries, and thus to limit a therapeutic experience to any one expressive modality. Rather, it seems natural and right, with groups as with individuals, to allow people to move freely in accord with their inner dictates (cf. Lewis, 1993; Oaklander, 1988; N. Rogers, 1993).

Experience with these older youngsters in a free, creative approach contradicts the notion that "the expressive methods are most rewarding with very young children" (Rabin & Haworth, 1960, p. 10). It further corroborates what others have said, that "the inner life of fantasy never loses its meaning" (Davidson & Fay, 1964, p. 506). "When we help children to see, hear, taste, and smell a variety of things, their feelings can lead them from art into poetry, drama, music, song, movement, and back into art again. Many relationships occur in the child himself as he moves among these experiences. Joyous, active participation in all of the arts, develops both the skill to create within the discipline of each art form, and the insight which selects the right form to express the need of the moment" (Snow, 1968, p. 20; see also Levine & Levine, 1999; Knill, Levine, & Levine, 2004).

I am not advocating that we should all be generalists in the creative arts therapies. Although the relationships among different expressive modes within humans seem evident, it also seems clear to me that to be proficient in the discipline of any one art form requires years of patient learning and integration, especially in order to use it effectively with others. What I *am* suggesting is that we be more open-minded in our approach and in what we make available. Although the creative materials in my office are still mainly art media, I also have some puppets and miniature life toys for dramatic use. More important, I try to be open and receptive to expression in any modality—which may take the form of art, drama, movement, music, or creative writing.

Dr. Marvin Shapiro, a child psychiatrist/psychoanalyst, wrote the following words, which constitute an excellent rationale for a multimodality approach to treatment: "In many ways the full experience has an analogy to the growing child. The baby, in learning about the world, mouths the object, feels it, presses it against himself, and uses as many sense modalities as he possibly can to integrate his concept of what the object is. In this way, the child learns and expresses an interest and curiosity in the world around him. In the same sense, we too must use more than one sense modality in grasping the full impact of an activity, an experience, or an object, out of the swirling, confusing life around us. By taking such a multi-medium approach of varied sensory participation, the therapeutic potential is greatly enhanced, and increases the possibilities for change in the children" (Irwin, Rubin & Shapiro, 1975, p. 116).

PART IV

ART THERAPY FOR DISABLED CHILDREN

CHAPTER
15

Art as Therapy for
Children with Disabilities

The Universality of Creativity

Desmond Morris, an anthropologist, once published a book about man's closest relatives and their picture-making activities, called *The Biology of Art* (1962). It is fascinating to learn therein that apes and chimpanzees can be genuinely interested in drawing or painting (DVD 15.1). In fact, when deeply involved in their work, they are at times oblivious to other normally prepotent needs, including hunger and sex. Their surprising investment led Morris to suggest that picture-making is for apes a "self-activating activity" that satisfies an innate "exploratory urge" (15.1A).

Visually clear in the book, and equally interesting, is the stylistic individuality in the art of different animals: Alexander the Orangutan has a way of painting that is distinct from that of Congo the Chimpanzee! And, based upon some experiments with their apparently deliberate use of picture space, Morris concluded that the apes seem to have an intuitive sense of compositional order.

While one might object to the use of the word "art" to describe their creations, it is significant that critics were fooled at several staged openings in fashionable galleries, actually praising the unknown painters' work. The purpose of this illustration is not to suggest a parallel between disabled children and apes, but rather to emphasize the universality of that exploratory or "making" urge, and to underline the biological roots of stylistic individuality and a sense of order (15.1B).

It took some imagination on Morris's part to find ways of making painting and drawing possible for apes and chimpanzees. Once the mechanics

263

had been solved, however, the art activity itself seemed to come quite naturally, with little training or teaching necessary. Remarkably, this is also true for dolphins (15.1C) and elephants (15.1D) as well.

The similar challenge in working in art with the disabled is often one of needing to stretch one's own creativity and imagination in order to make it possible for what will still come naturally to happen (cf. Aach-Feldman & Kunkle-Miller, 2001; Anderson, 1992, 1994; Henley, 1992). "Wherever there is a spark of human spirit—no matter how dim it may be—it is our sacred responsibility as humans, teachers, and educators to fan it into whatever flame it conceivably may develop. . . . We are all by nature more or less endowed with intrinsic qualities, and no one has the right to draw a demarcation line which divides human beings into those who should receive all possible attention in their development and those who are not worth all our efforts. One of these intrinsic qualities is that every human being is endowed with a creative spirit" (Lowenfeld, 1957, p. 430).

For myself, it is now a firm belief "that every human being is endowed with a creative spirit" (DVD 15.2), for at many times and in many places I have been told that children with a certain disability would be unable to do anything productive, creative, or even nondestructive with art materials. And time after time, the children have proven the prophets wrong, and have surprised even their most hopeful advocates.

Children with Schizophrenia in a Psychiatric Hospital

The first such group I met, in 1963, were hospitalized, and suffered from one of the most severe forms of psychotic illness possible for youngsters—childhood schizophrenia.[1] They were all performing at a level below their chronological age, though the degree of real or functional retardation varied. It was thought in advance by some professionals who knew them that they would eat or smear the art materials, become disorganized and destructive, or get further lost in a world of autistic fantasy.

Nevertheless, the chairman of the Department of Child Development and I were allowed to try out a plan of art sessions on a voluntary individual basis. Thus, once a week for 8 months, I went to a small room on the sixth floor of the psychiatric hospital where these 10 schizophrenic children were being treated. The youngsters would come to the room one at a time. Once there, they were free to choose what art materials they would use, where they would use them, and what they would make.

---

[1] Like many youngsters in this book, they might now be given different diagnostic classifications, such as autism, pervasive developmental disorder, etc.

As with the apes, it was soon clear that each child had a style and a way of working that was all his or her own (DVD 15.3). Dan, for example, would pull his chair up to the easel, put a brush in each color of paint in the tray, and, holding his brush with a relaxed grip like a Japanese Sumi painter, would move it up and down, up and down, rhythmically and visibly relaxing. Selma also painted often at the easel, with a similar motor-kinesthetic rhythm. Yet her work was unique in her preference for repetitive circular motions involving the whole body. Karen, too, preferred easel painting, and engaged in an active rhythmic and vocal dialogue, with and through her bright splotches of color. She danced as she worked, moving away, coming back, intently tuned into her picture and its dabs and swirls of bold, rich color (15.3A).

They each grew, each in his own way. Dan learned to know and to indicate when he was done swabbing paint on one piece of paper, and was ready for the next. Selma enlarged her repertoire to include not only monochromatic circular sweeps, but also linear splashes and bouncy dabs of varied hue. Four-year-old Jonny's easel paintings changed over time, from tense, small blobs above each jar in the tray to free, sweeping movements of the brush, in which colors, at first separated, later mingled and blended in lovely tones.

Mike concentrated on linear drawings of objects, animals, and above all, people. For months, he worked on human-figure possibilities (see Figure 2.3), exploring a wide range (15.3B) of graphic body-image statements (15.3C), finally settling on a stable symbol (or "schema") of a boy (15.3D). Bobby loved to talk while he worked, telling imaginative stories about his drawings and paintings. One favorite theme was a scene of his uncle's farm with many details (15.3E), of which there were several versions (15.3F). Another was the creation of pictorial charts on such topics as "Holidays of the Year," "How to Stay Healthy," and "How a Pumpkin Grows from a Seed" (see DVD 2.2B). As described earlier, both Dorothy (see DVD 8.2) and Randy (see DVD 8.3) used their art time in equally unique and varied ways (see Chapter 8).

It is important to remember that all of these children had been diagnosed as suffering from the same disease—childhood schizophrenia. Yet, while they shared a descriptive label, what stood out most strongly in their artwork was their individuality, despite a literature which implies a greater uniformity. Thus, they used the opportunity in different ways—some primarily for manipulative play, some for clarification of realistic and fantastic concepts, and some for organizing and mapping out their words. Because they were individualistic and varied, their products often displayed a normality, perhaps reflecting capacities rather than deficits.

There is much to be learned from this experience, and from a study which grew out of it, where judges were unable to discriminate randomly selected products by the schizophrenic children from those by a matched group of nonschizophrenic youngsters (Rubin & Schachter, 1972; see DVD 21.3). One implication is that a diagnostic category like childhood schizophrenia, while useful and valid for some purposes, cannot adequately describe an individual's wholeness, richness, or creative language. Neither in comparison with the control subjects nor with each other can the artwork of these children be described with any meaningful generalization. The only one that makes any sense is that, like all children, they demonstrated through art the essential uniqueness of their individual selves—in spite of the degree of alienation from self and world from which all of them suffered.

While extremely rich as a source of information, a child's art cannot be translated through some neat process, form, or symbol guidebook into a diagnostic label. The preceding experience serves as a reminder that, as with any other group of people, children who have been judged to belong in the same diagnostic category may still be, think, feel, paint, and draw in ways that are radically different from one another. It is well to remember that "every person, from the moment of birth, is a unique individual, unlike any other being that ever existed" (Moustakas, 1959, p. 66).

Children with Physical Disabilities in a Residential Institution

There are yet others who have taught me a great deal about human capacity and growth potential. Four years after the experience with the schizophrenic children, in 1967, I was asked to help start an art program at an institution for orthopedically and multiply handicapped children where none had ever existed (DVD 15.4).

I shall never forget the first meeting with the dozen or so staff members involved with the children who had cerebral palsy. They presented me with a list of about 10 names. When I discovered that there were perhaps four times as many who had already been ruled out for a variety of sensible-sounding reasons, I suggested that we try evaluating everyone, just to see what might be possible. As a result of these individual assessments, it was found unnecessary to exclude anyone from the art program (15.4A).

Most amazing, those with severe orthopedic disabilities, such as extensive spasticity or athetosis, seemed able to mobilize unimagined resources, so that they could function both independently and creatively (Figure 15.1). Some of the hyperactive children, especially those with neurologi-

15.1 A Boy in a Wheelchair Paints His Ceramic Slab Pot

cal damage, who were expected to be destructive in the art room (15.4B) were so very constructive there that, when a token-reward behavior modification program was introduced for them, the most popular reinforcement was a period in the art room (although it cost the highest number of tokens). Equally amazing, those with severe orthopedic and muscular handicaps, such as extensive spasticity (15.4C) or athetosis, seemed able to mobilize unimagined sources (15.4D), so that they could function both independently and creatively (15.4E).

We learned a great deal from children like Claire (15.4F), a deaf-mute of 10, whose drawings were so articulate that they helped the staff to change her label from profoundly to mildly retarded (Figure 15.2). Because she could not talk and could make few gestures, picture-making became a vital expressive tool for her. One day she came into the art room, propelling her wheelchair, screaming inside with the agony of a visit to the dentist. She wheeled herself in, up to the table, grabbed a marker and paper, and drew a picture that, more eloquently than any words, told what it feels like to be attacked by a dentist—to be all teeth and mouth, stretched wide open, helpless as the intrusive tools of the doctor enter your body (Figure

15.2 A Drawing of the Art Therapist, by Claire. Age 10. Crayon

15.3). Her drawings also helped her in the classroom with learning concepts, and in speech therapy, where they became a bridge to spoken language through her "talking book" (15.4G).

Deaf Children in a Day School

In an experience at a school for the deaf in 1983 I was again reminded of the communicative value of art for those with language handicaps. Asked to explore the possibility of an art therapy program by working for a term with individual students, I found myself debating among a developmental approach (Aach & Kunkle-Miller, 2001; Malchiodi, Kim & Choi, 2003; Uhlin, 1972; Williams & Wood, 1977), an adaptive or behavioral one (Anderson, 1992, 1994; Rozum & Malchiodi, 2003), a cog-

15.3 Claire's Drawing, Done Immediately after a Visit to the Dentist. Marker

nitive one (Silver, 1978, 1986, 2001), and a psychodynamic one (Henley, 1992; Kramer, 2000). I had already learned from Claire and others like her the special need for art as an alternative form of speech, but I was genuinely uncertain about just what kind of visual communication would be most helpful.

The 16 children referred by their teachers for art evaluation interviews quickly told me, by saying quite eloquently that what they needed—even more than an opportunity to organize their thinking—was a chance to express and cope with powerful feelings through expressive art therapy (DVD 15.5). Since an art education program was already available for cognitive and creative growth, it seemed that the best approach would be a psychodynamic one, in which the individuals who participated used art and dramatic play to express and then deal with confused and conflicted feelings and fantasies (15.5A).

The intensity of their need for this kind of help was reflected in their ability to relate to me, despite my complete lack of signing skills (15.5B). Although I could understand some of the speech of the few who talked, and could use writing with some others, our communications were largely nonverbal—art, gestures, facial expressions, pantomime (15.5C).

As an illustration of the intensity of their response to the opportunity to express themselves in art, I shall share a middle session with Eleanor, the adolescent whose initial art interview was described in Chapter 5 (when I suggested that she draw "a feeling"). Eleanor, whose suicidal impulses had been known to the staff for some time, had tried to cut her wrist the night before our fourth art therapy session. Realizing, after describing to me what had occurred, that she had hurt herself rather than the real target of her rage, she drew—with much excitement—a picture of what she would like to do to the grownup who had made her so angry.

In the drawing (Figure 15.4), a many-toothed, monstrous creature is

15.4 Eleanor's Drawing of "What She Would Like to Do." Marker

holding a huge knife over a small, fearful person. Eleanor first said that she was the big one and the adult was the small one; then she reversed herself, explaining that in reality she felt helpless to deal with the power of those in charge. I suggested that she might also feel frightened of the extent of her rage, of what she would really like to do to the grownup in the picture. I wondered if she had turned the anger on herself as a punishment, as well as a way to protect the adult, who she then said cared a lot about her.

She spent the remaining time in the session drawing a volleyball net, as if to screen out the fearful imagery of her first picture, and then used colorful fingerpaint to make four balloons tied together. Eleanor was thus able to use the art therapy session first to express the feared impulse and then to defend against it; both were helpful to her in the ongoing task of self-awareness and self-control.

I informed school personnel about the homicidal impulses which had been expressed in Eleanor's first picture. Since dangerous fantasies are often drawn in art, and since one never knows whether they will be acted out in reality, art therapists—like all mental health professionals—are legally and morally required to report such information to someone in authority. This is equally true for artwork which suggests that the child has been abused, whether physically or mentally.

Responding to violent or provocative imagery is a delicate matter, and depends on the setting, the individual(s), and many other variables. In "Censorship or Intervention: 'But You Said We Could Draw Whatever We Wanted!'" art therapist Martha Haeseler (1987) described a range of possible interventions, based on the meaning of the imagery for the adolescents in the group, as well as the probable impact of its display on the inpatient unit they were in.

On the basis of the pilot study, which involved Eleanor and several others being seen weekly for a term, a part-time art therapist was hired and worked at the school for a number of years, seeing both individuals and groups. I had the pleasure of remaining involved as a consultant, and of helping the therapist design and evaluate an outcome study, which indicated some positive behavioral changes in those children involved in the art program (Kunkle-Miller, 1982).

Children with Developmental Delays in a Preschool

Another inspiring experience was working for several years with a group of retarded preschoolers and their teachers (DVD 15.6). Much to our delight and (I confess) surprise, these tiny tots of limited intellect were able to choose and to initiate independent artwork in a variety of media, with

271

gradually reduced support and assistance from adults (15.6A). Some revealed unknown abilities to concentrate and to organize themselves, and all responded with joy and vigor, albeit on a primarily manipulative level (15.6B).

The range of capacities, even within this young, fairly homogeneous group, was impressive. Asked to draw a picture of a person, for example, one child produced a labeled scribble of "A Kid", while another created a well-organized face called "A Monster." Both children were 4, both were clearly delayed, yet one was obviously functioning at a rather age-appropriate level, and even the labeled scribble was within the norm for young children's drawings.

In their imaginative play with the art materials, many of the children helped us to see their capacities for expression in other forms. Thus, although the program began with an emphasis on the visual arts, it later expanded to include various kinds of creative play—with sand, water, blocks, musical instruments, dolls, puppets, dress-up clothes, props, and housekeeping equipment. This expansion came as a natural development, as the children revealed their interests and propensities for expression in other modalities.

Blind Children with Multiple Disabilities in a Residential School

The largest group of such children from whom I learned were blind and partially-sighted (DVD 15.7). They were also mildly or greatly retarded (average IQ, 65), and suffered from other disabilities, such as cerebral palsy, speech and language disorders, deafness, brain damage, and emotional disturbance (cf. Rubin & Klineman, 1974).

As in the instances already described, the prior expectations of those who knew them were far from hopeful. An experienced teacher of art to blind children, for example, predicted chaos, saying that these multiply handicapped youngsters would have clay on the ceiling and a mess on the floor without step-by-step instructions. Once more, the experience with art was a pleasant surprise, and is documented in visual and auditory detail in a film, *We'll Show You What We're Gonna Do!* (Rubin, 1972), some excerpts from which are on the DVD.

Since the children had not had any art activities before, I began with individual assessments, evaluating each child's responses (15.7A) to different media and to various sensory stimuli (15.7B). On the basis of the degree of vision, intellectual level, and behavior in these interviews, the program director, Janet Klineman, and I arranged small, homogeneous groups of two to five children, who met for 7 weeks in half hour sessions. We hoped to explore the children's potential for creative growth, given a free choice of materials within a planned learning environment.

Indeed, the exploratory art program truly opened the eyes of the sighted adults involved, while it broadened the children's worlds (15.7C). It made us acutely aware of their creative potential and of their unexpected capacity for growth. Not only did they not mess as feared; they responded enthusiastically and constructively. We saw children, some in their first contact with new materials, creating artwork of sometimes surprising beauty.

While initially uncomfortable with freedom of choice, the children soon understood that we really expected them to make their own decisions about medium, theme, and place of work. They then exercised their newly acquired privilege (or is it a right?) with gusto. These experiences contradicted the "frequent arguments . . . that handicapped persons need the security and confidence which result from mere imitative occupation, such as copying or tracing" (Lowenfeld, 1957, p. 431).

Often, the children opened our eyes to previously hidden capacities. Jimmy's meaningful response to color, for example, led to an individualized visual stimulation program. Carl's skill and interest in wood scrap constructions resulted in a successful after-school woodworking club (Figure 15.5). All of them revealed a surprising ability to function independently in a setting that involved freedom of choice, leading to an "open classroom" the following school year.

In yet another way, the art program revealed to us the values, the uniqueness, and the beauty in their different ways of perceiving and knowing. Although in our society, "handicaps are not recognized as differences or unique aspects of self, but [are] seen as inadequacies" (Moustakas, 1959, p. 247), the children with whom we worked enabled us to revise our perception of handicap as primarily *defect* to primarily *difference*.

It was impossible to deny the existence of their disabilities, or the many painful feelings they caused. One could not, in candor, say that their perceiving and creating in art were the same as the sighted, as some have suggested (Freund, 1969). What we did find, however, was "that blindness may become the basis of a specific and unique creativeness" (Lowenfeld, 1957, p. 446), and that "sighted individuals may be missing great riches by the lack of kinesthetic awareness" (Haupt, 1969, p. 42).

As we opened ourselves to their unique ways of being, we learned to value their otherness, to treasure the ways in which they sensitized us. The children expanded our sensory awareness by referring to "clay that smells like candy," "ether markers," or "soft paper." They tuned us in to sounds, like Billy, who took intense pleasure in "a marker that squeaks a whole lot . . . that makes a whole lotta noise." Although one would not have chosen a

15.5 Carl Making One of His Many Wood Scrap Compositions

felt-tip marker as the most appropriate tool for a boy with no vision, Billy taught us not to allow our own preconceptions to interfere with what media we might offer a handicapped child. Indeed, rather than finding a best medium for these blind children, we discovered that almost every one selected his or her own preferred material from those available (clay, wood, wire, paint, chalk, markers, crayons, and so on).

Through their sensitive use of their hands, those who could see nothing taught us about a kind of free-floating tactile attention in their approach to shape, form, and texture. They seemed to know where to position their wood scraps, suggesting a "tactile aesthetic" different from a visual one, later explored in a pilot study (Rubin, 1976). Indeed, when we put blind-folds on, we found that their sculptures *felt* quite different to us than they *looked* (see DVD 21.2). We wondered if there could be a kind of "tactile thinking," analogous perhaps to "visual thinking" (Arnheim, 1969).

Similarly, those with limited vision sensitized us to the excitement and impact for them of new visual experiences. Peter, for example, responded with a kind of color shock to the intense tempera paint hues. And deaf-blind Terry literally jumped for joy after accidently discovering that wet clay pressed on white paper made a visible mark, and that *she* had made it happen herself.

Their use of materials was often quite free and inventive, perhaps in part because of a genuine naïveté and openness. David made, with foam tubes and pipe cleaners, a delightful "sweeper," and then zoomed around the room with it, making sweeper noises. His frequently uncontrolled aggression, which had gotten him into a lot of trouble, was able to be channeled into art activity, to be sublimated (15.7D).

There was poetry in Peter's painting titles, such as "A Mountain Hilltop Way out West and a Coyote Howling in the Night, with a Full Moon." And there was charm in his animistic description of his wood scrap sculpture, "The Memorial Toll Bridge," which "lets the people walk across it, and it lets cars through it" (15.7E). Perhaps because of their developmental immaturity, they were less self-critical than most children their age. Thus, Peter could say of his creation with unself-conscious pride, "It's a pretty good sculpture!"

The children also opened our eyes to the intensity of their feelings about being blind, and their needs for expression. One day, four youngsters who had no functional vision sat around a table, each working on a different project of his or her choice, and shared an intense discussion of disabilities—of people who are out of shape, who are deaf, crippled, or retarded. They recalled when people close to them had been injured, or had been seriously ill (15.7F). They talked of themselves, and the danger of other losses. Larry (15.7G), for example, said, "This is very, very important. Everybody listen! This could happen to you guys, too. When you get sick, you know, you could lose your hearing—and see—the time I got my earache, I almost got deaf. . . . And something else—if you don't sleep and wake up, you'll feel sickly too! You'll get sick—Yeah! I don't think you'll *lose* anything." Larry's eyes had been removed when he was 5, and when he later spoke of his dad's kidney stone operation he said, "*He* still has everything."

The group continued to work on their projects, and shared scary experiences, worrying aloud about what would happen to themselves. As Larry put it, "like if I got hit by a car—see, say like if I *die*—say like now, if I *die*." Finally, Tammy told of a person she knew who "couldn't hear and couldn't *see* either." I asked the children how they felt about that, and Larry said, "That's one thing I got right now! I can't see. . . . And I'm sad about it."

I asked Bill how he felt about it, and, with much blocking and stammering, he explained his attempt at denial: "I don't care. Even if I can't see, I'm—I just don't—I just pretend that—I just pretend—you know." [You just pretend that you really *can* see?] "Yeah, I don't even—I don't like—I don't even let—I don't even *talk* about it. I just pretend it's not even there!" Larry quickly empathized, saying, "That's what I do too. . . . You know what I do at night? Every night when I sleep, I just pretend it's not even there! That's all." The group was relieved, and went on to talk about how sad and angry it made them to be blind, and how badly they wished they could see.

It seemed that the children in this art program grew perceptibly in the formal quality of their work, in the controlled freedom of their working process, and in their good feelings about themselves. It was as if, in the process of creating their increasingly complex and personalized products, the children were also discovering and defining (and perhaps actualizing) themselves as unique individuals. And, paradoxically, they were in the process teaching us—in spite of their blindness, they opened our eyes.

We learned that "eventual levels of attainment may be curtailed not only by whatever inherent limitations may be present in the children themselves, but also by the restrictions imposed upon them by adults" (Weiner, 1967, p. 7). We learned, too, that "the only meaningful readiness . . . is a flexibility and a willingness to meet the child as he is, and a belief in him as a whole person of immeasurable potential" (Moustakas, 1959, pp. 217–218).

Changes over the Years Since the First Edition

The skepticism about the creative capacities of the disabled that I faced in the sixties and seventies has been largely overcome (DVD 15.8), thanks to the early pioneering work of people like Lowenfeld (1952, 1957) and Schaeffer-Simmern (1961), as well as later organizations like the National Committee, Arts for the Handicapped, formed in 1975 (now Very Special

Arts) and individuals such as Donald Uhlin (1972), Rawley Silver (1978), Frances Anderson (1992), Sally Smith (1979), and Claire and Robert Clements (1984). Many art therapists, like Uhlin, Silver, Anderson, and David Henley (1992,) began their careers as art teachers who specialized in work with the disabled.

Some art therapists now work in public schools usually with children whose emotional disabilities interfere with their ability to learn. In a program started by Janet Bush (1997) 25 years ago in Dade County, Florida, a large staff of art therapists serves children of all ages (15.8A). Special schools for children with disabilities are now much more likely to offer art therapy to youngsters with various kinds of social and emotional problems (15.8B), as well as learning disabilities (15.8C), neurological impairments (15.8D), physical handicaps (15.8E), blindness (15.8F), and deafness (15.8G). In most, children are seen both in groups and individually, depending on their needs.

In 1985 Carole Kunkle-Miller, whose background is in special education, rehabilitation, and art therapy, identified the special competencies needed by art therapists whose clients have physical, cognitive, or sensory disabilities. Whether a disability is temporary, permanent, or unpredictable, it affects a person's self-concept, mood, and outlook on life. It is important that anyone working with disabled individuals be clinically sensitive, and that he or she understand the conditions that are especially vital for successful art therapy with these children.

Special Considerations in Art for Children with Disabilities

The first, and perhaps most essential, condition, is to believe sincerely what Lowenfeld was able to say with such conviction—"that every human being is endowed with a creative spirit" (1957, p. 430). It is not something that can be learned, but if felt honestly and conveyed to the child, can have immensely positive effects (DVD 15.9). It seems equally important to believe that all human beings have an inherent and natural tendency toward growth, order, and integration. In order to permit any kind of freedom within a facilitating framework, one must have confidence in the child's ability to become him- or herself, to make choices and decisions about his or her own work.

It may also be necessary to expand one's notion of "art," so that it can encompass the manipulation of collage materials with feet by an armless child, or the rhythmic, repetitive swabbing of paint by a psychotic child. In a way, such manipulative and making activities are to art as babbling and jargon are to speech. They are a preparation for formal expression, and constitute as legitimate a part of art with the handicapped, as reading readiness for the average learner.

There may be some severely disabled children for whom formless, sensory play with art materials is the most they will ever be able to achieve developmentally. Why deny them these pleasures, and why impose upon them our need for them to produce more legible work? Such an imposition is found in the prepared outlines within which the children are still asked to color—meaningless for a child at a pre-figurative level of graphic development. It seems ironic that such filling-in of others' boundaries should be considered more legitimate as art than the independent manipulation of media by the child. Art with the handicapped can and should include the whole possible range of manipulative and making activities, with any media or tools controllable by the child, not necessarily the traditional ones .

Values of Art for Children with Disabilities

While true for work with all children, it seems especially important to clarify the goals and values of art for the handicapped child, for whom a good thing like art is often provided for the wrong reasons. This is not to say that such activities are not useful for filling leisure time, developing manual dexterity, or learning to share, but there are even more important values in art for a handicapped child (DVD 15.9).

Pleasure and joy, for example, are luxuries often denied those with disabilities, who need sensory-manipulative and motor-kinesthetic pleasures for tension-release, as well as for permissible regression. The blind children, who at first seemed lifeless and depressed, who were characterized by an observer in the first session as compliant and docile, came alive as they became involved in art (see DVD 3.2). They began to smile, to move and laugh and speak more freely, and to show real pleasure in both process and product (15.9A). Some have suggested that the need to play may be as fundamental as the need to love (Curry, 1971), that "the opposite of interplay is deadness" (Erikson, 1972, p. 13), and that "playfulness makes life worth living" (Sutton-Smith, 1971, p. 21).

Art provides these children with important opportunities to function as independently as possible, while they must so often be dependent on others. Through independent choice and decision-making, they are helped to define themselves in symbolic-productive terms, developing their personal tastes and styles. While some avenues of learning or expression may be blocked, art experiences can help children to further develop those sensory and productive avenues open to them—such as touch for the blind, vision for the deaf, and manual dexterity for those whose legs are immobilized.

Through practice, handicapped children can develop mastery of tools, materials, and processes. They thus learn the joy and pleasure of skill development, and the pride in a product which is truly their own (see DVD 7.5). Since disabled children so often feel out of control, both physically and psychologically, it seems especially important for them to have materials and a modality in which they can indeed be in charge (where they can be the boss).

One major value of art for exceptional children is that they can be the active ones who do something to and with materials, since so often they are passively led, dressed, doctored, and so forth. In another way, they are able to achieve mastery through dramatic play with art media. In reliving traumatic situations the blind children often assumed the stronger and more controlling role, rather than the original and often helpless one.

Thus Karen, a victim of child abuse, played the role of an angry, punitive, withholding mother to her clay babies, screaming, "You go to bed! You don't get no more food. You don't get nothin' to eat today!" (see 14.2F). These children certainly have greater stresses, more traumas, and many fewer ways of coping with them, as in Peter's memory of his hernia operation (15.9B).

In art, they can safely let go and regress, especially when anxiety about fluid media is allayed through the use of physical boundaries, like bowls or trays. They can also symbolically let go and express strong feelings of anger or fear that are hard to express directly, especially when one feels vulnerable and dependent on others.

Feelings may be released and evoked through media contacts as well as through symbolic representation. Larry, for example, smelled "ether markers," which stimulated much of his doctor play, and with clay he created symbols of free movement—his many rockets (Figure 16.4). Thus, it is possible for a disabled child to express many feelings in and through art, safely relieving inner tensions while creating aesthetic forms.

The ensuing task, then, in providing art for children with disabilities, becomes one of stretching the imagination in order to adapt the art-learning situation to the needs of that particular individual. This may mean a physical adaptation, like chocolate-pudding finger paint for those who cannot always inhibit the putting of hands in mouths, or taping paper on a table, so that an athetoid child can concentrate his or her energy on controlling the drawing tool.

It may mean thinking anew about time, and the attention span of which a retarded preschooler is initially capable, measured in seconds, or at best, minutes. It may mean arranging space and groupings, so that a very needy or extremely hyperactive child will have the lack of distraction required for involvement in art. It means, in other words, being open to and making any and all necessary adaptations so that these children can be as much in control as possible (Anderson, 1992, 1994).

In order to find a preferred medium or modality the disabled child must have the opportunity to explore and to choose. Only then can any child discover his or her personally congenial way of making things. Thus, a broad choice of media, and an openness to the use of other related expressive modalities, is as essential for these children as for others. If self-definition and independent functioning are two of the main goals of art for the handicapped, the structure within which these occur is critical. One aspect of such a facilitating structure is consistency and predictability in the availability of art materials, and the arrangement of these materials in such a way that even a blind child may be maximally independent in procuring and using them (15.9C). Another is being sure that the materials offered are responsive (15.9D).

Several who have taught art to the visually and orthopedically handicapped have noted the helpfulness of providing physical outlines or boundaries within which the children could work comfortably (Lindsay, 1972). Bowls and trays indeed seem to be helpful containers, not only because they reduce the chance of mishap, but because they enable the regressive and potentially "naughty" or disorganizing behavior to remain contained psychologically as well (Figure 15.6). Messy media, like clay or finger paint, initially stimulated anxiety in many of the blind children, but such physical boundaries eventually helped them to master the discomfort.

Perhaps an equally important facilitating condition is a psychological framework that permits true freedom and exploration. By this I mean primarily an acceptance, an attempt at understanding the meaning of the experience to the child—not what it means to the adult who observes, but who cannot ever fully enter the child's frame of reference.

This is not easy, because it requires a kind of openness and empathy that are extremely difficult, even with normal children, and especially hard with the disabled. It means accepting any honest response on the part of the child, no matter how unexpected, bizarre, regressive, or messy, so long as it does no realistic harm. A child may, for example, first need to explore a new medium; this may mean smelling, tasting, banging, squeezing, smearing, playing, and possibly never making a finished product. It means accepting the unexpected, like Billy's love for squeaky markers. With a handicapped child, it means valuing even the most agonizingly slow progress, the painstaking efforts to put things together.

280

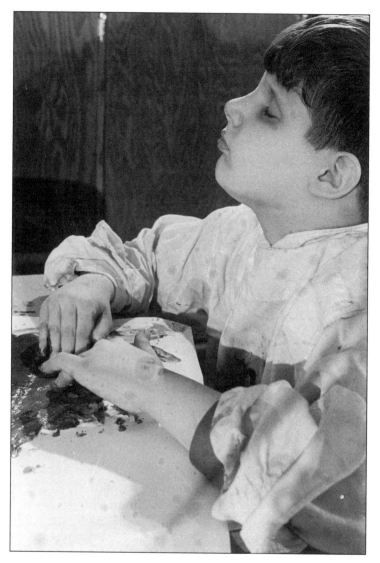

15.6 A Blind Child Experiencing Finger Paint

There may be a greater need with these children, especially at first, for adult intervention; sometimes to help them get started, as in Lowenfeld's "closure" technique (1957, p. 435). It may be necessary more often to join into the play, as with disadvantaged children who do not know how to play spontaneously. Often it means doing what Wills recommended to mothers of blind children, functioning "as the child's auxiliary ego, helping him to . . . organize his world without the aid of sight" (1965, p. 363).

Most important, perhaps, it is essential to value the child's own work above any product made even in part by another. While the crude creations of those who are severely disabled may seem inartistic or ugly to some, I agree with Lowenfeld that "the most primitive creative work born in the mind of a blind person and produced with his own hands, is of greater value than the most effective imitation" (1957, p. 446).

Just as it is essential to accept and value what the individual can produce as independently as possible, so one must be able to accept all of the feelings and fantasies that are expressed symbolically or verbally. In the process of helping children freely create their own work, and express their honest feelings, ideas may emerge for which an adult's calm acceptance can be a truly therapeutic experience. It is vital to remember that there can be no right or wrong in art, or in inner thought.

But it can be difficult to accept the vitality and the violence of the feelings hidden inside these often quiet and submissive youngsters. Perhaps because they dare not oppose those on whom they are truly dependent, feelings of anger at adults seem even more common among the handicapped, and more often hidden. As if bursting for release, they often emerge quickly and spontaneously in symbolic play and work with art media. The child may wish, for example, to smash his or her product, in fantasied destruction of another person. He or she may need to tell a gory or scary story about the art activity or creation.

Terry, for example, reacted with intense anger during her first art interview at the School for the Blind. First she squeezed, then pounded the clay, while speaking resentfully of "my sister . . . she just sits there and she laughs at me. That ain't funny! It's not! She laughed at me, and I squashed her half to death. I squashed her half to death! I just spanked her!" Pounding the clay with vigor, it was safe for Terry to imagine her make-believe revenge. Thus, the framework of fantasy, inherent in the symbolic nature of art, helped provide a safe release for such otherwise frightening impulses.

Despite their greater needs, there are real problems for an adult wishing to play a supportive, empathic, accepting role with exceptional children, due to the fact that they stir up such strong, irrational feelings in others. It seems especially vital here to be aware of one's own feelings, impulses, and wishes, so they do not get in the way. For example, one can unwittingly keep a child too dependent, through a need to give or to compensate for the disability, yet conversely may deny a necessary degree of dependency, through anxiety about too great an attachment. One must be watchful that expectations are neither too high nor too low, and must avoid interfering with the children's progress through premature interventions or excessive restrictions. Similarly, one must be careful not to pressure or seduce the children to work in a way that one knows would impress other adults, such as parents or colleagues.

One must be careful not to join the child in an attempt to deny the reality of the handicap, like Bill, who said, "I like to pretend it's not even there." Of course, one must also be sensitive to the child's wishes, and the need to pretend, as part of the process of coming to grips with reality. The ultimate, painful, but necessary challenge is to help them to come to an acceptance of the reality of their disability, and of all their feelings and fantasies about it. Only then will they be free to grow, and to develop fully the healthy parts of themselves.

Disabled youngsters are not easy to work with in art, but the rewards are immense. They do need more help from the adult—not in being told what to do or how to do it—but in being understood, and being helped to articulate their unique creative strivings. It may require more energy to empathize, to understand a child who is so different from oneself. It may require more imagination to find a way for that child to have independence and personal definition in and through art. It may require much patience and much time for the learning to begin to show. But to help a child to become him- or herself is a much more beautiful experience than nudging, leading, or seducing that child into some prearranged mold, no matter how attractive. It is also much more exciting, because it is totally unpredictable.

Art cannot give a blind child sight, a retarded child clear comprehension, or a crippled child free mobility—but it can and does give a child an exciting, stimulating, and pleasurable way to enjoy and explore the sensory world. It gives the child a way to be in charge, even in a limited sphere, of a medium or tool which is controlled as he or she wishes. It gives a youngster an opportunity to master whatever tools or processes are appealing and within reach, and to savor the pleasure of skills achieved with practice. It gives the child a way to safely let loose, to regress and smear and pound and release body tensions, or to let loose and express symbolically or verbally powerful scary feelings.

It gives them a way to control, to order, and to map out a confused sense of their body or environment, of time or space—to make sense out of things through organizing them, or to organize themselves in the productive activity. It gives them a way to discover and define themselves through genuine choices, decisions, and creations which are uniquely theirs. It gives them a way to create products of which they can be proud, which they can give to others, through which they may at times add true beauty to the world (cf. Selfe, 1977). More important, in the productive-creative experience, they can add true meaning to their lives—to their reality as well as to their fantasy.

Art for the handicapped can and must be more than a way of filling time, or a means of improving manipulative skills. For all human beings, and especially for the disabled, "art experiences can also be a way of performing mentally a desired activity which it is impossible to do physically" (Alkema, 1971, p. 3).

If it is true that "man creates, as it were, out of his mortal wounds" (Meerloo, 1968, p. 22), then the child with a disability has a need for creative experience that is much greater than that of the youngster who has not suffered irreversible wounds. Since he or she must ultimately learn "to live in a world that is made by and for the fully functioning," art is especially important as "one area where a symbolic world can be indeed adapted to the handicapped's needs, and where he is not only at liberty to tell of his world and experiences, but where he is *expected* to do so." Moreover, by so doing, "he contributes to our general understanding by giving form to his own [unique] experiences" (Kramer, 1983), something Lowenfeld must have known when he titled the book about his work with the blind, originally published in 1939, *The Nature of Creative Activity*.

CHAPTER

16

Art Therapy with Disabled Children and Their Parents

Similarities and Differences

Therapy with disabled children is generally similar to work with those who look and act normal, but who have emotional problems. It is true that the child with a physical or sensory handicap has a problem that shows, and even one with an invisible deficit, such as retardation, is usually discernibly different from other children. The disabled, however, are much like other children in their interest in media, desire to be independent, concern with mastery, and feelings of fear, jealousy, and anger.

Yet they are different, too, mainly because their handicaps seriously affect their perception of and relationship to their world. Because they are in many real ways deprived, even with the best of care they tend to be very "hungry," more ready—starved, in a way—for sensory and creative, as well as affective and interpersonal experiences, and for the kind of safe situation necessary for effective therapy. Thus, a blind child needs to be spoken to more often than a sighted one, needs to be told what is available and where it is located, and needs to be reassured vocally of the adult's continuing presence.

Because their handicaps are a reality for them—unlike the fantasies of the child whose bodily integrity has never been genuinely threatened—they often have particular problems in dealing with feelings and fantasies about their disability—especially how and why it happened to them, and how they can cope with it now and in the future. Since I have had the privilege of learning a great deal from some blind children who have come to our clinic, I should like to use the work with them to exemplify some of what occurs when one deals with a troubled child with a sensory deficit that is a reality.

First, you will hear about Candy's two individual art evaluations; then a family art evaluation that was part of her assessment; and finally, the therapy with her parents as a couple. Because I was not sure how easily she would be able to relate to me and adjust to the art media and the clinic, I suggested two individual evaluation sessions.

Candy: Individual Art Evaluation

The provision of materials that the blind can appropriately use is important, and helping them to get started may involve more instruction and demonstration than for a sighted child with more previous creative experience. Once begun, however, an art interview with a blind child is not very different from one with a sighted child.

What *is* different, however, is that the problem of coping with the fact of a missing or malfunctioning body part is a big one, and one that every blind child must confront. The fantasy that it is mother who has either not given the child the proper equipment, or has taken it away because of some "badness," is a common one.

This emerged rather quickly in 10-year-old Candy's first art evaluation session. Blind *and* cerebral palsied, she initially made a clay "doggy" (actually labeling a mass of clay as a dog), and went on to spontaneously create a drama in which a mother dog is eventually taken away. One of the inhibitions for a blind child in expressing anger toward a parent is the child's very realistic dependency on that parent, and the feelings of helplessness and vulnerability at the thought of separation.

Candy first put her clay dog "down in the cellar," and the dog yelled, "She dropped me!" She went on: "Let's pretend the dog is a mother. They're cuddling up with each other, and they're sleeping" (putting a smaller piece of clay next to a larger one). "This is the mother doggy, and this is the baby doggy. . . . The baby doggy goes right behind the mother. Then they give the mother doggy away!"

When asked who would do that, she said, "The little boy. He took her to the dog pound." Smacking another piece of clay vigorously, she shouted angrily, "Bad boy! You know better than to give those doggies away! I'll let you have it! You bring those doggies back!" She then stabbed a hole in the boy, saying, "Boy! You're gonna die! There! You're dead! Pretend this [a wooden clay tool] is like a knife. I killed him for good." In a later story during the same session she told of a father who "died of old age. . . . Nobody killed him. I didn't kill him."

In another drama built around claywork at the end of the same hour,

Candy expressed anxiety about being hurt: "Don't kill me! Oh! The bad guys are gonna kill me! I didn't do anything wrong! Oh, help! I didn't do anything wrong! I didn't do anything wrong!" I asked who she was in the story, and she said she was the mother.

She then pretended that I was her little girl and she was my *new mother:* "You need a new mother. You can get one right this minute. . . . I'll make the pancakes. I'll take her place, and she's dead. . . . My children punched me and they pulled my hair." Having worried aloud about being a mother and being the target of that aggression herself, Candy decided to undo the fantasied mother-killing and replacement. With a surprised tone she announced, "Your mother's back! You can tell her how well she was in the heaven." Then, as if the impulse was still too strong, she went on, "Maybe your mother—maybe she got sick. I guess she'll come back tomorrow."

In addition to the mother-killing wishes, blind children often have fantasies, and sometimes symptoms, which involve stealing. In part, this seems to reflect a feeling that something has been stolen from them (their sight), that they are missing something that is rightfully theirs, and that they are entitled to retrieve it. In Candy's second art interview, she pretended to be both a robber and a policeman, saying, "I'm gonna steal your money . . . because I like it."

As a very strict policeman (conscience), she then arrested the robber and put him in jail. The persistent robber returned, however, and the policeman said, "You're back again! What is the *matter* with you?" That question, however, may have been too close to home, as it was followed by an abrupt shift (disruption) in her play.

In the subsequent drama, holding one piece of wood and one of foam, Candy moved both objects toward and away from each other, enacting an approach-avoidance conflict, saying, "And the wood came along and asked if it could go out and play. And they play, and then they hit each other. You're bad! No, you're bad!" "Finally the stick says, 'I don't wanna play any more!' then both say 'I'm leavin'! No, *I'm* leavin'!' and the wood stick shouts and hits the scratchy thing, and it's all killed. . . . 'Oh no! I'm killed! Why did you kill me? You've done something wrong! No *you!* No *you!*'" The pressing dilemma seemed to be whether the *mother* had done something wrong, or whether the *child* was bad and had caused the disability herself as a punishment.

Using finger paint next, enjoying the feel of the creamy substance, Candy imagined someone not being pleased with the finger paint, which says, "I'm too *mushy* for you!" Continuing to use the paint, she went on to talk about funny and then scary stories about ghosts, potions, and especially, "magic potions that make you sick, which means you have a hard time breathing. . . . A witch is also scary. She could give you loads of bad stuff. . . . She gives you a potion, and you attack her, and she goes away." The fantasy that maybe a witch-mother's bad food (potion) caused the disability is also a common one.

In an equally common attempt to master the anxiety caused by this fantasy, Candy then pretended to put her finger painted hands into and onto lots of things, saying *she* was "polluting." She said to me, "Pretend you walk funny,[1] and you—Who's gonna wipe the pollution out? Pretend you felt sick. I'm gonna put pollution inside your smile. I'm gonna put—I'm gonna put pollution inside your *eye*. . . . Pretend I put pollution in your sock. Pretend you hurt your arm with pollution. . . . I'm gonna put pollution on your dish. Now you eat it, and you die!"

Having pretended to blind me as well as to kill me off, Candy became anxious, and there was an abrupt shift in the play, as she attempted to undo the effects of her angry retaliatory impulses: "There's never gonna be pollution again. The pollution will all go away. I'll never be a pollutor!" She then stuck a piece of clay on her finger, and enjoyed having it there, resisting removing it as the hour ended.

Candy: Family Art Evaluation

After I had met twice with Candy herself, her family was invited to come in for an art evaluation (DVD 16.1). Those attending were Candy, her parents, her 14-year-old brother, and her 6-year-old sister. So that the evaluation would be meaningful, it was necessary to modify the format according to Candy's special needs. Instead of a scribble or a group mural, the family was first asked to make up a story together, something in which Candy could participate as easily as the others (16.1A),

This was followed by a request to represent the family in any medium, but there were thin flat wood scraps of different shapes and sizes, along with glue and cardboard, in addition to the usual art supplies. Candy selected five pieces of wood, each one different, and glued them on a piece of cardboard in a way that reflected many of her wishes and perceptions about her family (16.1B).

After selecting a shape for each person, she placed her mother at the left, then her father (noticeably bigger than the others) on the right, then her older brother in the center "by himself," then herself (the smallest and thinnest piece of wood) right next to Daddy, and finally her younger sister "near Mommy." Her deliberate selection of sizes, shapes, and thicknesses,

---

[1] The reader may recall that Candy, in addition to being blind, had cerebral palsy and did indeed "walk funny."

along with her conscious placement of people, gave us a good understanding of her perception of intrafamilial relationships, despite the fact that she could not draw a family.

Her 14-year-old brother, clearly unhappy about being there, had been sulking silently after first saying that he couldn't make a family. However, he was stimulated, perhaps through rivalry, perhaps because it was less threatening, to use the wood shapes himself (16.1C). He placed his self-symbol alone in the center, showing it shooting missiles at the other four family members, each in a corner—a fairly accurate image of how things were at the time. Thus, the materials proved to be useful not only for the child with the sensory handicap, but also to overcome the resistance of her older brother.

Candy: Her Parents' Couple Therapy with Art

Art therapy can be used not only with individual parents whose children are in therapy (as described in Chapter 12), but also with couples (Wadeson, 1973; Riley, 2003). After the evaluation, which I conducted with a child psychiatry resident who wanted to learn how to do art therapy, I saw the parents for weekly child-centered counseling (I also supervised the resident's individual work with Candy).

Although art was not the primary medium of communication for this verbal and concerned couple, it became especially useful in dealing with the most loaded and difficult areas of their marital relationship, when these had emerged as significant factors in Candy's problems. Her dad, like many fathers of severely disabled children I have known, had largely escaped into his work and had left Candy's rearing, and parental worrying, primarily to his wife.

During one couple session, after much veiled and indirect expression of resentment from each concerning unmet needs and disappointment in the partner, I wondered if they could draw each other, since their perceptions of one another seemed to be an area of difficulty. After working on opposite sides of an easel, they looked at and discussed their drawings, both of which became critical reference points for the remainder of the treatment.

Candy's father had represented his wife as "The Rock of Gibraltar" (Figure 16.1), a tower of strength and stability in the shifting currents of life. At first he said that was how she *was*. Later, he responded to her hurt and anger at such unrealistic expectations with the admission that he had *wished* that she would never show vulnerability or weakness, but that he had been disappointed.

Candy's mother, on the other hand, was finally in tears about how impossible it was to please him, and how hard it was to get his sympathy and

16.1 Mr. C.'s Picture of His Wife: "The Rock of Gibraltar." Marker

concern when she herself was needy, conveying her own sense of deprivation. She represented Candy's father as all wrapped up in his hobbies and his work, with no time left for his family (Figure 16.2). Her drawing showed him playing his guitar and daydreaming about his various interests, none of which included her or the children.

While at first defensive about what he felt was an unfair portrayal, her husband finally agreed that perhaps there was some truth in it after all. In fact, it was he who then recalled how he had placed himself far away from the others in his family drawing a year earlier.

Perhaps 6 months after this session, a good deal of work was done for 3 weeks with nonverbal dyadic drawings, in which communication issues could be experienced and then discussed in an affectively charged manner (16.1D). Since both parents tended to intellectualize frequently and successfully, art was often used to help them get in touch with their feelings.

Tommy's Terror about His Vanishing Vision

Tommy was referred for therapy because he refused to learn Braille or go to Mobility Training (DVD 16.2). While he could thus maintain his denial

16.2 Mrs. C.'s Picture of Her Husband and His Many Interests. Marker

of his rapidly worsening vision, he needed those skills in order to cope with his blindness. Like Larry, whose eyes had been removed (16.2A), Tommy often used art materials to make extensions, like a cast, extra finger, or bigger hand of clay or Pariscraft (16.2B).

It was a way of compensating in fantasy for the missing body part or function, and may have also served as protection against the ever-present threat of further injury. Similarly, he created a superhero, a powerful, indestructible sculpture called the "Bionic Susquash" (Figure 16.3), who—according to Tommy—could see, hear, and perform perfectly.

His true feeling of being irreparably damaged and totally vulnerable was poignantly conveyed in two drawings of "Tommy Martian." The title's thin disguise told me that Tommy was almost ready to face those feelings as his own. In the first picture (16.2C) a boy is shown with "tentacles [and] a beam-arm," along with "the ship he was in." Although the figure looks intact, Tommy said, "He *crashed*. He bumped into a *bomb* flying saucer." He went on: "They were *after* him," as if the boy had done something wrong, revealing Tommy's unconscious guilt.

Talking while he drew the second picture (16.2D), Tommy went on with the tragic story: "He wasn't dead when he crashed into that ship. They're trying to kill him. A blade-type ship cut him right in half. They're trying to kill him. He was flying *his* ship. Then this one came over, got beside him, drew its blade, smashed into him, and now he's dead. . . . There's his body laying down on the ground. His head flew over here, his neck is here, one leg is over here, and one leg is over there. *He's all messed up!*"

Though articulate, Tommy couldn't put his anger about his progressive loss of vision into words, probably because he was so afraid of being further maimed—as in the story. He first safely expressed such dangerous feelings by making clay puppets who yelled at me (16.2E), banging on a drum, and later on a xylophone. In the process, we discovered that Tommy had a marvellous rhythmic and melodic gift, and we recorded his compositions and concerts on tape.

In the course of several months of weekly therapy, Tommy was able to deal with and work through many of his complicated feelings and fantasies about his disease. He could then go on growing and learning the needed skills—no longer stuck in his rageful fears. Because he was basically an emotionally healthy child, even though his retrolental fibroplasia was real and traumatic, Tommy's therapy did not take long.

Julie's Multimodal Brief Therapy

Although Julie's therapy had not been planned as time-limited, it became just that when her father prematurely pulled her out of treatment. Unlike Candy's parents, neither her mother nor father participated in Julie's treatment, but had agreed to allow her to come for therapy as long as school personnel transported her. She had been referred because she was very inhibited and, like Tommy, was resisting learning Braille, in spite of the fact that she had only a little light and color perception.

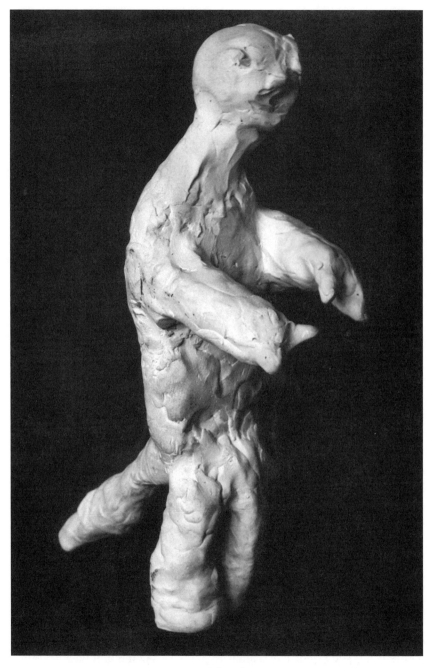

16.3 Tommy's Super-Powerful Sculpture: "Bionic Susquash"

Sessions 1 to 3

At first Julie, who was 9, expressed surprise at the playroom with its art media and sink; "I thought it was going to be like an office." She selected finger paint, noting, "I used to have finger paint at home. Something happened to it. My sister always loses it." After this reference to things that get lost because of someone else's intrusion, she went on to tell me about her art classes in school, and that the arts and crafts room was "a busy room," in contrast perhaps to the quiet of the clinic.

While she was tentative at first with the finger paint, Julie soon relaxed and moved more freely, beginning with one fingertip and finally using both hands. As she rocked and swayed rhythmically, smearing the paint, she began to talk about things she disliked, saying, "I *hate* shots and time tests and TB tests. . . . I had to have an operation. I got scared. I don't remember it too well." She quickly switched from this uncomfortable topic to a more manageable one—problems at home with her two younger sisters. She finished her finger painting, washed her hands at the sink, and then asked to use markers, then crayons, making tight little squiggles in a line, saying it reminded her of "writing Braille."

While she spoke in her first two sessions about angry feelings toward sisters, by the third she was drawing on sandpaper ("so you could feel it"), and talking about the "old and crabby" woman escort who walked her over from school. She then made brief references to anger at her parents, especially for sending her away to school on a scary bus. This was clearly difficult, however, so that much of the anger toward parents, especially mother, was displaced onto siblings and adult women at school. Pounding the clay with vigor at the end of the third session, Julie said of her housemother, "Some kids say I don't like her. She's so rotten and so nervous and contrary, so mean and contrary."

Session 4

Julie scribbled with markers more freely than before and discussed other children's handicaps and fears, and then some of her own wishes and feelings. She wondered if by coming to the clinic she might get her eyes magically fixed; "I thought Child Guidance gave you glasses, that they would check your eyes."

She said she liked coming to the clinic, but wished I could stop being a consultant to her school; "I don't want you to go to school." When I commented that she might feel jealous that I would come and be with other children, she nodded her head vigorously, all the time scribbling intensely. She tried to identify crayon colors, was unsuccessful, and seemed sad but relieved, saying she has to "pretend" some of the time that her limited light and color perception is greater than it really is.

Session 5

Julie announced that she wanted to make a movie, and then proceeded to arrange building blocks and clay figures she had made on the floor in a living room setting, using them to enact a scary story (DVD 16.3).

In the drama, two children, a girl of 7 and a boy of 9, are sitting near a stage built of blocks, when they hear a knock on the door. One asks, "Who is it?" to which a deep, scary voice responds, "Dracula!" The children then say, "Come in," and afterwards, "What do you want?" Dracula, still menacing, growls, "I want to kill you. I want to kill you!" The girl defiantly replies, "Kill me? Go ahead!" to which the monster responds by trying to do so, and in the process knocks off the upper level of the block stage. The girl says angrily, "See what you did? *You ruined my stage!*" to which Dracula replies, "What did I do? I didn't ruin anything. *We've got the lower stage still.*"

The boy then asks, "What would you like?" Dracula replies, "To eat you and to kill you," to which the boy compliantly answers, "*Go right ahead.*" Dracula then proceeds to kill both children and weakly moans, "Ooooooo, I died. I killed one lady, and now I must suck her blood." Another Dracula monster arrives and joins the first in sucking blood—Julie (as Dracula) sucking water out of a baby bottle she had previously rejected.

When asked about the motive for the killing, Julie explained, "He's mad at them—at—um—that lady because she gave him some bad food." It appeared that aspects of Julie herself had been present in all of the roles, from the fearful-brave children to the angry monster. The stage, whose upper portion had been knocked off, might also have symbolized Julie, whose upper receptors (eyes) had been damaged ("ruined"), despite the fact that the lower-stage body parts were still intact.

Session 6

The following week, Julie began by using clay and recalling times when she still liked to suck out of a bottle, even in kindergarten, but feared her mother might object. She then worried that I might disclose (presumably to her mother) what went on in the sessions, saying, "You never told anybody what we do, did you?" I commented that it must be very hard for children to believe that adults would keep secrets, and she said solemnly, "It's very hard for children, and the thing is, they see movies and they get very frightened. . . ."

"You know what I'm scared of? In the car by myself, if the car would move. If somebody's in the car with me and it moves, it's okay—my sister or somebody. What's the best thing to do?" Julie asked this with some urgency, and then went on to explain that this was a worry she had had for a long time, and that she even has "bad dreams" that a car starts and is moving, and she is alone and can't stop it. I wondered why she was thinking about this sort of problem, since she had also told me that it had never happened in reality. She responded, with evident anxiety, "Because they say that people have been getting killed!"

She then went on, "You know how I started that? I dreamed that I was in a car and I heard the car go out of gear, and the wheels too, and it started to move, and I jumped out of the car, and I cried." She remembered having such a dream several times, most recently after she had returned to school following Easter vacation. She went on, by then sucking water with anxious intensity out of the baby bottle: "I dreamed that several girls came, opened up the door, and the car stopped. You see, if there's somebody with you they do something. Three girls all opened the door. . . . I think I dreamed about one where my Aunt Ruth left me in the car, and the car rocked back and forth and I just stopped. I've even told my sisters not to mess with the gears. Every time my sister talks in the car I get nervous. . . . I have the dream at home and at school."

When I asked what she thought the danger was, she replied, "You'll be mashed." Continuing to suck the water, she spoke of other scary things, like thunderstorms and electricity. She recalled a time when she had almost gotten hurt by touching an electrified fence, saying "I wanted to see what it was like. I guess it was just my curiosity. I had to touch it with just my finger. It shakes you up really good."

She went on to worry more about cars rolling and people getting hurt, while working with sandpaper on some soft wood. She liked the sounds made with the sandpaper, and experimented with various rhythms, saying, "Did you ever hear of a song called the 'Sandpaper Ballet?' Well, that's it!"

Session 7

The next week's appointment was canceled by her dad because of his anger over the clinic bill, ironically due to a misunderstanding of the amount owed. Julie came in a week later, but was aware of her father's threat to abruptly pull her out of therapy. As she modeled some clay, I asked her how all this fuss made her feel. She said, "Kind of terrible. It made me think that they were poor . . . I want to be a grownup."

When I asked how coming to the clinic made her feel, Julie expressed her ambivalence, noting that she had to miss a club meeting at school, and that, "Last week I felt very sad not coming; no, I guess I had mixed feelings."

She said she was feeling bossed about coming or not, and also about taking part in a school play. "I really don't like people bossing you around." When I asked what she does when that happens, she replied sadly, "Nothing. I just get mad. I go in my room and I put my head down, and I might be punished. When people tell me I don't speak up, I get mad too. I *do* speak up! Whenever I have a headache I tell the nurse. I was worried about it—about not getting to come here. I was afraid you'd get angry!"

I wondered why she thought I'd be angry, and she said, "Does it scare you? Does it scare you in the lobby?" I said that perhaps it scared her to feel angry and that it led her to worry that I might not approve. She explored aloud the idea of getting angry at me, but dismissed it, saying, "Go ahead and talk back, and you'll get in trouble." I wondered how she thought I would react, and she said, "I'm a little worried about you. If it's a *he* that comes before me, then I'll really be angry. Sometimes I wish I could see, but even though your parents can see, they could still learn a little bit of Braille." I noted that she seemed to wish people understood more about what it was like to be blind, and she explained how hard it is at the seashore, saying, "Because pebbles hurt your feet. There's real big waves and I'm still scared. I'm gonna tell people it's not true." She then said there were some other things she would like to tell people, including, "I wish I could see," and, "Nothing—what I really *can* see," and, "I can read Braille," "I can wash dishes," and, "I can sweep the floor—with your hands, with your hands!" She went on, "Some blind children can be *cured*. They *could* be— but they were probably born that way."

I wondered why she thought children became blind who were not born that way, and she said quite clearly, "Their parents prob'ly beat them. And this guy beat this little boy. So I just feel like shooting the parents. Did you ever read in the paper about some children? They put them against the wall and then stamp on their stomach. That's the way to murder them!" I said she seemed concerned about parents being angry at children, or maybe vice versa, and she said that she sometimes got mad when her mother did things for her that she wished she could do herself. "Maybe it's hard things, like tying your shoes or something. *She* does it. Well, I *try* to do it. If we're going somewhere, I don't do it 'cause she's in a hurry."

She was making a container out of clay, and called it "a bowl, a cup, a dish, or a basket," asking, "Could you paint this kind of clay if you wanted?" I said she could do that if she came back next week, and she said, with fervor, "I *do* want to come. Could I pretend about being in a car next week?" I said we had a big cart that she could sit in, and she went on, "Our car shakes and vibrates. I get scared it is really moving. Our garage door scares you to death." When I wondered about the basket, she grinned and said,

"The basket is yours. We'll paint it next week." I had the feeling at that point that I was indeed being used as a container, one into which she could risk pouring previously unspoken fears and fantasies. Probably the threatened termination led her to want to dramatize the scary dream quickly, in the hope that I might help her with it.

Session 8

When she arrived the following week she immediately began the drama, announcing, "For this week there is a long car accident, and people committing suicide. The story takes place in a shopping center. The characters are: the policeman, nurse, housemother, doctor, and a schoolteacher, and Julie—me." Before she started the story, she commented with irritation that it makes her angry when people rush her in the morning, and recalled how mad she had gotten at her housemother: "Some people really boss you. I got really angry yesterday. She made me pick up those books—from playing school. And everybody else played, but I had to do the cleaning up. That also makes me angry. It makes me mad. I'm sick and tired of it!" Following this direct ventilation of angry feelings, she began what Susan Aach-Feldman called a "genesis" drama, an attempt at explaining in a fantasy the origin of her blindness.

"It is about a car accident. I'm waiting in the lobby for a nurse. The mother left the child at home. My mother went shopping without me in another car and she locked me in. And then the car started moving, and it went out of gear by itself, and. . . ." She hesitated to play it out, saying she'd just *tell* it, so I wondered if I could interview the characters, and she agreed.

As the mother, she said, "My daughter was in the car. I do *not* like my daughter. She shall be beaten and killed, because I *hate* her, because she never does anything but lay around, because there is nothing to do. She will not go outside, and it was a nice day. . . . It makes me think she's sick. She is *pretending* to be sick. She is *pretending* to be sick! Because she does not want to do any chores!" I asked the mother if she had any other children and she named Julie's real younger sisters. "But it is only the *oldest* who will not do her chores." She then yelled viciously, "Get over here, young lady! Get over here! You're gonna be beaten!"

As the interviewer, I wondered if maybe her oldest child had trouble with chores because she was blind, and wondered too if the mother had any idea of how that happened. She replied, "I think I socked her in the eye with a stone!" She then turned to her daughter and went on, "Young lady! I want you to get out of that chair. We're gonna go home and lock you in the car. The trip is over." I then asked Julie if it would be all right if I were the policeman. I said I would not let a mother do such a terrible thing to her child, at which point Julie got some clay, made a round, big bomb, and pretended to kill the bad mother.

We discussed the story at the end of the session.

Session 9

The following week Julie wanted to replay her story, first dictating the following distorted review:

"The Accident. Once upon a time I was in this car, and I pretended that I was going to the Monroeville Mall. And then some old lady locked me in the car. And I had a car accident and broke my leg. And then I went to the hospital. And then I called the police, and the police was going to bring in this old woman that locked me in the car. So I had a session with the judge, a trial. I was the witness. At the trial I had a clay time bomb, and I blew the witch up, and the witch died. And then there was this nurse who pretended to be a housemother. I mean, there was this housemother pretending to be a nurse, and she-she-she-blew up too. And then there was another one who was a very nice nurse. She took the bandage off and let me out of the hospital, and that was the end of the story."

She then went on to tell what the story for this week was to be, though it was eventually played out with much more violence and gore than in the preview. "This week there was a long car accident and people committing suicide. It takes place in a shopping center. The characters are: a policeman, nurse, housemother, doctor, and schoolteacher—and there's me, and I'm the one that has the car accident. I'm supposed to go a long way down a great big hill and bump into something—crash!"

In both stories a girl gets injured in a car accident caused by her mother, who has left the child in the car alone and "forgotten" to put on the brakes. The implication is that the mother had deliberately caused the blindness, and in both stories the girl's rage is expressed through bombing and killing the mother, with support from the policeman, the judge, and the nurse. When asked what the moral of the stories would be, Julie said, "Mothers shouldn't hit kids hard." Of course, it is essential in work with all children not only to help them get in touch with their rage, but also to help them protect their loved ones from it by finding appropriate ways of expressing their frustrations.

Session 10

Julie's father continued to be upset about the clinic bill, and decided that she could come only one more time. In this goodbye session, we talked about how hard it was that a child could not be the boss of her own therapy, and how angry she felt at all the grownups, including me, for not preventing the premature termination. Fortunately, enough work had been done that significant changes in Julie's symptoms had taken place; she was less inhibited in self-assertion, and in the use of her hands for learning Braille. While she had not resolved all of the underlying conflicts, she had come to know her anger and her helplessness, and was finding that she could speak up without hurting anyone she loved.

Coming to Terms with Blindness

All blind children, whether or not they end up at mental health centers, go through a process of trying to come to terms with their disability, a process that usually involves denying, wondering, wishing, raging, mourning, and then attempting to accept it. At first, it is most common to try to deny the reality, to say, like Candy did in her first session, "I know color. I can tell colors, like green, red, pink, yellow, blue, white, orange. I like purple. Purple's my favorite."

Knowing that she did not have either color or light perception, I wondered if she meant that she knew color names, but she insisted that she could see the different hues. Larry, with his two artificial eyes, at first asserted that he was the only child at the school who wasn't "really blind." These, of course, represented attempts to deny the reality of the handicap, which, as Tommy said symbolically, can feel like being "all messed up."

The awareness that one is different and more vulnerable is not always verbalized, but may be powerfully conveyed through art. Janice, in her first art interview, spoke symbolically of her greater vulnerability and anger at feeling so helpless. She drew a "Snowman Family" of three, and when asked who they were, wrote the names of herself and her parents below the figures. She said that the parents don't fight, but, "I get angry the most." When asked the cause of her anger, she said with vehemence, "I just never want the sun to come out!" I wondered if that was because her snowman would melt, and she said, "Yes." I then said, "Doesn't the sun melt the parents too?" to which she bitterly replied, "No, 'cause they're unmeltable!"

During a session held several months later, Janice went on to express her resentment and retaliatory rage at the sighted, especially those on whom she felt dependent. She painted "a building which is a hospital, and in this hospital—there's just one patient in this hospital. . . . The one patient is Mrs. Rubin. . . . she had an accident. She bumped into another lady's car and . . . she punctured her eye" (DVD 16.4).

When asked what would happen, she said, with a grin, "It's gonna blind her," going on to explain how Mrs. Rubin would then be unable to work with children in art. When asked how she herself felt about it, she asserted with a sly smile, "I don't feel anything. My sight's coming back!" Having verbalized this wish, she went on to deny her handicap completely, saying, "I can see just like a regular person!"

Larry: A Long Therapeutic Journey

Working with blind and otherwise handicapped children in therapy is not an easy thing to do, but is always a challenge as well as a powerful learning experience. Sometimes progress can be painfully slow. It required 6 years of work for Larry, about whom you have already read, to move from his statement that he was the only child at school who was "not *really* blind," through his fantasies, wonderings, wishes, rages, and mournings, until he could rather calmly talk about "the *real* Larry, you know, the one at the School for the Blind." It took 6 years for him to be able to *talk about* his impulses, rather than *act* on them—to not break a window, but to tell a story about "Larry, and how he would *like* to break a window when his sister calls him a blind cripple" (DVD 16.5).

Larry's therapy had begun with many indications of feeling vulnerable. In his first art interview he had carefully poked rows of holes into clay with a tool, and had spoken of falling down a deep hole, "where maybe you couldn't get out!" (16.5A) Like many, he had attempted to achieve freedom from the constrictions imposed by his handicap, creating numerous clay rockets (Figure 16.4) and stories about being an astronaut in outer space (16.5B).

These wishful denials of reality included such thoughts as, "It would be fun to go, because you could *see* things, and you could walk on the moon." As if he could not, even in fantasy, escape from danger, however, he added, "If I walk on the moon myself, I'm afraid I'd fall through." Nevertheless, like other handicapped youngsters, he was full of compensatory omnipotent fantasies, imagining himself as the "King of Space" or the "President" of the country.

Because his world was so constricted, his therapy became for him, as for other such children, a central event in his life. He not only developed a strong and initially positive transference, but fantasized that it was returned, as when he asked in the second month of therapy, "When you go home, do you always think about me?" While such wishes are common for many physically intact, troubled youngsters, they are intensified for a child whose existence is really restricted, for whom the expression of strong feelings may seem more risky.

Because of his particular disability, he, like others, relied not only on art media, but also on sounds (16.5C), music (Figure 16.5), and dramatic play, with a special function for the tape recorder, which he would use to sing

301

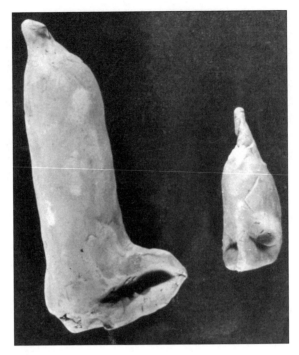

16.4 Two of Larry's Many Clay Rockets Used for Space Fantasies

(16.5D) and to review what had occurred, much as a sighted child could look back at artwork. Much of the time, he was working on his feelings of guilt for the death of his baby sister from cystic fibrosis, which in his fantasy was the cause of his final operation on his eyes—to have them removed because of his congenital glaucoma.

As you know from reading about him in earlier chapters, Larry used art, and especially drama, to work through his problems. Indeed, he had an internal split between two self-images: a "Good Larry" and a "Bad Larry," the one who escaped reality or was very aggressive. To integrate both parts of himself was hard work, during which I consulted with his teachers and houseparents, while his parents met with a blind social worker at our clinic, and occasionally with me.

Despite having experienced a powerfully negative transference as well as a positive one (those good and bad feelings about others mirroring his internal division), Larry had a hard time deciding to end his therapy, which had been a big part of his life. Eventually, however, he made the decision to do so.

On his last day, with his usual dramatic flair, he announced that he was

16.5 Larry Playing a Recorder during a Therapy Session

going to give a speech announcing his resignation from the Child Guidance Center, a fairly realistic reflection of how far he had come:

"I've asked for this time to speak directly to you all about my resignation at the Pittsburgh Child Guidance Center. During the past several weeks I've been thinking about this plan to resign, and two weeks ago, I told my therapist I was done. But as I resign, let me resign in good spirits. For the past few years we worked on problems, how I've handled things, and tempers I've lost.

I'm through all that. There are a lot more things to accomplish. . . . It's hard to do, but I have to, because I believe that the time has come that I should resign here. I hope all will be well. After this I'll go back home and work with problems and do heavy work. . . . I leave with no bitterness. I leave with this conclusion to the years of work. Sometimes we will have fights, we will be angry, sometimes we will be all right.

303

Hopefully, I might report and come back and visit the people here. . . . I trust you all will remember the past and think of the future. I want to say goodbye to everybody over here—Mrs. Rubin and Miss Driben [a blind social worker] and the ladies in the waiting room. I came here in 1969 and ended in 1975. My conclusion is this—I told a few school friends that I was resigning Child Guidance Center after I made the decision. They said good. My girlfriend is just as proud as I am. . . .

I hope I'll get through this blind school. I may be an elevator operator. I can't be an airplane pilot. . . . I'd like to be a radio reporter. . . . I've been working hard in class, in school—in social studies and math. As I leave, I conclude with one final word: I hope nothing goes wrong here. I hope everybody remains the same shape, and all the people I know—I'll be talkin' about you, and I hope in the future things become better off for you. So farewell, goodbye. For the past number of years, we worked hard on courageous problems at home and at school. Farewell."

As Larry listened to a replay of the tape of his speech he was solemn, but seemed sure of his decision, which was indeed difficult after such a long time. He did call every few months "to see how things are over there," and 6 months later asked to come in for "just one visit" in order to tell me his latest New Year's Resolutions.

In the years while Larry was still at the school for the blind he kept in touch with me, through occasional phone calls. He still liked to create rockets—his symbol of unrestricted freedom, his fantasied escape from the constrictions of his blindness. He no longer believed, however, that he could be an astronaut or an airplane pilot.

Instead, he worked hard as a student and became an active citizen in high school, then went on to secure and keep a job at the Guild for the Blind, traveling to and from work on a bus. He continued to develop his dramatic gifts, too, performing at a local cabaret on amateur night as a comedian, calling me proudly to let me know, in case I could attend.

In his periodic telephone contacts during the years since he terminated therapy, I have had the impression that Larry has found a way to not only succeed as a blind person coping in a sighted world, but to be reasonably happy as well. Fifteen years after he terminated, I ran into Larry on the street. He recognized my voice immediately, and greeted me warmly.

He told me proudly about the life he had made for himself: his friends, his job at the Guild for the Blind, and his performances at a local comedy club (he had always done wonderful vocal imitations). He recalled our times together fondly, and grinned as he announced that he was no longer "mental!"

In the summer of 2004 I not only heard from Larry, but received a request to get together. It seemed that his mother had died, he was living with his father and sister, and he wanted to tell me about his life as an adult. The red hair and the sense of humor were still present, as we met for an intense hour of catching up on what had happened over the years since we had met on the street.

He remembered our meetings fondly, although he also assured me that he was never "mental." I asked how he felt about coming for psychotherapy for all those years, and he replied that that was different, and good. On the phone, Larry had asked for a copy of the 1972 film in which he had appeared, and for which he had provided some scat singing (Rubin, 1972). I brought him a videotape.

He had also requested the audiotapes we had made during our therapy sessions, which had provided him with a way to reflect on what happened during those hours. I found a few, which I lent him, which he copied and then returned to my office. He asked if we could meet again some time, and we agreed to do so next year. On the Jewish holidays in the fall Larry, now a devout Catholic, left a warm message on my answering machine.

In addition to seeing Larry for individual therapy I had also consulted to his school, where the art therapy program described in Chapter 15 was followed by a summer program. This included a mothers' group as well as groups for the children.

Mothers' Art Therapy Group: School for the Blind

In a 6-week summer program, Larry's mother was one of eight who had weekly group art therapy at the school, while their children had art and drama therapy (DVD 16.6). One week they had a joint session with their children (16.6A). The mothers' group, which met for 90 minutes, was initiated because parents need to face their own feelings about a child with a disability before they can understand what it means to the child.

The mothers began each of their meetings with art activities designed to help them understand their children's experience as well as their own. These included modeling with blindfolds or closed eyes, family drawings, life-space pictures (16.6B), scribble drawings, and free drawing or modeling.

Looking at her *family drawing*, in which her blind son and her husband were given shaky outlines and looked weaker than the others, Larry's mother began to talk about how frustrated she was in trying to help her assertive son: "I want to be his right arm, that's what I want. I want to be his buddy. I want to be his mother and his very good friend, and I don't have it!"

During the joint art session 3 weeks later, she and Larry successfully completed a joint drawing they had planned at home—a "Pizza," a subject of deep significance for both (16.6C). It was one of the few things she made for him that he trusted as a communication of her love. After that, however, they were unable to work together on a joint project to their mutual satisfaction.

She next took him to an easel, where she attempted to paint a picture (16.6D) with him, with much attendant frustration and resistance on Larry's part (16.6E). Despite his desire to do something on his own, his mother had persisted in trying to get Larry to make further joint products with her, but to no avail. They finally ended up, still side by side, at a table near another mother-child pair, with each working alone (16.6F). Larry was happy, but his mother was sad (16.6G).

In the discussion following that experience, she said with much feeling, "He was just agitating me! He wouldn't take any suggestions. He has a mind of his own, a definite mind of his own . . . I was just frustrated. I tried real hard to get him to work with me, but he had a mind of his own, and I was just agitating him by trying to. But after the pizza, forget it! That was it! He will not let me help him. He won't let me see for him, in other words. He can do it himself, and I thought I could show him about it. But he don't want no part of it. And I think that's why I loused it up. He just didn't want me to do anything with it!"

Her need to help, to keep him dependent on her in an overprotective way, as if to compensate for his loss, was shared and empathized with by many other mothers. Some, however, while sympathizing with her frustration, were able to show Mrs. N. how she could enjoy a blind child's growing independence. One mother told proudly about how her usually timid boy had played a teacher role with her. "He told me to draw like he was drawing, but I tried it, and I didn't like it so much. So I used clay and that was okay too."

Another woman spoke of her daughter, Terry, whose inoperable brain tumor was gradually worsening, with a warm appreciation of the child's assets: "She has so many ideas. She does her thing, and I do mine. She's under so much pressure at school, why pressure her any more?" (16.6H)

Mrs. N. thus began to see her own possible motives for trying to pressure her son into doing only joint projects. "I think I feel guilty, like I'm somehow to blame for him losing his eyes. I know it's crazy, but I hit him hard, and the next day the doctor told us the news. I feel like I just have to make it up to him."

Larry's mother's wish to deny the reality of his two artificial eyes had been poignantly evident in an inappropriate request for him to hand her a red crayon during the pizza drawing. Asking him to make a *painting* with her was similarly impossible for him to do (see 16.6E). In the mothers' group discussion following the joint session, her choice of visual media stimulated an intense and frank discussion of the difficulty of accepting the reality of a blind child. The following week, in the mother's group, Larry's mother stated with relief, "It's all over now. He's a new kid. You said tell him about his handicap? Well, we told him. I think he's realizing it. He even talks about it. He told the bus driver this morning, 'I can't see.' He never said that before!"

Some mothers were able, through the joint art session, to see their children in a new light. One totally blind boy surprised his mother and others by being interested in art at all, and especially by being willing to use and even enjoy fluid media like finger paint.

Another woman, herself an artist (16.6I), spoke of her cerebral-palsied, partially sighted son with genuine astonishment: "He seemed very much at ease. He likes to paint! And I'm surprised because he didn't used to like to do anything that would make his hands dirty, and I notice now that he doesn't seem to mind a lot of the materials. You know, I was kind of surprised" (16.6J).

Her remarks, however, about how rapidly he worked, revealed less approval, even a deprecating attitude: "When he was finished with it, I thought I'd die! I didn't know, you know. . . . Those paintings, he just knocks them off, one a second! Quantity not quality! I think his talent lies more with the verbal than with something like this." This mother also made a poignant nonverbal statement about her perception of her son's artistic ability, laying her hand on his and guiding it during the making of a joint mural (Figure 16.6).

While all of these mothers found the joint art session to be rather embarrassing and uncomfortable, half of them referred to it spontaneously in their post-program evaluations, suggesting more such activities. One woman wrote with candor, "Having to work with my son was the hardest. I know it was the best and most important for both of us, but it wasn't easy. . . . But we should do more things together like this" (16.6K).

Another mother, also self-conscious about being on display, stated, "More involvement with the children and the parents together, I think would make for a better relationship, say, even for just a half hour. . . . I think when the parents are happy, the kids are happier and more adjusted to their handicap."

Outpatient Mothers' Therapy Group: Sustenance and Support

When I left the psychiatric hospital (where I worked after the clinic), I often got referrals of children with disabilities. I ended up seeing youngsters

16.6 An Artist-Mother "Helps" Her Blind Child to Paint Better

with a wide variety of physical, sensory, and cognitive problems, and frequently met with their parents as well. One mother, whose other child was seeing my colleague, Dr. Irwin, met another mother in our waiting room, and began to share notes. They requested a group, to which I invited two others.

In the beginning they did art as a way of introducing themselves and reflecting on their perceptions of their disabled youngster. After a while, the pressures of parenting these complicated children led to frank and open discussions, in which the group became a therapy for them as individuals, and mutual support for them as mothers of children whose special needs would last a lifetime. In the end, I learned much more from them than I was able to give. Fortunately, therapy is always such a mutual growth experience.

PART V

ART AS THERAPY FOR EVERYONE

17

Helping the Normal Child through Art

Making art available to more children in a way that allows them to honestly express themselves is good medicine, like taking vitamins or getting regular checkups—a form of primary prevention.

When Fred Rogers invited me to be the "Art Lady" on *Mister Rogers' Neighborhood*, a public television program for young children (1966–1969), our goal was to demonstrate the value of art expression for self-esteem, self-definition, and dealing with feelings (DVD 17.1).

Therapeutic Values in Art Education

Art educators recognized the broadly therapeutic and growth-enhancing potential of their subject soon after it became an accepted part of the school curriculum (DVD 17.2). During the heyday of progressive education, art was seen as a vehicle for self-expression and as a way of dealing with feelings (cf. Petrie, 1946; Schaeffer-Simmern, 1961; Shaw, 1938). Walden, the school Margaret Naumburg (1928) founded in 1914, was based on such ideas. The art classes at Walden were taught for a period of time by her sister, Florence Cane (1951), herself an art therapy pioneer.

In the first edition of *Creative and Mental Growth* (1947), Viktor Lowenfeld proposed an "art education therapy." Like Edith Kramer, he felt that art contributed to psychological integration because of the synthesis involved in the creative process itself. "Because whenever we move from chaos to a better organization in our thinking, feeling and perceiving, we have become a better organized individual. And this, indeed, is the common goal of any therapy. Therefore, aesthetic experiences are greatly related to this harmonious feeling within our own selves" (1982, p. 30).

Indeed, art enables children to look with open eyes, to encounter the world without fear, to acquire a perceptual vocabulary that helps them organize their experiences. In art, children learn concepts related to things like change (as in color mixing) or stability (as in construction), that relate not only to the arts, but also to dealing with life. Art helps children to think divergently, to explore alternative solutions to problems, to take risks, to fail, and to cope in a flexible way.

In art children learn to manage tools and media in order to make personal statements, helping them to feel better (because they have mastered something), and to speak more clearly (to express themselves). Creating helps children define themselves and their experiences, through forming unformed media, developing their own themes and styles, and discovering and delineating their identities (17.2A).

Art also helps children learn to share, to respect each other's work, and to live together in a social environment. Moreover, in art children can give form to their feelings, especially those which are difficult or impossible to put into words (17.2B). Philosopher Susanne Langer (1958) believed that "there is an important part of reality that is quite inaccessible to the formative influence of language: that is, the realm of so called 'inner experience,' the life of feeling and emotion" (p.4). "The primary function of art is to objectify feeling so that we can contemplate and understand it" (p. 5).

This value may be the one most clearly related to therapy, but it seems to me that in a broader sense, all of the values inherent in art can be thought of as therapeutic—in helping children to feel better about themselves as competent people who can meet the challenges of living, including the painful ones that are part of everyone's childhood.

There is also considerable evidence that troubled or disadvantaged children can be helped to develop more positive attitudes toward learning, toward others, and toward themselves, as a third grade teacher once observed: "Time and again, I have noted the catalytic effect of art in a student's life. The shy one becomes confident—the slow-learner shows a new eagerness. For it is by creating something unusual that he discovers his worth" (Lehman, 1969, p. 46).

It seems to me that the most therapeutic thing one can do in a classroom, as in a therapy group, is to provide a setting in which each child can become him- or herself. First, it is necessary to watch and listen, to understand just who each child is, and where he is, and where he seems to want to go. Then one can try to help him get there, by honestly valuing his or her own creative definition of himself. Through understanding, through provision of appropriate conditions, through permitting and focusing on areas of concern and conflict, art in the classroom can be a powerful tool in preventing problems, as well as in helping each child to grow as well and as beautifully as he or she can (17.2C).

Over the years, more and more art therapists have been working in schools (Cohen, 1974), with preschoolers undergoing transient stress (Salant, 1975), elementary students with learning disabilities (Smith, 1979), or emotional disorders (Wolf, 1973). Most often, they help children of all ages overcome psychological problems enough to be able to do what is central in school: to learn (Allan, 1988; Allan & Bertoia, 1992; Bush, 1997; Case & Dalley, 1990; Henley, 1992, 2001; Moriya, 2000; Ross, 1997; Stepney, 2001).

Dealing with Normal Stresses through Art

In addition, there is also a therapeutic role for the classroom or art teacher who can help to prevent emotional difficulties from mushrooming and causing significant problems that require therapy. This is especially true for the normal stresses that children experience as part of growing up, as well as those that stem from difficult situations they may encounter at home or in the community. Having materials available for expression enables children to use art to deal with urgent feelings. Sometimes feelingful art emerges spontaneously; at other times it is deliberately evoked by a sensitive teacher or therapist.

No one is in a better position to understand and to help children deal with stress through art than teachers or parents. Unlike therapists, they know the child over time, both extensively and intensively. They are in a position to recognize signs of situational stress, by noting variations in a child's usual working style. When Lisa's mother went to the hospital to have a baby, for example, Lisa's painting was a smeary regressive mass, done with agitation (Figure 3.10b), radically different from her usual well-controlled decorative designs (Figure 3.10a)—a clear signal to her teacher that she was extremely upset.

Joan, usually quite sociable, was uncharacteristically quiet when she entered the after-school workshop room one day. She said a perfunctory hello to her best friend, threw her coat on the chair, and went straight to the easel. Taking a brush out of the black paint, with vigorous, slashy strokes, she quickly sketched a picture of a boy in tears, a bicycle in the background (Figure 17.1). When she was finished, she sighed and stepped back to look at her painting.

As the workshop leader, I asked if she felt like talking about the picture,

313

17.1 A Boy Crying Because He Lost His Bike. Age 10. Tempera

and she said, "Oh, it's just a boy." After a pause, however, she went on: "He's crying, because he lost his bike, and he's afraid to tell his mom, 'cause she might be mad at him." I then wondered if she knew anybody like that, and, with tears in her eyes, she blurted, "Me. Just this afternoon. I couldn't find it. And I'm really scared!" The picture-making helped Joan to deal with what had happened, to look at both feelings and consequences.

All children have such stresses, changing in impact as they grow older and more able to cope (DVD 17.3). Nona, at 3, had gotten lost in a store, and was fearful about leaving the house. As if to further communicate this anxiety to me, she showed me her drawing and explained, "It's a man crying for his mommy 'cause he got lost in the dark. He can't find his way home, 'cause it's too dark, and he's afraid" (17.3A).

Viola tells about a mother whose child was having nightmares: "The mother with her right instinct asked her boy if he would not like to draw the bogey man and the other unpleasant things he dreamt of. After a time the dreams ceased" (1944, p. 59). Like Nona's nightmare picture (Figure 1.1), the creation of forms that are symbolic of the feared object can often help; as when Ruth Shaw's (1938) students finger painted "awful things" or when Natalie Robinson Cole's (1966) pupils were encouraged to draw and write about "secret crimes" and other such loaded subjects.

314

Separation Anxiety

All children deal with separations, whether the parent is leaving them or vice versa. Nona, about to enter a new school at 12, did a drawing about a girl who was doing the same (17.3B), and described it: "The father is bringing the daughter to school, and she's kind of frightened by it, because she's never been to school before . . . and she doesn't know anybody, and she's frightened of a big school."

I asked her why the girl was frightened, and she explained, "Because she's afraid of what the teachers will be like, and if they will be mean or nice. And she wants her dad to stay in school." Then, reflecting upon her own early experience, she added, "I remember I wanted you to stay, but I knew you couldn't, and I was embarrassed, so I told you to go away." In her drawing she was letting me know how this new school revived some of the same anxieties she had felt when she was little.

Sibling Rivalry

Almost all children have to cope at one time or another, with the birth of a sibling, the separation from mother, and the advent of a new rival that such an event entails. During the pregnancy they may be preoccupied with curiosity about what is growing in mother's tummy, sometimes imagining it to be food or an animal which moves about inside. Many of the children in a kindergarten class had mothers who were pregnant, and were buzzing with questions, so the teacher suggested that they draw pictures of babies inside and then discuss both fact and fantasy (17.3C).

Sammy's drawing, on the other hand, was done spontaneously in his kindergarten, and reflected, to his understanding teacher, his anger at the new baby (Figure 17.2). His mother had just brought home a little girl, the first one in the family, and everyone was making a big fuss over her. Sammy made a fuss, too. He helped with the diapers, kissed the baby, and told all his friends and relatives about how much he loved his new sister.

But Sammy was jealous, too. His mother used to have more time for him, and now she was always busy or tired, and seemed less interested in him than before. So one day at school he drew a picture of a bird diving down toward a nest, and told his teacher, "That big boy bird's gonna knock that other one off the nest. There ain't no room for two!" Sammy could not get rid of his sister in reality, nor would he want to all the time; but he could safely express that wish in symbolic disguise in his drawing.

Tommy was a little farther along than Sammy in accepting his new baby, when he drew a picture at home. He told his mom, "It's a mother pushing a baby in a carriage. It's a *new* baby, and it's crying—wha! wha! It's raining,

17.2 A Bird Knocking Another Bird off the Nest. Age 5. Marker

and they want to go home." Tommy seems to have accepted not only the presence of his new sibling, but even the fact that his mother must give the infant a lot of attention. The only sign of any hostile feelings is that the baby is crying and is getting soaked by Tommy's rain.

When baby brothers get bigger, they can be a real problem for the older child, who both likes and resents the presence of another in his play space. Nona at 5 drew a picture of a crying girl (Figure 17.3), and explained, "She's sad, because her baby brother broke the head off her teddy bear." Nona's teddy bear had indeed been damaged by her infant brother, and was a highly prized "transitional object" which comforted her at bedtime (Winnicott, 1971a).

Her ability to use crayons and paper to express her sadness helped her to avoid more destructive ways of dealing with her feelings. Nona could easily have withdrawn to her room to cry, or refused to eat supper. She might have felt guilty over her anger and provoked punishment from others, she might have expressed her anger physically at her brother, at his toys, or she could have displaced it into someone else. Moreover, she might easily have denied her sad and angry feelings to herself, repressing them, so that they might then or later have emerged in distorted or confusing behavior.

Meanwhile, Jonathan, the youngest child and only boy in the family, also had some problems with aggression. When he was 4, he dealt with his scary monster dreams by painting pictures (17.3D) of his fears (17.3E). As

316

17.3 A Girl Crying because Her Brother Broke Her Doll. Age 5. Crayon

he got older, he mastered his impulses through pictorial attacks on family members. Later, he drew armed ships and planes, as well as powerful soldiers and superheroes. By adolescence, he was reading science fiction and creating humorous fantasy creatures (17.3F).

Five-year-old Vince's dad was a minister, who encouraged his children to articulate their wishes and fears in both words and images. One day he brought me some drawings done by Vince, one expressing destructive wishes toward a sibling, the other reflecting anxiety about punishment. The first was a drawing of "a Bad Scissors," about to cut off the very long nose of a brother (Figure 17.4). Vince assured his dad that the big brother on the right was not going to let the scissors hurt his sibling, but instead was going to save the one who was being attacked.

Worries about punishment for such angry wishes are also common for young children. In his other picture, entitled "I Hope This Didn't Happen" (Figure 17.5), he worried aloud about what might happen to someone who got thrown off a mountain because he was bad. He also worried about the rescue party, and added men and a net to his drawing.

Getting older does not necessarily reduce the rivalry and competition between siblings. Nona, at 8, followed a fight with her older sister by making an "ugly" drawing of Jenny (Figure 17.6). Four years later, Jon, her

17.4 A "Bad Scissors" about to Cut Off a Brother's Nose. Age 5. Pencil

younger sibling, made a similarly nasty drawing of her, distorted with a beard and elongated nose, following an argument (Figure 17.7).

Meanwhile, Jenny, the oldest, had herself attacked not only siblings but parents too, following the birth of Jonathan. Although she was behaving like a model big sister, being very helpful, I found a drawing in her room of an "Ugly Mommy" and an "Ugly Daddy," missing eyes, hair, and limbs, along with a "Beautiful Jen" (Figure 17.8). The parents, she explained, had gotten "ugly" by making "too many children." A few months later, her family drawing included everyone, although the males are minimized (17.3G); and a year later, she was able to represent the whole group more realistically (17.3H).

Anger toward Adults

Angry feelings may be the most difficult for all of us to deal with, especially when they are felt toward those we also love—as is usually the case. Actually, "violence" and "vitality" have the same Latin root (*vis*), and can be conceptualized as related but different. "Violence is the life force turned in a negative and destructive direction; vitality is the life force channeled into constructive and creative forms" (Barron, 1970). In other words, love and hate are two sides of the same coin.

17.5 "I Hope This Didn't Happen." Age 5. Pencil

Grownups need to accept angry feelings in order that children feel comfortable expressing them (17.31). The workshop leader must have been at ease with such thoughts, or the 8-year-old girl could not have drawn and shown him her humorous attack on adult authority, "Jerky Teacher" (17.3J), and Jonathan could not have left an angry pictorial message on my chair—a picture of a "Killer Shark" devouring me—had he not been secure that I could understand and accept it (Figure 17.9).

Art also allows a child to fantasize being stronger and getting back at the adult safely. When Nona was 4 she was angry with me, because I had said she would have to get a haircut if she wouldn't allow anyone to brush her long, thick hair. She still refused to let her dad or me do it.

17.6 Ugly Drawing of Older Sister Jenny, by Nona. Age 8. Crayon

17.7 Ugly Drawing of Older Sister Nona, by Jon. Age 7. Pencil

17.8 Ugly Drawing of Parents, by Jenny. Age 5. Crayon

The day her hair was cut, she brought home two paintings from preschool. The first was entitled "A Girl who has Grown Long Hair and Locked her Mommy in the Garage" (17.3K). In the second, the girl is sitting triumphantly on top of the garage, the mommy (smaller) is still inside, and "The Girl Has the Key" (17.3L). Although Nona couldn't control me in reality, in her art (as in dramatic play) she could have all the power.

Expressions of anger are often mingled with and caused by feelings of affection, especially during the time when a child is struggling with the oedipal conflict, wishing to have each parent all to him- or herself, yet aware of and fearing the other parental rival. Such wishes may be reflected in 4-year-old Carol's drawing of her family.

She first drew her mother, "holding on to someone's hand. Now I'll make my dad," she said (the central figure). "He's going out the door because he's holding something" (mother's hand?). Finally, she drew herself on the far left, commenting on her pretty ears and hair, like mother (omitted on father).

"She's holding *his* hand, and he's holding *my* hand. They're going to Vicky's wedding, but not me!" Looking angrily at the picture of father about to leave with mother, she drew a vertical line through the figure and

321

17.9 Killer Shark Devouring Bad Mother, by Jon. Age 8. Pencil

said, "Oops! He's got a line down him!" She giggled nervously, as if her symbolic revenge had been successful.

Jon, asked to make a "funny family drawing" at 8, made a picture of three clowns in a circus (17.3M). "The big one is the father. The little one in the middle, the son, is very curious. He likes to see if it hurts when he sticks his arrow point into his mother's butt. The mother is yelling because she's being stuck, and the father is kicking and yelling at the boy for sticking the arrow point into his wife."

When asked about the ambiguous extensions on the mother's body, Jon giggled and said, "I started to make boobs, but decided on arms instead." His thinly disguised oedipal wish, and associated anger because it was not gratified—along with the expected punishment from father—is as common for young boys as his anal-aggressive humor.

Jon's ugly portrait of his dad at 9 (Figure 17.10) followed an argument about privileges that he had lost. A spontaneous drawing, discovered days after it had been made, might well have stemmed from a similar defeat at the hands of his father, for it shows a little dog frightening a big one; yet another drawing depicts a big man being shot by a little boy (17.3N).

On the other side of the paper, as if to extend his fantasy of potency and victory, is a young man in a snappy racing car with a trophy for having won the race. Images of superheroes like Batman (17.3O) are created by children of all ages, representing the child's wished-for strength in the face of his or her realistic weakness. The same kind of wish is probably represented in the images of phallically potent cars, tanks, ships, planes, and rockets so common for young boys, often bristling with weapons for both aggression and protection (17.3P).

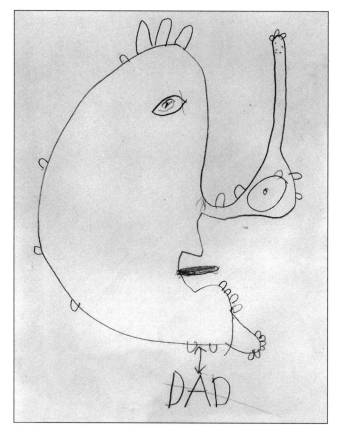

17.10 Ugly Drawing of Father, by Jon. Age 9. Pen

Separation and Divorce

As separation and divorce become a way of life for half our children, more and more youngsters have to cope with that difficult, painful situation in which they are, indeed, helpless victims (cf. also Betts, 2003). Michael, a 5-year-old whose parents had recently separated, became very involved in drawing superheroes full of action, like his flying Superman or Spiderman (Figure 17.11). Often, as in this image, the superhero would have a smaller figure attached to it. Maybe he was representing his own wish to hang on to his dad, who had moved out of their home, and who he saw only on weekends.

Lori, the depressed 4-year-old you met earlier, sometimes did drawings in her therapy about her parents' separation and planned divorce. She had seen little of her father since he left the home. He was first omitted from her family drawing, but was later added as the largest figure, wishfully re-

323

17.11 A Flying Superhero with a Little Boy Hanging onto Him. Age 5. Marker

instated at a family picnic. Sadly she said, "I love my daddy. He is beautiful. But he is not a live-at-home daddy."

Several months later she drew a sad girl (17.3Q) and said, "That girl is crying . . . because her house falled apart . . . 'cause there was a big, big storm, and lightning cut it in half." Perhaps this was Lori's way of saying how her own life had been torn apart, and how the divorce seemed to her like a painful bolt from the blue.

Art as Therapy in Times of Trauma

A trauma, something that is too great for the ego to manage, can be something as minor as getting lost, if the child is very young. Sometimes, children are exposed to overwhelming events that are unquestionably traumatic for people of all ages (DVD 17.4). At such times art can be vital. The children in the Nazi concentration camp of Terezin (17.4A), for example, were fortunate to be offered art by the mentor of art therapy pioneer Edith Kramer (17.4B), a woman named Friedl Dicker-Brandeis (Jewish Museum of Prague, 1993; Makarova & Seidman-Miller, 1999; Volavkova, 1962). It was an island of hope in a sea of despair (17.4C).

After a firestorm destroyed many dwellings in Oakland, CA, art therapists went into area schools to help the children and families deal with the emotional fallout (DVD 17.5).

In situations of extreme stress, it helps children to write and draw about their experiences (DVD 17.6). This was true for youngsters in Israel (17.6A) after the Six Day War (17.6B; Kovner, 1968); for those from Croatia (17.6C), and for many in the United States after the terrorist attacks of 9/11 (17.6D).

Making art was also helpful to children living in ghettos racked by violence following the murder of Martin Luther King in 1968. In a book published that year, Washington, D.C. youngsters drew about the horrors (17.6E) of the riots (17.6F), and of their hopes for a more peaceful future (17.6G).

Medical Stresses: Acute and Chronic

Although it was rare when the first edition of this book was written, art therapy is increasingly available to children with medical problems (DVD 17.7), such as chronic diseases, like diabetes (17.7A) or asthma (17.7B). It is also more often offered to children undergoing all kinds of medical procedures, from brief hospitalizations (17.7C) to long-term treatment for such things as severe burns (17.7D) and quadriplegia.

When a teenager named Eddie became a quadriplegic after an accident, art therapist Irene Rosner helped him to create, drawing and painting according to his verbal instructions. Over time, Eddie was gradually able to do more and more himself, using his mouth to hold a pencil or paintbrush. At all stages, Irene functioned as his "auxiliary ego," supporting Eddie's own creative strivings.

Abuse and Posttraumatic Stress Disorder

Over the years, like other art therapists (Gil, 1991; Klorer, 2000, 2003; Malchiodi, 1997) I have worked with many children who have been abused. Jackie had not only been sexually abused by her father, but had also witnessed a horrifying event. She could not talk about either, and was clearly suffering with Posttraumatic Stress Disorder (PTSD).

Jackie had scary nightmares and intrusive waking imagery. She was also miserable, because her grumpy behavior with both adults and peers left her feeling very lonely. She had been in play therapy for almost a year, with no change in her symptoms. Her child care worker, who had attended an art therapy workshop, finally decided to see if art therapy might help, although it required a long drive (DVD 17.8).

At age 5, after being sexually abused by her father, who had left the family, Jackie had watched her mother shoot and kill her younger brother (17.8A). Like most children with abusive parents, Jackie could not safely know or acknowledge anger at her mother. She was afraid of losing what little good feeling she clung to on her infrequent visits to the jail. But she could safely direct her rage at me—as the mother in the transference—in "ugly" drawings of "Dr. Rubin's Face" (Figure 17.12).

For several weeks, she put signs on my office door, warning other children not to believe what I said, and—projecting her own envy and neediness onto me—accusing me of being "a *beggar*" (17.8B). Thus, using art and the relationship, Jackie was able to work through her confused feelings about herself and others (17.8C). She eventually integrated good and bad images of both of us (17.8D), and was able to leave therapy with a warm attachment (17.8E).

Loss of Parental Figures

Most children suffer some losses, like the death of their pets, but the most traumatic are those involving parental figures (DVD 17.9). Unable to talk easily about their pain, often acting out their distress in disruptive ways, youngsters can be helped through art to deal with the trauma. The loss of the person may have been due to an accident (17.9A), a fight (17.9B), a disease (17.9C), or the terrorist attacks of September 11, 2001 (17.9D). Whatever the cause, many children who have lost significant others are being helped to cope by creating (17.9E).

It is difficult to imagine any loss more traumatic than a parent committing suicide, voluntarily abandoning a child. As hard as it is for adults to comprehend, such a death is impossible for children to understand (DVD 17.10).

Billy and His Father's Suicide
Two-year-old Billy, whose father had killed himself, would paint a blob of color, then angrily cover it over—compulsively repeating this ritual for many weeks. He next turned to the sand table, first playing with water and sand, then having plastic animals engage in fierce battles. This was followed by play with people figures—a boy and a man.

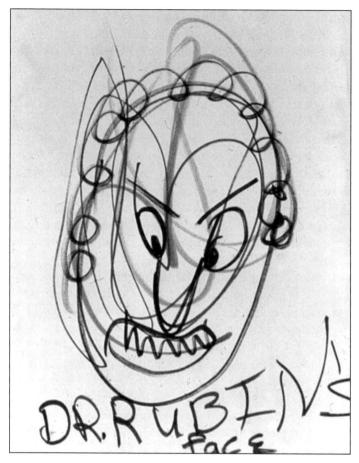

17.12 Ugly Picture of Dr. Rubin's Face. Age 7. Marker

They too would fight, and Billy would furiously bury the father figure in the sand, while I would talk about how angry he was at his dad for leaving him and his mom so suddenly. After several months of this drama—which was interspersed with quiet times of painting shapes that were no longer obliterated, and pretending to be a grownup (17.10A), Billy's mother reported that he was no longer oppositional or clingy, but was his former cheerful, agreeable self.

Christopher and His Mother's Suicide

Seven-year-old Christopher knew that I helped children through art. When I visited his home after his mother had made a suicide attempt, he showed me his magical creation. Using cut paper and glue he had made a flag, writing "Trouble" (17.10B) on one side and "Save Me" (17.10C) on the other. Inside, he had hidden a cardboard hatchet and knife. It was a poignant attempt to keep her from destroying herself.

Alas, it was not successful, but Christopher himself requested an art session following the funeral. His visit to my clinic was just a few weeks after his mother's death. He worried about getting messy with chalk or finger paint, because "my Mommy would yell at me." Projecting an image of "A Dog" onto his scribble (17.10D), he said it must be the one he had wanted so badly, but was not allowed to have because of his mother's depression.

Christopher then made a dark, messy finger painting, commenting anxiously on how mad his mother would be if she could see him. He wondered aloud whether she was angry at him, and if his being naughty or wanting bad things like the dog had anything to do with her leaving him.

His story about the finger painting, as he drew lines in it with a stick, was that it was "A Road." "But," he continued, "you'll never find your way out. . . . No one can stop me. . . . They'll never find their way out. They'll feel so sad. . . . They'll be stuck there forever." I asked what "they" would do. Christopher placed his hand in the black paint, lifted it up to show me, and then smashed it onto the paper, splattering the paint.

One year later Christopher asked to come in again. This time he symbolically represented his mother's suicide in his painting (17.10E); a person "falls" off a road, as she had "fallen" (jumped) off a bridge. Later, he dramatized with clay and tools a crash, an emergency, and an operation in which he, as the doctor, tried unsuccessfully to restore the injured patient. Creating in the presence of another gave Christopher a way to release his overwhelming rage and frustration. It also gave him an opportunity to clarify the event, and to cope with the painful reality he needed to accept.

Conclusion

As you have seen in these brief vignettes, art can be very helpful to normal children in school and at home, as a way of expressing, clarifying, and coping with some of the complicated feelings like jealousy, anger, and fear that every child has when growing up. These are not always easy to talk about, and some feelings are really difficult—if not impossible—to put into words, no matter how articulate a child may be (see DVD 17.2B).

Moreover, you can hurt somebody in make-believe, as did Vince in the "Big Scissors" drawing (Figure 17.5), without anything really bad happening. Because art is symbolic, no one actually gets hurt, and the wish has been expressed in a safe and manageable way. Maybe if more children had a chance to express their feelings in and through art there would not be so many who would need specialized help for their emotional problems. Art is a very natural form of primary prevention.

Perhaps as important as expressing feelings is the fact that children can define themselves (see DVD 17.2A) and can feel very good about themselves as competent people, through mastering the skills involved in using art materials. They not only experience the pride and pleasure of mastering a medium; they also learn that they can do something and can do it well. If there is a finished product, they may feel additional pride in their creation, along with the admiration of those who view it. So, whether you think of art as helping children to master skills or feelings, or as a way of developing respect for self and others, the broadly therapeutic values and the educational goals for children in art do not seem so far apart (see DVD 17.2C).

CHAPTER

18

Helping Parents
through Art and Play

Art as Therapy for Normal Adults

Art can be therapeutic for individuals of all ages, not just children. Amateur painters, like British Prime Minister Winston Churchill, have found making art to be immensely helpful, especially during periods of stress—such as the kind he was under during World War II.

Art classes can also be therapeutic (DVD 18.1), like those conducted by Florence Cane (18.1A) in New York during the thirties and forties, who released the creativity of many (18.1B) in her studio.[1] Art therapist Elinor Ulman (1972) taught art to adults at a Washington museum, and described the therapeutic value of the classes. Art therapist Robert Ault (18.1C) opened an art school after 18 years at the Menninger Clinic. In "Art Therapy with the Unidentified Patient" (1989), he noted the therapeutic benefits of learning art for students of all ages.

Creative art activities are also therapeutic for normal adults when they are used in sensitivity, encounter, or human potential groups, as in Janie Rhyne's (18.1D) early work at Esalen and later in her own studio (18.1E) (1973/1995; Vich & Rhyne, 1967). Growth centers, like Omega, offer many workshops using art for self-development.

And normal people of all ages, dealing with the ups and downs of everyday life, can be helped to cope and to grow through the therapeutic use of

---

[1] Florence Cane conducted art classes for adults as well as children, which were written up in newspapers and periodicals of the time. Copies of these were sent to me by Mary Cane Robinson, her daughter, who became an art therapist.

art. Making art provides practice in creative problem-solving, useful in all aspects of living. It also helps people to articulate a clearer sense of themselves, through their own unique creations. This is true for adults in their role as parents as well, as I discovered in my own work.

Education in the Community

Since it is my firm belief that art is good for all people—parents as well as children—I derive great satisfaction from making art activities available to families. At the Pittsburgh Child Guidance Center, a part of the community mental health system, half of my job was in Community Services, or Consultation and Education. Through this department, I was able to work in many different settings, which included those serving normal, healthy children—like those described in the preceding chapter—and their parents.

Three Rivers Arts Festival: Family Creative Arts Center

In Pittsburgh there is an annual Three Rivers Arts Festival, which lasts for 3 weeks. In 1973, the creative arts therapists were asked to design and staff an area where children could make art. Because the clinic's focus was on the whole family, my colleagues and I ended up with something we called the Family Creative Arts Center (DVD 18.2). There, parents and children were invited to work with clay, paint, wood scraps, and other art materials, sometimes expanding into the surrounding environment, like sailing styrofoam boats on a small pond near the working area. In addition to basic art media, there were areas for the creation of mobiles, stabiles, and the showing of animated films.

Since there were also drama, dance, and music therapists at the clinic, activities in all of the arts were made available to families attending the festival. These included making simple instruments, puppets, and movement sessions. Led by volunteer arts educators and therapists, they were a great success. As a result, an art activity center for youngsters and their families has become an integral part of this annual event, enabling thousands of children and parents to have the pleasurable experience of creating side by side for 3 weeks every year (Figure 18.1).

While some might be concerned about the risks of adult pressures on the youngsters, I agree with Viktor Lowenfeld that "just as children of different age levels can work happily, respecting each other's way of expression, so can parents participate without influencing their children's concepts" (1954, p. 44). Lowenfeld added: "I dare say that our world would be quite different if parents would set aside weekly 'creative afternoons' for them-

18.1 Children and Parents Working on an "Endless Easel" at an Arts Festival

selves and their children. . . . Above all, parents would learn more about themselves, their children, and their relationships to them" (p. 46). In to-day's busy world of working parents and overly scheduled children, that statement is even more true.

Being part of the Community Services department allowed me to spread the word about the therapeutic benefits of art to many settings, such as preschools, community centers, and churches. There were art groups for parents, where they created with media and, through their own experience and discussion, understood the value of art for their children. There were also family and mother-child art sessions—where the art activity was fol-lowed by discussion groups for the adults, so that they could reflect on and learn from the joint experience.

Family Art Workshop: Elementary School

One summer (DVD 18.3) I offered animated filmmaking (18.3A) to children in a parent-run summer recreation program (18.3B) at an elemen-tary school (18.3C). Their parents also requested a family art workshop, which was held toward the end of the summer (DVD 18.4). It was attended by 20 mothers and 30 children, ages 4 through 12 (Figure 18.2a).

a

18.2a,b *Mothers and Children at a "Family Art Workshop" in a School*

b

The joint art activity took place in a comfortably large kindergarten room, where paint, crayons, and clay were available in separate areas (18.4A). As each family entered, it was suggested that they might like to do something together, though this was optional (18.4B). The groups ranged in size from dyads to one mother and three children, and included one of three generations (18.4C).

The art activity lasted just 45 minutes, but it was busy and productive, with a surprisingly relaxed atmosphere considering the number of people involved. The most striking thing was the obvious enjoyment on the part of almost all participants. With the exception of one mother who looked anxiously around the room for most of the time, the parents seemed to be having as much fun as the children. In most cases, at least one joint project was undertaken, although there was also a good deal of observing and parallel creative activity (Figure 18.2b).

The mothers then met in groups of 10 for hour-long discussion groups led by psychiatric social workers. The mothers shared with each other many of the feelings and thoughts that had been aroused by the joint art session. One emphasized the pleasure for herself and her son to be alone without the new baby: "For me, I think, the important thing was this: the very fact that it was *just* David and me going to a *special* place at a *special* time was very important and very exciting. And we do it very rarely—once in a while, but generally with [the new baby] tagging along."

Another mother eloquently expressed the personal impact of the experience of working with her 9-year-old daughter: "She and I both grew. Things I wanted *from* her and *with* her I couldn't get really in any other way. It was a pleasure to see her loosen up and to let herself flow. As we went from one project to another, I felt we were moving together. It was a very important moment for me."

In addition to sharing a special activity with the child in a place away from home, several mothers referred to the increase in understanding that the joint experience had provided. "First, I was able to share my daughter's thoughts about the creative process. That is, she explained to me why she painted in a particular way, or why she would use specific colors."

Parent Art Workshop in a School

The following fall the same parents requested another family art workshop, to include husbands and older children. Then they changed their minds and asked for an evening workshop for parents only, saying they wanted something "just for us, without the kids around" (DVD 18.5).

A large number came and worked in a big classroom set up with supplies, for a full hour and a half (18.5A). Though they enjoyed themselves, those who had participated in the summer workshop were surprised by how much harder it was to get started and how much more inadequate they felt compared to the session with their children (18.5B). The momentous discovery that evening, in fact, was that the children had helped and given support to their parents—who felt unexpectedly ill at ease without them.

Mothers and Toddlers in a Church

Once a month a group of women gather for a Mothers' Morning Out at a local church, bringing their toddlers and preschoolers, who are cared for away from their parents. The mothers usually spend their time listening to a speaker, drinking coffee, and having a discussion following the presentation of the morning. I had visited these women twice before to give talks, and one woman, having heard of the program at the school described previously, asked if such a session would be possible at the church (18.6).

A joint art session (18.6A) was therefore held one morning, with 25 mothers and 22 children attending (Figure 18.3). The children ranged in age from 19 months to 5 years (18.6B). After an hour spent working together, the children went back to their rooms, and the mothers had a large group discussion, sitting in a circle, surrounded by artwork on the walls.

18.3 Mothers and Toddlers at a Parent-Child Workshop in a Church

These mothers focused on feelings about themselves and their children in terms of competency, creativity, and artistry.

Many spoke of the jealousy they had felt while watching their children work with ease and freedom, and some worried aloud about their own lack of creative ability. As one mother stated, "I could find this myself, that my rigid upbringing showed, because I was making Christmas trees and Santa Clauses that looked like those things, and my daughter made a psychedelic tree, and changed the season. She's certainly uninhibited about expressing herself, and I envy her freedom, really, especially here."

Another mother recalled her own painful art experiences in school, and how no one ever said a word about her pictures: "I can remember shedding tears over it! . . . And anything that I ever made always was uglier, or graded down, and this tended to go through somehow. When I try to sit with my children and do things with them, I have a bit of an inferiority complex, which is sad, I think—it doesn't have to be that way."

Another expressed feelings of inadequacy, saying she was "inhibited. I find myself, when I pick up a piece of clay, totally inhibited. I just have no idea what to do with it! I'd like to just sit there and squeeze it, but to make anything!" The fear of exposure was well-articulated by one mother, who said, "The feeling I got was—I didn't really want to do anything. Because, as I said to my neighbor, after these papers are all put together and she holds them up, she'll say, 'Oh, look at this. This looks like about a five-year-old did it,' and it'll be my paper!"

Some were genuinely concerned that their own felt lack of artistic ability might hurt their children, either genetically or through learning. "I know myself that I'm not a very creative person. But I noticed it also in my son, at least I did this morning, and those around me seemed to be quite creative. But I felt like my lack of creativity showed up in what he did." Or, as another woman said of her son, "I don't want him to have the same feelings about art that I have."

Toward the end of the hour, a previously silent woman tried to settle the issue for the group: "It always bothers me when a parent talks about a child, in that they put their child into themselves, and then they throw off this thing, that 'I'm not creative'. And I have heard it so much in my life, that parents come to you and say, 'I'm not creative. I don't know how Johnny can be creative'. And the hairs on my back just bristle, sort of, because it's not fair. You haven't had the opportunity and the experience and the marvelous thoughts that have been started, just recently really, in art for little people."

Or perhaps it was sentiments like these that settled the issue for those many concerned parents: "Well, I was excited by the materials, and I—I hate art! But I really had fun with those oil things [paintstiks], and they made such great colors, and I couldn't really make anything, but the colors were exciting and I enjoyed myself! I was really surprised. I found that my daughter stayed with the magic markers, and really liked that, and wasn't very interested in what I was doing, but that we both really enjoyed it."

The mothers also dealt with some interactional issues, like how dependent or independent their child had been, or how their behavior that morning compared with their behavior at home—"My little three-year-old goes to nursery school and smears colors, but at home she draws things."

They talked of how sometimes their wish for their children to achieve had prompted behavior they knew was not best for them: "I found this myself today, because I walked up to him and I said, 'Don't scribble—make something!' . . . And I realized that if he wants to draw a house or a man, he can very easily, but if he wants to scribble, he can too. He was up there having a ball with a paint brush, but I couldn't resist asking him to make something!"

Another mother spoke warmly, telling a tale that brought forth laughter: "So often—we always go up to a child and say, 'What're you making?

What does it look like?' And at one point, a little boy over at the easel—I don't even know who he was—he looked at me. I hadn't even said anything. He looked up and he said, 'I don't know!'"

On a more practical level, the mothers found themselves sharing ideas about how to provide art activities at home. They told of cooperative arrangements, with mothers of same-age children taking turns, of a basement workshop set up where there is no concern about mess, of crayons and shelf paper on the refrigerator door for the active toddler during dinner hour, and so on. They also shared realistic concerns about household maintenance when making art media available to young children: "I think our lives, and mine included, are so ordered and so orderly in our home, that it's very difficult to do this kind of thing that we were doing here in our homes, unless you have a room for it. And yet you don't, and you think, besides the paper that's on the wall, they're gonna go on through the hall and the bedroom! But we're hung up on this, and I think it's just a tragic thing in our lives."

Some expressed annoyance at the presence of the children, at being "too busy supervising, just supervising. If they hadn't been here, then of course I could've done more of my work." The majority, however, seemed to find, as did the elementary school mothers described earlier, that their children helped them to feel more comfortable.

"I think it was Steichen who said, 'Happily, growth is not for children only.' . . . We're all lucky, really, and we really needed our own children to kind of let us do it legally, to slop in the paint, and paint with them, and color. Really, it's part of the fun." Or, from another point of view, "You know, I think it's important that they can see their mother do these things. You know, so many times we just do things mothers do, and I think it's great if we can just sit down with paint and clay in their world—on their level. It's kind of like, when you make a mistake, it's good for them to see that we're not always up here and they're just the little people."

The art activity took place in mid-December, and one mother stated, "I found this particularly valuable this week. Everything's so tense, with Christmas coming and getting things for four children and all that stuff, and I really found that we relaxed together this morning." Stressful seasons aside, many felt that spending time together was not easy. "I think it was of value for me to do something with them."

"As they get older and can do more on their own, you're more apt to say, 'You go color.' And you need to make an effort to do things together, you need to set a time aside." The majority echoed these sentiments, with a final decision to repeat the experience at some future date: "It would be fun to have a longer session, mothers and children again. I thought it was valuable for the kids and mothers just to do something together. At home, you're so busy, you don't sit down together, even if you know you should!"

Clearly, the use of joint or separate art experiences, followed by some discussion or reflection, can be useful in parent education. The nature and goals of the particular group should determine in large part the precise format. Such an experience might well be related to more or less structured instruction in normative stages of child development, a discussion of how one feels about one's child, or any of a number of other possible topics. It is my feeling that, in most cases, allowing the content of the discussion to come from the group provides the opportunity for most participants to use the experience to the fullest.

Parent Play Groups

Whether attention is drawn to process or product, whether artwork is done in groups of mothers, couples, or families, art activities can be a useful tool in parent education. One of the most imaginative approaches was developed by a psychoanalyst, Tobias Brocher, in the 1950s in Ulm, Germany—"Parents Schools" (Brocher, 1971).

In this approach, parents are asked to participate in play activities, many involving art media, as a way of "understanding children by repeating childhood behavior" (Smart, 1970, p. 14). The emphasis is on the experiential or process aspects of the adults' play with art media, and other modalities. The activities are conceived of "as a bridge to the essential reexperiencing. It was important that the parents should experience again the way they themselves felt as children, and in this manner discover an easier, more direct access to their own children" (Brocher, 1971, p. 1).

With the conviction that "the peer group of parents is other parents" (Smart, 1970, p. 15), Brocher and his colleagues devised a curriculum centered around play, in which a series of carefully selected activities were designed to stimulate feelings and fantasies from infancy, childhood, and adolescence, based on psychoanalytic theory (Erikson, 1959).

Following participation in the play activities, parents share feelings and memories in group discussions, relating the here-and-now experience of the play to the there-and-then feelings of their own childhood, and then to the current rearing of their own children. Through the direct experience of the play, and in "giving expression to the thoughts that arise along with the play" (Brocher, 1971, p. 4), parents are led to contribute to their own and each other's experience—to consider the past and its connections to the present.

Inspired by Dr. Brocher, who worked in Pittsburgh for several years, a movement and drama therapist and I developed our own activities for each developmental level, and worked with both parents and group leaders in a training context, using the parent play model (Rubin, Irwin & Bernstein, 1975). The following are examples of activities we developed for the successive developmental phases listed in Table 3.1 (p. 56) (DVD 18.7).

Sample Activities to Help Parents Understand Developmental Phases

Infant: Core Issues

Trust versus mistrust, sensorimotor exploration, differentiation of self and non-self, primacy of oral zone.

Body Awareness. With participants on the floor, eyes closed in a darkened room, the leader speaks softly. At first, verbal suggestions may encourage relaxation of body boundaries, symbolically simulating the primary nondifferentiated relationship with the environment. Eventually, attention is called successively to different body parts and their relationships, and to environmental stimuli (sound, temperature, shadows, etc.).

Sensory Awareness. Seated in a circle, the lights still dimmed with soft, flowing music and no talking, the participants are given by the leaders a series of items of different shapes and textures (cloth, sponge, fur, paper, steel wool) and encouraged to explore these thoroughly. As with tactile awareness, other senses are stimulated in a similar way, with participants being given items of different smells (cotton saturated with various odors), and of different tastes and colors (fruit, candies, cheeses, drinks). These are all passively received by the participants, "fed" by the leaders.

Oral Sensations

1. *Sucking.* Activities involving oral-incorporative sensations, such as sucking a lifesaver, drinking sweet liquids through straws of various widths (necessitating more or less effort), holding sweet objects in the mouth, and holding onto soft, warm, cuddly objects like pillows or blankets.

2. *Biting.* Activities involving oral-sadistic or aggressive actions, such as biting, chewing, spitting (gum, chewy candy, licorice), and bobbing for apples; blowing bubbles (Figure 18.4) of gum or soap (18.7A), and blowing thin paint, using a straw or the mouth to direct the liquid on smooth, glossy paper.

18.4 An Adult Blowing Soap Bubbles in a Parent Play Group

Interaction with Another. Participants are guided in dyadic movement activities, with both individuals seated back to back, mirroring each other's patterns, so that there is no leader or follower, and the movement is felt as originating from a symbiotic fusion. Similarly, one person may gently rock another, trying to get into that other's rhythm. Individuals are asked to feed each other toward the end of the sensory-awareness activities, and typically become involved in playful interactions around various stimuli, especially tactile ones. Bobbing for apples may become competitive. Another useful biting game is to have two participants chew from either end of a licorice string to see who can get to the lifesaver in the middle first.

Toddler: Core Issues

Impulse control, autonomy, ambivalent power struggle with mother, independence/dependence, control of locomotion.

Unstructured Media-Play. Participants are encouraged to play with such fluid media as finger paint (on trays, paper, and walls, often used spontaneously as makeup on faces). They also play with sand (with and without water), and various plastic modeling materials: homemade play dough, water-base clay, plasticine, and so on. In addition, wearing plastic smocks, they are encouraged to play with water—filling, emptying, mixing, pouring, sailing toys—and, more aggressively, shooting water pistols at targets.

Letting Go versus Holding On. Participants are directed to engage in activities involving seizing and releasing, such as a tug-of-war with a rope or a piece of elastic cloth; or the towel game, in which one partner has the towel and teases the other with it; the objective is to try and get it away from the other.

Assertion-of-Self Games. One participant is the child, the other the parent; the parent tries to get the child to do something (go to bed, put toys away, eat), while the toddler stubbornly says a foot-stamping, loud-shouting, "NO!"

Preschooler: Core Issues
Curiosity, inclusion/exclusion, rivalry and competition, intense fantasy play, concern about retaliation and punishment, sex-role identification.

Inclusion/Exclusion. This element is present in a game where one member "fights," pushing and shoving to get into a circle of the others, who cling together and try to keep him or her out. A triad may also be emphasized, in a role play where two people are engaged in doing something together, while the third tries to join the activity.

Constructive Play. Building or constructing with wood scraps and glue (three-dimensional) or collage (two-dimensional), and using construction toys like blocks, Tinkertoys, or Lincoln Logs. They also may use tools with wood and nails, engaging in sawing and hammering.

Fantasy Play. Individually, participants may construct miniature worlds or microcosmic symbolizations of reality, which they then play *on* and *in* using miniature life toys. In pairs or small groups they may use or make puppets, or engage in dramatic play, using dressups and props to act out a spontaneous drama.

Active Coordinated Movement Play. Participants are encouraged to play movement games, involving leaping or jumping (as in jump rope), or invoking ballistic patterns of a masculine nature (any competitive sport), or more feminine, undulating, ballet-like movements.

School-Age Child: Core Issues
Competence, mastery and learning, peer group interaction and acceptance, same-sex groups, development of rules and standards.

Creative Activities Involving Skills. Participants are asked to practice with a new tool, medium, or process, to experience mastery; emphasis is on doing it well (e.g., drawing, painting, or sculpting) or making something useful (e.g., weaving, printing, large-scale building, sewing).

Peer Group Interaction. Males and females can work separately in same-sex groups at any of the above tasks, or can use found materials to build clubhouse or hideway environments. Males and females can each prepare for and stage a "birthday party," deciding on the games, refreshments, favors, and soon.

Games With Rules. Participants may engage individually or in groups in games of skill (darts, jacks, marbles, hopscotch), chance (board games, card games, dice games), and/or competition (games with teams, and choosing sides like tag, red rover). It may stimulate participants to be asked to use structured pieces of paper or plastic to make up a game with rules for small groups—to play it, and then to write a description of it so others can try it out.

Adolescent: Core Issues
Revival of oedipal wishes, dependence/independence, autonomy and control, concern for privacy, future and work choice, sex-role orientation established, interest in identity in general: self-consciousness, self-definition, self-esteem.

Privacy and Control. In a Discovery Game two people role-play a situation in which the parent makes a symbol (or pretends to have one) for something found in the young person's room which causes concern; both then play out the discovery and confrontation. Participants take both roles in turn and discuss the transaction.

Triadic Power Game. In a Boss-Slave game, one parent of a mother-father-teenager triad bosses the teenager in a task (usually making or doing something) while the other parent observes and intervenes (or not) as he or she wishes. Roles are changed so that all can experience bossing and being bossed. A similar role-play can occur around planning a floor model of a new house together, with the same triad, focusing on the adolescent's room and planning for it.

Identity Issues. Participants may be asked to draw, write, or role-play about such themes as, "Who I Am Now," "What I Like and Dislike in Me," "How I Want to be Five Years from Now," "The Ideal Mate for Me," and so forth. Poetry may be a useful medium here, and the issue of finding one's preferred modality may be used as an example of discovering and defining individuality.

Possible Ways to Proceed

Parent play groups, like art therapy groups, can be conducted in many ways, for differing time periods, with different numbers of participants and various configurations of leaders and meeting times. In our work, we most often combined play and discussion in one session of 2 hours, though they can also occur at alternate meetings of an hour or more.

Leaders can follow a normal developmental sequence, which is most appropriate if teaching child development to students or professionals. When working with parents, one can begin where the group seems most comfortable, or at the age level of most of their children, and move in either direction, depending on what occurs over time.

As with any other group, it is vital to maximize comfort and minimize stress. A brief discussion and explanation of the meaning and purpose of the activity helps those who need "permission" to regress and to play. It also seems to help to suggest that people let go and become as involved as they can, but keep an observing ego watching what goes on in themselves as they play, so they can discuss it later.

As with other groups, leaders may play multiple roles: as observers, co-players, protagonists, and role models, teaching others how to play. At times, there may be a need for reassurance and support; at others, a leader may need to serve as a teacher or as a symbolic "good parent." On occasion, the group may request the leader to act as an authoritative parent and to control the bad children, especially if play with regressive media (like finger paint or water) gets out of hand. Such wishes become grist for the mill in the group discussion which follows the play.

Karen, for example, became frightened during water play, and said to the leader, "Don't you think you ought to stop them?" In the discussion afterward, she acknowledged that she was angry with the leader for "not stopping the play, because someone might have gotten hurt." Such thoughts led to her childhood, where her mother, an anxious woman, did not allow the children to play or jump because they might get hurt. With some awareness, she then spoke of her own overprotectiveness toward her two latency-age children.

During the discussion phase, as with any activity-discussion art therapy group, leaders act as facilitators, trying to help all participants to be involved. It is important to keep the discussion centered on the shared group themes, and to clarify, if necessary, the comments of the participants. It is often essential to help people to make sense of the experience—in that way, to gain control over it. Most important is for participants to perceive and use the group as an opportunity for learning through play.

The emphasis in the parent-school approach is on the recall of childhood memories and feelings stimulated by the creative experience. While the qualitative and symbolic aspects of the art activities still exist, the focus in both doing and discussing is on process rather than product. Instead, one looks at the totality of the experience, especially its connection to the childhood past and parental present of the adult group member.

Even in more orthodox approaches to art therapy or parent education through art, one may always choose whether to focus on process or product, form or content, conscious or unconscious dynamics. In these groups, participants learn about child development, and they learn about themselves—their impulses, fantasies, feelings, ideas, and wishes. They also learn something about media and the use of materials with children, the facilitation of play, and the pleasures of creative experience.

Often a parent discovers the fun of participation in one or more art forms, as a work-weary adult who does not care to become an expert, but who can still have an awfully good time and feel much better after fooling around with clay, paint, on a drum, or in a drama. Many a parent has spoken of the renewal felt following a creative play experience (18.7B).

Such renewal is one source of the strength of art in therapy and growth in all places—that it comes from a deep sense of being in touch with one's self, of exploring one's full potential for becoming a creative person as well as a better parent. Perhaps the poet was right, after all, when he said "Man is human only when he plays" (Schiller, 1875).

PART VI

GENERAL ISSUES

19

What Child Art Therapy Is and Who Can Do It

S ince a good deal of space and energy in this book is devoted to describing the therapeutic aspects of art for normal and handicapped children
and their parents in the community, I think it necessary to clarify the distinctions between art in therapy and art in other contexts. One common
misconception is that art therapy means working in art with those who are
different from the norm.

But the definition of art therapy does not depend on the population with
which one works, any more than it is a function of the setting in which the
work occurs. When art activities are made available to disabled or disturbed children, they may be educational or recreational. When one is
teaching or providing art for the purpose of constructively filling leisure
time, one is *not* engaged in art therapy. Even when the setting is a psychiatric one, if the primary purpose of the art activity is learning and/or fun,
then it is *not* art therapy (cf. Rubin, 1981b).

The essence of art therapy is that it must partake of both parts of its
name—it must involve both art *and* therapy. The goal of the art activity,
therefore, must be primarily therapeutic. This might, of course, include diagnosis as well as treatment; in order to be an effective therapist, you must
understand who and what you are treating. In order to be an effective *art*
therapist, you must know a great deal about both components of this hybrid discipline.

You must know *art*—the media and processes, their nature and potential. You must know the creative process—the language of art, the nature
of symbolism, form, and content. You must also know *therapy*. You need to

know about yourself and about others in terms of development, psychodynamics, and interpersonal relations. Finally, you must know about the nature of the treatment relationship, and the mechanisms that underlie helping others to change.

Art Therapy and Art Education

Because the work includes helping others to create, there is also an element of education involved. The teaching in art therapy, however, is secondary to the primary aim, which is diagnostic or therapeutic. In other words, if an art therapist teaches techniques, it is not for the sake of the skill itself, but rather in order to help the person to achieve, for example, a higher level of sublimation or an increased sense of self-esteem.

Conversely, there are therapeutic aspects of art education, as noted in the previous chapter. Indeed, I think that the very best art teachers are growth-enhancing personalities who nurture the student's sense of self and of competence in a broadly therapeutic way. There is no question that art activities, even in a classroom for normal children, may be conducted in a way that promotes social and emotional development. Art itself is in many ways therapeutic, for it permits the discharge of tension and the representation of forbidden thoughts and feelings in socially acceptable forms.

I believe, however, that we must distinguish between art in *therapy* and art activities which happen to have some therapeutic components. The field of psychotherapy is itself a complex one, encompassing many different ways of understanding human beings and of helping them to overcome difficulties in development and adjustment. In order to offer art as *therapy*, it is essential to know what one is doing as a therapist. Even the most sensitive artist or art teacher is not automatically a therapist, no matter who the student happens to be.

Just as it takes years of training and discipline to master the visual arts, so it takes time and learning to master what is understood about psychodynamics and psychological change. It also takes special training, involving hundreds of hours of supervised work with patients, to be able to integrate what one knows about art with what one knows about therapy. Indeed, that task is a lifelong one, and it is not one which can be mastered without experienced clinical guidance. This is as true for the art therapist working in a school for exceptional children as for the art therapist working in an outpatient clinic or a psychiatric hospital.

One reason why it is so important to distinguish between art for primarily educational purposes and art for mainly therapeutic goals is that the activities themselves may not appear different to the untrained observer. An individual art interview with a child or adult may look and sound like an art lesson, and an art therapy group with members of any age level or with a family may look much like an art class (DVD 19.1).

The difference is not necessarily visible on the surface, for the materials are the same and the approaches in both can range from open-ended to highly structured. Even the verbalizations of the therapist, depending on the setting and age level, may be indistinguishable from what a friendly teacher might say. The primary distinctions are *invisible*—inside the head of the worker and, eventually, of the patient(s).

When I am doing a diagnostic art interview, for example, I am looking with a clinically-trained eye and listening with a psychologically-sophisticated ear to what is happening. I am tuned in to all aspects of behavior, hoping to understand not simply what people can do with art materials, but where they are developmentally, what their primary conflicts are, and how they are coping with them. Their messages to me are received in terms of assessing them as complex beings, to be understood on as many dimensions as possible, in order to be helped with whatever problem has brought them for therapy.

Similarly, when I am working with a family, I am interested in what they make and how they create; I am also interested in their individual and interpersonal dynamics, in how they relate to one another as a group, and in how that interaction may help me understand the specific problems of the identified patient. Anyone watching a family art evaluation would see an interesting exercise in which family members make things individually and jointly and then talk about them with one another. If they are relaxed about it, it might look like a pleasant recreational activity for the family. And yet, while they may have fun or learn new skills, the therapist's primary goal is understanding family dynamics through the symbolic medium of their art, within the context of their behavior.

Eventually, the individuals involved in art therapy themselves become aware that this is a different kind of art experience, even when the goals have not been made explicit. While it is customary to explain the diagnostic or therapeutic purpose of the art activity to those who can understand, that is not always possible. The very young, and those with communication problems, however, soon grasp at some level the special nature of art therapy. Roger Arguile, a British art therapist who works in a special school, also feels that the children know the difference between art in therapy and art in education (DVD 19.2).

I was impressed with such a response in some children I was seeing individually at a school for the deaf. When two of the teachers asked to observe what went on in an art session, both youngsters declined, apparently sensing a need for privacy which had never been stated. Given the powerful nature of the feelings and fantasies they were already expressing in their art after only three meetings, it was not surprising that they were uncomfortable with the idea of letting others view their violent images or their sometimes messy play with media. They were probably right in assuming that their teachers would have had difficulty understanding or accepting either the aggression or the regression, despite the fact that both were "contained" in the art itself. Another youngster, a teenager, signed out the window to his friend that he was with "an art lady who helped him with his problems," though we had never discussed the purpose of his visits to me. These events impressed upon me once again the unique quality of art in a therapeutic situation, even when the word "therapy" has never been spoken.

There is a difference, then, but it is not always visible or easy to explain. Of course, there are times when what goes on in art therapy becomes primarily educational or recreational, when learning or pleasure is focal for the moment. Similarly, there are times in art classes when what is occurring is mainly therapeutic, whether at the level of release or of reflection— but the differences in the primary goals remain, and it is these to which we must look when trying to comprehend the distinction between art therapy and art education.

Art Therapy and Play Therapy

There is a similar lack of clarity for many people about the relationship between play therapy and art therapy with children. As with art therapy versus art education, the differences are not always visible to the unsophisticated observer. A session of art therapy with an individual child or group might look very much like play therapy, especially if there is sensory play with media or if there is any kind of dramatization. Of course, there is a close relationship between art and play; playfulness is often part of a creative process, and there is much artistry in good play therapy. These overlappings are, however, analogous to the educational aspects of art therapy and the therapeutic aspects of art education; here, too, there are important distinctions.

In thinking about the differences between art therapy and art education, it became clear to me that the modality (art) was the same, but the goals (therapy versus education) were different. Similarly, in the two kinds of child therapy, the goal (therapy) is the same, but the modalities (art versus play) are different. Theoretical orientation is not the key to distinguishing the two, since both art therapy and play therapy include a wide variety of approaches, orientations, and attitudes toward the activity itself.

There are those, for example, who feel that a child, given a supportive environment and a reflective therapist, can play out his or her problems (Axline, 1947; Moustakas, 1953). Similarly, there are those who feel that the creative process itself is the main healing element in art therapy with children (Kramer, 1958; Lowenfeld, 1957). Conversely, there are clinicians for whom the child's play is seen mainly as a communication of unconscious conflicts, which must then be interpreted and understood in order for change to occur (A. Freud, 1946; Klein, 1932). There are also child therapists who view the child's art as symbolic speech, to be explained and grasped as an essential part of the therapeutic process (Naumburg, 1947, 1966; Ude-Pestel, 1977).

Despite my advocacy of other expressive modalities in child art therapy, I do believe that there are real differences between art therapy and play therapy, and that they lie both in the expertise of the worker and in what is presented to the child. Although most play therapists provide some art materials, they are usually rather limited in scope and variety and are offered along with a wide variety of other play equipment, including games.

An art therapist, on the other hand, usually makes available a much greater range of art media and tools, and is able to teach and to facilitate the use of materials—something the average play therapist is not equipped to do. Since the creative process itself is so often central to the art therapeutic encounter, the clinician's ability to facilitate that process is as important a component of successful art therapy as his or her equally refined understanding of the symbolic meanings of the child's visual communications.

As for the other expressive modalities advocated elsewhere in this book, I do not see them as play any more than I see art as equivalent to play, though the two are clearly related. The drama, movement, music, or creative writing which can also be facilitated for a child by an art therapist are other art forms, available like the visual arts for both sublimation and communication. However, if no expert in another expressive therapy is part of the work, as in the groups I ran with Dr. Irwin, there are limits to how far an art therapist can help a youngster to express him- or herself in music, drama, writing, or movement, just as there are limits to the play therapist's expertise in art. In addition, the age limits for play therapy are narrower than those for art therapy, which can be used with young people of all ages.

Qualities of Good Child Art Therapists

Both play therapists and art therapists who work with *children* need to possess some special qualities that, while desirable, may be less critical in work with adults. Perhaps most vital is a liking for—indeed, a loving of—children. Child patients can create severe strains and stresses, and in order to endure these with good humor a sincere enjoyment of the young is essential. Not only does a liking of children ease those difficult moments, it also enables one to respond with honest delight to the creative and progressive steps they take, even when these are tiny. If one does not warmly regard children in general, it is highly unlikely that one could enjoy being with many of those in need of therapy, who can easily stimulate negative reactions in others.

In order to like children enough to want work with them in art therapy, a clinician must also like the child inside themselves. The therapist must be comfortable with childish thoughts, feelings, and impulses. Only when peace has been made with one's youthful/primitive self is it possible to help a child to accept what an adolescent once called "the green creature within." It is those green, primitive impulses of love and hate, merger and destruction, which are evoked so powerfully through art, and which are often hard for the therapist to handle.

Since moments of strong feeling often involve impulses to action as well, they call on another essential element in the child therapist's repertoire. It is as important to be able to limit as to be able to permit, and the child who feels like destroying the art supplies or the room or the worker requires a calm, firm, adult hand to contain such chaotic feelings. Only a clinician who feels the inner capacity to contain affect and impulse can provide the kind of framework for freedom described earlier.

In order to sustain a containing role at times of urgent pressure, it helps if one has sincere confidence in the ultimate efficacy of the therapeutic process, as well as in the child's ability to grow therein. Such an optimistic attitude is best built not on blind faith, but on a coherent frame of reference for understanding what goes on within the child, within oneself, and between the two parties in the therapeutic transaction. Such a theoretical underpinning is best if it includes not only developmental considerations, but psychodynamic ones as well.

My own bias is for a psychoanalytic framework, which I find most useful in understanding what is going on, and in deciding how best to intervene. Any clear and consistent theory of personality and psychotherapy helps the child art therapist to know where to go, and to do so consistently. Consistency is especially vital in work with children, who require the security inherent in dependability.

Because their verbal skills are not as highly developed as those of adults, children need therapists who can communicate and receive messages in all nonverbal modalities. Movement, gesture, imagery, and sound are the basic vocabulary of the arts as well as of play. Anyone working creatively with children does well to nurture an ability to "swing" with the child in different expressive dimensions. This capacity to flow with all forms of communication used by the young requires, in addition to ease in nonverbal modes, a fluency and flexibility in the therapist, an ability to shift gears as well as to follow, permitting the child to move naturally and with comfort.

Both fluency and flexibility are hallmarks of the creative process, and suggest that the effective child art therapist is also a creative person. One ought to be able not only to promote freedom in the child, but also to regress in the service of one's own ego. In addition to facilitating one's ability to empathize with the child, it also enables one to fully experience the role in which one is placed by the child, whether in the transference or in a drama. The judicious use of the self as a facilitator in the expression and working through of conflict can be a powerful tool in child art therapy. Like all direct involvements, however, it is fraught with hazards, and should be undertaken only with a full awareness of the meaning of the event to the child and to the treatment process.

In fact, all of the elements noted so far as critical to effective child art therapy may be thought of as two-edged swords; they are powerful if used thoughtfully, dangerous if used naively or under the pressure of countertransference reactions. But, you may ask, how can that be? Is it possible to like young people too much or to be too supportive with them?

Yes, in a sense, for while there are times when a warm holding in lap or rocker is the most appropriate action, there are others at which touching is too threatening or seductive. In addition, while genuine appreciation of the child's art is often just the "gleam in the eye" that will be most useful to their shaky self-esteem (cf. Lachman-Chapin, 2001), there are times when too much applause for creative products would promote an unhealthful narcissism and dependency on the responses of others.

While it is essential to be able to like even the most unlovable and provocative child patient, it is not helpful for a youngster to be rewarded for destructive behavior, or to engage in a sado-masochistic relationship with the therapist. Although a good child art therapist should like and accept his or her own childish impulses, to give into them freely in work with children would be self-indulgent and potentially frightening to the youngster. Even a spirit of playfulness, while often liberating, can be threatening to a withdrawn child, overstimulating to an impulsive one, and quite insensitive when the issues demand an earnest and respectful response.

It is important to accept even the most primitive art and fantasy, but it is not good to exult in or to glorify unmodulated impulse. Promoting aggression is just as detrimental as suppressing it. On the other hand, too many limits can be as harmful as too few, especially if the therapist's own anxieties lead to premature or harsh limit-setting, presumably in the child's best interests. What better way is there to confirm the youngster's conviction about the malignant power of impulses? And how sad it is when the limit-setting is not on behavior but on symbolic fantasy, which should know no boundaries.

Even therapeutic optimism can be dangerous, if the desire to rescue or to cure blinds the worker to problems within the child, the self, or the process. And even a consistent theoretical framework can be detrimental, if it is understood and held too rigidly, perhaps obscuring the therapist's vision of events that do not seem to fit. The best clinicians I know, including the most orthodox, are also the most open-minded and modest about their uncertainties. A similar kind of flexibility is needed in behavior as well as in perception. In other words, the notion of consistency and predictability is not to be wrongly understood as rigidity.

Too much flexibility is not best, either, for flowing with the material is not always the optimal stance in art therapy with children. There are many times when stopping, stepping back, looking, and organizing what has occurred are the most helpful clinical behaviors. While it is generally good to be creative in areas like interviewing, such creativity in the therapist must always be used in the service of the child's treatment rather than of the clinician's own exhibitionistic or narcissistic needs.

Further, it would seem evident that characteristics, such as those noted previously, are by themselves not sufficient for good child art therapy. Although they may indeed be essential conditions, without which the worker could not be effective, they alone—like love or art—are not enough. Being able to communicate nonverbally or symbolically, for example, is of little use without an understanding of the meanings of such transactions. Similarly, a tolerance for ambiguity or a love of children has only limited value in the absence of a clear sense of overall direction in the treatment process. While confidence in oneself, as well as in the child or process, is essential, a grandiose disregard for the scientific aspects of treatment is hardly helpful. Rather, a modesty about one's magical powers is an essential condition of a continuing search for understanding.

I believe that any kind of therapy is neither a scientific nor an artistic endeavor alone, but in its highest form is a synthesis of the two modes. Creative thinking in science is the wellspring of new discoveries, while any art form involves a large element of skill and technique. I believe that it is possible for a child art therapist to be quite thoughtful and scientific in orientation, while at the same time valuing artistry and spontaneity in the refinements of method. Since children, like all humans, are creatures of both thought and feeling, it makes sense that in order to reach and help them as whole people one would need to engage both cognition and affect. It also makes sense that in order to communicate both thought and feeling one would need to be equally open to either.

I think that an ability to be at home with both feeling and thinking is related to the art therapist's comfort with images and words, with primary process and secondary process, with mentation dominated by either the right or left hemisphere. To be able to synthesize these apparently distinct aspects of the self in a constructive way may be the essence of mental health. To be in charge of one's capacities, rather than being at the mercy of one's passions or ruminations, is a reasonable therapeutic goal for children as well as for adults.

For a therapist to be able to help a youngster achieve such an end, the clinician must have access to what lies within. When an art therapist is able to use both heart and mind, both thought and feeling, in the service of another's growth, and to do so with creativity and enthusiasm, then the child who is treated is indeed a fortunate person.

The quality of the relationship may be the key element, as implied in this description of effective child therapists: "To discuss this natural facility for therapy a bit more, we see it as being very similar to that possessed by those we call natural teachers. . . . We see them as therapeutic personalities, whether or not they are therapists by profession. Something nice happens to us when we are with them" (Hammer & Kaplan, 1967, pp. 35–36). If the teacher, therapist, or parent behaves sensitively, providing appropriate conditions for human expansion, "this kind of experience provides the child with the climate conducive to change and growth" (p. 36).

Those who pioneered art therapy with children are many, and we are all in their debt. Not all of them are recorded on film or videotape, but a few have been, and it is worthwhile for the reader to catch a glimpse of them at work. Those on the DVD all made major contributions by writing books at an early stage of the development of this specialty (DVD 19.3).

When I interviewed Margaret Naumburg in 1975, she recalled her beginnings with the children at the New York State Psychiatric Institute (Naumburg, 1947) under the sponsorship of its director, Dr. Nolan D.C. Lewis (19.3A). Edith Kramer, whose work began in 1951 (Kramer, 1958), conducted a demonstration session in 1975 (19.3B). Mala Betensky's first book came out in 1973 (19.3C), Violet Oaklander's in 1978 (19.3D), and Helen Landgarten's in 1981 (19.3E).

Why and How the
Art Therapist Helps

The Need and Capacity to Create

Central to understanding and helping children and their families through art is an assumption, a conviction, that "every person is, by nature, a potentially creative being" (Moustakas, 1969, p. 1). Though not yet actualized, such a spark is assumed to be present, and able to blossom if nurtured, even if long dormant. I believe, too, that all human beings have within them a natural tendency toward growth, toward actualizing that creative potential at increasingly mature levels. And I feel equally certain that each individual is likely to have some preferred media, modalities, and themes, which must be discovered or even invented, in order for that person to fulfill his or her promise.

I assume that all humans have an inner desire to create form in some way. The impulse to touch, to make contact, to manipulate, and to make marks is evident in the sand play of the toddler. It is also present when a child is irresistibly drawn by the seductive power of moist clay, glowing tempera paints, or a brand new box of crayons. Even apes and chimpanzees take naturally to art media; when a hungry ape prefers finishing a painting to eating dinner, one must wonder whether such an activity could not be a fairly basic, perhaps universal, impulse or need (Morris, 1962).

The philosopher Martin Buber felt that there is "an autonomous instinct, which cannot be derived from others, whose appropriate name seems to . . . be the 'originator instinct.' Man, the child of man, wants to make things. He does not merely find pleasure in seeing a form arise from material that presented itself as formless. What a child desires is its own share in this becoming of things. . . . What is important is that by one's own intensively experienced action something arises that was not there before" (1965, p. 85).

Freud said that a healthy person is able to love and to work; Erikson (1970) suggested that he or she also needs to be able to play. If play and art include each other, and I think they do, then the creation of one's self through art is not only a right and a possibility for all children—it may even represent a *need* that, if unfulfilled, leaves a kind of deprivation all the more insidious, as its effects are not easily visible.

Perhaps the need to make one's mark through creative endeavor stems from a simple sensory response to attractive materials, from a primitive desire to give form to that which is formless, or to interact with a manipulable environment. Perhaps, too, it comes from a more complex psychic need to reconcile, to integrate, and to give order and balance to one's experience. Man is uneasy when things do not fit, make sense, or rest comfortably. In the effort to reestablish an optimal level of comfort, it is necessary to reduce cognitive and affective dissonance and conflict.

There appear to be strong inner pressures toward both constructive and destructive acts, seen in responses to art media as well as elsewhere. In order for progressive and integrative tendencies to gain ascendance, internal conflict must be reduced. Energy can then be free, both to express and to control that expression aesthetically. The stimulus for unrest may come from inside, outside, or some combination of the two. The child may feel a need to make sense out of feelings, fantasies, and thoughts from within, as well as to sort and map out the confusing reality without. And it is then still necessary to both integrate and separate the two, in order to be free to grow, and to be in touch with both.

Here is where art can be so helpful, for as Elinor Ulman so eloquently said, it is "the meeting ground of the inner and outer world" (1971, p. 93). "Its motive power comes from within the personality; it is a way of bringing order out of chaos—chaotic feelings and impulses within, the bewildering mass of impressions from without. It is a means to discover both the self and the world, and to establish a relation between the two. In the complete creative process, inner and outer realities are fused into a new entity" (1961, p. 20).

The Creative Process as a Learning Experience

In art, even a child may have what Maslow called a "peak experience" (1959), or may feel a sense of heightened awareness and aliveness, what Ulman called "a momentary sample of living at its best" (1971, p. 93).

Through art, a youngster may experience not only the momentary release of tension through a discharge of surplus energy, but also the release of unconflicted energy, newly available for constructive use, through the sublimation and resolution of conflicts once draining resources.

Through art, a process in which one is in touch with all levels of consciousness (Kubie, 1958), and with external stimuli, one's level of awareness may be enlarged, expanded, deepened, and sharpened. "This openness to experience may itself be experienced: first, as a mood; secondly, as understanding; and thirdly, as expression" (Kaelin, 1966, p. 8).

During a creative activity there are times to stop and look, in the middle as well as at the end, and times to reflect upon and think about the experience of the process as well as the product. This reflective mode is as much a part of a total creative process as immersion in doing, and a good art experience—at home, in school, or at a clinic—partakes of both. In learning to be involved as well as to step back, to do as well as to think, children learn to make use of their energies in ways that enable them to create formed aesthetic statements.

Children can, in art, develop autonomy and independence, taking responsibility for both process and product. They can learn to choose, to make, to act, to revise decisions, to appraise and evaluate, and to learn from past experiences. In art, children can experiment symbolically, and may try out in both process and product feelings and ideas that may eventually become possible in reality.

Children can manipulate media which do not talk back, enabling them to experience a kind of power and mastery at no risk. They can master tools and processes, and can feel competent. They can learn to accept their regressive/aggressive symbolic selves, and can come to value their creative/productive selves, leading to a deep feeling of self-worth. They can discover, develop, and define their uniqueness, creating in and through art a sense of themselves as special. They can experience the pleasure of an aesthetically fine product, the joy of sharing it with a loved one, the pride in the affirmation of another.

Gendlin has said that "Feeling without symbolization is blind; symbolization without feeling is empty" (1962, p. 5). The artistic symbol is a way for children to communicate to themselves and others about vague, nonverbal, essentially ineffable feeling experiences. It is important to remember that "It makes no basic difference whether a child, or an adult artist paints circles and triangles or animals and trees. Both methods represent the inner world and the outer world, and neither psychology nor art separates the two" (Arnheim, 1967, p. 341). The awareness of what has been expressed may not and need not be translated into words, often remaining at the level of perceptual-emotional impact; there are times when it seems that "knowing for one's self on the perceptual level is the most valid kind of knowing" (Rhyne, 1971, p. 274).

In a nonlinguistic fashion, it is the peculiar power of art to be able to symbolize not only intrapsychic events, but interpersonal ones as well, and to collapse multileveled or sequential happenings into a single visual statement. The artistic symbol is a condensation, a carrier of many meanings, and by its very nature able to integrate apparent polarities—like reality and fantasy, conscious and unconscious, order and chaos, ideation and affect.

There is much experiential evidence in art therapy that the giving of form to complex feeling is in itself helpful. Perhaps this is true because it enables the creator to feel some control over the confusion, as Frankl suggests: "Emotion, which is suffering, ceases to be suffering as soon as we form a clear and precise picture of it" (1959, p. 117).

Throughout these values in the art experience runs a thread called "person," the individual whose energy, potential, exploration, expression, mastery, autonomy, release, awareness, acceptance, liking, pleasure, and growth are both cause and outcome of all the rest. I believe there is a false dilemma in the dichotomy of process versus product. For me, it is always "person" that matters most, without whom there could be neither process nor product, nor art itself.

Thus, the values in art for me are human values, which is probably why I went from art history and the impersonal iconography of the museum to art education and the life of the classroom, to art therapy and the challenge of unblocking people who are stuck, detoured, or constricted in their growing. Thus, it is not "art for art's sake" nor "art for the sake of therapy," but *"art for the sake of the person"* which makes the only human(e) sense to me, whatever the context.

The Art Therapist as a Real Person and Symbolic Other: Transference

Perhaps one of the ways in which art therapy differs from art in other contexts is the importance of the relationship between the therapist and client(s). For creating art within a therapeutic relationship is different from drawing by oneself or working in a class. It is a kind of special protected situation, where one person creates an environment, physical and psychological, in which one or more others can fully explore, expand, and understand themselves through art.

In this relationship, the child voluntarily exposes him- or herself to another, and learns to look with that other person at their creative statements and at themselves. Often there are few or no words, yet the being together and sharing of both process and product offer protection, validity, even permanence, to the event, which could otherwise be so vulnerable, so fragile.

While the art therapist in his or her encounter with a child is in many ways a very real person, there are symbolic aspects of the role which are important, especially in clinical settings. In one sense, these refer to the distorted symbolic ways—the transference—in which the relationship is experienced by the client(s). In another sense, they refer to the particular activities of the art therapist, which themselves carry symbolic meanings. The two are related, for the behaviors of the art therapist inevitably influence the kind of transference that develops, as well as its understanding and use as a vehicle for change.

The concept of transference is a useful one for an art therapist to know, and is quite congenial, for it is simply an extension to the human sphere of what is already suspected about the meaning of artistic symbols (DVD 20.1). That a color or theme can stand for something to an individual in terms of past experience, is not so different from the notion that people project similar meaning and feeling ideas onto other people.

In general, human beings always have a need to make sense out of the stimuli with which they are presented; the unknown of a new person must be filled in mentally, like a visual gestalt. We all tend to perceive new people on the basis of past experience with similar others, and to color that perception affectively in terms of unresolved wishes and conflicts.

In therapy, we can make good use of that human tendency to distort what is perceived in terms of what is inside. In many ways, the conditions that facilitate transference perceptions are not unlike those that foster the emergence of meaningful material in art. In the latter, we present primarily unstructured media in a free situation, allowing people to find and express their own images.

Similarly, the therapist can present him- or her-self in a relatively neutral fashion, so that the individual can project upon the clinician feelings and ideas related to still-active inner conflicts. The neutrality and non-judgmental attitude of the therapist thus allow the child to project onto the adult feelings and fantasies, in the same way that a youngster projects onto the material *their inner world*.

Such distortions in perception become evident over time, as the child responds in a way that is out of proportion or in some way inappropriate to the stimulus, suggesting that they have colored their view of the therapist on the basis of inner issues. While the meaning of a particular distorted perception may not be immediately clear, any more than one can at first be sure of the meanings of a symbol, one can first identify and then explore such apparently unreasonable reactions.

Sometimes they are in relation to the art process or product, such as concern over the therapist's anger because of the messiness of a finger painting, or an expectation that the therapist will be critical of a drawing. At other times they relate primarily to the relationship, as when Barry asked, after 2 months of therapy, "Do you think about me all the time when I'm not here?" or assumed that when he didn't come to the clinic, I didn't either (20.1A). Such thoughts as these conveyed his wish to be the therapist's "only child," not surprising in a boy from a family with five children and much sibling rivalry.

But the art therapist is not and cannot be totally neutral. The role demands certain behaviors that themselves carry symbolic meaning, and tend to influence the transference. For example, in giving the child materials and supplies, the art therapist is feeder; the food sometimes being experienced as good, and sometimes as not enough, or not quite right.

On the other hand, in offering messy materials in a permissive setting, the art therapist may be felt as a seducer, inviting the child to engage in potentially "bad," forbidden experiences. In expecting children to think for themselves, the art therapist may be seen as asking too much, while in limiting destructive uses of media, the clinician may be felt to be mean and restrictive.

In the expectation that the child use the materials, and in the implicit request for a product, the art therapist may be felt as too demanding. In the looking-at function, the clinician may be experienced as exposing the child, or perhaps encouraging excessive voyeurism. In asking questions, the art therapist is often felt as an intrusive prober, and is sometimes seen as a judge of what is produced. When an art therapist teaches a child about a medium or process, he or she may be experienced as giving, or, conversely, as getting in the way. In all of these functions, the art therapist is responded to by the child in ways reflective both of the roles and of the child's reactions to them.

Children often reflect transference reactions in art therapy through their behavior with the materials. Sometimes they refuse to use them at all, as when angry in a withholding way; sometimes they will show their anger at the adult by using media in a destructive, aggressive, or regressive manner. At other times, that same anger may be reflected more directly by making a parent or authority figure in clay and chopping him or her up. With even less disguise and more control, it may be revealed in a funny or ugly picture of the therapist (Figure 20.1).

20.1 An Ugly Picture of the Art Therapist during a Period of Angry Feelings

Conversely, the therapist may be represented directly or symbolically as omniscient, omnipotent, or all-giving; and the relationship may be represented in a positive fashion, as when Terry gave me a baby doll, who felt affectionate towards me (20.1B). What is important is to be alert to the symbolic meanings of the therapist, the relationship, and the treatment as these evolve over time, using them as a way of understanding how the child perceives and copes with feelings (cf. Rubin, 1982b).

Because the art therapist is also an artist, there are some peculiar risks in the symbolic aspects of the transaction. One must be careful, for example, not to overvalue the production of multiple or skilled products for their own sake, always trying to tune in to what they mean to the client. One must be careful, too, that one's own media, content, or style preferences do not subtly interfere with the appreciation and facilitation of an individual's mode of expression. If art therapists have needs to control, they may unwittingly influence what a child uses, or may find reasons to impose tasks or methods more often than is really necessary.

If they have needs to give, they may do more feeding or teaching or even doing for a child than is helpful to that child's developing autonomy. If art therapists are especially curious, they may inadvertently pressure a child with more direct questions than the child can handle, perhaps precipitating withdrawal. What matters here is to be as tuned in to one's own inner life as to the child's, so that the therapist's conflicts do not get in the way of the child's treatment.

An Artist and a Therapist

In order to be maximally helpful, the art therapist should combine in one person the virtues of both artist and therapist, of creator and facilitator. These two roles and perspectives are not so opposed or so different as they may seem. Both artists and psychologists, for example, are concerned with making sense out of human experience (assessment), as well as with uplifting the souls of men (therapy). Both reach for contact with unseen forces, and seek an understanding and articulation of them.

Sandor Lorand, a psychoanalyst, wrote of the artist: "He seems to combine psychoanalytic knowledge with artistic intuition of the way in which the human emotions work. . . . He seems to have been led by an insight of his own, and the results are an inspired accomplishment" (1967, p. 24).

The artist, like the psychologist, affirms "the validity of the inner view" (Shahn, 1960, p. 50), but differentiates their perspectives, as did Ben Shahn, a painter: "So while I accept the vast inner landscape that extends off the boundaries of consciousness to be almost infinitely fruitful of images and symbols, I know that such images mean one thing to the psychologist and quite another to the artist" (p. 51). The art therapist—artist, educator, and clinician (Kramer, 1971)—hopefully has made peace with those differences, and indeed finds them complementary.

In that sense, the art therapist combines both an intuitive, inspired approach with a rational, analytic one, alternating and integrating them in tune with the needs of the situation. An art therapist's comfort with both words and images enhances the possibility of helping people to use both for expression and understanding.

I think that any art therapist's comfort with both free association and discipline, with passive and active modes, and with looking as well as making, serves to broaden the range of possible communication for those with whom they work. Thus, they can be most creative, free to use their resources most imaginatively, because they have access to different modes of thinking, including different ways of thinking about art. There are moments when words can get in the way, and there are moments when words can create relief, order, or calm. The important thing is to be able to sense and to choose.

The Art Therapist as a Change Agent

Whether diagnostician or therapist, teacher or group leader, collaborator or supervisor, consultant or public educator, artist or researcher, art therapists try to use what they understand and feel about people and art to help others to grow. Whether the goal is growth in an individual, a family, a group, a classroom, an institution, or a community, there are certain general steps in the process of being a change agent which seem to me common to all.

In the challenge of finding ways to utilize the strengths and capacities of the individual, family, or institution for growth, it is first necessary to know how the person or system with which one is dealing functions—in general, and in particular. Thus, in work with individuals, developmental and intrapsychic phenomena are part of one's frame of reference, while in work with groups or institutions, group and systems phenomena are necessary for understanding the specific situation.

The history and peculiarities of the particular person, family, or community are also important to know, for only then can one begin to analyze how it is and what it can become. So it makes sense to start not only in therapy, but also in teaching and consultation, by observing, listening, and trying to learn as much as one can about the particular person, group, or place at hand.

Then, in collaboration with that person, place, or group, it is possible to begin to formulate goals, to create a design for change, using one's perspective of the situation and understanding of the background. Having set general objectives, it is then possible to think about what might be done to reach them, what artistic and human events might be likely to help a child to get better, or a school to develop a more therapeutic art program. As the work progresses it is important to be open; no curriculum for change can be tightly planned, or can predict the organic, uneven, and unexpected nature of growth.

At various points it may be necessary to step back and assess where one is, perhaps to refine or revise goals, perhaps to test certain assumptions. And when it seems that the individual, family, or institution is ready to go on functioning independently, then it is necessary to start planning and working toward termination of the formal contract, working through the feelings—as well as working out the facts—of that event. At the end, one says goodbye, one lets go; one might even engage in a review and critique, and perhaps a pictorial or printed publication or display of what has been accomplished, always with the permission of those involved.

Extending Opportunities: Art Therapy Consultation

If one is convinced of the therapeutic importance of art for children and families, one may also be able to influence others to facilitate such experiences. Art therapy is in a peculiarly favorable position as a base for mental health consultation. This is especially true when the agency requesting help is not a clinical one, but is instead educational, recreational, or custodial.

A school, a community center, or an institution for the retarded will already have, or can easily envision, activities in art. If an art program doesn't exist full-blown, chances are that its seeds are there, if only in the form of an occasional box of crayons, and a stack of old (perish the thought!) coloring books. Many institutions see a therapeutic art program as somehow more in keeping with their goals than a regular one, perhaps because it serves a disabled or deviant population, or a normal population under conditions of exceptional stress.

In any case, the art therapist can use art as a *wedge* to open many doors commonly closed to mental health consultants, or open only under narrow and limited conditions. Art can be a *bridge* to minds formerly fearful of and hostile to the "shrink." In this sense, art in consultation may be a *tool* analogous to its sometime-function in therapy; it may be a way of reaching and communicating with a resistant institution in a safe and mutually meaningful way.

In some cases, art serves to sugarcoat the bitter pill of emotional awareness, which may need later to be swallowed and eventually digested. In
others, a taste of mental health thinking through art therapy may help to
develop a greater appetite for more information on the part of a previously
resistant staff or administration. Through art, it is often possible to meet
felt needs for program improvement, while establishing the kind of mutually respectful relationships that permit later ventures into new and potentially fearful territory.

At the end of a year of programatically prolific consultation to an institution for children with disabilities, for example, the agency was ready to
consider a previously rejected proposal for a part-time art therapy effort, in
addition to the existing art and craft programs. That institutions, like
people, can be led to look at, understand, and cope with previously avoided
issues is no great discovery. That art therapists are in a particularly good position to use art as a wedge, a bridge, and a tool in such cases is now quite
apparent to me, and no doubt to others doing similar work.

The peculiar hybrid identity of the art therapist, as artist and mental
health worker, is perhaps part of the potential effectiveness. For, just as in
therapy teaching or supervision or in consultation, too, art therapists can
use themselves in any number of possible ways. I would submit that art
therapists are best equipped to function with maximal flexibility when
their understanding of mental health concepts is as deep and rich as their
feeling for art.

Consultation requires the same interpersonal sensitivities and skills as
any helping relationship. From the first contact through the final leave-
taking, one must explore in a fashion that is both careful and caring of what
is asked, wished, and even feared. Then, if one is open to different possibilities, one may use oneself to help the institution, program, or individual
to grow in a natural and organic fashion.

An art therapy consultant may serve as a resource for practical information, such as appropriate materials, supplies, and equipment—where to get
them and how to use them once secured. An art therapy consultant may
also serve as a resource for other kinds of information, such as relevant
readings, similar arts programs, and opportunities for training.

If the information requested is conceptual, it is vital to find ways of getting it across which are neither beyond nor beneath the learning capacities
of the people wanting to know. Sometimes minimal input can achieve
maximal results, especially when those asking for help need only a small
amount of information, guidance, or permission, in order to build on already existing strengths.

An art therapy consultant may find it useful to show or to demonstrate, modeling behaviors which might be misunderstood or hard to visualize if conveyed only verbally. Conducting pre-program art evaluations at various institutions has served not only to help me to assess the children's potential, but also to expose observing staff members to a radically new child-centered way of working with youngsters in art. In order to help staff members to function in this different way, it may be necessary not only to meet with them and hear from them about their work, but also on occasion to observe what they do or to work alongside them.

Helping people and places to grow in providing healthful art experiences for children is an exciting and challenging task. The particular form a consultant's activities take may change, even in the course of one contact, and will almost certainly vary over time. During a year of consultation to an institution for physically disabled children, my activities included ordering supplies, arranging equipment, organizing schedules, training staff members, meeting and negotiating with administrators, and, even over that brief period of time, overseeing the organic development of a therapeutic art program.

What began with one art classroom grew into an additional full-time craft program, a part-time roving art teacher for bedridden children, and an elaborate series of bulletin boards and display cases for the children's products. Less visible developments were the changed attitudes of the staff toward the children's creative capacities and the therapeutic values of art.

Sometimes I have had the pleasure of remaining in contact with an agency over a long period of time, as with The Western Pennsylvania School for Blind Children, where I have participated in its struggles to grow, seeing many spinoffs and developments from an initial input. A 12-week after-school exploratory art program led to a 6-week summer art-and-drama program for children and parents, as well as ongoing mothers' groups. Eventually, I trained mothers to lead the groups; there was a part-time, and later a full-time arts specialist, who worked with both children and staff in ongoing program development.

My consulting role varied over the years, and included work with the children, the parents, the staff, and the administration. What has developed in the school is a bigger and more secure place for the arts and mental health, as well as a deeper understanding of the children's needs to express and to deal with their feelings in creative ways. What has also developed is a wiser me, enriched as much by contacts with institutions as by those with individuals or groups.

How the Art Therapist Learns through Research

Introduction and Issues

In all of the experiences described in this book, the patients and the institutions are not the only ones who grow and change. Such work is infinitely complex, and I find quite consistently that the more I do and learn, the more I become aware of how much I do not know. Then I develop a further motivation to learn some more, which sometimes leads to the kind of systematic inquiry known as "research."

Earlier chapters have dealt with assessment through art for individuals and families. The precise form taken by the evaluative procedure and analysis of the data depends on many variables, primarily the particular questions being asked. A worker must therefore be clear about goals before it is possible to decide intelligently how to reach them. This reasoning applies to helping as well as to understanding, to treatment as well as to diagnosis, to service as well as to research.

For many years, those who worked in the arts were hostile to research, in large part because they knew that some things important to them were not easily quantifiable, measurable, or even visible. One leader in art education research eventually turned from an approach emphasizing quantification and statistical analysis to one valuing subjective, introspective reports of internal processes (Beittel, 1973). A similar position has been espoused by an experienced art therapist (McNiff, 2000).

The question, however, is not an either/or one, any more than it is ever an issue of process versus product or affect versus cognition. All are false dichotomies. What matters is to formulate one's questions and to explore ways of asking and answering them, settling finally on an approach that seems best fitted to the problem in an authentic and practical way.

It is possible to create a situation for purposes of assessment with varying degrees of structure, utilizing all of the options at hand—space, time, media, theme, and manner of work. For example, one might offer a child a choice from among two or more alternatives, suggest a selection from among a class of materials, or specify the use of a particular medium.

The theme may be left open, as in the individual art interview, or may be more or less specific, such as representing the family in the family art evaluation. The manner in which the task is to be performed may be left open or specified, so that the drawing may be timed (as in a 1-minute gesture drawing), or the person may be required to work with someone else, possibly in a specific way (as in a nonverbal dyadic drawing).

How one then looks at the behaviors and/or products that emerge also depends on the purpose of the assessment. For example, with a family mural, one might focus either on the family's decision-making behavior, the cohesion of the finished product, or the underlying themes therein. I think of research, assessment, evaluation, and diagnosis quite broadly, as slightly different semantic ways of expressing systematic attempts to understand. Sometimes we are most interested in comprehending a child's developmental level, sometimes a child's problems, and sometimes the role of a child within the family. It is useful not only to think of alternative ways of eliciting particular behaviors about which one is concerned, but also to explore different means of noting and assessing them as objectively as possible.

It is important to remember that research can be more or less formal. It is fascinating, once one has decided just what it is one wishes to investigate, to create situations or to look at available data in terms of a particular question. Sometimes an informal examination lessens the motivation for systematic study; at other times, hypotheses get refined for more formal investigations. Because some degree of objectivity in describing behaviors or products is central to all assessment and research, I shall begin by describing ways of helping people to become more accurate and more empathic observers.

Objective Observation

In order to help therapists-in-training sharpen their art process observation skills, so vital to accurate assessment, I have found it useful to print up various *Observation Guides*, such as the one used by Hartley, Frank, and

Goldenson (1952, pp. 346–350), as well as to develop some of my own. The value of such guides, I think, is that they serve to alert the neophyte to behaviors involved in the art-making process, and to the kinds of things about each behavior that may be noted through careful observation. They serve both to define and to focus what might otherwise be a kind of confused looking, determined as much by the observer's past and present experiences as by what is being observed.

I have often involved people in workshop experiences designed to sensitize them to observing and being observed, and have found that even experienced art therapists can have trouble being objective. It is a skill that needs to be practiced and, like all clinical work, is probably as much of an art as a science, even when one is using a printed guide.

Subjective Clinical Assessments

While guides help one to focus one's viewing, there are many times when observations meant for assessment must, given the conditions under which they may be obtained, be quite global and subjective. In a follow-up study at the Center of a group of toddlers with schizophrenic mothers, we decided to observe and to keep samples of artwork produced spontaneously in a play group situation. There was no attempt to systematically control what was presented or how, since the activity was going on within the context of an essentially free, unstructured play environment. Nevertheless, it was possible for me to attend the first and last of six group meetings, to make detailed observations of each child's work with art media, and to look at the first and last week's art behaviors of the children.

I could note "a large and observable difference" in one girl's behavior, "in general being more expansive and freer than she had been during the first session," an impression gleaned from her artwork, her behavior with materials, and her way of relating to me. Another child was observably "more focused" in her artwork and behavior than had been true at the first session. While impressionistic, such clinical observations at different points in time by the same individual can be useful adjuncts to quantifiable measures.

Grouping and Goal-Setting

Quite often the purpose of assessment is pragmatic and practical, as with a project at a preschool for retarded children. A new "creative art and play room" was being set up, so it was necessary to decide how to group the children, and to set goals for work with individuals. The teacher and I therefore devised an evaluation interview, which consisted of a series of tasks in each of the creative play modalities available in the room (drawing, painting, modeling, block construction, sand play, miniature life toys, and dramatic play). Though one task was specified ("draw a person"), the rest were simply presentations to the child of the equipment, along with an invitation to use it. If a child was unable to begin independently or with verbal stimulation, he or she was briefly shown by the teacher how the materials might be used, after which most of the children were able to proceed on their own.

The teacher who conducted these individual interviews began to get a sense of the range of behaviors among the 30 children at the school, and by noting them briefly on a recording form, learned how to observe each activity. The products or play in each area were then ranked according to rough developmental norms (Table 21.1), and the quality of the child's play was also assessed in terms of issues like independence and spontaneity. From these evaluations it was then possible not only to group the children, but also to map out preliminary goals for each child, which would be met not by prescription, but by selectively reinforcing desired behaviors.

Assessing Change in Blind Children I

In an exploratory art program, blind children were also first seen individually, in order to be able to group them most effectively (DVD 21.1). Because of their disability, they were presented with a wide range of sensory stimuli (21.1A), such as foods (taste, smell), musical instruments (hearing), and objects of different sizes, textures (21.1B), and consistencies (touch). When giving them a choice of art media, it was necessary to state the available options, which included wood scraps and glue, clay, finger paint, and drawing tools.

Two observers were given a 24-item nine-point rating scale, in order to note where each child was on each of the behavioral dimensions that seemed most relevant for grouping. These included items descriptive of their overall behavior, such as passive/active, tense/relaxed, distractible/involved, and depressed /alert. Other items referred to the nature of their interaction with the adult, such as dependent/independent, suspicious/trusting, and withdrawn/outgoing. Still others related to their use of the materials, such as awkward/coordinated, impulsive/deliberate, stereotyped/original, and to their attitude toward their work, such as critical/pleased. Yet others related to the creativity of their thinking, such as barren/fluent,

Name _____

Date _____

	1.0–1.5	1.5–2.0	2.0–2.5	2.5–3.0	3.0–3.5	3.5–4.0	4.0–4.5	4.5–5.0	COMMENTS
Age in Years									
Age in Months	12–18	18–24	24–30	30–36	36–42	42–48	48–54	54–60	
DRAWING	Disordered Scribble	Swing Scribble	Circular Scribble	Figure-Ground and Vertical Line	Suggested Shaping	Definite Shapes	Primitive Figurative Representations	More Detailed Figures	
CLAY	Pinch Pound	Roll (Coils)	Making a Ball	Naming	Decorate Surface	Definite Labeled Shapes	Primitive Figures	Detailed Figures	
BLOCK PLAY	Carrying and Dumping	Rows	Towers	Bridging	Enclosures	Simple Labeled Constructions	Elaborate Labeled Constructions	Drama Around Block Play	
DRAMATIC PLAY	No Evidence of Dramatic Play	Solitary Dramatic Play	Elaborate Solitary Dramatic Play	Parallel Dramatic Play with Others	Dramatic Play With Others (Interaction)	Cooperative Dramatic Play With Others	Sustains Role Through the Play	Creates Roles and Stories in Dramatic Play Cooperatively	

Table 21.1 Chart for Assessment of Developmental Levels in Art and Play: Preschoolers

rigid/flexible. An average of the two observers' ratings on each dimension was used, although they agreed surprisingly often (close to 90 percent of the time).

Following 7 weeks of group art sessions, we were interested in seeing how and where individuals had changed, if at all, on these same dimensions. We therefore repeated the individual interviews with each child (21.1C), and again used the mean of two observers' ratings on each dimension (21.1D). Differences between pre- and post-program ratings were all in the desired direction, and were significant for the group of 13 present both times on the following dimensions: independence, flexibility, relaxation, involvement, and originality. These more objective assessments were seen as supplementing our subjective sense of individual and group gains, and were especially meaningful since they supported each other (Rubin & Klineman, 1974).

In the developmental scales used at the preschool for retarded children, the interest was primarily in *what* (descriptively) the child could do in each play area. In the behavioral scales used at the school for the blind the interest was primarily in *how* (qualitatively) the child reacted to the art media and the invitation to create. In another study at the same school, described in the following section, existing and homemade instruments were used to assess both developmental and affective issues, with particular focus on the areas thought to be most relevant and likely to change through the arts program.

Assessing Change in Blind Children II

In a later study done with Susan Aach, Creative Arts Specialist, at the same school for the blind, pre- and post-program assessments of individuals were developed in order to evaluate possible changes during the school year in areas of particular interest (e.g., creativity, body-image representation, independence, and awareness of feelings).

Because an existing instrument had already been used successfully with blind children (Halpin, Halpin & Torrance, 1973), three items from the *Torrance Creativity Tests* (Torrance, 1966) were administered, and scores of fluency, flexibility, and originality were used as a measure of verbal creative thinking. Since Witkin had reported successful use with the blind, a five-point body concept scale was also used, as a measure of articulation in the clay representation of the human figure (Witkin, Birnbaum, Lomonaco, Lehr, & Herman, 1968).

It was necessary to create measures of both independence and feeling awareness, however, since none were known to exist or to be applicable to this population. Independence was measured inversely, in terms of the number of times during the making of the clay figure that the child asked the adult for assurance, ideas, or assistance. The number of dependent statements, so defined, became the child's score on this measure. In order to get at awareness of feelings, each child was asked to make up a story about the clay figure that had been created, and the score was the number of feeling words, like "happy," "angry," "sad," spontaneously utilized therein.

When the 12 children were tested at the end of the year, after having weekly group sessions in art, drama, movement, and music, changes on all measures were in the predicted direction. Only a few, however, reached a statistically significant level, among them one of the creativity measures (fluency on unusual uses of cardboard boxes, $p < .01$); and the independence measure ($p < .01$), with the change in the feeling awareness scores approaching significance ($p < .10$). While the body image scores improved, the five-point scale devised by Witkin proved not to be sufficiently sensitive to the fine differences apparent in the relatively primitive products of these young, multiply handicapped blind children, and a more differentiated scale seemed to be needed.

Several years later, even less success was had using an existing instrument, the teacher's rating scale of a widely used Self-Esteem Inventory (Coopersmith, 1967). In this attempt to assess change, teachers referring children for individual art therapy filled out the questionnaires both before and after the intervention, most often at the beginning and end of the school year.

Although their informal reports of growth in the youngsters had been rich, especially in the area of self-esteem, the items on the scale failed to reflect such change clearly or consistently. Indeed, the inherent difficulties of measuring such complex areas as creativity or self-esteem are formidable, and are further magnified by the associated problems of using instruments designed for the normal child with disabled youngsters.

What is clear from this example is the need, first, to define what it is one wants to assess, then to explore available instruments in terms of the particular situation or population involved, then to modify these or develop new ones if necessary, and finally to administer them under controlled conditions, in order to be able to use such data as an index of the behaviors being studied.

In the case of the blind populations just described, it was not possible to have a matched control group, since there were not enough of such multiply handicapped children to make up such a sample, and because it was important that all such children have access to the arts program. In order to assess change at the end of the school year, therefore, the same children were retested, becoming their own controls.

A Phenomenological Investigation

Many questions regarding children and art must be approached not only with an open mind but also with an open kind of design, which does not preclude valuable information. A recent study on the aesthetic responses of blind children was first conceptualized in terms of a series of choices among paired comparisons. After consultation with psychologist Jack Matthews, PhD, familiar with work in experimental aesthetics, it was decided to include only two such tasks (DVD 21.2).

First, I presented the blind, partially sighted, and sighted judges with comparable (21.2A) three-dimensional artwork (21.2B) created by all three populations (21.2C), asking each child-judge to select which ones he or she most liked and most disliked, and to tell why (21.2D). This procedure elicited a wealth of information, not only in terms of the specific choices made (21.2E), but also in regard to all items noticed (touched and/or commented upon) by all of the judges (21.2F). There was, in fact, quantitative support for the hypothesis that children would prefer artwork (21.2G) done by someone like themselves (21.2H), in regard to useful vision ($p < .05$) (21.2I).

What may have been a more important outcome, however, were the qualitative similarities and differences in the responses of the three groups of judges, useful clues to the basis for an equal but different aesthetic for the blind. Most of the children preferred sculptures with some degree of variety, as well as those with a sense of order.

The visually impaired were different from the sighted, however, in their need to label the objects as representational, as well as their lack of response to abstract elements in general. They also reacted more strongly to certain structural features, particularly projections (which they disliked), holes, and enclosures (which they usually liked).

While the sighted judges tended to be fairly objective in their responses, the visually impaired were more subjective, often relating things to themselves, and reacting with some anxiety to anything that might be perceived as dangerous or unstable. A blind girl preferred one sculpture to another, for example, "because it won't get knocked over as easy as this one. Things make me nervous that can fall over easily." What thus became apparent was not only that the blind have a different aesthetic, but that it is in some ways related to their experience of their disability (Rubin, 1976).

375

Self-Assessments of Art Products

Some questions, however, are fundamentally subjective ones, and can only be answered in that way. Such was the case with another sort of evaluative art interview, held with each of 50 children following a summer program in which every child had 6 weekly 1-hour sessions of group art therapy.

The format of these individual review sessions was to lay out before the child all of the products made over the 6-week period. They were then asked to react to their creations, first in an open-ended fashion, then with more directed questions concerning most- and least-liked products, experiences, and so forth. This provided an opportunity not only for children to assess themselves, but also for the worker to judge what was recalled, repressed, valued, rejected, and so on from the short but intensive program.

Don (Chapter 13) reviewed the sequence of his artwork, from its first compulsive beginnings in a design redone because at first it did not meet his standards (Figure 13.3a). This 10-year-old boy looked at this as well as at all his other products, and finally chose as the favorite his clay sculpture of "somebody" dead in a pool of blood (Figure 13.3b).

His production of this sculpture during the fourth session had represented a breakthrough, and had made possible insight into his intense rivalry with his younger brother, the symbolic victim. This enabled this previously tense and constricted child, who had spoken in a whisper, to begin to move freely, to speak loudly, and even to smear and mess without fear of loss of control or overwhelming guilt. Although some rather smeary paintings were his last products of the summer, his choice of a later, more balanced painting (Figure 13.3c) as a gift for his therapist when he finished individual art therapy reflects the integration he was by then able to achieve.

Measurement of Media Popularity

In order to investigate the subjective aspects of work with different art media, one would need to record and observe all facets of expressive behavior, while to simply gauge which is most popular, all one needs to do is to count. Thus, it was possible to review the records of 50 individual art interviews conducted in the Center with children of different ages, all of whom had been offered the same choice of materials, to get a picture of which media were used most frequently. It was found that the most popular material was clay (24.1 percent), closely followed by tempera paint (22.4 percent), then dry drawing materials—crayons, chalk, and pencil

376

(20.5 percent), watercolor markers (16.1 percent), finger paint (8.9 per-cent), and, finally, wood scraps and glue (8.0 percent).

Clearly, how one organizes such data influences the results, for it would also be reasonable to group clay and finger paint as contact media, clay and wood scraps as sculpture, tempera and finger paint as fluid media, or to group watercolor markers with the other drawing tools. Any of these changes would modify the resultant sequence.

Similarly, it would be possible to analyze the data according to age, sex, or diagnostic category. One could look also at sequences of choices within the hour, in order to see if there were any repeated patterns. All of these questions, however, can be answered by looking at the recorded facts, while other kinds of questions about why and how people use different media are less simple to answer in such a numerical fashion.

Group Drawings and Group Dynamics

In another kind of attempt to understand just what can be inferred from products, a psychologist colleague and I looked at the relationship between certain judged aspects of group murals and the group members' perception of their interaction while creating them. A preservice training session for staff members of a children's residential treatment unit provided the op-portunity to collect the necessary data.

Three small groups (five or six members) were asked first to silently cre-ate a chalk drawing standing around a table, each person using a different color of chalk. Each group then did a wall mural with markers, following discussion of a theme. Finally, each member represented the group with pieces of cellophane, using a different color for each individual. A month later, each person answered a questionnaire on which he or she indicated the most and least dominant people in the group on each task. Individuals also rated the group's degree of cohesion, order, freedom, and disorganiza-tion on each joint activity.

Judges in an expressive therapy course rated the two murals by each group on the same dimensions: degree of cohesion, order, freedom, and dis-organization. The judges also assessed the most and least dominant colors on each chalk mural, as well as on the cellophane representations of the groups.

The data analysis focused on the question of how the judges' ratings—of color dominance and the nature of the group product—related to the members' assessments of individual dominance and the nature of the group interaction. Results indicate widely different degrees of correlation, varying noticeably both by group and by task. Some are significantly high, but some are low or negative, suggesting that what one sees in a picture may or may not reflect what members felt went on in the group (Rubin & Rosenblum, 1977).

Diagnostic Questions about Child Art

Some of my earliest work with disturbed children was with a group of schizophrenic youngsters who were on a special inpatient unit at a psychiatric hospital. The chairman of the department for which I worked asked if and how their art was more disturbed than that of normal children, whom I also saw weekly in an after-school recreation program. I had difficulty delineating significant differences in the artwork itself, though there was no question that their behaviors in regard to materials and in relation to me were radically different, and generally quite bizarre.

In order to look more systematically at the question of whether and how their art work differed, a study was designed in which a group of normal youngsters, matched for age and sex, were seen for a series of individual art interviews, identical in format to those of the hospitalized children. Products were then randomly selected from work by both populations, and presented as slides to judges who varied in their experience with children, art, and pathology.

The judges were asked if they thought they could discriminate the work of schizophrenic from that of normal youngsters, and most of them replied in the affirmative. They were then asked to identify each of 40 items (half from each population presented in random order) as schizophrenic or non-schizophrenic, and to note their degree of certainty (unsure, fairly sure, sure), as well as the reasons for their decision.

Thinking that they might be able to be more accurate with a larger sample of artwork, groups of products from a single session were also presented in the order in which they had been done, and the same judgments requested. Having begun with a skeptical hypothesis born of my own difficulty in answering the department chairman's question, it was still surprising that only 3 of 40 judges were able to judge correctly beyond chance expectation on both single items and groups of products. Two of these three individuals were in the group of 10 judges with no experience in child art or psychopathology!

Even when given information on chronological age and sex, their accuracy was no greater. What did emerge, however, was a significant correlation between judged normality and judgments of aesthetic value (which were made at the end, on the 40 single products), suggesting that what looks "good" also looks "normal" to most judges (Rubin & Schachter, 1972). Some paired comparisons are included on the DVD (DVD 21.3).

What also emerges from the brief description of this study is the necessity of first formulating the question, devising a way to answer it, and formulating subsidiary questions regarding important variables (such as groups of items versus individual products, information on age and sex, or the experience of the judges) in order to find some answers from a controlled investigation.

Another study, part of a large series on schizophrenic mothers and their children, enabled us to look briefly at the possible relationship between some measurable aspects of drawings and pathology (Rubin, Ragins, Schachter, & Wimberly, 1979). In this study, we wondered whether there would be any judged differences between the artwork done by two matched groups: schizophrenic and nonschizophrenic mothers and their respective school-age children.

In order to maximize the likelihood of finding some significantly discriminating measures, we used a variety of drawing tasks and treatments of the data. The children's tasks included specific topics for which standardized measures are available (person, self), or which have been thought significant by clinicians (family, kinetic family), as well as free drawings and a free media choice. The mothers did person, self, and family drawings, as well as one free drawing each.

Developmental scores were assessed on all person and self drawings (Harris, 1963), "Emotional Indicator" scores (Koppitz, 1968) on the first two person drawings, and Self-Concept scores (Bodwin & Bruck, 1960; Porter, 1971) on the self drawings. Heights of figures in person and self drawings were measured, as well as the distance between the self and mother figures in each child's family drawing.

Some attempts were made to analyze content, using such quantifiable aspects as: sex of figure drawn, frequency in person drawings of children versus adults, and frequency in free drawings and paintings of figurative versus nonfigurative work. Finally, blind judgments of pathology were made by graduate art therapy students on some of the artwork, as in the earlier study. The family drawings were rated globally for such things as degree of anger and of organization.

The two groups of children and the two groups of mothers were then compared, and were found not to be differentiated significantly on any of the measurements employed. The two groups of children differed significantly, however, on some of the content analyses, such as the frequency of fantasy figures, or the inclusion of family members in person drawings, and the frequency of nonfigurative work in free paintings. As in the earlier study, even with the drawings of the (diagnosed) schizophrenic and control group mothers, the judges were unable to discriminate pathology significantly often.

None of the qualities of the family drawings were significantly different as judged. In general, the implications for the use of artwork as an early warning signal of incipient pathology in the children of schizophrenics were far from hopeful, at least in regard to formal drawing characteristics.

Variability in Children's Art

Based in part on the judges' difficulties in these two studies, my colleagues and I decided to look at what might have contributed to some of their inability to give children's artwork accurate diagnostic labels—the variability that seemed so often to be present in groups of products by the same child. This phenomenon was one that I had often noted in my clinical work, though I was not sure whether it occurred more often with any age level or type of disability.

In order to study variability as a developmental phenomenon, it was finally decided to utilize human figure drawings—since the scoring system for them was most reliable—and to collect artwork from children ages 4 to 12; 20 subjects (10 boys and 10 girls) at each level. Teachers of art and elementary school in the public schools, in a course with me at that time, were willing to collect the data in their classrooms, omitting the work of any child suspected to have any emotional disturbance or intellectual handicap (Rubin, Schachter, & Ragins, 1983).

The children each did four drawings of "a person" with pencil on 9-by-12-inch paper ("the best you can") (DVD 21.4), at the same time of day on a Monday and a Tuesday, and again on the the following Monday and Tuesday. The coded drawings were scored by trained judges using the Goodenough scale (Harris, 1963); variability was assessed by determining the standard deviation among the four drawing scores (21.4A). In addition to *score variability* (21.4 B, C, D, E), we also developed a code for *content variability* (man, woman, boy, girl), and one for *visual variability* (how alike or different the four pictures looked) (21.4 F, G, H, I).

The correlations between each pair of variabilities were significant, suggesting that they were all aspects of the same phenomenon. The developmental line that emerged, however, was a surprise, since it was not a straight line of gradually decreasing variability with advanced age, as I had expected, but rather an up and down picture with lows at 5 and 10, peaks at 4 and 8, and an upswing at 12 (21.4A).

One obvious implication of these findings is that scores based on one or even two figure drawings, whether used to determine developmental level (Harris, 1963) or emotional problems (Koppitz, 1968), are more reliable at some ages than at others. In addition to developmental factors, one must also wonder about other possible correlates—creativity (if variability is seen as flexibility), or emotional disturbance (if variability is seen as instability).

I believe that this study is a good example of the kinds of research questions that can emerge from the practice of art therapy, but that have implications for the decision-making processes of other professionals. Perhaps even more exciting, such studies open the door to a better understanding of how the mind works when it expresses itself pictorially, something that is just beginning to be investigated systematically.

Free Association in Art Imagery

Such a motivation to understand the mind's imagery processes lay behind yet another study. Fascinated by the experience of free association in words and mental imagery in psychoanalysis, both as patient and as analyst, I decided to see what would happen if people were invited to follow one picture or sculpture with another, allowing images to emerge in as free and nondeliberate a fashion as they could achieve.

A class in Imaging was offered through a Psychoanalytic Center, in which 10 people with art or mental health backgrounds came for 5 weeks and, in 2-hour meetings, experimented with free association in drawing, clay modeling, painting, and collage—in the final session choosing one image to develop in a more finished fashion.

Six participants responded to my invitation to come in for individual interviews reviewing both products and process, from which I got a deeper understanding of the nature of their experiences. In addition to my relief at how relatively easy the process seemed to be, I was even more surprised to discover during these interviews that a large number of individuals had found the class to be personally therapeutic, often in a dramatic way (as in overcoming long-standing creative work blocks), though that was neither promised nor expected.

The process itself turned out to be a complex one, not having a consistent pattern from one person to another or from one medium to another. Patterns emerged, but they varied from those with a climax at the end (a culminating image to which all else seemed to lead in a straight line), to those with a rhythmic up-and-down or back-and-forth flow (one kind of imagery or direction alternating with another), to those where the peak seemed to be somewhere in the middle (with a feeling of dénouement following a central pictorial statement). Existentially, participants reported a high level of emotional involvement, sometimes a feeling of being swept along by the flow of images that seemed to come from somewhere other than themselves, often in rapid succession.

Work in the field of mental imagery (Nucho, 1995) indicates a much greater presence of visual images in the mind at all times than had been supposed. Not only are they utilized for organized problem-solving, but they are also available for other, nonconscious modes of mentation, including creative thinking. This investigation opens further windows on the inner world upon which art therapy draws, with possibilities for future study as well as for eventual clinical applications (Rubin, 1981a).

Relationships between Creativity and Mental Health

In a study of teachers-in-training, I attempted to look at the relationship between creativity and mental health, a critical one for the field of art therapy. Although it was difficult to find reliable and valid measures of either variable, a standardized instrument for measuring dimensions of personality was finally chosen (Edwards Personal Preference Schedule—Edwards, 1959), and creativity tests were developed, based on the work of Wallach and Kogan (1965).

Eight students chose to take a 10-week "Self-Designed Learning Process" (SDLP) led by a clinical psychologist, a kind of sensitivity group in which trust, expressiveness, caring, separateness, and empathy were taught via exercises and discussions. Ten randomly-selected students participated in a 10-week "Creativity Workshop" led by me; here, the weekly 2-hour sessions involved an experiential exploration of creative approaches to all elementary school curriculum areas, via the arts. The 10 control subjects took the same required block of methods courses as the others throughout the term, and all took the EPPS and the creativity tests before and after the 10 weeks, during which some had the special experiences.

The hypothesis was that students exposed to either the Creativity Workshop or the SDLP group would demonstrate changes on both creativity and personality measures. All subjects tested comparably on both pre-program measures, as well as on a test of perceptual rigidity (Breskin, 1968) and on faculty ratings of creativity.

Although the interventions were brief, there were some statistically significant differences in post-program scores on both the creativity tests and the EPPS. All were in the predicted direction, indicating limited support for the hypothesis; there were significant increases in the creativity test scores and changes in the direction of greater personal freedom on the

EPPS for members of both experimental groups, and no change in either category for members of the control group. Given the brevity of the interventions, it is surprising that any changes at all were visible, and we speculated optimistically that the hints of movement in the test results would have shown themselves more strongly had there been more time for the special experiences (Rubin, 1982a).

Reviewing the literature in writing up the study, I was reminded that the area of creativity and its relation to mental health is still full of speculation, with few relevant empirical studies—and even those had conflicting results. The finding, however, that experiences in the Creativity Group led to some growth in mental health suggests that experiences in the arts are also therapeutic, perhaps measurably so.

Since there was both doing and talking in the Creativity Workshop, it is not known how much of the growth may have been due to the creative experiences themselves, and how much to their possible integration through discussion and reflection. This question relates to one of the central debates in art therapy; the relative value of art *as* therapy versus art *in* therapy, an issue that, as far as I know, has yet to be addressed experimentally.

Comparing Products from Art and Drama Interviews

This particular study grew out of an earlier investigation. A drama therapy colleague, Eleanor C. Irwin, PhD, and I had asked five experienced clinicians to read the protocols of 10 boys seen in art and drama interviews on the same day, and to try to match them (cf. Rubin & Irwin, 1975). We were stunned that they were able to do so only one fourth of the time. This unexpected outcome stimulated a later study during which we spent several years rereading, reviewing, and finally evolving a meaningful analysis of the material.

It was possible to make comparisons, because we had been able to see the same children for both kinds of interviews on the same day (half in each sequence), could keep the conditions constant, and had sufficient subjects (24) to be able to generalize about conclusions. The collection of data occurred in the course of interviews held prior to placement in the treatment groups described in Chapter 14.

The analysis of the data required a long period of examining and discussing the material, in order to find appropriate dimensions on which to compare the two art modalities. We eventually looked at those elements of form and content in both areas that were genuinely comparable.

We considered productivity, specific form elements, and different aspects of the content: primary themes, developmental level, and the nature and degree of disguise, including the treatment of time and space. We also included the child's attitude toward his or her product, because this was quite different in the two modalities. We discovered that what was most apparent in art was form, while in drama it was content, and that anxiety in the art sessions almost always related to some regression in form, while in drama it was usually associated with the content of the story.

Conclusion

There are special problems with doing research in and through art therapy, since all the elements we want to study are so complex and hard to measure. As is evident from the studies in this chapter, finding really appropriate, valid, and reliable ways to assess psychopathology or progress through art *products* is extremely difficult. Observing the art *process* in a truly objective and at the same time empathic way is very hard, even with normal children (Brittain, 1979; Gardner, 1980).

How much more difficult it is to do so when the child is different, especially since observers wish to find commonalities between themselves and others. Although distortions in perceptions of those with disabilities tend to be unfairly negative, there is an equal danger in not seeing and accepting the very real differences in their life-experience, including their creative work with art (Rubin, 1981c).

The most difficult and yet most important area for study is that of *progress*—the *outcome* or effect of art therapy on the children we serve. Again, the problem is considerable, since we so often work with populations for whom normal assessment instruments are invalid, and because so many of the kinds of changes we expect from art therapy are so hard to see externalized in measurable indexes. In addition, when dealing with children, we often find that the developmental variables are so hard to disentangle from those whose effects we hope to measure that they present yet another complication in an already confusing situation. Art therapist and glass artist James Minson was recently able to demonstrate significant positive behavioral changes in Guatemalan children as a result of his intervention using a variety of measures (DVD 21.5).

However, despite all of these difficulties and complexities—and they are very real—doing research in and through art therapy can be enormous fun. While identifying the questions to be asked and ways to ask them are the formal steps necessary for any kind of assessment or research, most studies derive their motive power from multiple sources. It is probably not accidental that most of the studies described in this chapter were stimulated less by the needs of the institution, than by those of the investigator(s).

Such wishes to comprehend an observed phenomenon, to explore territory as yet uncharted, or to question widely-held assumptions are based on inner strivings as much as are making and looking at art.

As with art activities, the fact that research derives from unconsciously determined motives makes it possible to understand why it is so deeply satisfying. Like looking at art, research is an acceptable way to indulge one's curiosity; like making art, it is a valid way to try to bring order into one's view of the world and to explore new areas within controlled boundaries. What is important here, as elsewhere, is to be aware of one's private motives for systematic question-asking, so that they do not in any way impede or distort the research undertaken. For myself, the process of formulating questions and discovering answers through research is as deeply satisfying for the mind as helping people through art is pleasurable for the heart.

A Cautionary Note

The procedures described in this book may seem simple, perhaps deceptively so. Art is a powerful tool—one that, like the surgeon's, must be used with care and skill if it is to penetrate safely beneath the surface. Using media with those who are significantly handicapped or disturbed (even without analysis of process or product), requires an understanding not only of art, but also of the world of those with whom one is working. The use of art with all kinds of children or families as a symbolic communicative medium is a clinically demanding task, which carries with it both a tremendous potential and an equally great responsibility.

A parent or teacher without clinical training can indeed provide children with genuinely helpful—and in many ways therapeutic—art experiences. Caution is required, however, in the use of such experiences for a deeper understanding or remediation of internal psychological problems. There, in both assessment and treatment, close clinical supervision in the learning phases and early work stages of art therapy seems to me to be not only desirable, but essential.

Dealing with those who are already vulnerable, or opening up others in a way that creates a certain vulnerability, can be either helpful or harmful. One need not be afraid to do many wonderful and meaningful things with children in art, but one must always respect the importance and the uniqueness of a child's emotional life. One also grows to respect, with some awe and humility, the potency of art, especially in the context of those special human relationships promoted in art therapy.

Finally, one must always respect, when working with children, the primary relationship with the family. It may appear, from some of the highly

GENERAL ISSUES

condensed vignettes in this book, that art therapy with a troubled child consists simply of helping the youngster to express his or her repressed hostility toward significant others.

One must always maintain a delicate balance, however, in order to protect the child from either excessive guilt feelings or possible retaliation from the environment. This is one reason why someone should work with the parents when a youngster is involved in a change process like therapy, which can unleash overt behaviors that may be threatening if the family is not prepared. Even with parental support for the treatment, one must always respect the child's need for sufficient defenses, as much as his or her need for tolerance of forbidden impulses.

The message of this note, therefore, is this: be neither fearful nor fearless, but proceed with open eyes, and with respect for the value of the child as well as the power of art. If you are just beginning, be sure you have someone who understands assessment and therapy much better than you do to guide you. If that person also understands art, so much the better. Even "natural" clinicians can add depth of understanding to their intuition. All who undertake the awesome task of helping others, I think, have a responsibility to carry out their work with as much sensitivity and skill as they can possibly develop. This book ends, therefore, with the hope that those who have read it will indeed carry on, but that they will do so with care.

References

Aach-Feldman, S., & Kunkle-Miller, C. (2001). Developmental art therapy. In J. A. Rubin (Ed.), *Approaches to art therapy* (2nd ed., pp. 226–240). New York: Brunner-Routledge.

Adler, J. (1970). *Looking for me*. [Motion picture]. Pittsburgh, PA: Maurice Falk Medical Fund.

Alkema, C. J. (1971). *Art for the exceptional*. Boulder, CO: Pruett Publishing Co.

Allan, J. (1988). *Inscapes of the child's world*. Dallas, TX: Spring Publications.

Allan, J., & Bertoia, J. (1992). *Written paths to healing*. Dallas, TX: Spring Publications.

Allen, P. B. (1995). *Art is a way of knowing*. Boston: Shambhala.

Alschuler, R., & Hattwick, L. W. (1969). *Painting and personality* (Rev. ed.) Chicago: University of Chicago Press.

Anderson, F. E. (1992). *Art for all the children* (2nd ed.) Springfield, IL: Charles C. Thomas.

Anderson, F. E. (1994). *Art-centered education and therapy for children with disabilities*. Springfield, IL: Charles C. Thomas.

Appel, K. E. (1931). Drawings by children as aids in personality studies. *American Journal of Orthopsychiatry, 1*, 129–144.

Arnheim, R. (1954). *Art and visual perception*. Berkeley, CA: University of California Press.

Arnheim, R. (1967). *Toward a psychology of art*. Berkeley, CA: University of California Press.

Arnheim, R. (1969). *Visual thinking*. Berkeley, CA: University of California Press.

Arrington, D. B. (2001). *Home is where the art is*. Springfield, IL: Thomas.

Ault, R. E. (1989). Art therapy with the unidentified patient. In H. Wadeson,

J. Durkin, & D. Perach (Eds.), *Advances in art therapy* (pp. 222–239). New York: Wiley.

Axline, V. M. (1947). *Play therapy*. New York: Ballantine Books.

Axline, V. M. (1964). *Dibs: In search of self*. New York: Ballantine Books.

Bach, S. (1990). *Life paints its own span: On the significance of spontaneous pictures by seriously ill children*. Zurich: Daimon.

Barron, F. (1966). Creativity in children. In H. P. Lewis (Ed.), *Child art: The beginnings of self-affirmation* (pp. 75–91). Berkeley, CA: Diablo Press.

Barron, F. (1970). Commentary for *No war toys*. Los Angeles: No War Toys.

Barron, F. (1972). *Artists in the making*. New York: Seminar Press.

Baruch, D. W., & Miller, H. (1952). Developmental needs and conflicts revealed in children's art. *American Journal of Orthopsychiatry, 22*, 186–203.

Beittel, K. E. (1973). *Alternatives for art education research*. Dubuque, IA: Wm. C. Brown.

Bender, L. (Ed.). (1952). *Child psychiatric techniques*. Springfield, Illinois: Charles C. Thomas.

Berlyne, D. E. (1971). *Aesthetics and psychobiology*. New York: Meredith Corporation.

Bertoia, J. (1993). *Drawings from a dying child: Insights into death from a Jungian perspective*. New York: Routledge.

Betensky, M. G. (1973). *Self-discovery through self-expression*. Springfield, IL: Charles C. Thomas.

Betensky, M. G. (1995). *What do you see?* London: Jessica Kingsley.

Betensky, M. G. (2001). A phenomenological approach to art therapy. In J. A. Rubin (Ed.), *Approaches to art therapy* (2nd ed., pp. 121–133). New York: Brunner-Routledge.

Bettelheim, B. (1950). *Love is not enough*. Glencoe, IL: The Free Press.

Bettelheim, B. (1964). Art: A personal vision. In *Art: The measure of man* (pp. 41–64). New York: The Museum of Modern Art.

Betts, D. J. (2003). *Creative arts therapies approaches in adoption and foster care*. Springfield, IL: Charles C. Thomas.

Blos, P. (1962). *On adolescence*. New York: The Free Press.

Bodwin, R. F., & Bruck, M. (1960). The adaptation and validation of the Draw-A-Person Test as a measure of self-concept. *Journal of Clinical Psychology, 16*, 414–416.

Boenheim, C., & Stone, B. (1969). Pictorial dialogues: Notes on a technique. *Bulletin of Art Therapy, 8*, 67–69.

Breskin, S. (1968). Measurement of rigidity: A non-verbal test. *Perceptual and Motor Skills, 27*, 1203–1206.

Brittain, W. L. (1979). *Creativity, art, and the young child*. New York: Macmillan.

Brocher, T. (1971). Parents' schools. *Psychiatric Communication (WPIC), 13*, 1–9.

Brooke, S. (2004). *Tools of the trade: A therapist's guide to art therapy assessments*. (2nd ed.). Springfield, IL: Charles C. Thomas.

Brown, E. V. (1975). Developmental characteristics of clay figures made by children from age three through age eleven. *Studies in Art Education, 16,* 45–53.

Buber, M. (1965). *Between man and man.* New York: Macmillan.

Buck, J. N. (1948). The H-T-P Test. *Journal of Clinical Psychology, 4,* 151–159.

Burns, R. C. (1987). *Kinetic house-tree-person drawings.* New York: Brunner/ Mazel.

Burns, R. C., & Kaufman, S. H. (1970). *Kinetic family drawings.* New York: Brunner/ Mazel.

Bush, J. (1997). *The handbook of school art therapy.* Springfield, IL: Charles C. Thomas.

Buxbaum, E. (1949). *Your child makes sense.* New York: International Universities Press.

Cane, F. (1951). *The artist in each of us.* Craftsbury Common, VT: Art Therapy Publications.

Carey, L. (1999). *Sandplay therapy with children and families.* Northvale, NJ: Jason Aronson.

Cartwright, D., & Zander, A. (Eds.). (1981). *Group dynamics: Research and theory.* (3rd ed.). New York: Harper & Row.

Case, C., & Dalley, T. (Eds.). (1990). *Working with children in art therapy.* London: Tavistock.

Cassidy, J., & Shaver, P. (Eds.). (1999). *Handbook of attachment theory.* New York: Guilford.

Chazan, S. (2002). *Profiles of play.* London: Jessica Kingsley.

Children of Cardozo . . . Tell it like it is. (1968). Cambridge, MA: Education Development Center.

Clements, C. B., & Clements, R. D. (1984). *Art and mainstreaming.* Springfield, IL: Charles C. Thomas.

Cohen, B. M., Hammer, J. S., & Singer, S. (1988). The Diagnostic Drawing Series. *The Arts in Psychotherapy, 15,* 11–21.

Cohen, F. (1974). Introducing art therapy into a school system: Some problems. *Art Psychotherapy, 2,* 121–136.

Cohen-Liebman, M. S. (2003). Drawings in forensic investigation of childhood sexual abuse. In C. A. Malchiodi (Ed.), *Handbook of art therapy* (pp. 167–180). New York: Guilford.

Cohn, R. C. (1969–1970). The theme-centered interactional method: Group therapists as group educators. *Journal of Group Psychoanalysis and Process, 2,* 19–36.

Colarusso, C. A. (1992). *Child and adult development.* New York: Plenum.

Cole, N. R. (1966). *Children's arts from deep down inside.* New York: John Day.

Coles, R. (1992). In M. Sartor (Ed.), *Their eyes meeting the world: The drawings and paintings of children.* New York: Houghton Mifflin.

Comins, J. (1969). Art motivation for ghetto children. *School Arts, 69,* 6–7.

Coopersmith, S. (1967). *The antecedents of self-esteem.* San Francisco: W. H. Freeman.

Corcoran, A. L. (1954). Color usage in nursery school painting. *Child Development, 25*, 107–113.

Councill, T. (1999). Art therapy with pediatric cancer patients. Physiological effects of creating mandalas. In C. Malchiodi (Ed.), *Medical art therapy with children* (pp. 75–94). London: Jessica Kingsley.

Cox, M. V. (1992). *Children's drawings*. London: Penguin Books.

Cox, M. V. (1993). *Children's drawings of the human figure*. Hillsdale, NJ: Erlbaum.

Cox, M. V. (1997). *Drawings of people by the under-5's*. London: Folmer.

Culbert, S. A., & Fisher, G. (1969). The medium of art as an adjunct to learning in sensitivity training. *Journal of Creative Behavior, 3*, 26–40.

Curry, N. E. (1971). Consideration of current basic issues in play. In N. E. Curry (Ed.), *Play: The child strives toward self-realization* (pp. 51–61). Washington, DC: National Association for the Education of Young Children.

Davidson, A., & Fay, J. (1964). Fantasy in middle childhood. In M. R. Haworth (Ed.), *Child psychotherapy* (pp. 401–406). New York: Basic Books.

Denny, J. M. (1972). Techniques for individual and group art therapy. *American Journal of Art Therapy, 11*, 117–134.

Despert, J. L. (1938). Technical approaches used in the study and treatment of emotional problems in children II. *The Psychiatric Quarterly, 12*, 176–194.

Dewdney, S., Dewdney, I. M., & Metcalfe, E. V. (1967). The art-oriented interview as a tool in psychotherapy. *Bulletin of Art Therapy, 7*, 4–19.

Dewey, J. (1934). *Art as experience*. New York: Capricorn Books.

Di Leo, J. H. (1970). *Young children and their drawings*. New York: Brunner/Mazel.

Di Leo, J. H. (1974). *Children's drawings as diagnostic aids*. New York: Brunner/Mazel.

Di Leo, J. H. (1977). *Child development: Analysis and synthesis*. New York: Brunner/Mazel.

Di Leo, J. H. (1983). *Interpreting children's drawings*. New York: Brunner/Mazel.

Drachnik, C. (1995). *Interpreting metaphors in children's drawings: A manual*. Burlingame, CA: Abbeygate Press.

Dubowski, J. K. (1984). Alternative models for describing the development of children's graphic work: Some implications for art therapy. In T. Dalley (Ed.), *Art as therapy* (pp. 45–61). New York: Routledge.

Dunn, M. D., & Semple, R. A. (1956). *"But still it grows": A use of spontaneous art in a group situation*. Devon, Pennsylvania: Devereux Foundation.

Edwards, A. L. (1959). *Edwards Personal Preference Schedule*. New York: The Psychological Corporation.

Edwards, B. (1979). *Drawing on the right side of the brain*. Los Angeles: Jeremy Tarcher.

Edwards, B. (1986). *Drawing on the artist within*. New York: Simon & Schuster.

Ehrenzweig, A. (1967). *The hidden order of art*. London: Weidenfeld and Nicholson.

Elkisch, P. (1945). Children's drawings in a projective technique. *Psychological Monographs, 58*, No. 1.

Elkisch, P. (1948). The 'Scribbling Game'—a projective method. *Nervous Child,* 7, 247–256.

Erikson, E. H. (1950). *Childhood and society.* New York: W. W. Norton.

Erikson, E. H. (1959). Growth and crises of the healthy personality. *Identity and the Life Cycle, Psychological Issues,* 1, 50–100.

Erikson, E. H. (1972). Play and Vision. *Harvard Today,* May, p. 13.

Erikson, J. M. (1988). *Wisdom and the senses.* New York: Norton.

Evans, K., & Dubowski, J. (2001). *Art therapy with children on the autistic spectrum.* London: Jessica Kingsley.

Finley, P. (1975). Dialogue drawing: An image-evoking communication between analyst and analysand. *Art Psychotherapy,* 2, 87–99.

Fraiberg, S. M. (1955). *The magic years: Understanding and handling the problems of early childhood.* New York: Scribner's.

Frankl, V. E. (1959). *Man's search for meaning.* New York: Pocket Books.

Freud, A. (1936). *The ego and the mechanisms of defense.* New York: International Universities Press.

Freud, A. (1946). *The psychoanalytical treatment of children.* New York: Schocken.

Freud, A. (1965). *Normality and pathology in childhood: Assessments of development.* New York: International Universities Press.

Freud, S. (1908). Creative writers and day-dreaming. In J. Strachey (Ed. & Trans.), *The standard edition of the complete psychological works of Sigmund Freud* (Vol. 9, pp. 141–156). London: Hogarth Press.

Freud, S. (1910). Leonardo da Vinci and a Memory of his Childhood. In J. Strachey (Ed. & Trans.), *The standard edition of the complete psychological works of Sigmund Freud* (Vol. 2, pp. 63–138). London: Hogarth Press.

Freud, S. (1921). Group psychology and the analysis of the ego. In J. Strachey (Ed. & Trans.), *The standard edition of the complete psychological works of Sigmund Freud* (Vol. 18, pp. 67–145). London: Hogarth Press.

Freund, C. (1969). Teaching art to the blind child integrated with sighted children. *New Outlook for the Blind,* 63, 205–210.

Furman, E. (1969). Treatment via the mother. In R. A. Furman & A. Katan (Eds.), *The therapeutic nursery school* (pp. 64–123). New York: International Universities Press.

Furth, G. M. (1988). *The secret world of drawings.* Boston: Sigo.

Gantt, L., & Schmal, M. (Eds.). (1974). *Art therapy: A bibliography.* Rockville, MD: National Institutes of Mental Health.

Gantt, L., & Tabone, C. (1998). *The rating manual.* Morgantown, WV: Gargoyle Press.

Gantt, L., & Tabone, C. (2003). The Formal Elements Art Therapy Scale and "Draw a person picking an apple from a tree." In C. A. Malchiodi (Ed.), *Handbook of art therapy* (pp. 420–427). New York: Guilford.

Gardner, H. (1980). *Artful scribbles: The significance of children's drawings.* New York: Basic Books.

Gardner, H. (1982). *Art, mind, and brain.* New York: Basic Books.

Gendlin, E. T. (1962). *Experiencing and the creation of meaning*. New York: Free Press.

Gerber, N. (1996). *The brief art therapy screening evaluation*. Philadelphia: Author.

Gil, E. (1991). *The healing power of play*. New York: Guilford.

Gillespie, J. (1994). *The projective use of mother-and-child drawings*. New York: Brunner/Mazel.

Ginott, H. G. (1961). *Group psychotherapy with children*. New York: McGraw-Hill.

Ginott, H. G. (1965). *Between parent and child*. New York: Macmillan.

Goldstein, S. B., Deeton, K. D., & Barasch, J. (1975, March). *The family joint mural: Family evaluation technique*. Paper presented at the California State Psychological Association Convention, Anaheim, CA.

Golomb, C. (1974). *Young children's sculpture and drawing*. Cambridge, MA: Harvard University Press.

Golomb, C. (1992). *The child's creation of a pictorial world*. Berkeley, CA: University of California Press.

Golomb, C. (2002). *Child art in context: A cultural and comparative perspective*. Washington, DC: American Psychological Association.

Goodnow, J. (1977). *Children drawing*. Cambridge, MA: Harvard University Press.

Grözinger, W. (1955). *Scribbling, drawing, painting*. New York: Humanities Press.

Gussak, D., & Virshup, E. (Eds.). (1997). *Drawing time: Art therapy in prisons and forensic settings*. Chicago: Magnolia Street Publishers.

Haeseler, M. (1987). Censorship or intervention: "But you said we could draw whatever we wanted!" *American Journal of Art Therapy, 26*, 11–16.

Hagood, M. (2000). *The use of art in counseling child and adult survivors of childhood sexual abuse*. London: Jessica Kingsley.

Halpin, G., Halpin, E., & Torrance, E. P. (1973). Effects of blindness on creative thinking abilities of children. *Developmental Psychology, 9*, 268–274.

Hammer, E. F. (Ed.). (1958). *The clinical application of projective drawings*. Springfield, IL: Charles C. Thomas.

Hammer, E. F. (Ed.). (1997). *Advances in projective drawing interpretation*. Springfield, IL: Charles C. Thomas.

Hammer, M., & Kaplan, A. M. (1967). *The practice of psychotherapy with children*. Homewood, IL: Dorsey Press.

Hanes, K. M. (1982). *Art therapy and group work: An annotated bibliography*. Westport, CT: Greenwood Press.

Hare, A. P., & Hare, R. P. (1956). The Draw-A-Group Test. *Journal of Genetic Psychology, 89*, 51–59.

Harms, E. (1948). Play diagnosis. *Nervous Child, 7*, 233–246.

Harris, D. B. (1963). *Children's drawings as measures of intellectual maturity*. New York: Harcourt, Brace, and World.

Hartley, R., Frank, L., & Goldenson, R. (1952). *Understanding children's play*. New York: Columbia University Press.

Haupt, C. (1969). Creative expression through art. *Education of the Visually Handicapped, 1*, 41–43.

Haworth, M. R. (Ed.). (1964). *Child psychotherapy*. New York: Basic Books.

Hays, R., & Lyons, S. (1987). The bridge drawing: A projective technique for assessment in art therapy. *The Arts in Psychotherapy, 8,* 207–217.

Hedges, L. E. (1983). *Listening perspectives in psychotherapy*. New York: Jason Aronson.

Henderson, P., & Lowe, K. (1972, November). *Reducing focus on the patient via family videotape playback*. Paper presented at the annual meeting of the American Association of Psychiatric Services for Children, Washington, DC.

Henley, D. (1992). *Exceptional children, exceptional art*. Worcester, MA: Davis Publications.

Henley, D. (2001). Images in the lessons: Art therapy in creative education. In J. A. Rubin (Ed.), *Approaches to art therapy* (2nd ed., pp. 326–339). New York: Brunner-Routledge.

Hill, A. (1945). *Art versus illness*. London: George Allen and Unwin.

Hill, A. (1951). *Painting out illness*. London: George Allen and Unwin.

Horovitz-Darby, E. (1988). Art therapy assessment of a minimally language skilled deaf child. In *Mental health assessment of deaf clients: Special conditions* (pp. 115–127). Proceedings from the 1988 University of California's Center on Deafness Conference. Little Rock, AK: ADARA.

Horowitz, M. J. (1983). *Image formation and psychotherapy*. New York: Jason Aronson.

Howard, M. (1964). An art therapist looks at her professional history. *Bulletin of Art Therapy, 4,* 153–156.

Hulse, W. C. (1952). Childhood conflict expressed through family drawings. *Journal of Projective Techniques, 16,* 66–79.

Irwin, E. C. (1983). The diagnostic and therapeutic use of pretend play. In C. E. Schaefer & K. J. O'Conner, (Eds.), *Handbook of play therapy* (pp. 148–173). New York: Wiley.

Irwin, E. C., & Malloy, E. S. (1975). Family puppet interview. *Family Process, 14,* 179–191.

Irwin, E. C., & Rubin, J. A. (1976). Art and drama interviews: Decoding symbolic messages. *Art Psychotherapy, 3,* 169–175.

Irwin, E. C., Rubin, J. A., & Shapiro, M. I. (1975). Art and Drama: Partners in Therapy. *American Journal of Psychotherapy, 29,* 107–116.

Irwin, E. C., & Shapiro, M. I. (1975). Puppetry as a diagnostic and therapeutic technique. In I. Jakab (Ed.), *Psychiatry and art*, vol. 4 (pp. 86–94). New York: S. Karger.

Jakab, I. (1956/1998). *Pictorial expression in psychiatry: Psychiatric and artistic analysis*. Budapest: Akademiai Kiado.

Jewish Museum of Prague. (1993). *I have not seen a butterfly around here*. Prague: The Jewish Museum.

Jung, C. G. (1964). *Man and his symbols*. New York: Doubleday.

Kaelin, E. F. (1966). The existential ground for aesthetic education. *Studies in Art Education, 8,* 3–12.

Kalff, D. M. (1980). *Sandplay*. Boston: Sigo Press.

Kaplan, F. (2003). Art-based assessments. In C. Malchiodi (Ed.), *Handbook of art therapy* (pp. 25–35). New York: Guilford.

Kaye, G. (1968). Color education in art. *Color Engineering*, 7, 15–20.

Kellogg, J. (1978). *Mandala: Path of beauty*. Clearwater, FL: Association for Teachers of Mandala Assessment.

Kellogg, R. (1969). *Analyzing children's art*. Palo Alto, CA: National Press Books.

Kinget, G. M. (1952). *The drawing completion test: A projective technique for the investigation of personality*. New York: Grune and Stratton.

Klein, M. (1932). *The psycho-analysis of children*. London: Hogarth.

Klepsch, M., & Logie, L. (1982). *Children draw and tell: An introduction to the projective uses of children's human figure drawings*. New York: Brunner/Mazel.

Klorer, P. G. (2000). *Expressive therapy with troubled children*. Northvale, NJ: Jason Aronson.

Klorer, P. G. (2003). Sexually abused children: Group approaches. In C. A. Malchiodi (Ed.), *Handbook of art therapy* (pp. 339–350). New York: Guilford.

Knill, P., Levine, E. G., & Levine, S. K. (2004). *Principles and practice of expressive arts therapy*. London: Jessica Kingsley.

Konopka, G. (1963). *Social group work: A helping process*. Englewood Cliffs, NJ: Prentice Hall.

Koppitz, E. M. (1968). *Psychological evaluation of children's human figure drawings*. New York: Grune and Stratton.

Koppitz, E. M. (1984). *Psychological evaluation of HFD's by middle-school pupils*. New York: Grune & Stratton.

Kovner, A. (Ed). (1968). *Childhood under fire: Stories, poems and drawings by children during the Six Days War*. Israel: Sifriat Poalim.

Kramer, E. (1958). *Art therapy in a children's community*. Springfield, IL: Charles C. Thomas.

Kramer, E. (1971). *Art as therapy with children*. New York: Schocken Books.

Kramer, E. (1979). *Childhood and art therapy*. New York: Schocken Books.

Kramer, E. (2000). L. A. Gerity (Ed.), *Art as therapy: Collected papers*. London: Jessica Kingsley.

Kramer, E. (2001). Sublimation and art therapy. In J. A. Rubin (Ed.), *Approaches to art therapy* (2nd ed., pp. 28–39). New York: Brunner-Routledge.

Kramer, E., & Schehr, J. (2000). An art therapy evaluation session for children. In L. A. Gerity (Ed.), *Art as therapy: Collected papers* (pp. 73–93). London: Jessica Kingsley.

Kris, E. (1952). *Psychoanalytic explorations in art*. New York: Schocken Books.

Kubie, L. (1958). *Neurotic distortion of the creative process*. New York: Noonday Press.

Kunkle-Miller, C. (1982). Research study: The effects of individual art therapy on emotionally disturbed deaf children and adolescents. Proceedings, 13th Annual AATA Conference.

Kunkle-Miller, C. (1985). *Competencies for art therapists whose clients have physical, cognitive or sensory disabilities.* Unpublished doctoral dissertation, University of Pittsburgh.

Kwiatkowska, H. Y. (1962). Family art therapy: Experiments with a new technique. *Bulletin of Art Therapy, 1,* 3–15.

Kwiatkowska, H. Y. (1967). The use of families' art productions for psychiatric evaluation. *Bulletin of Art Therapy, 6,* 52–69.

Kwiatkowska, H. Y. (1978). *Family therapy and evaluation through art.* Springfield, IL: Charles C. Thomas.

Lachman-Chapin, M. (2001). Self psychology and art therapy. In J. A. Rubin (Ed.), *Approaches to art therapy* (2nd ed., pp. 66–78). New York: Brunner-Routledge.

Landgarten, H. B. (1981). *Clinical art therapy.* New York: Brunner/Mazel.

Landgarten, H. B. (1987). *Family art psychotherapy: A clinical guide and casebook.* New York: Brunner/Mazel.

Langer, S. K. (1953). *Feeling and form.* New York: Charles Scribner's Sons.

Langer, S. K. (1957). Deceptive analogies: Specious and real relationships among the arts. In *Problems of art.* New York: Charles Scribner's Sons.

Langer, S. K. (1958). The cultural importance of the arts. In M. E. Andrews (Ed.), *Aesthetic form and education* (pp. 1–8). Syracuse, NY: Syracuse University Press.

Lantz, B. (1955). *Easel Age Scale.* Los Angeles: Test Bureau.

Lehman, L. (1969). Let there be art! *School Arts, 68,* 46.

Levick, M. F. (1983). *They could not talk and so they drew: Children's styles of coping and thinking.* Springfield, IL: Charles C. Thomas.

Levick, M. F. (2001). *The Levick cognitive and emotional art therapy assessment (LECATA).* Boca Raton, FL: Author.

Levine, S., & Levine, E. (1999). *Foundations of expressive arts therapy: Theoretical and clinical perspectives.* London: Jessica Kingsley Publisher.

Levy, S., & Levy, R. A. (1958). Symbolism in animal drawings. In E. F. Hammer (Ed.), *The clinical application of projective drawings* (pp. 311–343). Springfield, IL: Charles C. Thomas.

Lewis, J., & Blotcky, M. (1997). *Child therapy: Concepts, strategies, and decision-making.* New York: Brunner/Mazel.

Lewis, P. B. (1993). *Creative transformation.* Wilmette, IL: Chiron Publications.

Lindsay, Z. (1972). *Art and the handicapped child.* New York: Van Nostrand Reinhold.

Linesch, D. G. (1988). *Adolescent art therapy.* New York: Brunner/Mazel.

Linesch, D. G. (Ed.). (1993). *Art therapy with families in crisis.* New York: Brunner/Mazel.

Lorand, S. (1967). Preface. In A. Zaidenberg (Ed.), *The emotional self* (p. 24). New York: Bell Publishing Company.

Lowenfeld, M. (1971). *Play in childhood* (2nd ed.). New York: Wiley.

Lowenfeld, M. (1979). *The world technique.* London: Allen & Unwin.

Lowenfeld, V. (1952). *The nature of creative activity* (2nd ed.). London: Routledge and Kegan Paul.

Lowenfeld, V. (1954). *Your child and his art.* New York: Macmillan.

Lowenfeld, V. (1957). *Creative and mental growth* (3rd ed.). New York: Macmillan.

Lüscher, M. (1969). *The Lüscher Color Test.* New York: Random House.

Lusebrink, V. B. (1990). *Imagery and visual expression in therapy.* New York: Plenum Press.

MacGregor, J. M. (1989). *The discovery of the art of the insane.* Princeton, NJ: Princeton University Press.

Machover, K. (1949). *Personality projection in the drawing of the human figure.* Springfield, IL: Charles C. Thomas.

Makarova, E., & Seidman-Miller, R. (1999). *Friedl Deicker-Brandeis, Vienna 1891–Auschwitz 1944.* Los Angeles: Tallfellow Press.

Malchiodi, C. A. (1997). *Breaking the silence: Art therapy with children from violent homes* (2nd ed.). New York: Brunner-Routledge.

Malchiodi, C. A. (1998). *Understanding children's drawings.* New York: Guilford.

Malchiodi, C. A. (Ed.). (1999). *Medical art therapy with children.* London: Jessica Kingsley.

Malchiodi, C. A. (Ed.). (2004). *Expressive therapies.* New York: Guilford.

Malchiodi, C. A., Kim, D., & Choi, W. S. (2003). Developmental art therapy. In C. A. Malchiodi (Ed.), *Handbook of art therapy* (pp. 93–105). New York: Guilford.

Malraux, A. (1978). *The voices of silence.* Princeton, NJ: Princeton University Press.

Manning, T. M. (1987). Aggression depicted in abused children's drawings. *The Arts in Psychotherapy, 14,* 15–24.

Maslow, A. (1959). Creativity in self-actualizing people. In H. H. Anderson (Ed.), *Creativity and its cultivation* (pp. 83–95). New York: Harper & Row.

Mattil, E. L. (1972). *The self in art education. Research Monograph 5,* Washington, DC: National Art Education Association.

McFarland, M. B. (1978). Reality as a source of creativity. In E. A. Roth & J. A. Rubin (Eds.), *Perspectives on art therapy* (pp. 5–6). Pittsburgh, PA: Pittsburgh Child Guidance Center.

McKim, R. H. (1972). *Experiences in visual thinking.* Belmont, CA: Wadsworth.

McNiff, S. (1981). *The arts and psychotherapy.* Springfield, IL: Charles C. Thomas.

McNiff, S. (1998). *Art-based research.* London: Jessica Kingsley.

Meerloo, J. A. M. (1968). *Creativity and eternization.* New York: Humanities Press.

Michael, J. A. (Ed.). (1982). *The Lowenfeld lectures.* University Park, PA: Pennsylvania State University Press.

Mills, A. (2003). The Diagnostic Drawing Series. In C. A. Malchiodi (Ed.), *Handbook of art therapy* (pp. 401–409). New York: Guilford.

Milner, M. (1957). *On not being able to paint.* New York: International Universities Press.

Milner, M. (1969). *The hands of the living god.* New York: International Universities Press.

Montague, J. A. (1951). Spontaneous drawings of the human form in childhood schizophrenia. In H. H. Anderson & G. L. Anderson (Eds.), *An introduction to projective techniques* (pp. 370–385). Englewood Cliffs, NJ: Prentice Hall.

Moon, B. L. (1998). *The dynamics of art as therapy with adolescents*. Springfield, IL: Charles C. Thomas.

Moon, C. H. (2001). *Art therapy: Cultivating the artist identity in the art therapist.* Philadelphia: Jessica Kingsley.

Moriya, D. (2000). *Art therapy in schools*. Boca Raton, FL: Author.

Morris, D. (1962). *The biology of art*. New York: Alfred A. Knopf.

Mortensen, K. V. (1991). *Form and content in children's human figure drawings*. New York: New York University Press.

Moustakas, C. E. (1953). *Children in play therapy*. New York: Ballantine Books.

Moustakas, C. E. (1959). *Psychotherapy with children*. New York: Ballantine Books.

Moustakas, C. E. (1969). *Personal growth*. Cambridge, MA: Howard A. Doyle.

Murphy, J. (Ed.). (2001). *Art therapy with young survivors of sexual abuse*. Philadelphia: Taylor & Francis.

Namer, A., & Martinez, Y. (1967). The use of painting in group psychotherapy with children. *Bulletin of Art Therapy, 6*, 73–78.

Napoli, P. J. (1951). Finger Painting. In H. H. Anderson & G. L. Anderson (Eds.), *An introduction to projective techniques* (pp. 386–415). Englewood Cliffs, NJ: Prentice Hall.

Naumburg, M. (1928). *The child and the world*. New York: Harcourt, Brace.

Naumburg, M. (1947). Studies of the free art expression of behavior problem children and adolescents as a means of diagnosis and therapy. *Nervous and Mental Disease Monograph, 71*. (reprinted as *An introduction to art therapy*. New York: Teachers College Press, 1973)

Naumburg, M. (1950). *Schizophrenic art: Its meaning in psychotherapy*. New York: Grune and Stratton.

Naumburg, M. (1953). *Psychoneurotic art: Its function in psychotherapy*. New York: Grune and Stratton.

Naumburg, M. (1966). *Dynamically oriented art therapy: Its principles and practices*. New York: Grune and Stratton.

Neumann, E. (1971). *Art and the creative unconscious*. Princeton, NJ: Princeton University Press.

Nixon, A. (1969). A child's right to the expressive arts. *Childhood Education, 299–310*.

Nucho, A. O. (1995). *Spontaneous creative imagery*. Springfield, IL: Charles C. Thomas.

Nucho, A. O. (2003). *Psychocybernetic model of art therapy* (2nd ed.) Springfield, IL: Charles C. Thomas.

Oaklander, V. (1978). *Windows to our children: A Gestalt therapy approach to children and adolescents*. Utah: Real People Press.

Oster, G. D., & Crone, P. G. (2004). *Using drawings in assessment and therapy* (2nd ed.). New York: Brunner-Routledge.

Oster, G. D., & Montgomery, S. (1996). *Clinical uses of drawings*. Northvale, NJ: Jason Aronson.

Pasto, T., & Runkle, P. R. (1955). A tentative and general guide to the procedure for administering the diagnostic graphic-expression technique to children. *Ars Gratia Hominis, 2*, 30–31.

Peckham, M. (1965). *Man's rage for chaos*. New York: Schocken Books.

Peller, L. E. (1955). Libidinal development as reflected in play. *Psychoanalysis, 3*, 3–11.

Petrie, M. (1946). *Art and regeneration*. London: Paul Elek.

Piaget, J. (1950). *The psychology of intelligence*. New York: Harcourt Brace.

Piaget, J., & Inhelder, B. (1956). *The child's conception of space*. London: Routledge & Kegan Paul.

Piaget, J., & Inhelder, B. (1971). *Mental imagery in the child*. New York: Basic Books.

Play Schools for Parents. (1971, January 11). *Time*, p. 55.

Porter, J. D. R. (1971). *Black child, white child*. Cambridge, MA: Harvard University Press.

Prinzhorn, H. (1972). *Artistry of the mentally ill*. New York: Springer-Verlag.

Proulx, L. (2002). *Strengthening emotional ties through parent-child-dyad art therapy: Interventions with infants and preschoolers*. London: Jessica Kingsley.

Rabin, A. I., & Haworth, M. R. (Eds.). (1960). *Projective techniques with children*. New York: Grune and Stratton.

Rhyne, J. (1971). The Gestalt art experience. In J. Fagan & I. L. Shepherd (Eds.), *Gestalt therapy now* (pp. 274–284). New York: Harper Colophon Books.

Rhyne, J. (1995). *The gestalt art experience* (2nd ed.). Chicago: Magnolia Street Publishers.

Riley, S. (1999). *Contemporary art therapy with adolescents*. London: Jessica Kingsley.

Riley, S. (2001a). Commentary: Systemic thinking and the influence of postmodern theories on art therapy. In J. A. Rubin (Ed.), *Approaches to art therapy* (2nd ed., pp. 134–148). New York: Brunner-Routledge.

Riley, S. (2001b). *Group process made visible*. New York: Brunner-Routledge.

Riley, S. (2003). Art therapy with couples. In C. A. Malchiodi (Ed.), *Handbook of art therapy* (pp. 387–398). New York: Guilford.

Riley, S., & Malchiodi, C. A. (2003). Solution-focused and narrative approaches. In C. A. Malchiodi (Ed.), *Handbook of art therapy* (pp. 82–92). New York: Guilford.

Riley, S., & Malchiodi, C. A. (2004). *Integrative approaches to family art therapy* (2nd ed.). Chicago: Magnolia Street Publishers.

Robertson, S. (1963). *Rosegarden and labyrinth*. London: Routledge & Kegan Paul.

Rogers, N. (1993). *The creative connection: Expressive arts as healing*. Palo Alto, CA: Science & Behavior Books.

Rosal, M. (1996). *Approaches to art therapy with children*. Burlingame, CA: Abbeygate Press.

Rosenthal, R., & Jacobson, L. (1968). *Pygmalion in the classroom*. New York: Holt, Rinehart and Winston.

Ross, C. (1997). *Something to draw on*. London: Jessica Kingsley.

Roth, E. (2001). Behavioral art therapy. In J. A. Rubin (Ed.), *Approaches to art therapy* (2nd ed., pp. 195–209). New York: Brunner-Routledge.

Rozum, A. L., & Malchiodi, C. A. (2003). Cognitive-behavioral approaches. In C. A. Malchiodi (Ed.), *Handbook of art therapy* (pp. 72–81). New York: Guilford.

Rubin, J. A. (1972). *"We'll show you what we're gonna do!" Art for multiply handicapped blind children*. [Motion picture]. Pittsburgh, PA: Expressive Media.

Rubin, J. A. (1973). *Children and the arts: A film about growing*. [Motion picture]. Pittsburgh: PA: Expressive Media, Inc.

Rubin, J. A. (1976). The exploration of a 'tactile aesthetic'. *New Outlook for the Blind, 70*, 369–375.

Rubin, J. A. (1981a). Art and imagery: Free association with media. *Proceedings of the Twelfth Annual Conference of the American Art Therapy Association*, Baltimore: American Art Therapy Association.

Rubin, J. A. (1981b). Art for the special person: Roles and responsibilities of art therapists. In J. Rogers & J. Kahlmann (Eds.), *Art in the lives of persons with Special Needs* (pp. 15–19). Washington, DC: National Committee, Arts for the Handicapped.

Rubin, J. A. (1981c). Research in art with the handicapped: Problems and promises. *Studies in Art Education, 23*, 7–13.

Rubin, J. A. (1982a). Creating creative teachers: An experimental study. *The Arts in Psychotherapy, 9*, 101–111.

Rubin, J. A. (1982b). Transference and countertransference in art therapy. *American Journal of Art Therapy, 21*, 10–12.

Rubin, J. A. (1984). *The art of art therapy*. New York: Brunner/Mazel.

Rubin, J. A. (1999). *Art therapy: An introduction*. New York: Brunner/Mazel.

Rubin, J. A. (Ed.). (2001). *Approaches to art therapy: Theory & technique* (2nd ed.). New York: Brunner-Routledge.

Rubin, J. A. (2002). *My mom and dad don't live together anymore*. Washington, DC: 'Magination Press (American Psychological Association).

Rubin, J. A. (Producer). (2004). *Art therapy has many faces*. [Motion picture]. Pittsburgh, PA: Expressive Media.

Rubin, J. A. (2005). *Artful therapy*. New York: Wiley.

Rubin, J. A., & Irwin, E. C. (1975). Art and drama: Parts of a puzzle. In I. Jakab (Ed.), *Psychiatry and art* (pp. 193–200). New York: S. Karger.

Rubin, J. A., & Irwin, E. C. (1984). *The green creature within: Art and drama in adolescent group psychotherapy*. [Motion picture]. Pittsburgh, PA: Expressive Media.

Rubin, J. A., Irwin, E. C., & Bernstein, P. (1975). Play, parenting and the arts: A therapeutic approach to primary prevention. *Proceedings of the American Dance Therapy Association*, 60–78.

Rubin, J. A., & Klineman, J. (1974). They opened our eyes: An exploratory art program for vsually-impaired multiply-handicapped children. *Education of the Visually Handicapped, 6,* 106–113.

Rubin, J. A., & Levy, P. (1975). Art-awareness: A method for working with groups. *Group Psychotherapy and Psychodrama, 28,* 108–117.

Rubin, J. A., & Magnussen, M. G. (1974). A family art evaluation. *Family Process, 13,* 185–200.

Rubin, J. A., Magnussen, M. G., & Bar, A. (1975). Stuttering: Symptom-system-symbol (Art therapy in the treatment of a case of disfluency). In I. Jakab (Ed.), *Psychiatry and Art* (pp. 201–215). New York: S. Karger.

Rubin, J. A., Ragins, N., Schachter, J., & Wimberly, F. (1979). Drawings by schizophrenic and non-schizophrenic mothers and their children. *Art Psychotherapy, 6,* 163–175.

Rubin, J. A., & Rosenblum, N. (1977). Group art and group dynamics: An experimental study. *Art Psychotherapy, 4,* 185–193.

Rubin, J. A., & Schachter, J. (1972). Judgments of psychopathology from art productions of children. *Confinia Psychiatrica, 15,* 237–252.

Rubin, J. A., Schachter, J., & Ragins, N. (1983). Intra-individual variability in human figure drawings: A developmental study. *American Journal of Orthopsychiatry, 53,* 654–667.

Rutten-Sarris, M. J. (2002). *The R-S Index: A diagnostic instrument for the assessment of interaction structures in drawings.* Unpublished doctoral dissertation, University of Hertfordshire, UK.

Safran, D. (2002). *Art therapy and AD/HD: Diagnostic and therapeutic approaches.* London: Jessica Kingsley.

Salant, E. G. (1975). Preventive art therapy with a preschool child. *American Journal of Art Therapy, 14,* 67–74.

Sarnoff, C. A. (1976). *Latency.* New York: Jason Aronson.

Schaefer, C. E., & O'Connor, K. J. (Eds.). (1983). *Handbook of play therapy.* New York: Wiley.

Schaeffer-Simmern, H. (1961). *The unfolding of artistic activity.* Berkeley, CA: University of California Press.

Schiffer, M. (1969). *The therapeutic play group.* New York: Grune and Stratton.

Schilder, P. (1950). *The image and appearance of the human body.* New York: Wiley.

Schildkrout, M. S., Shenker, I. R., & Sonnenblick, M. (1972). *Human figure drawings in adolescence.* New York: Brunner/Mazel.

Schiller, F. (1875). *Essays, aesthetical and philosophical.* London: George Bell.

Schmidl-Waehner, T. R. (1942). Formal criteria for the analysis of children's drawings and paintings. *American Journal of Orthopsychiatry, 17,* 95–104.

Schmidl-Waehner, T. R. (1946). Interpretation of spontaneous drawings and paintings. *Genetic Psychology Monographs, 33,* 3–70.

Selfe, L. (1977). *Nadia: A case study of extraordinary drawing ability in an autistic child.* New York: Academic Press.

Shahn, B. (1960). *The shape of content.* New York: Vintage Books.

402

References

Shaw, R. F. (1938). *Finger painting*. Boston: Little, Brown and Company.

Silver, R. A. (1978). *Developing cognitive and creative skills in art*. Baltimore: University Park Press.

Silver, R. A. (2001). *Art as language: Access to thoughts and feelings through stimulus drawings*. New York: Brunner-Routledge.

Silver, R. A. (2002). *Three art assessments: Silver drawing test of cognition & emotion; Draw a story: Screening for depression; & Stimulus drawings and techniques*. New York: Brunner-Routledge.

Simon, R. (1992). *The symbolism of style*. NY: Routledge.

Sinrod, H. (1964). Communication through paintings in a therapy group. *Bulletin of Art Therapy, 3*, 133–147.

Site, M. (1964). Art and the slow learner. *Bulletin of Art Therapy, 4*, 3–19.

Slavson, S. R. & Schiffer, M. (1975). *Group psychotherapies for children*. New York: International Universities Press.

Smart, A. (1970). Play therapy schools for parents. *Menninger Perspective*, Aug.-Sept., 12–15.

Smith, N. (1981, Winter). Developmental origins of graphic symbolization in the paintings of children three to five. *Review of Research in Visual Arts Education, 13*.

Smith, S. L. (1979). *No easy answers*. Cambridge, MA: Winthrop.

Snow, A. C. (1968). *Growing with children through art*. New York: Reinhold Book Corp.

Sobol, B. (1982). Art therapy and strategic family therapy. *American Journal of Art Therapy, 21*, 23–31.

Sobol, B., & Williams, K. (2001). Family and group art therapy. In J. A. Rubin (Ed.), *Approaches to art therapy* (2nd ed.). New York: Brunner-Routledge.

Steele, W. (2003). Using drawing in short-term trauma resolution. In C. A. Malchiodi (Ed.), *Handbook of art therapy* (pp. 139–151). New York: Guilford.

Stepney, S. A. (2001). *Art therapy with students at risk: Introducing art therapy into an alternative learning environment for adolescents*. Springfield, IL: Charles C. Thomas.

Sutton-Smith, B. (1971). The playful modes of knowing. In N. E. Curry (Ed.), *Play: The child strives toward self-realization* (pp. 13–25). Washington, DC: National Association for Education of Young Children.

Swenson, C. H. (1968). Empirical evaluations of human figure drawings: 1957–1966. *Psychological Bulletin, 70*:20–44.

Thomas, G. V., & Silk, A. M. K. (1990). *An introduction to the psychology of children's drawings*. New York: New York University Press.

Torrance, E. P. (1966). *Torrance Tests of Creative Thinking*. Princeton, NJ: Personnel Press.

Tyson, P., & Tyson, R. L. (1990). *Psychoanalytic theories of development: An integration*. New Haven, CT: Yale University Press.

Ude-Pestel, A. (1977). *Betty: History and art of a child in therapy*. Palo Alto, CA: Science & Behavior Books.

Uhlin, D. M. (1972). *Art for exceptional children*. Dubuque, IA: William C. Brown.

Ulman, E. (1961). Art therapy: Problems of definition. *Bulletin of Art Therapy, 1*, 10–20.

Ulman, E. (1965). A new use of art in psychiatric diagnosis. *Bulletin of Art Therapy, 4*, 91–116.

Ulman, E. (1971). The power of art in therapy. In I. Jakab (Ed.), *Psychiatry and Art* (pp. 93–102). New York: S. Karger.

Ulman, E. (1972). Art classes as therapy. *Journal of the American Association of University Women*.

Van Sommers, P. (1984). *Drawing and cognition*. Cambridge: Cambridge University Press.

Vich, M. A., & Rhyne, J. (1967). Psychological growth and the use of art materials: Small group experiments with adults. *Journal of Humanistic Psychology*, Fall issue.

Viola, W. (1944). *Child art*. (2nd ed.). London: University of London Press.

Volavkova, H. (Ed.). (1962). *I never saw another butterfly . . . children's drawings and poems from Terezin concentration camp, 1942–1944*. New York: McGraw-Hill.

Wadeson, H. S. (1973). Art techniques used in conjoint marital therapy. *American Journal of Art Therapy, 12*, 147–164.

Wadeson, H. (1980). *Art psychotherapy*. New York: Wiley.

Wadeson, H., Durkin, J. & Perach, D. (Eds.). (1989). *Advances in art therapy*. New York: Wiley.

Wadeson, H. W. (2000). *Art therapy practice: Innovative approaches with diverse populations*. New York: Wiley.

Wallach, M. A., & Kogan, N. (1965). *Modes of thinking in young children*. New York: Holt, Rinehart & Winston.

Waller, D. (1993). *Group interactive art therapy* New York: Routledge.

Weiner, B. B. (1967). Arts and crafts for the mentally retarded: Some hypotheses. In D. Gingland (Ed.), *Expressive arts for the mentally retarded* (pp. 5–8). New York: National Association for Retarded Children.

Wiggin, R. G. (1962). Teaching mentally handicapped children through art. *Art Education Bulletin, 19*, 20–24.

Williams, G. H., & Wood, M. M. (1977). *Developmental art therapy*. Baltimore: University Park Press.

Wills, D. M. (1965). Some observations on blind nursery school children's understanding of their world. *Psychoanalytic Study of the Child, 20*, 344–364.

Wilson, L. (1977). Theory and practice of art therapy with the mentally retarded. *American Journal of Art Therapy, 16*, 87–97.

Wilson, L. (2001). Symbolism and art therapy. In J. A. Rubin (Ed.), *Approaches to art therapy* (2nd ed., pp. 40–53). New York: Brunner-Routledge.

Wilson, B., & Wilson, M. (1978). Recycling symbols: A basic cognitive process in the arts. In S. Madega (Ed.), *The arts, cognition and basic skills* (pp. 89–109). St. Louis, MO: Cemrel.

Winner, E. (1982). *Invented worlds*. Cambridge, MA: Harvard University Press.

Winnicott, D. W. (1964, 1968). The squiggle game. In C. Winnicott, R. Shepherd, & M. David (Eds.), *Psycho-analytic explorations/ D.W. Winnicott* (pp. 299–317). Cambridge, MA: Harvard University Press.

Winnicott, D. W. (1971a). *Playing and reality.* New York: Basic Books.

Winnicott, D. W. (1971b). *Therapeutic consultations in child psychiatry.* New York: Basic Books.

Witkin, H. A., Birnbaum, J., Lomonaco, S., Lehr, S., & Herman, J. L. (1968). Cognitive patterning in congenitally totally blind children. *Child Development, 39*, 767–786.

Wolf, R. (1973). Art therapy in a public school. *American Journal of Art Therapy, 12*, 119–127.

Wolff, W. (1946). *The personality of the preschool child.* New York: Grune & Stratton.

Woltmann, A. G. (1964a). Diagnostic and therapeutic considerations of nonverbal projective activities with children. In M. Haworth (Ed.), *Child Psychotherapy* (pp. 322–337). New York: Basic Books.

Woltmann, A. G. (1964b). Mud and clay, their functions as developmental aids and as media of projection. In M. Haworth (Ed.), *Child psychotherapy* (pp. 349–371). New York: Basic Books,

Yalom, I. D. (1995). *The theory and practice of group psychotherapy* (4th ed.). New York: Basic Books.

Zambelli, G., Clark, E., & Heegaard, M. (1989). Art therapy for bereaved children. In H. Wadeson, J. Durkin, & D. Perach (Eds.), *Advances in art therapy* (pp. 60–80). New York: Wiley.

Zierer, E., Sternberg, D., & Finn, R. (1966). The role of family creative analysis in family treatment. *Bulletin of Art Therapy, 5*, 47–63; 87–104.

Index

Aach-Feldman, Susan, 298
Abandonment:
  masks and, 81–83
  themes and, 130
Abstract artwork, 115–117
  mother-child art sessions and, 160
Abstract Family Portrait, 178
Accepting. *See* Therapeutic process, accepting
Acrylic paints. *See* Painting materials
Activities:
  activity-interview groups and, 219
  series of, 98
  See also Tasks
Adjunctive art therapy, 117
Affect, imagery sources and, 49
Affective understanding, facing and, 65
Aggression:
  acceptable, 4
  clay and, 124
  family art therapy and, 163–164
  fluid media and, 157
  group art therapy and, 159
    multimodality, 239, 245
  oral, 177 (*see also* Biting)
  responses to, 22–23
  setting limits and, 59
  targets and expressing, 83–84
  termination and, 236
  themes and, 130
  See also Anger
Alcohol abuse, 197, 203

Alliances, group art therapy and, 226
American Art Therapy Association (AATA), xl
Anal images, abstract artwork and, 117
Anderson, Frances, 277
Anger:
  masks and, 81–83
  progressive blindness and, 292, 294
  toward adults, 318–322
  See also Aggression
Animals:
  evaluation and drawings of, 97
  symbols, 149
Animation, 67, 331
Anorexia. *See* Eating disorders
Anxiety, xli
  blindness and, 280
  casual interviewing and, 113
  finger paint and, 108
  multimodality group therapy and, 241
  support and, 32
  themes and, 130
  time limits and, 221
  See also Separation, anxiety
Approach-avoidance behavior:
  disabilities and, 287
  symbolic messages and, 124
Approaches to Art Therapy: Theory and Technique,
  18
Archetypes, imagery sources and, 48
Arguile, Roger, 349
Arnheim, Rudolf, 52

Arrington, Doris, 197
The Art of Art Therapy, 18
Art-Drama therapy, 105. *See also* Multimodality group therapy
Artistic development, 34–36
  acceleration in, 46–47
  consolidating, 40–43
  delays in, 46–47
  forming, 36–38
  issues in
    developmental stages vs., 55–56
    imagery sources, 48–49
    regression, 55
  manipulating, 36
  naming, 38
  naturalizing, 44–45
  personalizing, 45–46
  representing, 38–40
Art Psychotherapy, 48–49
The Arts in Psychotherapy, 48–49
Art therapy:
  art education vs., 331–332, 348–350
  creativity, need for, 356–357
  learning experience, 357–359
  opportunities, extending, 365–367
  play therapy and, 350–351
  as sole mode of treatment, 65
  therapists
    as artist, 363–364
    as change agent, 364–365
    qualities of good, 351–355
    See also Research, learning through
  transference, 359–363
"Art Therapy with the Unidentified Patient," 330
Assertion-of-self games, 341
Association:
  free, 13–14, 381–382
  group art therapy and projected, 219
  scribble drawing and, 177
Asthma, 325
Athetosis, 266
Attention deficit disorder, xli
Attitude, toward product, 132–134
Ault, Robert, 330
Authenticity, setting limits and, 60
Authoritarian relationships, 77
Authority:
  aggressive impulses toward, 245
  group art therapy and, 223
  themes, 130
Autism:
  artistic development and, 47

mirroring and, 139
  mother-child joint sessions, 210
Autonomy, 340, 342, 358
  coping and, 69
  freedom and, 20
  themes, 130

Background information, limited:
  family evaluation and, 174
  individual evaluation and, 99
Behavior modification, 267
Bellevue, 48–49
Bender, Lauretta, 48–49
Betensky, Mala, 355
Betrayals, trust and, 61
The Biology of Art, 263
Bipolar disorder, xli
Biting, 339
Blindness, 300–307
  accepting, 68
  assessing change, 371–375
  attitude toward product and, 133
  coming to terms with, 65, 300–305
    mothers' art therapy group, 305–307
  family art evaluation and, 287–289
  freedom and, 24
  individual art evaluation and, 286–287
  multimodality group therapy and, 239
  with multiple disabilities, 272–276
  parents' couple therapy, 289–290
  partial, choice of medium and, 77–78
  progressive
    extending range of the medium, 92
    facing and, 64
    multimodal brief therapy and, 292–300
    parents and children, therapy for, 290–292
    picture-taking machine and, 90
    residential schools, treatment in, 272–276
  support and, 32
Blocking, casual interviewing and, 113
Board Certified (ART-BC), Art Therapy, xl
Body awareness, 339
  as imagery sources, 48
Borderline personality disorder, support and, 32
Boss-slave game, 213–214, 223, 342–343
Bragging, defensive, 133
Braille, learning, 290, 292
Brain damage, blindness and, 272
Bridge theme, 120
Brocher, Tobias, 338–339
Brushes, 120
Buber, Martin, 356
Bulimia. *See* Eating disorders

Burns, severe, 325
Bush, Janet, 277

Candles, 90, 92
Cane, Florence, 311, 330
Care, lack of protective, 130
Career choices, 342
Case illustration, 155–156
    family art therapy, 162–167
        evaluation, 161–162
        group art therapy, 158–160
        individual art evaluation, 156–158
        joint nonverbal drawing, 167–169
        mother-child art sessions, 155, 160–161
Case studies, 136–137, 152–154
    elective mutism, 137–145
    encopresis, 150–152
    schizophrenia, 145–150
Castration anxiety:
    mother-child joint sessions and, 212–213
    separating and, 71
Cephalopods, 38, 39
    regression and, 50
Cerebral palsy, 266
Certification, xl, 348–349
Chalk:
    regression and, 52, 55
    See also Drawing, materials
Chaos:
    fear of, 21
    See also Freedom, providing a framework for
Charcoal. *See* Drawing, materials
Child care workers, 17
Churches, art sessions in, 334–338
Churchill, Winston, 330
Clay:
    aggression and, 124
    forming stage and, 37
    manipulating stage and, 36
    naturalizing stage and, 45
    regression, 107, 108–110
        and disorganization, 125
    scribble, 221
    See also Modeling materials
Clements, Claire and Robert, 277
Closure techniques:
    disabilities and, 280–281
    See also Termination, therapy
Cognition:
    facing and, 65
    imagery sources and, 48, 49
Cognitive-affective ratio, regression and, 52, 54, 55

Cole, Natalie Robinson, 314
Collage:
    naturalizing stage and, 45
    self, 200
Colored pencils. *See* Drawing, materials
Communication:
    evaluation and, 113–115
    nonverbal, 129, 134, 270 (*see also* Drawing, joint nonverbal; Mural, nonverbal)
    products and content, 129
    shared therapy and, 214
    symbolic messages, 122–123
    therapist interaction, 123–124
    See also Therapeutic process, communicating
Community, art therapy in the, 331–332
Competence, 342
Competition, 341
    family art therapy and, 163
        sessions with siblings, 192
    group art therapy and, 226
    termination and, 70
    themes, 130, 160
Computers, facilitating expression and, 73
Condensation, 51
Conjoint family art therapy. *See* Family art therapy, conjoint
Consistency:
    placement of materials, 30
    time limits, 30
    trust and, 61
    working spaces, 30
Consolidating. *See* Artistic development, consolidating
Construction materials, 120
    conditions for creative growth, 29
Constructive play, 341
Consultation, art therapy, 365–367
Contemplative action, 20
Content:
    form and process as, 128
    products and, 128, 129
    regression in, 50–51
    scribble drawing and, 177
    variability, 380
Contour drawing, 45
Control, 342
    group art therapy and, 223, 224
    loss of, xli, 224
        mother-child sessions, 207
        symbolic messages, 189
    See also Impulse control; Locomotion, control of
Coping. *See* Therapeutic process, coping

Costumes:
  multimodality group therapy and, 241
  preschools, art therapy in, 272
Counselors, 17
Countertransference, 145. *See also* Transference
Court-mandated therapy, 105
Crayons:
  manipulating stage and, 36
  See also Drawing, materials
Craypas. *See* Drawing, materials
Creative connection, 238
Creative and Mental Growth, 311
Creative surrender, 20
Creative writing, 114
  as communication, 65
  coping and, 69
  See also Multimodality group therapy; Poetry;
    Stories
Creativity:
  freeing personal, 221
  universality of, 263–264
Croatia, 325
Curiosity, 341
Custody, court-ordered, 197
Cystic fibrosis, 302
  accepting, 68

Day school, art therapy in, 268–271
Deafness:
  blindness and, 272
  day school, treatment in, 268–271
  themes and, 74–76
  See also Hearing impairment
Defense mechanisms:
  casual interviewing and, 113
  imagery sources and, 48
  respecting, 66
Denial of disability, 283
Depression:
  individual art therapy, 201–202
  major, xli
  mother-child sessions and, 188–190
  multimodality group therapy and, 249, 250,
    255–256
  support and, 32
Desensitization, 68
Detention centers, art therapy in, xl
Determinism, psychic. *See* Psychic determinism
Development, normal artistic. *See* Artistic
  development
Developmental delays:
  artistic development and, 47

blindness and, 272
communication and, 63
coping and, 69–70
freedom and, 24
preschool, treatment in, 271–272
Diabetes, 325
Dicker-Brandies, Friedl, 325
Disabilities, 7, 15, 263–264
  special considerations, 277–278
  therapy for parents of children with, 285–286,
    290–292
  couple therapy, 289–290
  family evaluation, 288–289
  individual evaluation, 286–288
  mothers' therapy group, 307–308
  multimodal brief therapy, 292–300
  values of art and, 278–284
  See also specific type
Disadvantaged children, spontaneous play and,
  281
Disguise, symbolic messages and, 131–132
Disorganization:
  clay and, 125
  finger paint and, 125
Dissatisfaction, naturalizing stage and, 45
Dissociative identity disorder, family art therapy
  and, 197
Distortions:
  products and content, 129
  regression and, 51
Divorce, 323–324
Dolls, 272
Dramatic play:
  as communication, 65
  coping and, 69
  disabilities and achieving mastery through, 279
  facing and, 64–65
  genesis, 298
  group art therapy, 229–230
  masks and, 82
  themes and, 153, 229–230
  therapist involvement in, 80–81
  See also Multimodality group therapy
Drawing:
  conditions for creative growth, 29
  inhibitions and starters, 73–74
  joint nonverbal, 167–169
  materials, 119, 177–178
  naturalizing stage and, 45
  See also specific type
Dreams, 78–81. *See also* Nightmares
Dyadic drawing, 139

Easel Age Scale, 21
Easels, 120
Eating disorders, xli
    family art therapy and, 197, 198
Education, art therapy and. *See* Art therapy, art
    education vs.
Edwards Personal Preference Schedule (EPPS),
    382–383
Ego, observing, 132, 231–232, 343
Egocentrism, personalizing stage and, 46
Emotional disturbance, blindness and, 272
Empathy, 33
Encopresis:
    facilitating expression and, 77
    support and, 32
    See also Case studies, encopresis
Encounter groups, 330
Erikson, Eric, 109, 150
Esalen, 330
Evaluation:
    family art, 161–162, 173–174
        characteristics, 183–185
        diagnostic understanding, 182–183
        disabilities and, 288–289
        format, 174–182
        modifications, 185–187
    individual art
        abstract artwork, 115–117
        background, 97–99
        communicating through artwork, 117–118
        disabilities and, 286–288
        getting started, 103–106
        interviewing, 99–103
        materials, 106–110
        productivity, 118–119
        recommendations, 119–120
        space, 110–113
        talking about the art, 113–115
        See also Case illustration, individual art
        evaluation
Exaggerations, 129
Expression, facilitating, 73, 92–93
    candles, 90, 92
    dreams, 78–81
    extending the range, 92
    flashlights, 90, 92
    masks, 81–83
    mediums, 77–78
    picture-taking machines, 90, 91
    poems, 88–89
    starters, 73–74
    stories, 89–90

tape recordings, 85–88
targets, 83–85
themes, 74–76

Facing. *See* Therapeutic process, facing
Family art therapy:
    conjoint, 193–196
    occasional, 196–197
    family member dyads, 188–193
    multimodal sessions, 197–199
    See also Case illustration, family art therapy;
        Evaluation, family art; Parents
Family art workshops, 332–334
Family Creative Arts Center, 331–332
Family drawing:
    blindness and, 305
    evaluation and, 97
    family art evaluation and, 175, 178–180
    mothers' sessions, 203
    See also Kinetic Family Drawing
Family Puppet Interview, 184
Fantasy play, intense, 341
Father-child art sessions, 191–192
Fatigue, regression and, 52, 55
A Favorite Kind of Day theme, 120
Feely-Meely Box, 220
Fibroplasia, retrolental, 90
Film, 67–68
Fine-motor control, 46
Finger paint:
    freedom and use of, 24–25
    multimodality group therapy and, 238, 241
    regression and, 107–108, 241
        disorganization, 125
    rejection of, 201
    See also Painting materials; Regression, finger
        paint and
Flashlights, 90, 92
Flexibility, degree of, 42
Food play, creative, 230–231
Forensic evaluations, xli
Form:
    as content, 128
    products and, 126–128
    regression in, 50–51
Framework, 218–219. *See also* Freedom,
        framework for
Free association. *See* Association, free
Free products. *See* Products, free
Freedom, framework for, 19–29, 154
    conditions for, 29–33
    group art therapy and, 220

Freedom (*continued*)
   targets and, 85
Freudian framework, 218–219
From Isolation to Involvement, 144
Frustration:
   materials and, 106
   personal expression and, 7
Furniture, facilitating expression and, 73

Gantt, Linda, 221
Generalizations, decoding symbolic messages
      and, 127–128
Gestalt framework, 218
Gesture drawing, 45
Glaucoma, congenital, 302
Goals:
   drawing future, 222
   groups and setting, 370–371
Gouache, 120
Group art therapy:
   activities in, 222–225
   approach, structured and unstructured, 220–
      221, 228–229
   drawings, 377–378
   dynamics of groups, 377–378
   food play, creative, 230–231
   getting to know each other, 221–222
   growth
      group, 225–228, 234–236
      individual, 233–234
   history and development, 218–220
   interviewing
      each other, 231–233
      role-taking in, 231
   new members, 234–236
   reviewing, 233
   termination, 234–236
   themes and concerns, 229–230
   See also Case illustration, group art therapy;
      Multimodality group therapy
Growth, 233–235
   imagery sources and phase-appropriate tasks
      for, 48
Guernica, 6

Haeseler, Martha, 271
Haptic type, 48
Harms, Ernst, 48–49
Head Start, mothers' art therapy groups and,
      215–216
Hearing impairment, 145. *See also* Deafness
Hide and Seek, 6
Hide-and-seek game, 81

Homann, Juergen, 194
Hormone deficiency, growth, 77
Hospices, art therapy in, xl
House-Tree-Person drawing, evaluation and, 97
Human figure drawing, evaluation and, 97
Humanistic framework, 218–219
Human potential groups, 330

Identification, attitude toward product and, 132
Identity, termination and, 66–68
Imagery sources, 48–49
Impulse control, 340
Inclusion/exclusion, 341
Independence, 340, 342, 358
   disabilities and, 280
Injury, themes and, 130
Intellectualizing, 128
Interest, conditions for creative growth, 32
Interviewing:
   drama and, 383–384
   evaluation and initiating, 99–103
   family art evaluation and, 162
   group art therapy and, 231–233
      multimodality, 241, 244
   history-taking, 162
   puppets and, 184
   role-taking in, 231
Intrusions, unnecessary, trust and, 61
Irwin, Eleanor C., 383

Kinetic Family Drawing:
   evaluation and, 120
   See also Family drawing
King, Martin Luther, 325
Klineman, Janet, 272
Klorer, Gussie, 197
Kowska, Hanna, 221
Kramer, Edith, 7–8, 98, 120, 311, 325, 355
Kris, Ernst, 54
Kunkle-Miller, Carole, 277

Landgarten, Helen, 197, 355
Langer, Susanne, 240, 312
Language disorders, blindness and, 272
Leadership, group art therapy and, 226
   multimodality group, 257–258
Learning disabilities, stories and, 89
Letting go vs. holding on, 341
Lewis, Nolan D.C., 355
Life-space drawings:
   blindness and, 305
   group art therapy and, 222
   mothers' sessions, 203–205

Lighting, facilitating expression and, 73
Limits:
  setting, 59
  targets and, 85
Linesch, Deborah, 197
Listening, active, 122
Locomotion, control of, 340
Lorand, Sandor, 363
Loss, parental, 326–328. *See also* Mourning
Lowenfeld, Victor, 7, 311, 332

Magnussen, Max, 173
Malraux, André, 6
Manipulating. *See* Artistic development,
      manipulating
Markers. *See* Drawing, materials
Masks, 81–83
  multimodality group therapy and, 238, 251
Mastery, 15, 342
  disabilities and achieving, 279
Materials, 77–78
  evaluation and, 106–110
    arrangement of, initial interview and, 99
  facilitating expression and, 73
  free choice of, 77
  indecision and, 156
  popularity of, 376–377
  regression and, 52
  response to, 124–125
  sensory qualities of, 36
  See also specific type
Medical hospitals, art therapy in, xl
Medication, xli
Membership, new, 234–235
Mental retardation. *See* Developmental delays
Metaphor, 132. *See also* Symbolic messages
Minson, James, 384
Mirroring, 139
Mister Rogers' Neighborhood, 8, 311
Mobility training, 290
Modeling materials, 120
Modification, 267
  family art evaluation and, 185–187
Morris, Desmond, 263
Mother-child art therapy group, 202–203
  formats, possible, 213–214
  joint sessions, 206
    unstructured, 206–208
    working together, 208–213
  mothers' sessions, 203–206
  short-term, 214
  See also Case illustration, mother-child art
      sessions

Mother-Child Drawing, 120
Mothers' art therapy groups, 215–217
  disabilities and outpatient, 307–308
Mothers' Morning Out, 334
Motor-kinesthetic pleasures, 278
Mourning, 4, 6, 326–328
  free association and, 13–14
Movement:
  active coordinated, 341–342
  as communication, 65
  See also Multimodality group therapy
Multimodality group therapy, 237–240, 258–259
  art-drama therapy group
    adolescents, 249–257
    latency-age boys, 240–248
  leadership roles, 257–258
  See also Family art therapy, multimodal sessions
Mural:
  joint, 175, 180–182
  nonverbal, 221
Museum of Modern Art, 6
"Museum Without Walls," 6
Music:
  as communication, 65
  extending range of the medium, 92
  facilitating expression and, 73
  preschools, art therapy in, 272
  See also Multimodality group therapy
Mutism, elective:
  communication and, 63–64
  productivity and, 119
  support and, 32
  See also Case studies, elective mutism

Naming. *See* Artistic development, naming
Narrative framework, 218–219
National Committee, Arts for the Handicapped,
      276
Naturalizing. *See* Artistic development,
      naturalizing
The Nature of Creative Activity, 284
Naumburg, Margaret, 7–8, 311, 355
Neurobiological sources imagery and, 48
Neurological dysfunction, stories and, 89
Neutrality, art therapists and, 361
New York State Psychiatric Institute, 355
Nightmares:
  facing and, 65, 66
  multimodality group therapy and, 238–239
  patient understanding, 66–68
  scribble drawing and, 74
  trust and, 61–62
  See also Dreams

Nondominant hand drawing, 45
Note-taking:
  explanation of, 121–122
  trust and, 61, 79
Nurses, 17
Nurturance, therapy termination and, 66–68

Oaklander, Violet, 355
Observation Guides, 369–370
Observations:
  active, 122
  initial evaluation and, 111, 113
  objective, 369–370
  obtaining consent for, 61
Occupational therapists, 17
Oil crayons. See Drawing, materials
Omega, 330
Omissions, 129
  multimodality group therapy and, 255–256, 257
Oppositional disorder, support and, 32
Oral:
  aggression, 177
  images, 117
  sensations, 339
  zone, primacy of, 339
Order:
  conditions for creative growth, 30
  See also Freedom, framework for
Organic impairment, coping and, 69–70
Organization, regression, in, 50–51
Ownership, attitude toward product and, 132

Painting materials, 120
Parents, 17
  art therapy for disabled children and (see Disabilities, therapy for parents of children with)
  helping, 330–331
    community and, 331–339
    understanding developmental phases, 339–343
  individual art therapy and, 200–201
  parent-child therapy groups, short-term, 214
  play groups, 338–339, 343–344
  See also Family art therapy
Participation, therapist, 79–80
Pastels. See Drawing, materials
Peak experience, 357
Pediatricians, 17
Peer group interaction, 342
Pencils. See Drawing, materials
Person Picking an Apple from a Tree theme, 120

Personalizing. See Artistic development, personalizing
Phillips, Joan, 173
Physical abuse, 197, 325–326
Physical disabilities:
  treatment in residential institution, 266–268
  See also specific type
Picasso, Pablo, 6
Picture-taking machine, 90, 91
Pittsburgh Child Guidance Center, xxxvi, 173, 215, 303, 331
Plasticine. See Modeling materials
Play disruption, 109
  separating and, 70
Play therapy groups, 219, 350–351. See also Parents, play groups
Poetry, 88–89
  as communication, 65
  See also Creative writing
Posttraumatic stress disorder, 325–326
  family art therapy and, 197
Potter's wheel, naturalizing stage and, 45
Power struggle, ambivalent, 340
Preschool, art therapy in, 271–272
Privacy, concern for, 342
Process, working, 125–126
  as content, 128
Productivity, 118–119
Products:
  art and drama interviews, comparing, 383–384
  content and, 129
  free, 175–176, 182
Progression:
  group art therapy and, 159
  regression and, 52, 55
Projection, stimulus for, 115–116
Props:
  facilitating expression and, 73
  preschools, art therapy in, 272
Protection. See Care, lack of protective
Proulx, Lucille, 214
Psychiatric hospitals, art therapy in, 264–266
Psychiatrists, 17
Psychic determinism, 129
Psychologists, 17
Psychosis:
  animal symbols and, 149
  communication and, 63
  group art therapy and, 228–229
  repetition of themes, 149
  support and, 32
  themes and, 228

Punching bag, targets and, 83
Puppet drama:
    extending range of the medium, 92
    facilitating expression and, 73
    family art therapy and, 163, 197–199
    mother-child art sessions and, 160
    multimodality group therapy and, 238, 241,
        243, 244–245, 251
    naturalizing stage and, 45
    preschools, art therapy in, 272
    See also Family Puppet Interview

"Q" paintings, 21
Quadriplegia, 325
Quality, personalizing stage and, 46

Rationalizations, 128
Reality, suspension of, 248
Receptivity, passive, 20
Recommendations, 119–120
Recreational therapists, 17
Registered (ATR), Art Therapy, xl
Regression, 12, 50–51
    causes of, 52–55
    clay and, 125
    finger paint and, 125, 157, 159
    group art therapy and, 159
        multimodality, 241, 248
    healthy, 54–55
    permissible, 4
    responses to, 22–23
    stress and, 21–22
    termination and, 236
Rejection, themes and, 130
Reporting, 135–136
Representing. *See* Artistic development,
        representing
Research, learning through, 368–369, 384–385
    assessing change in blind children, 371–375
    creativity and mental health connections,
        382–383
    diagnostic questions, 378–380
    free association, 381–382
    group drawings and dynamics, 377–378
    grouping and goal-setting, 370–371
    media popularity, 376–377
    objective observation, 369–370
    phenomenological investigation, 375
    products from art and drama interviews, 383–
        384
    self-assessments, 376
    subjective clinical assessments, 370
    variability, 380–381

Residential:
    institution, art therapy in, 266–268
    school, art therapy in, 272–276
Respect, conditions for creative growth, 30
Retaliation, concern, 341
Reviewing, group art therapy and, 233
Rhyne, Janie, 330
Riley, Shirley, 197
Risk taking, freedom and, 20
Rivalry, 341
Rogers, Fred, 311
Rogers, Natalie, 238
Role-playing. *See* Multimodality group therapy
Rorschach inkblots, 7, 177
    evaluation, individual art, 104
    projection and, 115
Round-robin activities, 221
    multimodality group therapy and, 251
Rules, games with, 342

Safety, conditions for creative growth, 30
Same-sex groups, 342
Schehr, Jill, 98
Schemata, representing stage and, 39
Schizo-affective disorder, support and, 32
Schizophrenia, 8
    freedom of media choice and, 23–24
    multimodality group therapy and, 238
    psychiatric hospital, treatment in, 264–266
    See also Case studies, schizophrenia
Schools, xl, 271–276
    family art workshops in, 332–334
    parent art workshops in, 334
    See also specific type
Score variability, 380
Scribble drawing, 62, 73–74
    blindness and, 305
    evaluation and, individual art, 104
    family art evaluation and, 161
        individual and, 174–175, 177, 178
        responses to, 179
    multimodality group therapy and, 238
Sculpture, naturalizing stage and, 45
Security, setting limits to promote, 59–60
Self-consciousness, 242
Self-criticism:
    attitude toward product and, 133–134
    developmental delays and, 275
    naturalizing stage and, 44–45
    personalizing stage and, 46
Self-definition, 15, 342
    disabilities and, 280
    personal expression and, 7

"Self-Designed Learning Process" (SDLP), 382
Self-development, 330
Self-esteem, 342
  coping and, 69
Self-Esteem Inventory, 374
Self-fulfilling prophecies, interpersonal, 210
Self and non-self, differentiation of, 339
Self-portrait:
  evaluation and, 120
  group art therapy and, 159
  regression and, 50
  symbolic messages and, 131
Sensitivity groups, 330
Sensorimotor exploration, 339
Sensory awareness, 339
Sensory-manipulative pleasures, 278
Separation:
  anxiety, 315
  parents and, 323–324
  termination and, 66–68
  See also Therapeutic process, separating
Sex-role identification/orientation, 341, 342
Sexual abuse, 325–326
  multimodality group therapy and, 250
Sexuality, themes and, 130
Shahn, Ben, 363–364
Shapiro, Marvin, 259
Shaw, Ruth, 314
Shelters, art therapy in, xl
Siblings:
  rivalry, 315–318, 320
  sessions with, 192–193
Silver, Rawley, 276
Six Day War, 325
Skills, creative activities involving, 342
Smith, Sally, 277
Sobol, Barbara, 197
Social situations, regression and, 52, 55
Social workers, 17, 333
Space:
  conditions for creative growth, 29–30
  evaluation and, 110–113
  facilitating expression and, 73
  mixed plane and elevation, 41–42
  regression and, 50
Spasticity, extensive, 266, 267
Speech disorders:
  blindness and, 272
  therapists and, 17
  See also Stuttering
Standardization, evaluation and, 97, 98
Starters, 73–74
  using initials as, 222

visual, 221
Stimuli, selection of. See Imagery sources
Storage, conditions for creative growth, 29–30
Stories, 89–90
  multimodality group therapy and, 252–253
  See also Creative writing
Stress, 15
  dealing with normal, 313–326
  medical, 325
  regression and, 21–22
Stuttering, 155
Sublimation, 7–8
Substance abuse, xli, 197
  mothers and, 216–217
Sucking, 339
Suicidal impulses, 270–271
  coping and, 70
  expressing through
    poetry, 88–89
    tape recordings, 85–88
  family art therapy and, 197
  parental, 326–328
Sunflowers, 5
Support, conditions for creative growth, 32–33
Surfaces, 119
Symbolic messages, 359
  communication and, 63, 64
  control issues, 189
  decoding, 121–123
    content, form and processes, 128
    diagnostic implications of approach, 134–135
    disguise, degree of, 131–132
    interaction with therapist, 123–124
    note-taking, 121–122
    product
      attitude toward, 132–134
      content, 129
      form, 126–128
    reporting, 135–136
    response
      to materials, 124–125
      to task, 124
    self-representation, 131
    themes, common, 129–131
    unintrusive stance, 122–123
    working process, 125–126
  disabilities and, 279
  family art therapy and, 165–167, 168
  mourning and, 4
  representing stage and, 39–40
  separating and, 72
Symbolic speech, 7–8, 351

Tactile thinking, 275
Talent, as a distraction from treatment, 47–48
Tape recordings, 73, 85–88
  blindness and, 301–304
Target, 83–85
Tasks:
  assigned, 97, 98
    mothers' sessions, 203–205
  couple, 190
  free, 97–98
  family art
    evaluation, 181
    therapy, 167
  toddlers and, 340–341
  response to, 124
  See also Activities, series of
Tchelitchew, Pavel, 6
Teachers, 17
Tempera paints. *See* Painting materials
Terezin, 325
Termination, therapy:
  coping and, 69
  group art, 234–235
  separation and, 70–72
  treatment, 137–138
Territoriality, group art therapy and, 223
Testing. *See* Therapeutic process, testing
Themes, 74–76
  activities in group art therapy and, 222–223,
    228, 229–230
  articulation of, 63
  decoding symbolic messages and, 129–131
  evaluation and, 120
  family art therapy and, 165–167
  identity issues, 343
  indecision and, 156
  jointly-selected, 190
  multimodality group therapy and, 251
  psychosis and, 228
  repetition of, 149
  transactional, 223
  See also Dramatic play, themes and; *and*
    specific type
Therapeutic process, 57–58
  accepting, 68
  communicating, 63–64
  coping, 69–70
  facing, 64–66
  risking, 62
  separating, 70–72
  testing, 58–60
  trusting, 61–62
  understanding, 66–68

values, 311–313
Thought processes, regression in, 50–51
Three Rivers Arts Festival, 331–332
Time:
  conditions for creative growth, 30
  ending, 30 (*see also* Termination, therapy)
  facilitating expression and, 73
  spontaneity and limits on, 221
Torrance Creativity Tests, 373
Toys, miniature life:
  extending range of the medium, 92
  facilitating expression and, 73
Transference, 359–363
  dramatizing, 247–248
  group art therapy and, 227
    multimodality, 247–248
  negative, 227
  positive, 301
  separating and, 72
  See also Countertransference
Transitional objects, termination and, 69
Trauma, xli, 197, 324–325
  coping with, 4
  disabilities and achieving mastery, 279
Triadic power game, 342–343
Trust:
  vs. mistrust, 339
  See also Therapeutic process, trusting
Two People Doing Something in a Place theme,
    120

Uhlin, Donald, 276
Ulman, Elinor, 330
Unconscious scanning, 20
Understanding. *See* Therapeutic process,
    understanding
Unfreezing, 220–221
University of Pittsburgh, 8

Van Gogh, Vincent, 5
Variability:
  children's art and, 380–381
  intraindividual, 118
Very Special Arts, 276
Videotape recordings, mother-child joint
    sessions, 206–207
Vision impairment, 145. *See also* Blindness
Visual thinking, 275
Visual variability, 380

Wadeson, Harriet, 190
Walden, 311
Warmup techniques, 220–222

Watercolors. *See* Painting materials
We'll Show You What We're Gonna Do!, 133, 272
Western Pennsylvania School for Blind
    Children, 367
Western Psychiatric Institute and Clinic, xxxvi,
    173
Wolfe, Thomas, 6

World War II, 330
Writing, witness, 114. *See also* Creative writing;
    Stories

X-ray drawings, 41–42
    regression and, 50

About the DVD

Introduction

This appendix provides you with information on the contents of the DVD that accompanies this book. For the latest and greatest information, please refer to the ReadMe file located at the root of the DVD.

System Requirements

- A computer with a processor running at 120 Mhz or faster
- At least 32 MB of total RAM installed on your computer; for best performance, we recommend at least 64 MB
- A DVD-ROM drive

    * NOTE: Many of the video files on this DVD-ROM are in MP4 format. This format is playable with "Apple Quicktime" software. If you need to install Apple Quicktime onto your computer, visit **http://www.quicktime.com** to download a free copy.

Using the DVD with Windows

To install the items from the DVD to your hard drive, follow these steps:

1. Insert the DVD into your computer's DVD-ROM drive.
2. The DVD-ROM interface will appear. The interface provides a simple point-and-click way to explore the contents of the DVD.

If the opening screen of the DVD-ROM does not appear automatically, follow these steps to access the DVD:

1. Click the Start button on the left end of the taskbar and then choose Run from the menu that pops up.
2. In the dialog box that appears, type **d:\setup.exe.** (If your DVD-ROM drive is not drive d, fill in the appropriate letter in place of d.) This brings up the DVD Interface described in the preceding set of steps.

What's on the DVD

The following sections provide a summary of the software and other materials you'll find on the DVD.

Content

The attached companion DVD contains almost 500 image files, which have been carefully chosen and edited in order to bring the text alive for the reader. Since this book is about the use of art in therapy, it will come as no surprise that about 160 are of artwork, some of them color versions of the black and white reproductions in the book. About 230 show individuals of all ages creating with art media in a variety of clinical settings.

Perhaps most unusual are the video files—over 200 of them—in which the reader can hear and see what goes on when people use art in their clinical work. Although the majority of these are brief, one is a 10-minute excerpt from an interview by Natalie Rogers, daughter of psychologist Carl Rogers, in which a young woman uses drawings to help define her identity.

NOTE: Many of the video files on this DVD-ROM are in MP4 format. This format is playable with "Apple Quicktime" software. If you need to install Apple Quicktime onto your computer, visit **http://www.quicktime.com** to download a free copy.

Customer Care

If you have trouble with the DVD-ROM, please call the Wiley Product Technical Support phone number at (800) 762-2974. Outside the United States, call 1(317) 572-3994. You can also contact Wiley Product Technical Support at **http://www.wiley.com/techsupport**. John Wiley & Sons will provide technical support only for installation and other general quality control items. For technical support on the applications themselves, consult the program's vendor or author.

To place additional orders or to request information about other Wiley products, please call (877) 762-2974.

CUSTOMER NOTE:

IF THIS BOOK IS ACCOMPANIED BY SOFTWARE, PLEASE READ THE FOLLOWING BEFORE OPENING THE PACKAGE.

This software contains files to help you utilize the models described in the accompanying book. By opening the package, you are agreeing to be bound by the following agreement:

This software product is protected by copyright and all rights are reserved by the author, John Wiley & Sons, Inc., or their licensors. You are licensed to use this software on a single computer. Copying the software to another medium or format for use on a single computer does not violate the U.S. Copyright Law. Copying the software for any other purpose is a violation of the U.S. Copyright Law.

This software product is sold as is without warranty of any kind, either express or implied, including but not limited to the implied warranty of merchantability and fitness for a particular purpose. Neither Wiley nor its dealers or distributors assumes any liability for any alleged or actual damages arising from the use of or the inability to use this software. (Some states do not allow the exclusion of implied warranties, so the exclusion may not apply to you.)